The State, Ethnicity, and Gender in Africa

THE STATE, ETHNICITY, AND GENDER IN AFRICA

INTELLECTUAL LEGACIES OF CRAWFORD YOUNG

EDITED BY

SCOTT STRAUS AND AILI MARI TRIPP

The University of Wisconsin Press

Publication of this book has been made possible, in part, through support from the Anonymous Fund of the College of Letters and Science at the University of Wisconsin–Madison.

The University of Wisconsin Press
728 State Street, Suite 443
Madison, Wisconsin 53706
uwpress.wisc.edu

Printed in the United States of America
This book may be available in a digital edition.

Library of Congress Cataloging-in-Publication Data

Names: Young, Crawford, 1931– honoree. | Straus, Scott, 1970– editor. | Tripp, Aili Mari, editor.
Title: Cultural pluralism, the state, and gender politics in Africa : intellectual legacies of Crawford Young / edited by Scott Straus and Aili Mari Tripp.
Other titles: Africa and the diaspora.
Description: Madison, Wisconsin : The University of Wisconsin Press, 2024. | Series: Africa and the diaspora: history, politics, culture | Includes biographical references and index.
Identifiers: LCCN 2023054056 | ISBN 9780299349400 (hardcover)
Subjects: LCSH: Ethnicity—Political aspects—Africa. | Women—Political activity—Africa. | Africa—Politics and government—1960–
Classification: LCC DT30.5 .C85 2024 | DDC 305.80096—dc23/eng/20240415
LC record available at https://lccn.loc.gov/2023054056

Contents

v

Part III. Women, Gender, and Politics

Acknowledgments

This book owes its existence to the collective efforts of those who participated in two significant events: a Zoom Memorial in honor of Professor M. Crawford Young on September 21, 2020, held during the African Studies Association annual meeting; and the Symposium on the Intellectual Legacies of Crawford Young, held at the University of Wisconsin–Madison on April 1–2, 2022.

We extend our heartfelt gratitude to all the attendees of the Symposium and those who shared their insights during the event, as most of the chapters in this book draw upon the invaluable contributions and discussions that emerged from this gathering.

We would like to express our sincere appreciation to Aleia Ingulli McCord, Harry Kiiru, and the dedicated staff at the African Studies Program, whose tireless efforts were instrumental in organizing the Symposium. Their support and commitment ensured the success of the event.

Furthermore, we are deeply grateful to the Political Science Department for its support in making the symposium a reality and for its participation in the event. Special recognition is reserved for Louise Young, Estelle Young, Emily Young, and Eva Young, who supported us in many aspects of planning the symposium. We also extend our gratitude to Crawford Young's brother, Ralph Young, for his involvement in the event.

We would like to offer our special thanks to Monica Komer and Valeria Umanets, whose diligent work in preparing the manuscript for publication was invaluable in bringing this book to fruition.

The realization of this book is a testament to the collaborative spirit and dedication of many people, and we are deeply grateful for their contributions and support in honoring this remarkable man and scholar.

Prologue

Linda Thomas-Greenfield

Comments made by Linda Thomas-Greenfield, who received a master's degree from the University of Wisconsin, when she spoke at the Symposium on the Intellectual Legacies of Crawford Young on April 1, 2022. The views expressed here are hers and not those of the US government.

Good afternoon. It is truly an honor for me to be a part of the symposium and celebrate the extraordinary life and career of my UW mentor, Professor Crawford Young. Professor Young was an academic phenomenon. He wrote an impossible number of books and papers, and his body of work is all the more impressive when you consider he typed with just two fingers. I was always so amazed that he could type as fast with two index fingers on a manual typewriter as I could with all ten on an electric one. Professor Young was a sought-after expert on Zaire and politics across the African continent, and his teaching and scholarship made a major impact on countless lives across Africa and in the US, including mine. His teaching helped form an important foundation for my career as a diplomat in the foreign service, and I know that I'm not alone. In fact, at the UN, I have the opportunity to work now with my counterpart from the DRC [Democratic Republic of Congo], [Amb.] Nzongola Ntalaja, who just happens to be a fellow former student and mentee of Young's and who I know is in the room today.

In addition to Professor Young's extraordinary contributions to academia, he was a father figure and a friend to me. I felt fortunate to get to know his four daughters and his equally extraordinary wife, Becky. I'm sure that if Professor Young were here, he would tell you that his final book about Becky's life and accomplishments was his most important work. When I was a student at Madison, the Young family regularly welcomed me and other students into their home. And in the decades since, no matter what country or time zone I found myself in, Professor Young remained generous with his advice and his friendship. To this day, I still consider myself Professor Young's student for two reasons. The first is that I never completed my dissertation. The second is that I'm still learning from him. Professor Young made an enduring impact on everyone fortunate enough to know him. I know how much he would appreciate being remembered in this way, among so many people he loved and respected. And I'm grateful for the opportunity to be here among you to share my appreciation for such a tremendous person and mentor. Thank you.

The State, Ethnicity, and Gender in Africa

Introduction

The Legacies of Crawford Young

Scott Straus and Aili Mari Tripp

Crawford Young was an extraordinary man who changed the study of African politics, the state, and ethnicity. He was outstanding not only in his research but also as a mentor, colleague, teacher, administrator, and, above all, person. He was a man of great integrity, humility, and generosity of spirit. He left a huge legacy because of his prodigious scholarship and eloquent writing, because of the central role he had played in the lives of his graduate students and colleagues at the University of Wisconsin–Madison, because of his support for scholars in the broader field of African politics, and because of his spirit of service and administrative acumen. He was an intellectual giant and pioneer who made major scholarly contributions. He was also a gracious colleague and mentor who acted with exceptional generosity to junior faculty and graduate students.

This book celebrates the life and work of Crawford Young through the scholarship of his former students and associates. The liveliest and most powerful celebration, as Crawford himself would have noted, is a rich, thorough, and critical study of African politics more generally, and it is in this spirit that we honor him. In this essay, we argue that his scholarship, mentoring, and service were marked by openness, curiosity, kindness, attention to empirical patterns, and a ferocious comparative spirit. Young's enduring contributions are evident in the many books and articles he wrote and in the sensibility and approach that he modeled and inculcated in others. This volume seeks to capture aspects of those legacies for those who knew him or his work and for

3

those who did not. Indeed, his example and model of scholarship, mentoring, and service, we hope, will provide inspiration for future generations of academics.

In this chapter, we provide an overview of his life and professional accomplishments, and we offer a road map to the contributions of the authors in the volume. The writers are all former students of Young or students of his colleagues. While his influence is apparent in scholarship on African politics, identities, and the state, he fostered an approach to comparative politics that can be felt in the varied contributions. There is an emphasis on fieldwork and/or empirical patterns in the world, applying theory to make sense of those findings or letting the findings drive new theoretical insights and identifying patterns across countries and other units.

Intellectual Approach

Young's career and writing spanned much of Africa's postcolonial political history. His first book was on the origins of a postcolonial African state, essentially an analysis of the tumultuous birth of the Congolese state in the 1950s and 1960s, as well as a detailed account of the rise and decline of the same state through the 1970s and 1980s. He wrote synthetic books on Marxist models of development and ethnic politics in the 1960s and 1970s, as well as a major book on the colonial origins of the African state in the 1990s. His last works were on democratization and the multiplicity of African pathways since then. His scholarship thus tracked the first fifty or so years of postcolonial African political history. He was unquestionably one of the most important scholars of African and comparative politics of his generation—one of the founders of the field of the study of African politics—and he was arguably the most perspicacious. He had a remarkable ability for range. Even while always attentive to detail, he elucidated patterns and trends on a continental and sometimes global scale, and his work on Africa continued up until the 2010s. Indeed, his four-hundred-plus-page *Postcolonial State in Africa: Fifty Years of Independence, 1960–2010*, his last major work of scholarship, was a major stock taking of politics on the continent. When the book received the Best Book award from the African Politics Conference Group, in 2013, he received a spontaneous standing ovation.

As a scholar, Young wrote with exceptional elegance and lyricism. The son of an English professor and a journalist for his college newspaper, he loved vocabulary, careful sentence construction, and other flourishes in his writing. Rachel Beatty Riedl, a contributor and former undergraduate student of Young's and today a professor and director of the Mario Einaudi Center for International

Studies at Cornell University, recalls the first time she read *Politics of Cultural Pluralism*, saying, "the poetry of his language stays with me to this day, and when I teach the book (I still do! In my grad seminars) I take a moment with the students to make note of his writing style."[1] The work is also remarkable for its combination of simultaneous empirical specificity and effort at categorization. Young was a close observer of places, people, and history. Events and individuals mattered in his writing. But in those realities, he always looked for patterns and generality.

The Democratic Republic of Congo (formerly Zaire) was the place he knew best and to which he dedicated two major books. The first was his dissertation, published in 1965 by Princeton University Press. *Politics in the Congo: Decolonization and Independence* is still read today as an authoritative account of this period. Yet its chapter titles reference the key social science concepts of the day: elites, public administration, federalism, and nationalism, among others. *The Rise and Decline of the Zairian State* (University of Wisconsin Press, 1985), coauthored with Tom Turner, exemplifies his style even more so. On the one hand, the book is a detailed anatomy of Zaire. One can read the book to learn Congolese political history; it is, in fact, essential reading to understand the years of political rule under Mobutu Sese Seko (1965–97). But for Young and Turner, the empirics were a pathway to concepts and theory. The chapters are a compilation of the main themes in African politics in the first thirty years of the study of African politics: the state, civil society, inequality, ethnicity, patrimonialism, legitimacy, the military, and African international relations. The book is thus not just a case study of Zaire but a social science–inflected analysis of the country's politics.

Young was also a comparativist who looked for patterns across Africa and the world, using detailed empirics to illustrate the points. This is especially evident in one of his best-known books, *The Politics of Cultural Pluralism* (University of Wisconsin Press, 1976). The book identifies a general problem: the question of building national communities and managing differences in the context of postcolonial multiethnic, multireligious states. Young lays out an expansive list of types of identity differences, from ethnicity and religion to caste and race. He demolishes the concept of "tribe." His analysis is attentive to the fluid nature of identity and to the protean ways in which its contours and intensity vary in different contexts. He starts the book—as Tim Longman points out in his chapter in this volume—with a question that a Congolese person asked him in 1962, in particular, whether he was a Mubala or a Mupende, two Congolese ethnic categories whose salience had ebbed by the time the book appeared. Young was one of the first political scientists to underline the importance of ethnicity and other forms of cultural pluralism, identities that were thought initially to wash out in a wave of nationalism. Yet they persisted.

The ideas at the heart of the book remain salient, insightful, and to the point, as Joshua B. Forrest shows in his analysis of Ukraine and Russia in this volume. The book can also be read for its empirics. In it, one finds detailed analyses of Tanzania, Uganda, Nigeria, India, Indonesia, the Philippines, indigenous populations in Latin America, Bangladesh, South Sudan, and more. Young codifies and categorizes different kinds of plural arrangements in different kinds of states. Like his other work, the book can thus be read for its arguments, conceptualization, and theory, as well as for the careful, detailed empirics that are just as central to the presentation. If one wants to learn about the Biafran civil war or religious diversity in Southeast Asian archipelago states, the book is a good place to start. That the book won the most prestigious book award from the African Studies Association, then called the Herskovits Prize, is a testament to the quality of his empirical research and analysis.

The same can be said of Young's work on the African state. His conceptual analysis of the state in *The African Colonial State in Comparative Perspective* (Yale University Press, 1994) is a classic. Many cohorts of graduate students have read the chapter—or should! The book's argument endures; it remains one of the most influential in the study of African politics. The "vertebral thesis" (Young's words) argues that the coercive colonial state became encoded in and definitively shaped the postcolonial state. Who can forget the image of "Bula Mutari"—the crusher of rocks—as the metaphor to explain the nature of this state? And who can forget the painting reproduced on the cover, a painting by Tshibunda Kanda-Matalu, a Lubumbashi-based painter of popular history. In the image, a Belgian colonial officer smokes a pipe, looking on, while an African soldier stands with a whip in hand at the ready and various Congolese citizens experience different forms of abuse. The Bula Matari state is a state of violence, dispossession, and exploitation; that was the state that African leaders inherited at independence and that shaped their rule and how Africans experienced government, Young argues. His thesis is a classic, one that stands alongside Mahmood Mamdani's *Citizen and Subject* as a pillar of analysis in the study of African politics. In the book, one can find all manner of fascinating details about the British colonial state in Nigeria, the French colonial state in Algeria, the Belgian colonial state in Congo, and the colonial state in many other places. No wonder this book was also prize winning, receiving the Gregory Luebbert award for the best book in comparative politics from the American Political Science Association.

The point is this: from the vantage point of twenty-first-century political science, his work may look old-fashioned. In Young's major works, there are no datasets, no regression analyses, no attention to causal identification, and certainly no experiments. His selection of cases for comparison is often not justified. All in all, he does not wear methods on his sleeve in his work. Yet there are many merits to this approach, ones that contemporary scholars would do well to heed. His analyses were broadly comparative and empirically rich, and, as a result, the work has a lasting shelf life.

One reads his research today as major statements on ethnic politics and the state; those remain arguably his most enduring conceptual and theoretical interventions. His analyses of the state in general, the colonial state in Africa, and the postcolonial state remain fresh, and the arguments remain insightful. The same is true about ethnic politics. He was one of the first to see its importance for postcolonial states; he was prescient, and the book's concepts and categories still stand, as do the theoretical insights.

One also reads the work for political history. One cannot imagine trying to learn about the first thirty years of Congolese postcolonial history without reading Young's work. His two books on the Congo are flush with people, places, events, and historical processes. The books remain incredibly useful for the contemporary reader. The point applies to the more synthetic works as well: the books on cultural pluralism, the African colonial state, and the postcolonial African state are full of case studies and empirical descriptions that are sources of insight for the contemporary reader who wants to learn about the political history of those places.

The rootedness in place and specificity, while motivated by the ideas of a comparative social scientist, reflects not only a stylistic choice but an ethic and, ultimately, a method. He looked for patterns through comparison while seemingly in constant appreciation of the world he studied. He was not an overly normative scholar in the sense that he explored solutions offered by others but did not prescribe solutions himself. He approached comparative politics seemingly with a smile, curious about the world rather than judging it. There is openness, generosity, and empathy in his writing to the leaders and the citizens of the world, as well as to the scholars whose work predated him.

That approach—of openness, generosity, and empathy—extended beyond his books and articles to his teaching and mentorship. Young trained several generations of graduate students in political science. His intellectual lineage continues through his former students, one that has been passed on to their students. In many ways, this book speaks most concretely to that legacy. Across the contributions, one can see enduring commitments to the themes that animated much of Young's research agenda: the politics of identity, the state, democratization, and the DR Congo. One also detects a sensibility to the study of Africa, in particular—an appreciation for salient dynamics and patterns rooted in social science conceptualization and theory but in which the realities and empirics usually take center stage. Young—like many of his students—was interested in Africa for how it is and came to be rather than how it should be.

Young encouraged the various research topics pursued by his students. He also was open to criticism and sensitive to lacunae in his own work. Many of the contributors to this volume are students of the politics of gender, a concept that did not feature in his work. Yet he embraced and encouraged such work, starting with his mentorship of Kathleen Staudt, who wrote a 1976 dissertation on "Agricultural Policy, Political Power, and Women Farmers in Western Kenya" and went on to publish several books on women and international development as well as gendered violence along the US-Mexico border. His role in hiring Aili Tripp in 1991 was further evidence of his openness to gender studies and his support of the many advisees who joined his department and worked on gender and politics, including Kathleen Mulligan Hansel, Lynn Khadiagala, Alice Kang, Melinda Adams, and Kaden Paulson-Smith. Some former advisees like Gretchen Bauer and Ladan Affi adopted this focus after leaving Madison. Young's embrace of topics far afield from his own was evident in the reflections made at the African Studies Association memorial held in his honor in November 2020 and at a later conference in Madison in April 2022, which forms the basis for the chapters in this volume.

Before turning to that legacy, we present a brief biographical sketch so that readers can understand more about him; the chapter then reflects on Young as an administrator, a mentor, and as a person—all forms of his legacy.

Brief Biography

M. Crawford Young was born in Philadelphia, Pennsylvania, in 1931.[2] He lived there until high school, when his family moved to Washington, DC, where his father was appointed to the Federal Reserve in 1946. His mother, Louise Young, an English professor at the American University, having written a book on the League of Women Voters and its vital postsuffrage role, had a strong influence on his interest in the study of politics.[3] He graduated from Woodrow Wilson High School in 1949, completed his BA at the University of Michigan in 1953, and joined the army for two years. Young then worked for two years with the International Students Association in Paris. There, he met and married the love of his life, Rebecca (Becky) Young (1934–2008), on August 17, 1957. After completing his doctorate at Harvard, Young joined the Department of Political Science at the University of Wisconsin–Madison in 1963. Young also taught at Makerere University in Kampala, Uganda, from 1965 to 1966 as a visiting professor. Not surprisingly, Young was tenured only three years after being hired. He became chair of the Department of Political Science at UW–Madison in 1969, only six years after receiving his doctorate.

Administration and Honors

His stint as department chair was the first of what would become a career-long commitment to institution building. In interviews about his career, he insisted that his ambition was not to become an administrator. He wanted to remain a scholar, and he worried that staying too long in administration would undermine his credibility and acumen as a scholar. Yet his characteristic ability to help others and establish structures to do so came through in his administration.

At UW–Madison, Professor Young helped get the African Studies Program off the ground after its inception in 1961. That center became one of the most dynamic institutions for the interdisciplinary study of Africa, cultivating a vibrant culture for discussions of Africa, support for scholarship, and a place to congregate for those connected to Africa who found themselves in the heart of the upper Midwest.

At Madison, Young served as associate dean of the Graduate School (1968–71) and, later, as acting dean of the College of Letters and Science (1991–92). In between, he served a second term as chair of the Department of Political Science. He also served on a wide range of committees across campus, chairing the Search and Screen Committee for the Chancellor, which hired Donna Shalala, and chairing the Transportation Demand Management Committee, where he advocated strongly for greater bus use.

In the 2003 interview with Barry Teicher of the UW Archives Oral History Project, he reflected on how he thought about his academic service:

> Every one of these administrative opportunities I had (except for the one in Zaire Congo . . .), I had been asked to take on the function. I always found it was my civic duty if others made the judgment that I was the most appropriate person to fill the role, to be willing to make, what in some ways was a sacrifice of one's teaching [and] research to fulfill these responsibilities. I never thought of administration as attractive long term. Among other things, I was always very conscious of the fact that if you spend more than five years or so consecutively in an administrative role, sufficiently demanding to lay claim to most if not all of your time, you're going to lose your standing in your own field and there won't be an easy pathway back.

Perhaps his most enduring legacy at the University of Wisconsin—and one that has been generally overlooked—was his effort to get the Department of

African American Studies off the ground after the 1969 strike of Black students on campus.[4] One of the demands that the students made was for the formation of an autonomous African American studies department. Most of their demands were nonnegotiable, but this was one that the administration believed could be implemented. Chancellor H. Edwin Young appointed Crawford Young to chair the committee that formed the department and drew heavily on the faculty from the African Studies Program—including Jan Vansina, Edris Makward, David Wiley, and Donald Harris—to get the department off the ground. UW thus became one of the first universities in the United States to form such a department. Young was very proud of the fact that the steps they took resulted in the formation of a department "that had a very good academic reputation and solid standing within the university community."

He was particularly sensitive to the demands of the African American students at the time because of some of his experiences during his formative years in college and in the army. At the University of Michigan, Young spent forty to fifty hours a week working on the undergraduate newspaper, *Michigan Daily*, and eventually became managing editor. (His future wife was also working on the staff.) Civil rights was one of the most important political issues on campus during his undergraduate years (1949–53). His work on the newspaper brought him into contact with campus debates over whether the student government could impose some kind of ban on fraternities that persisted in maintaining a discriminatory clause.

His views on racism were further solidified when he carried out military service from 1953 to 1955. He was sent to Fort Benning, Georgia, for infantry training. Although there were a number of southern whites in the group, the largest contingent of infantry was from a historically Black university, Prairie View A&M, in Texas. One of the infantrymen was James Earl Jones. The commander asked Young if he wanted to be moved to another, presumably whiter contingent, and he said he preferred to remain with his Black mates. As he reflected later: "I thought it was an interesting experience. . . . It was very revelatory to have a sense of their concerns. It further reinforced my sense that racial justice was one of the key issues."[5]

Beyond Madison, in one of his most formative administrative roles, he served as dean of the Faculty of Social Sciences at l'Université nationale du Zaire, Lubumbashi (1973–75). This period was the height of the Mobutu regime, and his experiences and observations there ultimately shaped the insights that permeated *The Rise and Decline of the Zairian State*. Young was also a Fulbright scholar in Dakar, Senegal, at the Faculty of Law at Université Cheikh Anta Diop (1987–88), another formative experience for him.

Young's commitment to scholarship on Africa extended beyond the Madison campus. In addition to his mentoring of students and his time in Uganda, Zaire, and Senegal as a visiting scholar or administrator, he also was engaged in the African Studies Association, which is the premier scholarly association on Africa in North America. He served as president of the ASA from 1982 to 1983. He was later recognized in 1990 with the organization's Distinguished Africanist Award, an honor reserved for very few. His open approach to method and inquiry meant that he was welcomed by an interdisciplinary group of scholars.

Beyond Africa, Young also earned recognition. As noted, his book on the colonial state won the most prestigious book award for comparative politics, given by the American Political Science Association. In 1998, he was voted in a member of the American Academy of Arts and Sciences and earned an honorary degree from Florida International University that same year.

Scholarship

Crawford Young's productivity throughout his career and even after retirement was remarkable. Young had always been extremely prolific, even from his time as a graduate student at Harvard University. The economist Elliot Berg was visiting Harvard and asked Young about how his dissertation was coming along. Up to that point, he had been just reading. Berg warned him that he was courting disaster if he did not start writing. He would be demoted to the rank of instructor and would forfeit research support. Young immediately stopped reading and chained himself to his typewriter, writing up to ten pages a day. Between February and June, he produced a 620-page dissertation. This was the beginning of his very productive career in writing.

In the end, Young authored or coauthored eight scholarly monographs, two more personal histories, and more than 120 articles and book chapters. In addition, he edited seven volumes. We have already mentioned five of his books: *Politics in the Congo* (Princeton University Press, 1965), *The Rise and Decline of the Zairian State* (University of Wisconsin Press, 1985), *The Politics of Cultural Pluralism* (University of Wisconsin Press, 1976), *The African Colonial State in Comparative Perspective* (Yale University Press, 1994), and *The Postcolonial State in Africa* (University of Wisconsin Press, 2012). These books are among his best known, and they speak to the central themes of his work: the Congo, the state in Africa, ethnic and other forms of identity politics, and continental trends. In addition, he authored *Ideology and Development in Africa* (Yale University Press, 1982), which identified three major ideological streams in Africa (Afromarxism, populist socialism, and African capitalism) and looked at the different policy consequences of the various ideological preferences. The book was widely adopted by African politics classes until the breakup of the Soviet Union led to a decline in the Afromarxist orientation.

Some consider his last major academic book, *The Postcolonial State in Africa,* one of his best. In it, Young provides a breathtakingly comprehensive overview of the fifty years following independence, drawing on the perspectives he absorbed while working in Africa and his broad global points of reference. He identified three cycles of hope and disappointment, starting with the euphoria at the time of independence in the 1960s, followed by the emergence of single-party autocracies and military rule. The second period was one of state expansion in the 1970s, leading to state crisis and state collapse in the 1980s. Finally, there was the third wave of democratization, starting in the 1990s, and the proliferation of civil wars. His nuanced magnum opus shows how the African states increasingly diverged from one another over the half century in ways that would have been difficult to predict from the outset of independence. This book won the African Politics Conference Group award as the best book on Africa in 2012.

Throughout his career, Young also contributed numerous articles to professional journals and anthology chapters arising from many conference volumes. Professor Young's oeuvre, as he liked to call it, also includes a 695-page history of the Department of Political Science at UW–Madison, *Political Science at the University of Wisconsin–Madison: A Centennial History* (University of Wisconsin, 2006). This massive green volume was given to every entering graduate student in the PhD program at Madison. Up until his very last years, he would climb the four flights of stairs in North Hall, which houses the Department of Political Science at UW–Madison, to regale students with trends and dynamics in the department since its start.

His last labor of love was a self-published book, *Rebecca Young, a Life of Civic Engagement and Progressive Electoral Politics* (2019), honoring the pioneering efforts of his late wife as a prominent figure in Wisconsin politics. Young served in the Wisconsin State Assembly from 1985 to 1997. He was fiercely supportive and proud of her career as a politician, which informed his interest in the study of women and politics, a subject that he did not research but encouraged others to pursue.

Mentor and Senior Colleague

Young's outstanding reputation as a scholar of African politics naturally drew many PhD students to Madison to study with him. One of his students, Linda Thomas-Greenfield, became assistant secretary of state for African affairs and later the US ambassador to the United Nations. Georges Nzongola-Ntalaja served as DR Congo's representative to the United Nations. Another PhD student, Steven Morrison, became senior vice president at the Center for Strategic and International Studies. Young trained an entire generation of prominent Africa scholars, among them Michael Schatzberg, Catharine Newbury, Edmond Keller, Gretchen Bauer, John Harbeson, Joel Samoff, Thomas Turner, and Timothy Longman. An extraordinarily large number of his former students became presidents of the African Studies Association (ASA), including Newbury, Keller, Bauer, and Nzongola-Ntalaja, and others served on the board, including Longman and Samoff. Harbeson formed the African Political Science Conference group, which convenes political scientists at national and regional political science conferences as well as the ASA.

Young was as conscientious and efficient in his mentoring as he was in his scholarship. Both Crawford Young and Aili Tripp received a draft dissertation one day from a student, and Aili thought, "Okay, I will get to it the next day," fancying herself to be rather ambitious. In those days, there was no email, only snail mail. When Aili got to North Hall the next morning, there lay in her mailbox twelve pages of thorough, incisive, single-spaced commentary on the dissertation. And in the mail basket, there was a copy of the commentary in an envelope, stamped and ready to go. Young would work late into the night. His office was next to Aili's. Every day, she would hear him tapping away on his typewriter, long after everyone else had shifted to the computer (as Aili recalls, there were many times she wished he would embrace more quiet technologies). But there he would be, typing away from early in the morning to late at night in his fourth-floor office of North Hall, even on Friday evenings.

Young learned from everyone, including his students, and built on what he learned. One of his first students, the late Paul Beckett, who worked on Nigeria, describes going on a flight with him to Nigeria, and he said it was like sitting next to a human vacuum. Not only had Young done his own extensive preparation and reading, but, as Paul put it, "He literally sucked out every bit of knowledge that I had about Nigeria, so that by the time we landed in Nigeria, Crawford knew more about Nigeria than did I, who considered myself a Nigeria scholar!"

Scott Straus similarly recalled at the 2020 Young tribute,

> In my first few years as a professor at Madison, Crawford came virtually to every single public talk I did. He often invited me to lunch or for a beer afterward. And then, after a little small talk, he got right to the point: "So, Scott," he'd ask with that sort of deeply kind grin and a slight tilt of his head. "Who do

you think shot down Habyarimana's plane? What do you think about Paul Kagame? Because James Kabarebe really is number two. What do you think is really the relationship between Alassane Ouattara and Guillaume Soro? Do you think Katumbi could win a fair election in the Congo? Say, Scott, do you think that Bashir is funding the Janjaweed? Or do you think it's Salah Gosh?"

Young's insatiable curiosity meant that he always had his finger on the pulse of African politics, paying extremely close attention to events as they unfolded.

Young modeled what it meant to be a true intellectual for the rest of us. He pushed students not only to focus narrowly on Africa but also to expand beyond the continent and take a broader comparative perspective. Not only could he tell you about the Biafran war in Nigeria, but he could "hold forth," as he put it, with equal ease on Tajik-Uzbek relations. His frame of reference was truly astounding. He had amazing geographical breadth, but he also read widely outside the study of politics. He was an Africanist, and he believed in the value of various studies and interdisciplinary inquiry. This was evident in the syllabi for his courses and also his encouragement of students to take courses in areas such as African history and anthropology as well as language studies alongside the courses in political science, as Catharine Newbury recalled at the 2020 memorial.

The depth and breadth of Young's knowledge was humbling for those who came to know him. Cédric Jourde, professor of political science at Ottawa University, met Young on his first visit to North Hall in September 1995. As he recalls:

> I was twenty-two. Right away, I realized that this was a man who knew a lot about everything and yet wanted to know more. His intellectual curiosity had no limits. Recall that a few weeks later, in October 1995, Québec was about to have its referendum on independence, and Crawford wanted to know everything about what was going in Québec. So, we began discussing this whole independence thing. The problem was that I could barely answer his questions because I knew so little about my own province and country, compared to what he knew about them. I was the one who should have asked him questions about the political history of Québec and Canada. Then I remember we began talking about my doctoral project, which was about ethnicity and elite politics in Senegal and Mauritania. As we were talking, still in his office, he stood up, disappeared under a table that was standing between his desk and one of his bookshelves, reappeared on the other side of the table, and began picking books about Senegal (and the few about Mauritania), asking me if I had read this one, and that one, and this one, all in French, my own language. And of course, I had not read any of these books, and I realized that the learning curve was going to be quite steep.

Young took pride in his scholarship and his administrative skills, as well as his students, but he did not flaunt his achievements, nor did he seek accolades. It came from being secure in his own self-worth and accomplishments. As a former student and professor at Northwestern University, Will Reno, mused: "He had a good sense of self-awareness. What that meant was he always had concern for other people, and it was always about them. It was never about him. There wasn't an ounce of self-promotion. I mean in my view he didn't need to. But that is the authority; that is respect that he had. He was such a humble man."

Moses Khisa, an Ugandan professor at North Carolina State University, was another beneficiary. A former student of Reno's at Northwestern University, Khisa wrote, upon Young's passing: "Crawford has left an unmatched indelible mark not just in Africanist scholarship but also in many African academic institutions where he served. I was fortunate to benefit from his enormous intellectual resources, not just from his research, ideas, and warm conversations but also from the fact that he advised and mentored my mentor and adviser. We will greatly miss him."[6]

Young was not only an extraordinary scholar; he was also a truly singular colleague and mentor. Young's students and junior colleagues knew that Young had their back. As the UW–Madison political science professor Aili Tripp observed at the ASA memorial:

> I owe my career to him. He supported me in countless ways, in getting me through the difficult tenure process, in reading my work, and in writing letters of recommendation for grants. But he did so much more in providing moral support. He believed in me sometimes more than I believed in myself and could see value in my work in ways that I did not even fully appreciate at the time. I felt he had really high expectations of me, and I was sometimes afraid of not meeting them. A gifted intellectual, he set incredibly high standards, to which one could only aspire. He was so confident in his own abilities he did not need to diminish or minimize others. Instead, he lifted them up.

On rare occasions, he showed his playful side. The evening after the Department of Political Science voted to grant Aili Tripp tenure, Aili was playing the piano. She heard a car door slam in the driveway. By the time she got to the door, the car had pulled out of the driveway. There was no one in sight. Instead, she found on her doorstep a bottle of champagne with a card of congratulations written in Crawford's handwriting, signed, "from a fairy."

A few years before he died, he offered to read an entire manuscript of a book Scott Straus was working on. As was typical of Young, he wrote ten pages of single-spaced invaluable comments on the work. His feedback was devoid of

harsh comments, even if one could tell he didn't like something. He would usually offer something generous like "have you considered reducing some of the
pages you devote to X or Y?"

He was always encouraging of his students. He would tell them as they
went to defend their dissertations, as he did with John Harbeson, to think about
the defense "as the brightest class you're ever going to teach, so enjoy it." He
was very gentle, kind, and lighthearted in his interactions with students. He
challenged them and differed with them at times, but he listened, queried, wondered out loud, advised them, and, above all, encouraged learning. As Joel
Samoff of Stanford pointed out: "He took students as serious participants in
university life and in the academic enterprise. Crawford Young was not a faculty member who sought apprentices or junior copies. He valued independence
and initiative and, throughout my experience with Crawford, he created space
for me and others to do our work, even as we went our own ways, and for all of
us as educators that surely should be our model." Young's collegiality and
openness to different views had a palpable impact on his colleagues in the Department of Political Science, which to this day is known for its intellectual
pluralism and methodological eclecticism, in no small measure because of his
influence.

Young was open to different views and was always eager to learn from his
students. Catharine Newbury, Gwendolen Carter Professor Emerita in African
Studies at Smith College, recounted at the 2020 memorial:

> While David [her husband] did his dissertation research and I was writing up
> my dissertation, we flew to Lubumbashi for a brief visit during which we were
> able to see Crawford, who was then serving as Dean of Social Sciences at the
> University. That was very special, not least because we engaged in a friendly but
> lively debate with Crawford and Thomas Turner about the current state of
> politics in the country. I remember that the perspective of David and myself
> differed somewhat from that of those who focused more on national politics.
> We were living at the very local level, aware of widespread rural discontent over
> various policies of the regime. Crawford was very tolerant of divergent per-
> spectives and that's why it was a fruitful debate and a very informative one. It
> was educational.

Young opened his home to students and held both social and academic
gatherings with invited guests. This allowed students and faculty to interact in-
formally with leading scholars and politicians. Students especially appreciated
that informal touch. More than one student noted that he would serve large
hard pretzels, and, because of them, sometimes attendees had to struggle to
hear the speaker while not making too much noise crunching. Tim Longman,

associate dean at Boston University, recounted: "As I look back, I realize how really significant these evenings were. I took it very much for granted at the time. I realized the degree to which I just assumed all professors did this. In retrospect, I realize that's a wonderful model. He introduced us to important people, made nice connections, put us in touch with people who invited us to conferences, helped us get publications out there, without ever really making a big deal about it. . . . He was thinking of us even though we weren't aware of it."

His former student and close colleague Michael Schatzberg recalled how Young took faculty and graduate students to Camp Randall for football games in the fall and excursions to Milwaukee to watch the Brewers during the summer. Even during those beloved sporting events, African politics always found its way into his habitual lamentations about both the Badgers and the Brewers.

Many former students drew on Young's example as a model for their own mentorship, especially in being available to the students, respecting them, taking a keen interest in them, and having their backs. They later talked about the ways he provided useful, practical advice with the aim of helping them become the best academics they could become.

As Gretchen Bauer, a professor at the University of Delaware, recounted at the 2020 memorial:

> I left grad school just as email and the Internet were becoming more widely available. In my day, seeing Crawford involved climbing four flights of stairs to the top floor of North Hall. And he was always there, he was always available, and he at least acted happy to see us. That is a first takeaway. Second, he was deeply respectful of his students. He managed to telegraph that to us, I think, also by the way in which he interacted with his family, his four daughters, and his wife. As I noted previously, he always gave the impression that we had as much to teach him, as he us. Third, he exhibited a keen interest in us as human beings, not just as students. When I was doing dissertation research in Namibia, he visited Windhoek as a guest of the USIA [United States Information Agency], whose director he knew. He used the opportunity of my research and his acquaintance with Helen Picard to visit a place he had never been, to give lectures, and to convey interest and support.

Young was especially supportive of women graduate students in political science early on, at a time when they were few in number. Some of the first female graduate students who enrolled in the 1960s conveyed to Young that there was a feeling among the women graduate students that a good portion of the field of political science was not particularly sympathetic to women professionals. Young reflected on this period in the aforementioned 2003 interview: "I do look back with some pleasure at the number of women that were trained. . . . I think that it was also partly [because I] acquired a reputation of being reasonably sympathetic to women professionals. I remember well my own mother's struggle for professional recognition as a scholar . . . her inability to find an academic job for many years after she finished her English PhD. And I suppose, having an activist wife and four daughters has something to do with it too."

Young was well aware of his privilege as a white male who had obtained his PhD from a prestigious institution. However, unlike most male academics of his generation, he acknowledged his privilege. He had a deep understanding of how power and privilege operate in hidden and not so hidden ways within the academy. At his retirement dinner, in 2001, he spoke about how he had benefited from a form of privilege that favored white men. He talked about how he was hired through what he described as "an old boys network" at the time. The department chair, Leon Epstein, made a trip to Yale, Harvard, Princeton, and the University of Chicago to collect names of people the department ought to consider. Young was the only person interviewed for the Africa position and was subsequently hired. Three others were also hired at the same time. He admitted that it was an "inexcusable way of hiring. It's shocking to confess that this is the way that we went about it."[7] Needless to say, it was not a typical retirement speech.

Young as a Person

Young was a loyal man: loyal to his graduate students, loyal to his family, and loyal to the University of Wisconsin–Madison. He had a strong sense of institutional loyalty. Although he received numerous invitations to apply to positions at other institutions, especially after serving as dean, he regularly turned them down. As he explained in the 2003 interview with Barry Teicher of the UW Archives Oral History Project, "The reasons were firstly, I felt a strong sense of loyalty to the institution which always treated me well. Secondly, beginning in 1970, my wife had a political career, and . . . political careers are not transferable. She and I loved Madison. And so, it was absolutely pointless to . . . The last thing I would have wanted to do is to string along some other institution thinking they might be interested, and then getting to a final stage to pull out."

Crawford Young retired from the university in 2001 and remained in Madison. In the last years of his life, he lived in a wing of Capitol Lakes, appropriately named North Hall, until his death on January 21, 2020. Young was survived by his daughters, Eva Young, Estelle Young, Emily Young, and Louise Young, who followed in her father's footsteps, becoming a distinguished professor in the Department of History at the University of Wisconsin–Madison. The passing of this lovely prince of a man marks the end of an era. We are all the better for having known him, and his legacy lives on in his work and in the former students and colleagues who knew him.

Organization of the Book

The book is organized around three themes: the state, cultural pluralism, and gender and politics. The first two topics were central to Young's corpus of writing. The third is a theme that relates to his focus on the importance of social identity but was a theme that Young himself did not necessarily address directly in his writing. Yet he always supported scholarship on gender, and many of his mentees and their mentees came to write about gender, in particular in Africa.

The contributors are mainly Young's students or the students of his students. They gathered virtually at a memorial in his honor held at the 2020 annual meeting of the African Studies Association and/or at an in-person memorial held in his honor in Madison in April 2022 (once the COVID-19 pandemic had subsided). Their contributions to this volume represent not only a kind of thematic legacy but also an approach to the study of politics. We hope that both will endure.

The first section of the book is on the colonial and postcolonial state in Africa, which was a major theme in Young's writing. The volume opens with an incisive analysis of the African postcolonial state by William Reno, a former student of Crawford Young's. Reno asks whether Young's idea of a "crisis" in the African state, a frame for his 1994 book, still holds. Young had pointed not only to the authoritarian backbone of the African colonial and postcolonial state, as Paulson-Smith does, but also to the tensions between a European construct in an African social and cultural system. What now, some thirty years later? Reno argues that, while it is true that a number of African states are still in crisis, a large number are consolidating. He points to three main factors: smart use of increasingly cheap and accessible technology; improvements in public administration and, in particular, taxation; and, finally, the emergence of elite pacts. Not only broadly comparative and synthetic and hence written in a Youngian style, Reno's argument resonates with one of the central claims in Young's 2012 book, *The Postcolonial State in Africa*, which is about variation in the trajectories of African states during the past fifty years.

Reno's chapter is followed by a perspicacious examination of how democratization in sub-Saharan Africa has shaped state performance and legitimacy

on the continent. The author, John W. Harbeson, a former student of Crawford Young, has been an influential scholar on these themes and an institution
builder who started the now thriving African Politics Conference Group, as
mentioned earlier. Harbeson's chapter builds on Young's work and is written in
a comparative, stock-taking style that mirrors some of Young's scholarship.
The analysis is sobering: some three decades of democratization on the continent have not led to stronger, more capable states, and, while Africans favor
democracy on the whole, that commitment is wavering; indeed, the continent
is seeing an upsurge in nonconstitutional, nondemocratic military coups.

In the next chapter, Kaden Paulson-Smith, an assistant professor at the University of Massachusetts–Dartmouth and a Wisconsin PhD, develops an innovative argument about policing that resonates strongly with Young's central thesis
in *The African Colonial State in Comparative Perspective* (Yale University Press, 1994).
Paulson-Smith argues that oppressive policing in postcolonial Africa can be
traced to the colonial origins of the institution. Focusing in-depth on the repression of a dockworkers' strike in colonial Tanganyika, Paulson-Smith demonstrates how the logic of policing is maintaining order and suppressing resistance,
what he calls "the defining imperatives of the colonial state."

The second section of the book focuses on a second major theme in Crawford Young's research: ethnicity and other kinds of social identities. In the first
chapter of this section, Rachel Beatty Riedl, who was an undergraduate in
Young's final graduate seminar in Madison, builds on Young's monumental *The
Politics of Cultural Pluralism* to probe religion as the foundation of one major social identity on the continent. Cognizant of how religious identities in some
ways mirror and overlap ethnic identities—another major source of identification on the continent—Riedl argues for the specificity of religious identities.
Riedl builds on the foundational claim that all religion is grounded in the belief
in the supernatural and the divine. She demonstrates with great conceptual dex-
terity the different ways that religion shapes beliefs, social action, and politics.

In the second chapter of this section, Dauda Abubakar—a former student
of Crawford Young's and a professor at the University of Michigan, Flint—
extends the religious theme with a focus on sectarianism and Islam in Northern
Nigeria. Like Riedl, he argues that religion needs to be studied for its specificity
as a type of cultural pluralism; religion matters. In Youngian fashion, Abubakar takes history seriously, and he anchors his discussion of contemporary Nigerian political Islam in the nineteenth-century Sokoto Jihad of Sheikh
Uthman dan Fodio. Abubakar then delineates different Sufi orders and Islamic
sects in the north and traces the emergence of Salafist movements, with a focus
on Boko Haram, an armed group that has engaged in sustained rebellion and

violence against civilians. He shows how the nineteenth-century jihad served as a model for Boko Haram leaders, in particular Mohammed Yusuf. Abubakar extends this discussion to show how earlier Islamist mobilizations are invoked by contemporary movements in Mali, Sudan, and elsewhere. He concludes with a passionate call for Africans to reject "the weaponization of diversity" as part of a decolonization project.

In chapter 6, Timothy Longman, a former student of Young's, builds on one of Young's central insights about identity: ethnic and other identities are flexible, and they respond and are instrumentalized in particular political contexts. Longman's focus, like much of Young's, is the Democratic Republic of Congo. Focusing in particular on Congolese politics during the past forty years, with an emphasis on periods in Congolese politics that were less central to Young's work, Longman affirms the malleable, politicized, protean sense of identity. But he also argues that some ethnic identities are more fixed, and, by examining several specific Congolese groups, he argues that when identities become racialized, they become less flexible and subject to change. The chapter resonates not only with Young's research agenda but also with the Riedl and Abubakar chapters, which encourage observers to disaggregate and pay attention to the specificities of different identities.

Joel Samoff, a former student of Young's, in chapter 7, returns the reader to Tanzania. In his chapter, he builds on Young's insights about the constructed and situational nature of social identities. Yet Samoff pushes the analysis to argue that class and interests matter too and that these three explanatory foundations for identity and mobilization offer responses to different questions. To illustrate the argument, Samoff focuses on the Kilimanjaro region, which he sets in contrast to the Kigoma region in the west of the country. Through careful analysis, built on extended fieldwork in the country, Samoff demonstrates the constructed and situational nature of ethnic identity but also how focusing on cultural identities to the exclusion of class and interest groups misdiagnoses the dynamics of group formation and mobilization.

Young's last graduate student, Cédric Jourde, in his chapter, looks at how Crawford Young's research on state and political regime construction applies to the ethnic politics in the Mauritania–Senegal borderland. It highlights how the Haalpulaaren people experienced different political dynamics depending on which side of the border they were on. In Mauritania, state construction led to authoritarianism and the marginalization of non-Arabic-speaking minorities, while Senegal took a more inclusive approach. The chapter also delves into the historical context and its impact on current political events. It discusses the enduring caste system within the Pulaar-speaking community, which has deep historical roots dating back to the eighteenth century. This caste system persisted despite changes in state structures and affected intraethnic tensions. Jourde focuses on how state systems influenced interethnic politics without significantly altering intraethnic dynamics.

The final chapter of this section, by Joshua B. Forrest, also one of Young's students, extends the analysis of identity beyond Africa. Applying what he calls a "Young-ian" analytic paradigm of cultural pluralism to Ukraine, Forrest helps us understand the construction and durability of Ukrainian nationalism, as well as the origins of the interstate war between Russia and Ukraine, which was ongoing at the time of publication. Forrest focuses on two key dimensions: the emergence of grassroots ethnic mobilization and the authoritarian impulse to achieve domination over ethnic "others" in politics. Forrest's detailed and perceptive reading of contemporary nationalism and war demonstrates the continuing contemporary relevance of Young's core ideas.

In the third section of the book, on gender and politics, Ladan Affi in her chapter delves into the challenges women have faced in seeking a seat at the table in Somali politics. She shows how Somali women activists have fought for greater political representation dating back to the colonial era. She explores one of the gaps in Young's work: the tensions that can emerge between gender and other identities. One of the biggest challenges has been the ways in which clan politics has interfered with their claims to equal participation and representation. She shows how the idea of making the clan the foundation of the newly constructed state after 2000 clashed with the goal of increasing women's representation. The power-sharing arrangement between clans was based on an idea of politics as a zero-sum game in which women's participation was seen as a threat to clan control of a limited number of seats. Islamist parties also posed another threat to women's engagement in politics. She shows how women made limited gains, resulting in women claiming 24.4 percent of the lower house parliamentary seats and 26 percent in the upper house in the 2016 elections.

Building upon Young's work, Melinda J. Adams's chapter probes the intersection of gender with various facets of identity within the Cameroonian context. This emphasis on identity assumes particular significance in the crisis in Cameroon between the Anglophone minority and Francophone parts of the country. Adams's contention is that while Young's work furnishes a valuable framework for comprehending contemporary Cameroonian politics, particularly in relation to the territorial and identity aspects of the Anglophone crisis, a comprehensive understanding necessitates an exploration of how gender intersects with other facets of identity and the pivotal role that women play in shaping Anglophone national identities and peace initiatives.

In the last chapter in this section, Gretchen Bauer and Akosua K. Dark-wah's coauthored piece reflects the spirit of collaboration Crawford encouraged in his former students, and it also reflects his encouragement of scholarship by his students that went beyond his own many themes and interests. Bauer was his former PhD student, and Darkwah received her doctorate in the University of Wisconsin's sociology department. In their chapter, they discuss the historical exclusion of women from formal political office in Ghana, particularly after the country gained independence and during successive military regimes. The chapter highlights the very low representation of women in parliament since the early 1990s, even though women have had a somewhat higher presence in cabinets. The chapter suggests that interventions by political parties and government officials, including the president, could play a significant role in improving women's representation in the government. The chapter's insights are based on extensive research, including numerous interviews with women members of parliament, cabinet ministers, party leaders, and activists.

Notes

1. Personal communication, February 6, 2023.

2. He was named Merwin after his uncle. He never used the name other than to indicate its existence with an "M." preceding Crawford. He used to go to football games with Warren Tripp, who related that Crawford had once been at the doctor's office, where a nurse called out "Merwin . . . Merwin" several times. So rarely did he associate with this name that it was only a while later that it dawned on him that she was referring to him!

3. Louise Young, *In the Public Interest: The League of Women Voters 1920–1976* (New York: Greenwood Press, 1989).

4. At its inception, it was called the Department of Afro-American Studies.

5. Interview with Barry Teicher of the UW Archives Oral History Project, 2003.

6. "Crawford Young," Cress Funeral and Cremation Service, accessed January 17, 2024, https://www.cressfuneralservice.com/obituary/Crawford-Young.

7. Interview with Barry Teicher.

The Colonial and Postcolonial State in Africa

Part I

State Development in Contemporary Africa

William Reno

I s "crisis of the African state" a valid concept when describing and analyzing state development in contemporary Africa? The concept of a crisis of the state is a core feature of Crawford Young's classic *The African Colonial State in Comparative Perspective* (1994). In that book, Young presented a conception of states in Africa as reflections of the different characteristics of earlier European empires from the imposition of colonial rule through its consolidation and the process of decolonization. The crisis arises from the difficulties of indigenizing a European-designed grid of administrative hierarchies within precisely demarcated borders in a continent that had its own widely varying experiences with state building amid a great diversity of political structures. Young's work played an important role in shaping debates about this deep-rooted crisis that has defined the study of politics and economics in Africa for decades. Since then, political instability, the breakdown of state services, and the rise of Islamist insurgencies in the large states of the Sahel reflect the intensification of a long-term crisis of the state. Long-running conflicts in Central Africa and the Horn call into question the viability of Congo and Somalia in their present forms. At the same time, there are clear signs of divergence. Other states have found recipes for long-term political stability. Several have stopped patterns of repeated coups and reversed economic decline. Sustained high economic growth rates have enabled some of them to build more capable and, in some cases, more accountable government administrations.

This chapter explores Young's key role in defining debates about the character and, ultimately, the crisis of the state in Africa. Past events, particularly during colonial rule in Africa, affected options and decisions that led to crisis in a self-reinforcing feedback loop. That dynamic does not preclude remarkable discontinuities between historical periods. An observer of China in 1975, for example, would have been shocked to learn that a half century hence, China hosted the world's second-largest economy, nearly as large as the world's largest, and was able to challenge US dominance on the world stage. From the perspective of 1975, even with Chinese Communist Party rule, China was notable for its political instability and impoverished economy. The modern study of warlords took China's turmoil in the 1920s as a paradigm-defining model for the inquiry into state failure (Pye 1971).

Likewise, the observer of Latin America a half century after its wave of independence in the 1810s and 1820s would have painted a picture of weak and failed states. Its inheritance of colonial boundaries and weak and exploitative colonial administrations had put in place a dynamic that looked somewhat like Africa's path-dependent model of persistent state crisis, a pattern of sustained and mainly endogenous stagnation. By the end of the nineteenth century, much of Latin America had undergone big discontinuous changes, about as distant in temporal terms as much of Africa is from its colonial past. The rapid expansion of economies, the construction of new state institutions, and the reinforcement of old ones occurred alongside rapid social changes, such as shifts in center–periphery relations, the rise of urban middle classes, tensions between agriculture and industry, and the rise of worker activism. These big discontinuous changes are critical junctures because they drove social and political changes that upended political and economic relations that seemed frozen in time (Collier and Collier 1991).

Though Africa's crisis grows out of colonial legacies that are distinct from the patterns of colonial administration from the late nineteenth century to the middle of the twentieth—patterns that are at the core of Young's historical inquiry into the roots of the present crisis—China and Latin America show that political development proceeds at differential rates of change over time. Africa's crisis of the state is evident in the institutional stasis and decay in many places. But that path is distinct from that of the category of states that see institutional development, including institutions quite divergent from the state's earlier development. Once these institutions are in place, they can assume a life of their own, engaging with and extracting resources from society and even reinforcing societal changes. Thus, this chapter heeds Stephen Krasner's call for the character of the state, and its potential to undergo rapid change, to occupy a major place in scholarly debates about political development. As Krasner writes, "An imaginary that expects short bursts of rapid institutional change followed by long period of statis can be termed punctuated equilibrium" (1984, 242). Such displacements are rare, he argues, but when they occur they can potentially displace old patterns of political development (1984, 242). Young was attentive to this issue in his *African Colonial State*, asking: "Can a new state be invented that sheds the debilitating traditions of the past?" (1994, 292).

Young detected growing variation in African state development in his 2012 book, *The Postcolonial State in Africa: Fifty Years of Independence, 1960–2010*, reflecting nascent experiments with democracy in some countries and descent into armed conflict in others. He delineated a landscape, however, "with strikingly little change among the state actors but a dramatic transformation in their institutional content and social environment" (Mokube 2013, 125). By this time, Young recognized in the appearance of this variation in trajectories of state development that the groundwork for something like a critical juncture in Africa's state system had emerged.

The Weight of History and the Crisis of the African State

The colonial interlude was a short enough period that several presidents of independent African states, such as Sierra Leone's Milton Margai and Malawi's Hastings Banda, were born in places that had yet to come under colonial administration. Their circumstances and predilections reflected Africa's distinctive and shared colonial experience as much as they did precolonial legacies of governance. These legacies included the radical weakening of reciprocal obligations of rulers and ruled in the political realm. Where "traditional authorities" were incorporated into colonial administrations, they were stripped of their former sovereignty and survived as political agents engaged in the state's project of "ruthless extractive action" (Kandeh 1992). Young (2012) explained how the mediation of colonial rule through tribally organized local authorities created a distinct form of authoritarian rule. This administrative model created powerful forces of path dependency. Colonial forms of indirect rule that delegated the extraction of resources needed for basic state administration to these local authorities created "the shared interest of political elites in preserving extractive polities, on whose rents they rely for their livelihoods" (2012, 303).

This system of rule set up relations of domination and inequality linked to extraction, progressively shifting from extraction via formal state institutions to informal relations between patrons and clients. The path of upward mobility lay in securing a position in the state—and a place in political networks—that gave one access to these spoils. "Tribe" and other markers of identity were politicized in this manner. As Francis Deng noted, "there is always high pressure exerted on elected politicians to become benefactors to their kin group of ethnic constituencies, whether financially or in terms of social services. The abuse of power for the acquisition and disbursement of wealth under these conditions, rather than the result of some indigenous propensity toward corruption, may well be the outcome of a felt need caused by the demands of new standards of living and raised expectations" (2002, 379). The Nigerian sociologist Peter Ekeh conceptualized the duality of the political realm linked to moral imperatives and a civic realm that is amoral and expects that politics is used to extract resources and protection for personal benefit and for the benefit of kin. Like Young, Ekeh held: "It is to the colonial experience that any valid conceptualization of the unique nature of African politics must look" (1975, 93).

In broad terms, this afterlife of colonial rule predisposes many African states toward a distinct category of authoritarian rule that is intolerant of autonomous political power, such as business communities or mass movements. These colonial legacies of exploitation were primed for economic failure and the development of patrimonial autocracies based on various forms of asset stripping and dependence on external support to distribute resources to core supporters without any pretense of accountability. Young concluded that these legacies of colonial rule remained dominant into the start of the twenty-first century, even though a small number of states had succeeded in establishing modestly institutionalized democratic systems (Young 2004).

Young's conceptualization of African states stands alongside those who explored the "neo-patrimonial" aspects of African states. Jean-François Bayart (1989) and others highlighted cultural aspects of statecraft that, alongside the longue durée of subordination in a Europe-centric world order, produced a distinct "indigenization" of the European-inspired form of the state toward ever more diverse and externally oriented predatory strategies, including in illicit commerce, to support often hidden and collective structures of power that often were more influential than the official tenants of state offices. Young and Turner's *Rise and Decline of the Zairian State* provided a detailed survey of this process to the point that "the state risks becoming an irrelevancy, as well as a mechanism for predatory accumulation by those associated with its eroding power" (1985, 45). Though Young's analysis remained rooted in what is commonly termed comparative historical analysis (Mahoney and Rueschemeyer 2003), both Young's and more culturalist interpretations of state crisis raise the question Young posed in *The African Colonial State*: "History tells us that the patterns of the past remain embedded in the present. Can they be rewoven to permit the emergence of a new kind of polity, one that employs the discourse of democracy but connects itself to the deeper African cultural heritage?" (1994, 292).

Beyond Crisis?

Institutional and behavioral path dependencies in the processes of state development are difficult to break, short of bloody interstate war and the disruptions of social revolution. Both of those phenomena are notably rare occurrences on the continent. At the start of the century, states including the Congo, the Central African Republic, Somalia, and arguably Guinea-Bissau and a few others fit the model of persistent political and economic crises. Despite the end of complex multisided conflicts in West Africa, several large states of the Sahel joined the list. In each case, a political elite exhibits a variety of predatory modes of extraction to support its domestic structures of power, much in the manner Young and Turner found in Zaire (Congo) in their 1985 book. Military coups d'états, classic indicators of political instability, continue to be a feature of this dimension of Africa's political landscape. Since 2020, armed forces successfully staged coups in Mali (2020 and 2021), Guinea (2021), Sudan (2021), Burkina Faso (twice in 2022), Niger (2023), and Gabon (2023). Many of these large states of the Sahel region, including northern Nigeria, Niger, Burkina Faso, and Mali, struggle with persistent insurgencies that began in the early 2010s. Ongoing localized conflicts in eastern Congo are legacies of a much larger regional war at the close of the past century. Much of Somalia remains without an effective central government more than three decades after the start of a civil war in the late 1980s. Pope Francis criticized South Sudan's government during his January 2023 visit for "the inequitable distribution of funds, secret schemes to get rich, patronage deals, lack of transparency" (Walsh and Harowitz 2023). In 2021, Transparency International ranked South Sudan as the globe's most corrupt country, while Somalia bumped it to second place in the 2022 rankings (Transparency International 2022).

At the same time, some of Africa's states noted for political instability in the early decades of independence exhibit remarkable shifts toward stronger institutional channels of popular accountability in the form of stable civilian governance. Ghana was considered one of Africa's early "failed states" in the early

1980s after a succession of six coups d'état from 1966 to 1981 (Chazan 1983). Since 1992, Ghana has held competitive multiparty elections and undergone peaceful transfers of power and now has one of the continent's most professional armed forces. Despite Nigeria's many political and economic problems, after six coups d'état between 1966 and 1993, the country experienced a radical drop in military intervention into politics and has had a succession of elected civilian governments since 1999. Likewise, Benin experienced eight coups d'état between 1963 and 1975 and none since. Elected civilian governments have ruled that country since 1991.

These cases point to the basic principle that even extensive institutional reforms and training that characterize US and European Union security force assistance to African countries—as was the case for Mali, Niger, Gabon, and other states that experienced recent coups—are not sufficient to control Africa's armed forces in the long run. Instead, African governments that enjoy high or rising levels of legitimacy are less prone than others to military intervention in politics, a contrasting trajectory that stands in contrast to the recent round of coups in states with ruling elites of low and declining legitimacy (Aboagye and Clark 2022).

Several large African countries have among the world's better records of long-term economic growth (World Bank 2023). They include countries with significant legacies of conflict. Notable examples include Ethiopia's 9.5 percent average growth rate since the late 2000s. That growth rate doubled per capita incomes over a decade and eclipsed Côte d'Ivoire's overall 7.5 percent annual growth rate since 2011 and the sustained 8 percent annual growth rate in Rwanda, which doubled per capita incomes in under a generation (World Bank 2023). This group of relatively high-growth economies also includes countries with relatively stable elected governments, such as Ghana and Senegal. These higher material standards of living come with changes in social status, education, cultural norms, and lifestyles that have a bearing on political orientations and expectations about governance.

These social changes also motivate considerable academic debate over the meaning of the "African middle class." Earlier critiques of postcolonial states located the relatively affluent as adjuncts of corrupt and inefficient states, often beneficiaries of patronage-based hiring practices in state-owned enterprises and civil service (Shivji 1976). Since the turn of the century, this growth has occurred alongside reductions in public-sector employment. New strata of urban professionals and private-sector entrepreneurs may be less dependent on the state than their counterparts in past decades and thus are able to become well off without joining the rush for spoils (Lufumpa and Ncube 2015). How people

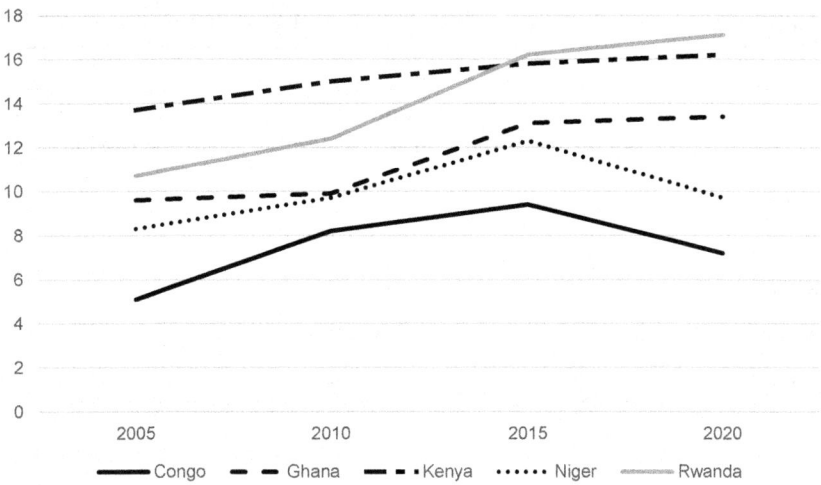

Figure 1.1. Tax revenues as percentage of official sector GDP in select countries. *Source*: UNU-WIDER 2023.

in this stratum pursue their own interests remains an open question. Do people with more money to spend demand greater accountability from the government, and do they tend to support policies that sustain higher economic growth and improve social conditions for the less well off? These questions surround real social changes taking place in some parts of Africa.

Increased state capacities to collect taxes, alongside reduced levels of corruption in the collection process, point to another vector of divergence. By the end of the 2010s, governments in sub-Saharan Africa were collecting about 15 percent in taxes as a share of their GDPs after bottoming out at about 11 percent in the late 1990s. That tax share is about half of the US rate and falls well short of the European average of 32 percent. There are, however, considerable disparities in revenue collection among African states. Congo collects taxes that are about a 7 percent share of recorded GDP. The real figure is likely well under that if one considers informal and clandestine activity that may exceed the size of the country's formal economy. As figure 1.1 shows, countries such as Ghana, Kenya, and Uganda register collection rates approaching half of the US and European averages after more than twenty years of steady increases (Tagem and Morrissey 2021).

The composition of tax revenues has diverged, too. Higher collection rates are associated with greater proportions of tax revenue collected through the application of value-added taxes on goods and on monetary transactions. The

Table 1.1. Cell and Internet Access in Select Countries

	Cellular subscriptions (per 100 inhabitants)	Internet access at home (percentage)	At least 3G access (percentage)
Congo	50	1	55
Ghana	120	19	96
Kenya	122	18	98
Niger	56	4	24
Rwanda	80	9	99

Source: International Telecommunication Union 2023.

collection of these revenues is dependent on making economic activities visible to the state, a difficult proposition when individuals could easily evade formal reporting procedures. Indirect taxation, through mechanisms such as value-added taxes, avoids the necessity of direct contact with the producer or purchaser of goods and services. That arrangement, in turn, limits the need for additional civil servants in tax collecting positions, a notorious source of spoils in many African state administrations. Those who pay taxes of this sort, including taxes on electronic transactions, do not have to meet tax officials, eliminating the practice of negotiating lower tax collection in return for bribes to tax officials.

Technology plays a growing role in this shift in tax composition and in the overall collection of revenue. After a decade of rapid growth, the penetration of mobile phones per one hundred inhabitants in sub-Saharan Africa reached about 75 percent in 2015 and continued upward at a slower rate (see table 1.1). Some African economies have achieved striking success with the adoption of mobile money services, such as Kenya's M-Pesa. Indeed, in Kenya, about 75 percent of the adult (age 15+) population has a mobile money account, with Uganda and Zimbabwe registering about half their adult populations using this service. Mobile money services take advantage of leapfrog technology and provide a range of financial services to people whose economic transactions have been largely beyond the purview of the formal economy. In the process, these services render transactions visible to the state, and thus they become taxable. Use of electronic systems to monitor tax compliance reduces the incidence of tax evasion. This digitized information also provides a wealth of information to tax administrations and economic planners, with programs built into the payment process to flag irregularities among transactions (Okunogbe and Santoro 2023).

Rwanda is at the vanguard of African countries using this digitized information to increase tax collection from businesses. Through archiving data on sales and payments, Rwanda allows businesses to access these data when paying taxes on e-filing platforms, which have become compulsory modes for tax payments. The necessity of computer equipment and technological savvy among users limits the reach of this mode of tax collection, though, as Rwanda's economy continues to grow, more people are included in this category of users (Mascagni et al. 2022).

The addition of GPS technology and publicly available satellite images such as Google Earth aids tax authorities' efforts to identify and locate taxable real estate. Administrative capacity is still needed to build a reliable property cadastral, though the collection of basic data is more insulated from efforts to evade the state's gaze.

Evidence from Ghana indicates that a geospatial database and (a still uncertain process) of valuation presents opportunities to integrate billing, payments, appeals, and enforcement into online systems. The integration of these different systems into a usable revenue collection mechanism requires a core of technology-savvy designers and operators who can update software and run usable platforms. Ghana's English-language education system and the cycling of skilled workers between Ghana and overseas educational opportunities and tech-sector employment give the Ghanaian state a comparative advantage in adopting this technology, particularly as Ghana has become a location in a global market of back-office data management and software production (Dzansi et al. 2022). This connection with a global supply chain in services provides another illustration of a widening divergence between crisis Africa, where conditions become more hostile to these sorts of complex systems, and postcrisis Africa, where the trend is toward applying new technologies to revenue collection and ultimately to increased state capacity to provide services outside inherited systems of patronage.

Surveillance technologies play a role in the divergences in state capacities in Africa. As with tax collection and communications technologies, surveillance technologies tend to favor state administrations that already possess the capacity to manage the data these instruments collect. Concerns have grown that governments in Africa have become more adept at using digital surveillance to track individuals' locations and intercept communications. A *Wall Street Journal* report, for example, revealed that Ugandan intelligence officers used spyware to penetrate a prominent opposition politician's WhatsApp chat group. That incident and another in Zambia pointed to the role of the Chinese telecommunications company Huawei in enabling domestic surveillance (Parkinson, Bariyo, and Chin 2019). Huawei has a dominant presence in the African market, having built telecom systems in at least forty countries since it started doing business in Kenya in 1998. Huawei's low-cost handsets have played a major part in enabling African consumers to access the Internet. As an example, I purchased a midrange model for $70 (which cost more than many other models) in Mali in 2019 and found that the device could do most of the basic functions that a much more expensive iPhone can do, albeit with less battery power.

The appearance of digital video surveillance, such as through CCTV cameras paired with facial recognition technology, is another potentially powerful tool for surveillance. Surveillance in Nairobi is linked to programs such as Huawei's Safe Cities project that interconnects video, tracking devices, and cloud storage systems to police urban areas (Jili 2022). Kano, a large city in northern Nigeria that has been the site of sectarian violence, has among Africa's densest CCTV coverage, with five thousand cameras or 1.19 cameras per one thousand population (CIPESA 2022, 17). These and related technologies merge policy initiatives to provide citizens with safety and predictability in their everyday lives through protection from crime, including growing cybersecurity threats, while combining those benefits with surveillance operations geared toward identifying unauthorized political activity. Beyond a threshold of basic state capacity to manage and use data, the commercial element of these systems relieve state administration and its treasury of a large portion of the financial burdens of setting up and maintaining these extensive systems. In sum, these systems are cheap ways, in relative terms, to extend state authority, when compared to the exercise of coercion through police or direct regulation of movements or behavior.

Observers express concern that these technologies worsen authoritarian tendencies when deployed to monitor citizens (Allen and La Lime 2021). Though it is not clear that "safe cities" projects contribute to reductions in urban crime, these technologies provide governments, which are capable enough to do so, the opportunity to manipulate these tools for their own purposes.

The relative capacity to exploit new technologies reflects the overall divergence in African state capacity. Even if governments rely on private companies, including foreign service providers, to manage data, the technical and organizational skills required to match data to government action demand relatively high levels of organizational capacity. For example, South Africa's large market for home protection services and the government's administrative capacity provide solid bases for the development of data management for other purposes. The more than five thousand CCTV units to monitor roads and public spaces in Uganda are effective tools because Uganda's police have the capacity to maintain a data management center that utilizes facial recognition technology (Special Correspondent 2022). Recent coups in Sahel states, however, show that technologies that were intended to provide more precise monitoring of citizens (Dalberto et al. 2018) were not used in ways that ultimately protected these regimes from those who overthrew them. No matter the sophistication of the technologies used for surveillance, fragmented governments still face the problem that those charged with protecting the regime may use positions that provide access to information to challenge their regimes.

Large-scale programs such as the World Bank's ID for Development (ID4D) aim to support national programs to provide citizens with government-issued ID cards linked to national digital data systems. The World Bank's primary goal is to help governments facilitate citizens' links to social registries. Legibility provides citizens with better access to state benefits and provides states with data to improve the targeting of social programs and provide a mechanism for digital payments. The purpose of these ID systems varies across countries, however, and they can be used them to deliver subsidies, streamline tax collection, and limit identity fraud.

Governments that already possess higher degrees of bureaucratic capacity emerge as the greatest beneficiaries of biometric ID systems. Lesotho, for example, extended a digital national ID system to 85 percent of the eligible population by 2020 to provide a common identification system for driver's licenses, voter registration, health records, and banking (Pule 2020, 10). Digital identification, in this case, aids the state's capacity to keep track of citizens in a country in which more than 40 percent of the population lives below the poverty line and many citizens work abroad as migrant laborers. Uganda goes a step further, adding data from DNA, fingerprints, and eye scans to the national ID registry "to eliminate crime." Reaching close to 80 percent coverage of eligible citizens, national ID registration increasingly is required for access to basic privately provided services such as telephone SIM cards and financial services (CIPESA 2022, 11). By contrast, significant failures to collect biometric data and link national ID numbers across systems occurred in Sierra Leone and the Central African Republic. Both countries passed legislative frameworks but lacked the basic capacities to collect information and manage the data they collect (CIPESA 2022, 14).

A New Path to Stronger States?

The growing divergence between governments that can maintain their states and those that succumb to crisis is striking. The latter category of states points to the next stage of a long-term process of failing and dysfunctional institutions and domestic turmoil; whereas the former category turns out to be stronger than expected, capable of surviving and addressing the challenges of colonial legacies and periods of political instability that dragged down other states. What accounts for this dramatic difference?

This divergence is unexpected, at least in terms of how many scholars have studied the African state. Charles Tilly's dictum "war made the state, and the state made war" has been influential in comparative macro sociology and in international relations explanations for the rise of strong states (Tilly 1975, 42). Tilly used Africa's weak states to illustrate the centrality of warfare in creating strong states. In Africa, boundaries appeared as a result of agreements among colonial rulers. Africa's independent states, for the most part, could not redraw boundaries to reflect realities on the ground. This static interstate architecture, writes Tilly, reflects a condition in which "states have ceased fighting each other over disputed territory, and border forces have shifted their efforts from defense against direct attack toward control of infiltration. Armies (and, for that matter, navies, and air forces) concentrate increasingly on repression of civilian populations, control of insurgents, and seizures of power. As a consequence, governments become more unstable as their borders become more secure" (Tilly 1992, 203). The international system recognizes this type of statehood, regardless of how lacking these governments are in terms of their institutional capacities and political will. These "quasi-states," in Robert Jackson's terms, "are now exempted from the power contest at least in part and treated as international protectorates. . . . Weaknesses or backwardness of countries is no longer a justification for conquest or colonialism" (1990, 23). Young's (1994) identification of colonial governments' "ruthless extractive action" to make their colonies self-financing, a process that left legacies of predation, played a critical role in shaping the domestic realms of what became "quasi-states."

The two-year Eritrean-Ethiopian war (1998–2000) was a notable exception to this dearth of interstate war. This war involved direct combat between national armies over territorial claims, and it ended with a UN-backed settlement that resulted in minor awards of territory to each side. Rwanda's efforts to control armed opponents in eastern Congo also led to interstate war. Rwanda's government has had a compelling reason to take risks and make sacrifices to increase its capacity to govern and defend its realm from hostile forces. These countries are examples of situations in which interstate war was a plausible stimulus to centralizing state power and building institutional capacity.

By contrast, the collapse of a central government in Somalia in 1991 and the failure of a successor to assert authority much beyond the capital city illustrates a more common pattern. This condition of weakness did not mean that Somalia lost territory to stronger neighbors through conquest or lost its seat in the United Nations. Similarly, crises in the large states of the Sahel do not create expectations that failure will expose these states to conquest or that outsiders will cease to recognize them as sovereign states.

In sum, the contemporary international system appears to contribute to the path-dependent trajectory toward a continued crisis of the state in Africa.

The appearance of governments that can maintain and even increase state capabilities stands apart from the crisis trajectory in important ways. Collectively, they point to the possibility of a model of state building that is not dependent on fighting wars. The survey in the preceding sections shares several common features that help to outline the contours of this exit from persistent state crisis. These common features include:

1. Constructing elite accommodations that are durable enough to permit political competition and provide a foundation of political stability.
2. Undergoing social transformations that produce professional/commercial communities that generate wealth that is not tied to control over some aspect of state administration.
3. Reaching thresholds of administrative capacity that are sufficient to take advantage of organizational and technological developments that are then used to further strengthen state capacities to provide services and engage (and control) citizens.

Durable elite accommodations have appeared in unexpected places, such as in previously coup-prone Ghana, Benin, and Nigeria. The removal of militaries from governance in these countries is an indicator of cooperation among elite members of diverse ethnic communities that refrain from politicizing armed forces to retain power. How and why these accommodations arose are complicated matters involving factors particular to each country. In any event, they share the significant involvement of local and regional authority figures—often outside the state's formal administrative system—who have the public credibility and capacity to mediate political conflicts.

Bolanle Awe's pioneering investigations into the role of prominent women in mediating political conflicts highlight how parallel systems of governance intervene at critical moments in Nigeria's political development to promote these elite accommodations (1991). Several Nigerian states that are sites of violent sectarian clashes incorporate religious leaders into "peace commissions" and recruit figures who have high degrees of public legitimacy into the conflict resolution efforts of these state governments (Kew 2021).

It is nothing new to note that there are forms of order beyond and outside the state. The importance of the interface of state and nonstate orders is that they create processes that are in line with what people in these societies regard as legitimate governance. Somalia, for example, did not descend into complete anarchy, despite the absence of a functioning state for significant periods over the past three decades. Business communities have sustained an efficient remittance system, provided services to some communities, and, in instances when they have teamed up with religious leaders, established court systems (Ahmad 2017). Local realities challenge the assumption that all these local arrangements are legitimate or necessarily contribute to states' capacities and legitimacy. But where they do, they play an important role in indigenizing state authority and offer a basis for theorizing the process of state building beyond Africa's colonial legacies and outside the conventional framework of "war builds states."

Africa's social transformations are central to thinking about how some African governments shift out of the patterns of predatory rule that Young and others investigated. Leonardo Arriola (2012) argues that democratic rule and accountable administration are more likely in African states where the main ethnic group that controls government is not the same ethnic group that is dominant in business. The idea that independent economic actors in pluralist political systems can promote more disciplined state administration and support for expanded economic activities is an old argument, but Arriola shows how a critical mass of entrepreneurs can acquire political clout. By the same token, politically marginal groups that are active in business, such as ethnic Somali entrepreneurs in Kenya who cannot rely on favor from politicians, have strong interests in supporting impartial judicial systems that can reliably settle disputes.

These pathways to independent political influence illustrate the ways that institutions beget institutions. These processes are more likely in states that already have institutional frameworks upon which to build. It also appears that these state-building processes are concentrated in large cities that have dense connections to the global economy, such as Nairobi, Dar es Salaam, Dakar, Accra, Abidjan, and Lagos. Most are coastal cities in countries that have large enough populations to support significant domestic markets. Most also have legacies of relatively dense local administration and are sites of infrastructure development. In sum, this departure from an old path-dependent trajectory toward crisis draws upon foundations that may be preconditions for a new path-dependent trajectory—a further widening of the divergent paths of African state development.

These two common features create conditions that support the third common feature—the ability to utilize technological and organizational developments to contribute to greater state capacity. Critical masses of IT specialists, whether as workers in offshore data processing and software development or even in clandestine cybercrime enterprises, provide expertise to manage data and apply findings to address practical problems. The largest talent pools tend to concentrate in large cities and countries with large English-speaking populations, the most attractive sites for outsourcing hubs. Kenya and Nigeria have emerged as the largest sources of startup finance and have made some of the largest advances in digitizing payments, thereby connecting new customers to financial services and ride-hailing services and small farmers to vendors. These startups utilize their comparative advantage in local knowledge about the organization of the informal economy, an advantage enjoyed by local ride-hailing apps over foreign competitors like Uber and Bolt. These firms also have the local knowledge to address issues of business partner and customer trust more easily, challenges that are difficult for foreign investors to master.

This third feature contributes to the divergence. Any aspiring tech entrepreneur in a state with a failing government and poor economic prospects has high incentives to migrate to one of these tech hubs. This concentration of talent draws more talent, which in turn encourages states to be more attentive to regulatory reform, streamlining licensing processes and introducing other changes that support the industry. The practical result is that Nigeria and Kenya have become Africa's dominant sites for digital business investment and digital business density, each significantly outpacing South Africa, with Ghana, Uganda, and Tanzania posting substantial growth in this sector (Begazo et al. 2023, 63). States such as Mali, Niger, and Burkina Faso do not register in these surveys, indicative of the widening divergence in the overall capacities of African states.

It is good news that, Ethiopia and Rwanda aside, there is a path to state capacity that does not involve fighting in interstate wars! The growing divergence between those that do master state building without warfare and those that do not points to a new set of state-building processes on the continent. Given this development, what is the future of the state in Africa likely to look like?

Looking Ahead

The widening divergence provides a basis for thinking about the future of Africa's state system. One Africa features the continued development of state administrative capacities in coastal states with large globally connected cities. These states will continue to draw the most talented from poorer and politically unstable neighbors. Their large diasporas will facilitate overseas connections and provide investments. Top universities in the United States already have established patterns of chain circulation between their economics departments and business schools and students from Africa who return to set up businesses. US government programs such as the Department of State's Young African Leadership Initiative support and partially subsidize these connections. The Mastercard Foundation supports students from Africa who study at elite US universities such as Stanford and the University of California at Berkeley. This more advantaged Africa includes states that already demonstrate the capacity to resist pressures from abroad to pick sides in the geopolitical competition between the US and China. They will be better able to maintain a "third-way" stance than their counterparts during the Cold War competition between the US and the Soviet Union. These states are becoming regional powerbrokers with the capacity to intervene in neighboring states when governments perceive threats to their interests. These states also will be able to marshal organizational and material resources to at least begin to address disruptions of climate change and other challenges.

Another Africa will consist of states that continue along the path of state crisis. The large inland states of the Sahel, along with Somalia, are notable examples. Their governments appear to be becoming less well equipped over time to address challenges such as climate change and large-scale migration. Series of coups, trending toward lower ranks with each iteration, point to the increasing fragmentation of their political systems. The popularity of these coups reflects to public disdain for corrupt and incompetent incumbent regimes. Military rulers sweep away parts of these old elite accommodations but struggle to replace them with an alternative that can rule their countries. Unlike in previous decades, there will be no UN peacekeeping forces to restore order. Aid from abroad will be scarcer as these old providers in Europe and the US conclude from their experiences in Afghanistan and Iraq that foreign-backed state building is a futile exercise. Many burdens of dealing with these crises already fall upon Africa's more successful states, which must absorb migrants (including some of these countries' most educated and energetic citizens who seek better environments in which to utilize their skills) and address the political instability of neighbors.

One might imagine a different Africa in which failing inland states were not independent states but instead hinterlands of large coastal states. Many problems then would be domestic affairs challenges to governments as they develop new capacities. But these are sovereign states, and their failures are international in dimension. Nigeria, Africa's sole surviving colonial-era federation, shows what could have been possible if other African federations had survived the transition to independence. Nigeria's North suffers from crises of governance as serious as those found in Sahel states. But because the North is part of a federated state, the resources and organization of the more dynamic parts of Nigeria are applied to dealing with its crisis—as a domestic matter. But this is not an option available to states in crisis. Instead, the divergence is likely to grow wider.

References

Aboagye, Michael Ohene, and John Clark. 2022. "Political Legitimacy and Military Interventions." In *Rethinking Civil-Military Relations in Africa*, edited by Moses Khisa and Christopher Day, 37–63. Boulder, CO: Lynne Rienner.

Ahmad, Aisha. 2017. *Jihad & Co.: Black Markets and Islamist Power*. New York: Oxford University Press.

Allen, Nathaniel, and Matthew La Lime. 2021. "How Digital Espionage Tools Exacerbate Authoritarianism Across Africa." Brookings, November 19. https://www.brookings.edu/articles/how-digital-espionage-tools-exacerbate-authoritarianism-across-africa/.

Arriola, Leonardo. 2012. *Multiethnic Coalitions in African Business Financing of Opposition Election Campaigns*. New York: Cambridge University Press.

Awe, Bolanle. 1991. "Writing Women into History: The Nigerian Experience." In *Writing Women's History*, edited by K. Offen, R. R. Pierson, and J. Rendall, 211–20. London: Palgrave Macmillan.

Bayart, Jean-François. 1989. *L'Etat en Afrique: La politique du ventre*. Paris: Fayard.

Begazo, Tania, Moussa Blimpo, and Mark Dutz. 2023. *Digital Africa: Technological Transformation for Jobs*. Washington, DC: World Bank.

Chazan, Naomi. 1983. *An Anatomy of Ghanaian Politics: Managing Political Recession, 1969–1982*. Boulder, CO: Westview Press.

CIPESA. 2022. "The Rise of Biometric Surveillance." Collaboration on International ICT Policy for East and Southern Africa. https://cipesa.org/wp-content/files/reports/State_of_Internet_Freedom_in_Africa_2022.pdf.

Collier, Ruth Berins, and David Collier. 1991. *Shaping the Political Arena: Critical Junctures, the Labor Movement, and the Regime Dynamics in Latin America*. Princeton, NJ: Princeton University Press.

Dalberto, Séverine Awenengo, Richard Banégas, and Armando Cutolo. 2018. "Biomaîtriser les identités? État documentaire et citoyenneté au tournant biométrique." *Politique africaine* 152:5–29.

Deng, Francis. 2002. "Beyond Cultural Domination: Institutionalizing Equity in the African State." In *Beyond State Crisis? Postcolonial Africa and Post-Soviet Eurasia in Comparative Perspective*, edited by Mark Beissenger and Crawford Young, 359–84. Baltimore: Johns Hopkins University Press.

Dzansi, James, Anders Jensen, David Lagakos, and Henry Telli. 2022. "Technology and Local State Capacity: Evidence from Ghana." NBER Working Paper 29923. National Bureau of Economic Research.

Ekeh, Peter. 1975. "Colonialism and the Two Publics in Africa: A Theoretical Statement." *Comparative Studies in Society and History* 17 (1): 91–112.

International Telecommunication Union. n.d. "Statistics." Accessed December 17, 2023. https://www.itu.int/en/ITU-D/Statistics/Pages/stat/default.aspx.

Jackson, Robert. 1990. *Quasi-states: Sovereignty, International Relations and the Third World.* New York: Cambridge University Press.

Jili, Bulelani. 2022. "The Rise of Chinese Surveillance Technology in Africa." Electronic Privacy Information Center. https://epic.org/the-rise-of-chinese-surveillance-technology-in-africa-part-4-of-6/.

Kandeh, Jimmy. 1992. "Politicization of Ethnic Identities in Sierra Leone." *African Studies Review* 35 (1): 81–99.

Kew, Darren. 2021. "Nigeria's State Peacebuilding Institutions: Early Success and Continuing Challenges." United States Institute of Peace. https://www.usip.org/publications/2021/06/nigerias-state-peacebuilding-institutions-early-success-and-continuing.

Krasner, Stephen. 1984. "Approaches to the State: Alternative Conceptions and Historical Dynamics." *Comparative Politics* 16 (2): 223–46.

Lufumpa, Charles, and Mthuli Ncube. 2015. "The Dynamics of the Middle Class in Africa." In *The Emerging Middle Class in Africa*, edited by Charles Lufumpa and Mthuli Ncube, 9–33. New York: Routledge.

Mahoney, James, and Dietrich Rueschemeyer. 2003. *Comparative-Historical Analysis in Social Sciences.* New York: Cambridge University Press.

Mascagni Guilia, Roel Dom, Fabrizio Santoro, and Denis Mukama. 2022. "The VAT in Practice: Equity, Enforcement and Complexity." *International Tax and Public Finance* 30 (2): 525–63.

Mokube, Eric. 2013. Review of Crawford Young, *The Postcolonial State in Africa: Fifty Years of Independence, 1960–2010. Africa Today* 60 (1): 125–27.

Okunogbe, Oyebola, and Fabrizio Santoro. 2023. "The Promise and Limitations of Information Technology for Tax Mobilization." *World Bank Research Observer* 38 (2): 295–324.

Parkinson, Joe, Nicholas Bariyo, and Josh Chin. 2019. "Huawei Technicians Helped African Governments Spy on Political Opponents." *Wall Street Journal*, August 15.

Pule, Nthabiseng. 2022. "Digital Identity in Lesotho." Research ICT Africa. https://researchictafrica.net/wp/wp-content/uploads/2021/11/Lesotho_31.10.21.pdf.

Pye, Lucien. 1971. *Warlord Politics: Conflict and Coalition in the Modernization of Republican China.* New York: Praeger.

Shivji, Issa. 1979. *Class Struggles in Tanzania.* Dar es Salaam: Tanzania Publishing House.

Special Correspondent. 2022. "Across East Africa, Big Brother Is Watching Your Every Move." *Nation* (Nairobi), December 8. https://nation.africa/africa/news/across-east-africa-big-brother-is-watching-your-every-move-4047340.

Tagem, Abrams, and Oliver Morrissey. 2021. "What Are the Drivers of Tax Capacity in Sub-Saharan Africa?" UNU-WIDER. https://www.wider.unu.edu/sites/default/files/Publications/Working-paper/PDF/wp2021-161-online-appendix.pdf.

Tilly, Charles. 1975. "Reflections on the History of European State-Making." In *The Formation of National States in Western Europe*, edited by Charles Tilly, 3–89. Princeton, NJ: Princeton University Press.

Tilly, Charles. 1992. *Coercion, Capital, and European States, AD 990–1992.* Cambridge, MA: Blackwell.

Transparency International. 2022. "Corruption Perceptions Index." https://www
.transparency.org/en/cpi/2022.

UNU-WIDER. 2023. "Government Revenue Dataset." Version 2023. https://doi
.org/10.35188/UNU-WIDER/GRD-2023.

Walsh, Declan, and Jason Harowitz. 2023. "The World's Newest Country Is Broken and
Forgotten. Enter Pope Francis." *New York Times*, February 3.

World Bank. n.d. "GDP Growth (annual%)." World Bank Open Data. Accessed December 17, 2023. https://data.worldbank.org/indicator/NY.GDP.MKTP.KD.ZG.

Young, Crawford. 1994. *The African Colonial State in Comparative Perspective*. New Haven,
CT: Yale University Press.

Young, Crawford. 2004. "The End of the Postcolonial State in Africa? Reflections on
Changing African Political Dynamics." *African Affairs* 103 (410): 23–49.

Young, Crawford. 2012. *The Postcolonial State in Africa: Fifty Years of Independence, 1960–2010*.
Madison: University of Wisconsin Press.

Young, Crawford, and Thomas Turner. 1985. *The Rise and Decline of the Zairian State*.
Madison: University of Wisconsin Press.

2

Third Wave Democracy and the State in Sub-Saharan Africa

John W. Harbeson

This chapter addresses the extent to which post–Cold War democratization has influenced sub-Saharan African state performance and, by extension, state legitimacy, a defining imperative of state making examined by Crawford Young in his magisterial works *The Postcolonial State in Africa: 50 Years of Independence 1960–2010* (2012) and his earlier *The African Colonial State in Comparative Perspective* (1994). Since the publication of *The Postcolonial State*, a considerable volume of data has attested to democratic decline in sub-Saharan Africa and worldwide following fifteen years of increasing democratization.

These results suggest that democratization has yet to result in improved state performance or even to forestall further state weakening. Meanwhile, though Africans continue to favor democracy, there is some evidence of their weakening democratic commitment. At a deeper, more fundamental level, data also suggest that the emergence of effective liberal democratic processes for strengthening, reforming, and relegitimizing contemporary weak, fragile states has continued to remain elusive.

Young's authoritative, comprehensive account records "five turbulent decades that have followed [independence] producing an African political landscape in which there was strikingly little change in the set of state actors but a dramatic transformation in their institutional content and social environment" (2012, 3). Given a premise that optimal state performance entails a stable democratic regime and sustained economic development, his account records outcomes "well beyond the outer bounds of analytical imagination" (Young 2012, 3).

This chapter offers a brief reprise of pertinent Cold War–era legacies before interrogating sub-Saharan Africa's thirty years of democratic experience, with a concentration on one dimension of this tripartite overarching issue: African democratization's bearing on the continent's many fragile states.

Legacies of Authoritarian Rule in Sub-Saharan Africa

The period of the late 1950s and the 1960s, beginning with Ghana's independence in 1957, was one Young characterized as "for the most part a bargained process whose consummation was mostly celebrated in a mutually reciprocated goodwill" (2012, 10). Meanwhile, the United Nations designated the 1960s a Decade of Development, anticipating that mostly independent sub-Saharan Africa would strive to throw off the shackles of colonially sustained poverty, ignorance, and disease, in support of which it established the United Nations Development Program (UNDP). Indeed, to a significant degree, international financial institutions (IFIs) accommodated African visions of rapid postindependence development as articulated by Africa's leaders.

Implicitly, trusting in the durability of the nationalism that enabled their independence, these leaders also tacitly appeared to assume that independence momentum would enable them to both sustain and reform the colonial states they inherited, including overcoming the hurdle of arbitrarily established national boundaries that bequeathed them societies of great ethnic diversity. They would come to realize, however, that most development would have to be carried out by the government. "There is no other way," said Kwame Nkrumah (Young 2012, 14). Thus, their nationalist parties became their primary institutional vehicle for development.

The independence generation leaders undertook to blend their own innovations with appropriate borrowings from both the socialist autocracies of the then-Soviet alliance and the liberalism and democracies of the West while generally eschewing formal alignment with either. They believed that democracy could best develop within the framework of a single party to blend development mobilization and democratic practice. With few exceptions, however, single-party regimes effectively accomplished neither objective. "Party and state flowed together into an exclusionary monopoly . . . raising questions about whether [prior independence] mobilization had been partly illusory" (Young 2012, 17). The single-party regime failed in all its claims to maintain either basic elements of democracy, representation, and free discussion or those of stable government or, "above all, to reconcile the differences between various regional groups" (Young 2012, 17; see also Lewis 1965). These regimes typically dissolved into military ones, laying bare underlying residual colonial states, repositories of repressive legislation, and intensified bans on opposition, which Young regarded as a "fundamental reconfiguration of political institutions" (Young 2012, 19).

In the 1970s, the dire results of the Development Decade prompted a comprehensive response that could have laid the foundations for a subsequent post–Cold War democratic era. Led especially by the World Bank, the IFIs and bilateral development agencies, during Cold War détente, propounded and urged African governments to adopt a fundamentally transformed development orthodoxy. Central to the new strategy was a focus on building development initiatives from the grass roots up to draw more upon the energies and wisdom of local peoples and communities. It mandated circumventing failing national governments by relying instead more upon host country nongovernmental organizations (NGOs) supported by the cooperation of donor country NGOs to reach the poor directly. The underlying premise of this comprehensive reform was that growth and equity could be effectively advanced simultaneously (Chenery et al. 1974). This renovation of development strategy was implicitly anchored in a revamped theory of governance focused on a citizen-centered, development-oriented state. The parallel obligation of national government institutions became to acquire durable political legitimacy by becoming more accountable for upholding and building on these local initiatives.

In the 1980s, the impact of this transformational development strategy was limited and cut short before its promise could be fully realized. Cold War antagonisms resumed, accompanied by a return to neoliberal economic orthodoxy in response to a burgeoning global debt crisis enveloping African and other developing nations. The IFIs exerted sustained, unrelenting pressure on African governments for more than a decade to liberalize their economies by sharply reducing public expenditures and devaluing inflated currencies. They urged export-oriented integration with the international economy as a condition for financial support for their generally debt-burdened, failing economies.

Together, these strategies planted seeds for a potential post-Cold War pursuit of democratic state reform. On one hand, Africans mired in entrenched underdevelopment rebelled against failed states by expanding informal economies that penetrated, marginalized, and threatened to bankrupt those states. Long-delayed fundamental reform of colonial states was needed, in particular by enfranchising democratically Africa's populations. In so doing, democratization might render these states more legitimate and viable over the long term (Young 1994).[1]

On the other hand, these new experiments with local participatory development were promoted by African development-centered organizations, making them potential precursors for national-level political advocacy in the ensuing democratic era. Their cultivation coincided with a rediscovery of civil society as a critical resource for achieving human rights and democratic governance in the post–Cold War years just ahead (Harbeson et al. 1994). The view emerged that state reform required political as well as economic reform (Young 2012). Africa's post–Cold War democratic era finally exposed and explicitly focused attention on the profound weakness and fragility of Africa's postindependence states. The IFIs also acknowledged that they had taken too long to recognize endemic poverty in Africa.

The arrival of democracy's "Third Wave" on African shores in the 1990s has been extensively examined (Bratton and de Walle 1997; Bratton, Mattes, and Gyimah-Boadi 2005). It followed the approaching end of the Cold War as earlier twentieth-century democratic waves followed the defeats of authoritarian-ruled states in World War I and World War II (Huntington 1991). Perhaps more for sub-Saharan Africa than for other regions, however, there has been a democratic opening juxtaposed with enduring, comprehensive poverty and inequality and with previously less than explicitly acknowledged pervasive state fragility.

Thus, sub-Saharan Africa's initiation of political liberalization and democracy has existentially challenged received theory positing that the existence of a stable state and some level of economic development are indispensable prerequisites for democratization (Linz and Stepan 1996). Inescapably, however, African countries have been existentially obliged to pursue all three objectives simultaneously without the opportunity to pursue them sequentially. After three decades, the critical questions have become the extent to which new sub-Saharan African countries have been able to meet and manage this simultaneous three-dimensional challenge.

A central purpose of this chapter is to examine evidence bearing on how African countries have fared in confronting one dimension of this complex problem: to what extent has democratization helped reform, strengthen, or at least sustain these weak, fragile states (Harbeson and Rothchild 2023). Two significant empirical limitations have inescapably attended this inquiry. As invaluable as democracy-measuring protocols offering statistical evidence are, they constitute only one form of the multidimensional evidence needed to fully address these questions. And some of the most granular data have become available only since about 2006, widely regarded as a critical year beginning democracy's decline worldwide and in sub-Saharan Africa.

Sub-Saharan Africa's Democratic Record, 2006–2021

Overall, taking 1990 as the base year as the Cold War was ending, sub-Saharan Africa's democratization trajectory has been one of ascending progress for fifteen years, notwithstanding a season of significant intrastate conflict, reaching an apogee about 2005, after which the democratic decline set in. This decline has steadily, albeit gradually, diminished but not yet canceled all the progress of the preceding fifteen years. There has appeared little to herald a halting or reversal of this decline. Meanwhile, sub-Saharan state fragility has remained essentially unchanged over this period, although individual country fragility has appeared to vary widely, reflecting Crawford Young's observation that the post–Cold War period has witnessed widely increased divergence in state performance (Young 2012, 28). Perhaps as significant has been evidence of a moderate correlation between changing levels of democratic performance and state fragility since the middle of the twenty-first century's first decade.

Of the many democracy measuring protocols, Freedom House's has been the oldest and among the most influential since 1972.[2] Freedom House measures all countries on a scale of 0 to 4 for twenty-five different criteria; data on these criteria have been public since 2013. Total scores of 74 or better indicate free and democratic countries, scores below 30 indicate unfree countries, and those between 30 and 73 indicate partially free democratic countries. It has made public since 2006 its scores in seven categories: three for political rights—electoral process, pluralism and participation, and governmental integrity and accountability—and four for civil liberties—freedom of expression, freedom of association, the rule of law, and personal autonomy and liberties. It further summarizes these scores by assigning scores of 1 to 7 each for the political rights and civil liberties groups. Scores of 1 or 2 indicate full democratic freedom; scores of 3 to 5 indicate partial freedom; and scores of 5 to 7 indicate nondemocracy or unfreedom.

Table 2.1. World and Sub-Saharan Africa
Overall Average Scores on Political Rights and
Civil Liberties, 1990–2020

	Political rights		Civil liberties	
	World	Africa	World	Africa
1990	4.29	5.62	4.09	5.11
1995	3.75	4.56	3.9	4.58
2000	3.64	4.48	3.7	4.4
2005	3.52	4.23	3.31	3.98
2010	3.6	4.48	3.42	4.19
2015	3.6	4.51	3.53	4.39
2020	3.67	4.76	3.52	4.42

Source: Freedom House, freedomhouse.org.

Table 2.1 records that the most pronounced democratic progress for sub-Saharan Africa and worldwide occurred from about 1990 through 1995. Sub-Saharan countries as a group improved more dramatically than all countries worldwide on average prior to 2005, including from the borderline unfree category to well into the partly free category before declining gradually, albeit more rapidly than all other nations on average thereafter.

Tables 2.2, 2.3a, 2.3b, 2.3c, 2.4a, 2.4b, and 2.4c present the democracy trajectories of forty-nine sub-Saharan African countries from 2006 to 2021. Table 2.2 presents average yearly overall numerical scores (0 to 100) for all sub-Saharan African countries as a group. The table records an 8-point nearly uninterrupted overall collective average decline from 49 points to 41. The table also portrays a significant range of trajectories, with a standard deviation of 23 to 26 points between individual country average scores over the period 2006–21.

Tables 2.3 and 2.4 discern six distinct democracy subtrajectories for sub-Saharan African countries from 2006 to 2021. Tables 2.3a, 2.3b, and 2.3c report three relatively encouraging, or at least less discouraging, trajectories for twenty-three countries. By contrast, tables 2.4a, 2.4b, and 2.4c report more discouraging trajectories for the other twenty-six countries. For each country, in both analyses, there are three scores, from left to right: its current 2021 score, its average score over the entire fifteen-year period, and the difference between each country's 2021 and 2006 scores.[3]

Table 2.2. Sub-Saharan Democratization,
Average Total Scores, 2006–2021

	Average score	Std dev
2006	49	23
2007	49	23
2008	49	24
2009	48	23
2010	47	23
2011	47	24
2012	46	24
2013	45	24
2014	45	24
2015	45	25
2016	45	25
2017	44	25
2018	43	26
2019	43	26
2020	42	25
2021	41	25

Source: Freedom House, freedomhouse.org

Three decades into sub-Saharan Africa's democratic era, tables 2.3a, 2.3b, and 2.3c record that while twenty-three countries are in relatively good shape in terms of democracy, only eight countries have sustained free and democratic status during the fifteen years of overall democratic recession. Although Senegal has an average score of 74, it dropped off the list of democracies with a 2021 score of only 68. Among the current democracies, Seychelles recorded the greatest 2021 improvement, 11 points. With the exception of South Africa, most are relatively smaller countries in terms of population.

In addition, the tables record that eight countries have improved their scores over the period, notably Côte d'Ivoire and Togo, though all remain in the partly free and democratic categories except for Zimbabwe, which still

Table 2.3a. Trajectories: Democracies

	2021	Avg	Change 2006–21
Botswana	72	75	−6
Cape Verde	92	90	2
Ghana	80	83	−4
Mauritius	89	90	−4
Namibia	77	76	0
São Tomé and Príncipe	84	81	4
South Africa	79	82	−9
Seychelles	79	69	11

Source: Freedom House, freedomhouse.org.

Table 2.3b. Trajectories: Improved

	2021	Avg	Change 2006–21
Côte d'Ivoire	49	37	28
Togo	42	42	17
Zimbabwe	28	24	13
Malawi	68	61	9
Sierra Leone	65	65	5
Liberia	60	59	4
Guinea	34	36	2
Angola	30	29	1

Source: Freedom House, freedomhouse.org.

Table 2.3c. Trajectories: Partly Free Sub-Saharan Countries

	2021	Avg	Change 2006–21
Burkina Faso	53	54	0
Madagascar	61	52	1
The Gambia	47	36	−2
Mauritania	35	36	−3
Zambia	51	58	−5
Comoros	42	53	−6
Nigeria	43	48	−6

Source: Freedom House, freedomhouse.org.

Table 2.4a. Democracies Lost

	2021	Avg	Change 2006–21
Mali	32	52	−42
Lesotho	63	69	−11
Benin	59	78	−11
Senegal	68	74	−8

Source: Free House, freedomhouse.org.

remains unfree. Another seven countries have remained partly free, though five have lost some ground. Mauritania appeared to be the most marginal member of that latter group, while The Gambia and Madagascar registered significant 2021 improvements over their average scores.

The other twenty-six countries counterbalance the first twenty-three. Four countries have slipped out of the democratic category, Mali into the unfree group, and Lesotho into the partly free category. Mali, in particular, had long been regarded as a model nascent democracy, partly as a result of its distinctive national conference democratic launch, notwithstanding its enduring poverty

Table 2.4b. Unfree Country Declines

	2021	Avg	Change 2006–21
Central African Republic	7	24	−37
Burundi	14	31	−35
Congo-Brazzaville	17	28	−20
Gabon	21	31	−19
Cameroon	15	23	−15
Ethiopia	23	23	−13
Djibouti	24	30	−11
Eritrea	3	6	−11
Chad	15	19	−11
Rwanda	22	27	−10
Somalia	7	4	−8
Equatorial Guinea	5	8	−5
Eswatini	17	20	−4
Sudan	10	11	−1
Democratic Republic of Congo	19	21	−1
(South Sudan)	1	13*	1

Source: Freedom House, freedomhouse.org.
*independent since 2011

Table 2.4c. Partially Free Countries Declining

	2021	Avg	Change 2006–21
Tanzania	34	56	−24
Kenya	48	54	−18
Guinea-Bissau	43	44	−16
Mozambique	43	55	−13
Uganda	34	40	−11
Niger	51	53	−11

Note: Freedom House considers countries with scores of 29 to 73 to be partially free.
Source: Freedom House, freedomhouse.org.

Table 2.5. Sub-Saharan African State Strength and Democracy

	State fragility (SF)	Democracy (D)	Correlation
	2007–21	2007–21	SF&D
Score	85.7 (2007) to 84.7 (2021)	49 to 41	r = .61
Gainers	25	12	
Losers	23	34	
No change	0	2	

DETAIL

	Fragility improved	Democracy change		Fragility declined	Democracy change
Cabo Verde	19.7	2.0	Burundi	−0.2	−35.0
Côte d'Ivoire	17.7	28.0	Benin	−0.5	−11.0
Seychelles	17.1	11.0	Burkina Faso	−0.8	0.0
Zimbabwe	12.3	13.0	Djibouti	−1.0	−11.0
Sierra Leone	11.0	5.0	Ghana	−1.1	−4.0
Botswana	10.3	−6.0	Mauritania	−1.2	−3.0
Malawi	9.2	9.0	Nigeria	−1.6	−6.0
Namibia	8.4	0.0	Democratic Republic of Congo	−1.8	−1.0

Country		
São Tomé and Príncipe	8.2	4.0
Gabon	6.6	−19.0
Sudan	6.6	−1.0
Rwanda	5.5	−10.0
Mauritius	4.8	−4.0
Liberia	4.7	4.0
Uganda	4.3	−11.0
Equatorial Guinea	4.1	−5.0
Lesotho	3.8	−11.0
Chad	3.1	−11.0
Kenya	3.1	−18.0
Togo	3.0	17.0
Guinea	1.7	2.0
Tanzania	1.1	−24.0
Eswatini	0.9	−4.0
Congo-Brazzaville	0.8	−20.0
Somalia	0.6	−8.0
Guinea-Bissau	−2.5	−16.0
The Gambia	−2.6	−2.0
Zambia	−3.0	−5.0
Angola	−3.2	1.0
Madagascar	−3.9	1.0
Ethiopia	−4.0	−13.0
Niger	−4.0	−11.0
Comoros	−4.5	−6.0
Senegal	−5.2	−8.0
Cameroon	−6.6	−15.0
Central African Republic	−7.1	−37.0
Eritrea	−10.4	−11.0
South Africa	−14.6	−9.0
Mozambique	−17.4	−13.0
Mali	−23.1	−42.0

and long history of restive pastoral communities. Mali's 2021 scores reflect its descent into military rule and the tenuousness and fragility of the Malian state itself (Wing 2008).

Benin moved out of the free and democratic category because of growing insurgency in its lightly served northern precincts, along with alleged governmental mistreatment of opposition leaders. Benin is also another country that had propelled itself into democracy with the benefit of a successful national conference early in the 1990s.

Tables 2.4a, 2.4b, and 2.4c reveal that six partly free countries have lost ground while still remaining partly free. Fifteen already unfree countries have all lost further ground. South Sudan falls into a different category since it has been independent only since 2011 but has remained in the unfree category.

Table 2.5 explores the possible connections between changing levels of democratic performance and state fragility. The Fund for Peace annually estimates state fragility in 174 countries across twelve criteria, using a 10-point scale that gauges levels of national cohesion, economic performance, political performance, and cross-cutting social issues (see https://fundforpeace.org). High total scores of 90 to 120 indicate the most fragile conditions, scores between 60 and 90 indicate a still significant concern about fragility, scores between 30 and 60 indicate state stability, and scores between 0 and 30 suggest sustainable state stability.

The State Fragility Index registered almost no change between 2007 and 2022 for all sub-Saharan countries as a group, declining by a single point from a relatively high (i.e., concerning) level of 85.7 to 84.7 for 2022. The table portrays very considerable individual country variation. It also indicates a moderately positive correlation of $r = 0.61$ between degrees of change in democracy and those for state fragility.

Citizen Perceptions of Democratic Performance

Scoring on dimensions of democratic performance in several prominent measurement protocols has largely been determined by expert opinion. As valid and indispensable as these are, at the end of the day, the opinion of African citizens themselves, as the prime beneficiaries of any democratic progress, should be especially influential. Afrobarometer surveys in more than thirty countries have supplied some of the best evidence concerning African citizens' experience with democracy (Afrobarometer.org). Afrobarometer's 2019–21 survey included thirty-two sub-Saharan African countries, where Freedom House has scored for forty-nine.[4]

Afrobarometer surveys conducted from 2011 to 2013, from 2016 to 2018, and from 2019 to 2021 have confirmed that Africans continue to prefer democracy to each of the best-known alternatives to democracy: military, one-party, and one-man rule notwithstanding a small overall decrease between the three surveys by 2.0 percent each between 2016 and 2018 and between 2018 and 2021. Table 2.6 indicates overall changes in levels of support by country over the decade between 2013 and 2021, including specific changes between 2013 and 2018 and between 2018 and 2021. As of 2021, democracy enjoyed majority support in all but four of the surveyed countries. Support for democracy by South Africans, however, shrunk by 31.5 percent over the decade to only 40.4 percent, the lowest among the surveyed countries.

Table 2.6. Citizen Preference for Democracy

	2021	2018	2013	Change 2018–21	Change 2013–18
Benin	**80.8**	72.5	75.9	**8.3**	−3.4
Botswana	71.1	79.8	81.8	−8.7	−2.0
Burkina Faso	70.3	62.7	71.4	**7.6**	−8.7
Cabo Verde	78.9	79.4	81.3	−0.5	−1.9
Cameroon	57.1	62.2	64.1	−5.1	−1.9
Côte d'Ivoire	72.3	72.2	82.7	**0.1**	−10.5
Eswatini	**49.1**	43.0	45.8	**6.1**	−2.8
Ghana	77.1	81.1	81.7	−4.0	−0.6
Guinea	**77.1**	76.3	77.0	**0.8**	−0.7
Kenya	**75.3**	66.7	73.0	**8.6**	−6.3
Lesotho	**52.4**	52.2	55.0	**0.2**	−2.8
Liberia	**83.2**	89.8	81.1	−6.6	**8.7**
Madagascar		47.0	39.3		
Malawi	52.2	61.7	65.6	−9.5	−3.9
Mali	**62.0**	67.4	61.8	−5.4	**5.6**
Mauritius	75.1	78.1	84.5	−3.0	−6.4

continues

Table 2.6. *(continued)*

	2021	2018	2013	Change 2018–21	Change 2013–18
Mozambique	48.7	57.4	62.5	−8.7	−5.1
Namibia	56.7	64.6	63.6	−7.9	**1.0**
Niger	64.3	69.3	65.7	−5.0	**3.6**
Nigeria	**75.2**	**69.2**	69.1	6.0	**0.1**
Senegal	**87.9**	82.3	87.5	**5.6**	−5.2
Sierra Leone	**84.8**	84.2	75.5	**0.6**	**8.7**
South Africa	40.4	54.2	71.9	−13.8	−17.7
Sudan	49.7	62.0	51.4	−12.3	**10.6**
Tanzania	77.3	78.1	84.5	−0.8	−6.4
Togo	72.8	74.8	76.5	−2.0	−1.7
Uganda	69.8	80.8	79.3	−11.0	**1.5**
Zambia	83.6	81.6	89.8	**2.0**	−8.2
Zimbabwe	77.8	75.2	78.9	**2.6**	−3.7
Average	68.7	69.9	71.7	−2.0	−1.8
Std dev	13.1	11.7	12.5	6.5	6.1

Note: Bold type signifies positive change from 2013 to 2018 and/or from 2018 to 2021.
Source: Afrobarometer.org.

The overall fairly strong continuing African support for democracy masks considerable variation among individual countries. Indeed, whereas only eight countries registered increased support for democracy between 2013 and 2018, twelve did so between 2018 and 2021, suggesting, at a minimum, some fluidity, a fluidity also exhibited to varying degrees by other specific measures of African support.

Citizen views on the upholding and exercise of democratic liberties are sampled in three areas. Overall, between 2013 and 2018, tables 2.7, 2.8, and 2.9 report significant declines from previous moderate levels of support for the exercise of these basic political liberties. However, between 2018 and 2021, citizen support for these liberties rebounded noticeably for reasons that remain to be fully explored. These reasons may potentially indicate durable increases in democratic beliefs or, alternatively, perhaps primarily responses to immediate circumstances in which they find themselves.

First, at an elemental level, how safe do citizens feel in expressing their views on issues in the public square? The strength of citizens' belief in their ability to speak out may hinge on the extent to which governments are perceived to be upholding freedom of expression, on how they assess tolerance for political expression among their neighbors, and/or on an evolving sense of empowerment to be able to speak out as needed. Table 2.7 records a 12.9 percent drop across twenty-nine countries in Africans' beliefs that they really can say what they think, from only 48.8 to 35.9 percent between 2013 and 2018, but support increased somewhat by 2021 to 41.2 percent. Only four countries essentially retained existing levels of confidence about the ability to speak out between 2013 and 2018: Cameroon, Côte d'Ivoire, Zimbabwe, and democracy leader Cabo Verde. Nine countries experienced drops of at least 20 percent,

Table 2.7. African Support for Exercising Democratic Liberties: Free to Say What One Thinks?

	2021	2018	2013	Change 2018–21	Change 2013–18
Angola	19.3				
Benin	36.1	36.0	**57.4**	**0.1**	−21.4
Botswana	**58.6**	45.5	**67.6**	**13.1**	−22.1
Burkina Faso	27.0	18.2	24.3	**8.8**	−6.1
Burundi		33.1			
Cabo Verde	**59.6**	**56.5**	**56.5**	**3.1**	0.0
Cameroon	26.0	32.9	30.0	−6.9	**2.9**
Côte d'Ivoire	17.7	21.4	21.4	−3.7	0.0
Eswatini	14.0	21.2	23.8	−7.2	−2.6
Ethiopia	40.1				
Gabon	16.4	11.2		**5.2**	
The Gambia	**71.4**	**52.4**		**19.0**	
Ghana	**71.2**	**67.1**	**73.5**	**4.1**	−6.4

continues

Table 2.7. *(continued)*

	2021	2018	2013	Change 2018–21	Change 2013–18
Guinea	**57.0**	29.7	**54.8**	**27.3**	−25.1
Kenya	48.0	43.0	**54.9**	**5.0**	−11.9
Lesotho	42.6	**50.8**	**65.0**	−8.2	−14.2
Liberia	**54.6**	**53.8**	**74.7**	**0.8**	−20.9
Madagascar		14.9	31.1		−16.2
Malawi	44.0	48.4	**78.6**	−4.4	−30.2
Mali	**53.8**	31.4	38.0	**22.4**	−6.6
Mauritius	31.0	26.9	44.8	**4.1**	−17.9
Mozambique	21.1	20.6	41.1	**0.5**	−20.5
Namibia	**54.4**	**50.0**	**60.0**	**4.4**	−10.0
Niger	36.2	36.1	**52.6**	**0.1**	−16.5
Nigeria	37.9	31.4	34.0	**6.5**	−2.6
São Tomé and Príncipe		**53.9**			
Senegal	46.0	40.9	**72.7**	**5.1**	−31.8
Sierra Leone	**54.4**	47.5	**61.9**	**6.9**	−14.4
South Africa	45.8	35.9	**52.2**	**9.9**	−16.3
Sudan	44.8	16.6	18.9	**28.2**	−2.3
Tanzania	**61.1**	45.5	**75.8**	**15.6**	−30.3
Togo	10.7	13.3	20.7	−2.6	−7.4
Uganda	49.5	40.1	**51.6**	**9.4**	−11.5
Zambia	42.6	35.3	**56.9**	**7.3**	−21.6
Zimbabwe	25.1	23.3	21.6	**1.8**	**1.7**
Overall	41.2	35.9	48.8	**5.3**	−12.9

Note: Bold type signifies improved and majority support between the two reporting periods.
Source: Afrobarometer.org.

including the relatively stronger democracies of Botswana, Senegal, Malawi, and (at the time) Benin. Between 2018 and 2021, however, country scores recovered almost half of that loss, increasing by 5.9 percent, led by Gambia, Mali, Guinea, and Sudan, and enabling ten countries to achieve majority belief in the viability of this right. Ten countries registered majority support in 2021, up from seven in 2018 but fewer than seventeen in 2013.

Second, how have African citizens assessed the merits of untrammeled freedom to join any organizations of their choosing, which is so critically important for political advocacy and civil society more generally (table 2.8). Sub-Saharan Africans sustained moderately strong levels of support for associational freedom at 64.4 percent in 2021, with losses between 2013 and 2018 mostly overcome in this most recent survey. All but seven countries registered declines in the earlier 2018 survey, while all but six registered gains in the 2021 survey, led by Cameroon, Ghana, Guinea, and Zimbabwe.

Table 2.8. African Support for Exercising Democratic Liberties: Should Be Free to Join Any Organization

	2021	2018	2013	Change 2018–21	Change 2013–18
Angola	42.2				
Benin	80.8	76.0	81.5	4.8	−5.5
Botswana	69.6	62.8	63.6	6.8	−0.8
Burkina Faso	71.6	67.4	76.5	4.2	−9.1
Burundi			85.5		
Cabo Verde	77.7	74.9	76.6	2.8	−1.7
Cameroon	69.3	56.7	70.5	12.6	−13.8
Côte d'Ivoire	82.6	76.7	86.1	5.9	−9.4
Eswatini	59.4	59.9	42.3	−0.5	17.6
Ethiopia	66.4				
Gabon	90.4	90.0		0.4	
The Gambia	60.2	54.2		6.0	
Ghana	59.5	47.6	69.0	11.9	−21.4

continues

Table 2.8. *(continued)*

	2021	2018	2013	Change 2018–21	Change 2013–18
Guinea	**77.1**	**66.5**	76.4	**10.6**	⁻9.9
Kenya	**47.7**	46.5	46.1	**1.2**	**0.4**
Lesotho	**84.0**	**78.6**	80.7	**5.4**	⁻2.1
Liberia	40.2	32.4	44.0	**7.8**	⁻11.6
Madagascar		**81.7**	66.4		**15.3**
Malawi	**74.5**	**76.7**	62.3	⁻2.2	**14.4**
Mali	**70.8**	**74.3**	79.4	⁻3.5	⁻5.1
Mauritius	**84.5**	**76.0**	73.7	**8.5**	**2.3**
Mozambique	47.4	46.3	50.3	**1.1**	⁻4.0
Namibia	**54.4**	**51.1**	70.9	**3.3**	⁻19.8
Niger	**73.6**	**64.1**	72.9	**9.5**	⁻8.8
Nigeria	43.8	43.4	48.7	**0.4**	⁻5.3
São Tomé and Príncipe		**66.0**			
Senegal	**79.0**	**84.2**	90.8	⁻5.2	⁻6.6
Sierra Leone	37.7	32.4	48.5	**5.3**	⁻16.1
South Africa	**64.3**	**64.0**	62.8	**0.3**	**1.2**
Sudan	48.4	**56.0**	45.2	⁻7.6	**10.8**
Tanzania	48.4	38.6	41.1	**9.8**	⁻2.5
Togo	**82.5**	**80.5**	86.2	**2.0**	⁻5.7
Uganda	**61.7**	**54.6**	72.2	**7.1**	⁻17.6
Zambia	**65.9**	**57.7**	59.3	**8.2**	⁻1.6
Zimbabwe	**73.0**	**59.8**	70.1	**13.2**	⁻10.3
Overall	**64.4**	**62.5**	66.5	**2.5**	⁻4.0

Note. Bold type signifies improved and majority support.
Source. Afrobarometer.org.

Third, African opinion on the merits of media freedom corresponded to expert opinion on its declining status (table 2.9), with all surveyed countries but Malawi, Mauritius, and Sudan registering significant declines between 2013 and 2018. By sharp contrast, however, the 2018–21 survey showed all surveyed countries except Botswana, Malawi, and Sudan registering increased support by 18.4 percent, more than overcoming the 10.4 percent decline in the earlier survey.

Table 2.9. African Support for Exercising Democratic Liberties: Media Should Be Free to Publish

	2021	2018	2013	Change 2018–21	Change 2013–18
Angola	52.0				
Benin	65.1	44.8	50.4	20.3	−5.6
Botswana	61.5	61.7		−0.2	
Burkina Faso	70.3	38.7	57.7	31.6	−19.0
Burundi					
Cabo Verde	76.1	56.7	83.1	19.4	−26.4
Cameroon	45.6	28.6	37.1	17.0	−8.5
Côte d'Ivoire	65.1	39.6	48.3	25.5	−8.7
Eswatini	61.7	41.2	50.8	20.5	−9.6
Ethiopia	51.3				
Gabon	80.2	61.6		18.6	
The Gambia	67.8	31.0		36.8	
Ghana	65.2	36.5	54.8	28.7	−18.3
Guinea	68.0	41.3	47.6	26.7	−6.3
Kenya	58.2	50.4	59.4	7.8	−9.0
Lesotho	68.3	33.8	40.1	34.5	−6.3
Liberia	61.2	32.6	46.5	28.6	−13.9
Madagascar		70.2	70.3		−0.1
Malawi	60.1	67.1	67.1	−7.0	0.0

continues

Table 2.9. *(continued)*

	2021	2018	2013	Change 2018–21	Change 2013–18
Mali	**68.8**	24.5	43.6	**44.3**	⁻19.1
Mauritius	**66.8**	**62.0**	**61.0**	**4.8**	1.0
Mozambique	49.2	44.5	**59.0**	**4.7**	⁻14.5
Namibia	**55.1**	43.6	**53.5**	**11.5**	⁻9.9
Niger	**59.3**	**50.2**	**63.8**	**9.1**	⁻13.6
Nigeria	**64.8**	44.9	**57.5**	**19.9**	⁻12.6
São Tomé and Príncipe					
Senegal	**62.3**	18.1	29.5	**44.2**	⁻11.4
Sierra Leone	**65.4**	44.8	**59.7**	**20.6**	⁻14.9
South Africa	**64.5**	**53.7**	**60.9**	**10.8**	⁻7.2
Sudan	**52.2**	**60.4**	48.7	⁻8.2	**11.7**
Tanzania	43.2	40.2	**73.3**	**3.0**	⁻33.1
Togo	**64.8**	**53.9**	**55.4**	**10.9**	⁻1.5
Uganda	**71.1**	**58.8**	**79.8**	**12.3**	⁻21.0
Zambia	**63.4**	41.5	**50.7**	**21.9**	⁻9.2
Zimbabwe	**75.8**	**53.0**	**57.8**	**22.8**	⁻4.8
Overall	**62.6**	46.1	**56.0**	**16.5**	⁻9.9

Note: Bold type signifies improved and majority support.
Source: Afrobarometer.org.

Support for Core Democratic State Institutions

Three measures of the bearing of African democracy on the condition of democratic state institutions include how citizens assess their states' transparency and accountability, and the extent to which they report trust in their core presidential and parliamentary institutions. Their views on these subjects then may be expected to influence the deeper issue, considered in the next section, of the degree to which they identify with their nation-states at all as distinct from the residual ethnic communities out of which those states were constructed and have been sustained over the decades.

Transparency and Accountability

The status of core democratic state institutions can be gauged usefully by querying citizens' estimates of governmental transparency and accountability. Table 2.10 portrays the results of a 2021 Afrobarometer survey of African perceptions of the extent of state accountability. The table inverts the Afrobarometer surveys on the extent of corruption in order to report the degree to which progress *is* being made rather than *not* being made on citizen-perceived current corruption trajectories, government effectiveness in addressing corruption, and citizen capacity to report corruption without perceived risk of retaliation. The index shows the average of those three scores and the ranking of the surveyed countries.

Table 2.10 indicates that in only two countries, Tanzania and Benin, did the majority of citizens believe progress has been occurring. Elsewhere in the surveyed countries, only 34 percent of African citizens believe that governments are effective in addressing corruption; 41.5 percent reported that corruption

Table 2.10. African Perceptions of Corruption Progress, 2019–21

	Corruption has not increased in last 12 months [1]	Government effective against corruption [2]	Safe to report corruption [3]	Transparency Index: the avg of columns [1], [2], and [3]
Tanzania	91.8	83.4	35.1	70.1
Benin	79.1	74.2	43.6	65.6
Sierra Leone	59.1	48.9	27.4	45.1
Botswana	49.5	56.9	28.0	44.8
Angola	68.2	33.5	32.6	44.8
Burkina Faso	53.3	40.2	28.2	40.6
Ghana	46.3	38.7	36.2	40.4
Ethiopia	57.8	31.8	27.6	39.1
The Gambia	39.1	19.4	49.4	36.0

continues

Table 2.10. *(continued)*

	Corruption has not increased in last 12 months [1]	Government effective against corruption [2]	Safe to report corruption [3]	Transparency Index: the avg of columns [1], [2], and [3]
Mozambique	45.4	38.1	24.1	35.9
Niger	48.0	31.4	24.9	34.8
Cabo Verde	**52.5**	17.0	32.1	33.9
Togo	40.3	31.1	21.6	31.0
Kenya	36.0	37.4	19.5	31.0
Guinea	37.2	19.5	33.2	30.0
Nigeria	44.9	28.5	15.2	29.5
Zimbabwe	45.2	25.6	16.9	29.2
Côte d'Ivoire	43.5	27.7	16.5	29.2
Sudan	33.1	17.2	37.0	29.1
Cameroon	35.4	29.7	20.7	28.6
Namibia	26.6	27.3	29.5	27.8
Eswatini	27.3	37.5	13.8	26.2
Malawi	33.2	27.1	17.2	25.8
Uganda	37.3	20.5	19.0	25.6
Mali	24.3	23.1	28.8	25.4
Liberia	28.1	15.1	31.3	24.8
Mauritius	22.8	26.8	22.4	24.0
South Africa	28.1	20.7	21.0	23.3
Zambia	28.6	15.4	19.3	21.1
Senegal	24.8	16.6	20.6	20.7
Lesotho	21.7	18.8	18.5	19.7
Gabon	18.2	14.0	8.8	13.7
Overall	**41.5**	**35.8**	**24.6**	**34.0**

Note: Bold type signifies majority approval.
Source: Afrobarometer.org.

had *not* increased over the preceding twelve months; Tanzania, Benin, Sierra Leone, and Angola were the most sanguine on that score. Only in Tanzania and Benin did majorities of respondents believe that their governments were addressing corruption effectively. In no country did majorities believe it was safe to risk reporting corruption without fear of retaliation. In The Gambia and Benin, citizens believed it safest to do so.

A safe hypothesis is that perceived poor performance in addressing corruption can only diminish citizen estimates not only of the viability of democracy itself but also of the likelihood of its capacity to reform and strengthen the region's chronically fragile states.

Trust in Democratic Institutions

An important measure of democracy's viability is the degree to which it builds, or at least sustains, citizens' enduring trust in its core democratic institutions over time, notably presidencies and parliaments. That requisite level of trust, in turn, plausibly generates or diminishes trust, belief, and perhaps ultimately a commitment to membership in states themselves. Those fundamental levels of trust are to be distinguished from perceived records of governments' performance at any given time, though those accumulated perceived records of performance are likely to influence underlying fundamental degrees of trust over time. Afrobarometer surveys have been careful to distinguish fundamental citizen presidential and parliamentary trust from governments' actual performance.

While citizen support for electoral democracy has remained relatively strong over the past decade, tables 2.11 and 2.12 suggest limited, even declining, citizen trust in presidencies and parliaments, their most fundamental institutions. That said, in a few countries, trust has increased.

On the one hand, table 2.11 reports declining citizen trust in democratic presidential institutions over the past decade, from 61.4 percent in twenty-nine surveyed countries in 2013 to a bare 50.6 percent majority view in 2021 in thirty-two countries. Only two countries, Mali and Nigeria, recorded less than majority trust in their presidencies in 2013, but the number doing so increased to thirteen in 2018 and fifteen in 2021. Only in Zambia and Eswatini did presidencies recover majority status in 2021. Nine countries swam against the tide, recording increased presidential trust in 2018; that number increased to eleven in 2021.

On the other hand, trust in parliamentary institutions has declined more than trust in presidencies in the surveyed countries (table 2.12). Whereas nine

Table 2.11. Trust in Democratic Institutions: President

	2021	2018	2013	Change 2018–21	Change 2013–18
Angola	**35.9**				
Benin	55.7	52.3	71.4	**3.4**	−19.1
Botswana	46.8	59.9	69.5	−13.1	−9.6
Burkina Faso	58.0	66.9	70.3	−8.9	−3.4
Cabo Verde	**49.8**	**49.5**	65.9	**0.3**	−16.4
Cameroon	58.2	59.3	56.0	−1.1	**3.3**
Côte d'Ivoire	60.8	59.5	52.5	**1.3**	**7.0**
Ethiopia	64.6				
Eswatini	56.2	**43.8**			
Gabon	**26.4**	**29.1**			
The Gambia	**46.1**	66.8			
Ghana	56.0	70.4	55.7	−14.4	14.7
Guinea	**49.9**	46.4	57.7	**3.5**	−11.3
Kenya	66.0	61.9	60.7	**4.1**	**1.2**
Lesotho	**13.6**	56.9	51.5	−43.3	**5.4**
Liberia	**39.4**	54.5	59.7	−15.1	−5.2
Madagascar		**37.6**	52.7		−15.1
Malawi	**43.2**	**35.6**	57.0	**7.6**	−21.4
Mali	**45.1**	55.6	**43.4**	−10.5	**12.2**
Mauritius	**41.1**	**26.9**	61.8	14.2	−34.9
Mozambique	65.8	69.4	72.2	−3.6	−2.8
Namibia	59.7	64.0	80.8	−4.3	−16.8
Niger	59.7	57.7	75.1	**2.0**	−17.4
Nigeria	**39.3**	**44.6**	**35.1**	−5.3	**9.5**
São Tomé and Príncipe		**30.1**			

Table 2.11. *(continued)*

	2021	2018	2013	Change 2018–21	Change 2013–18
Senegal	52.2	73.3	70.3	−21.1	**3.0**
Sierra Leone	55.4	69.6	69.9	−14.2	−0.3
South Africa	**38.1**	**38.2**	61.9	−0.1	−23.7
Sudan	**42.9**	**34.1**	60.2	**8.8**	−26.1
Tanzania	86.2	72.5	73.8	**13.7**	−1.3
Togo	**45.4**	**37.2**	52.6	**8.2**	−15.4
Uganda	62.7	63.8	58.7	−1.1	**5.1**
Zambia	50.4	**30.0**	65.5	**20.4**	−35.5
Zimbabwe	**48.1**	63.6	58.1	−15.5	**5.5**
Average	50.6	52.5	61.4	−4.3	−7.5
Std dev	13.3	14.5	10.1	14.3	13.9

Note: The bold type signifies majorities and positive change.
Source: afrobarometer.org.

Table 2.12. Trust in Democratic Institutions: The Parliament

	2021	2018	2013	Change 2018–21	Change 2018–21
Angola	**30.7**				
Benin	**41.5**	52.6	60.7	−11.1	−8.1
Botswana	**40.7**	51.2	54.0	−10.5	−2.8
Burkina Faso	51.4	64.6	60.4	−13.2	4.2
Cabo Verde	**33.3**	**39.8**	57.9	−6.5	−18.1
Cameroon	**37.0**	**43.0**	**41.8**	−6.0	**1.2**
Côte d'Ivoire	**40.1**	50.0	**46.9**	−9.9	**3.1**
Eswatini	51.0	57.9	53.8	−6.9	
Ethiopia	**47.7**				

continues

Table 2.12. *(continued)*

	2021	2018	2013	Change 2018–21	Change 2018–21
Gabon	**21.5**	**20.1**		**1.4**	
The Gambia	**44.2**	60.9		−16.7	
Ghana	**39.2**	55.7	**48.7**	−16.5	**7.0**
Guinea	**39.7**	**37.8**	51.4	**1.9**	−13.6
Kenya	**49.1**	**43.7**	49.2	5.4	−5.5
Lesotho	**20.6**	**48.1**	51.8	−27.5	−3.7
Liberia	**23.3**	**37.1**	**46.9**	−13.8	−9.8
Madagascar		34.3			
Malawi	53.1	**40.4**	63.9	**12.7**	−23.5
Mali	**36.1**	**49.2**	**42.4**	−13.1	**6.8**
Mauritius	**39.7**	**27.3**	64.9	**12.4**	−37.6
Mozambique	55.7	53.5	61.4	2.2	−7.9
Namibia	**44.7**	**47.1**	65.3	−2.4	−18.2
Niger	54.8	52.3	70.5	2.5	−18.2
Nigeria	**24.8**	**23.8**	**26.2**	**1.0**	−2.4
Senegal	**32.4**	**46.1**	55.8	−13.7	−9.7
Sierra Leone	**32.5**	63.1	55.5	−30.6	7.6
South Africa	**27.6**	**32.1**	56.1	−4.5	−24.0
Sudan		**23.8**	**31.4**		−7.6
Tanzania	89.2	**66.6**	76.4	**22.6**	−9.8
Togo	**39.3**	**29.4**	**36.7**	**9.9**	−7.3
Uganda	**46.5**	**51.1**	67.5	−4.6	−16.4
Zambia	**46.7**	**46.4**	53.5	**0.3**	−7.1
Zimbabwe	**44.1**	54.8	56.3	−10.7	−1.5
Average	41.6	45.3	53.8	−5.0	−8.3
Std dev	13.2	12.4	11.4	11.7	10.7

Note: Bold signifies majorities and positive change.
Source: Afrobarometer.org.

countries exhibited a lack of majority trust in their parliaments in 2013, nineteen fell into that category in 2018 and twenty-five in 2021, constituting a majority of all surveyed countries in both 2018 and 2021. Trust in parliaments diminished more in 2013 than did trust in presidencies: from 53.8 percent in 2013, it dropped to overall less than majority support in 2018, at 45.3 percent, and still further in 2021 to only 41.6 percent. Only in Malawi did parliamentary trust recover from less than majority support in 2018 to 53.1 percent in 2021. Trust in parliaments did increase in nine countries in 2021 compared to only five in 2018. Lack of trust is doubly significant because it also likely undermines support for parliament's important role in checking and overseeing the work of presidents.

Nation-State Identity

Beyond transparency, accountability, and trust in core democratic institutions of the presidency and parliament, as measures of democratic state formation, citizen identification with the nation-state itself is also critically important. In sub-Saharan Africa, states were generally constructed colonially by involuntarily grouping together numerous ethnic communities, often only parts of them. This surgery was accomplished pragmatically, generally with scant integrating vision in mind. A key indicator of the strength and legitimacy of those colonially formed states, six decades into the independence era, has become the degree to which African citizens have come to identify with and thus validate those states by subordinating and/or leaving behind identification with their residual ethnic communities.

Table 2.13 records evidence from Afrobarometer's 2013, 2018, and 2021 surveys in more than thirty countries that have measured citizen identification with their respective nation-states as they have experienced it over six decades of the independence era. In the second decade of the twenty-first century, these surveys have revealed significant declines in citizen identification with their nation-states. In 2013, only 47.8 percent of citizens in twenty-seven countries identified with their nation-states totally or more than they did with their ethnic communities. That number declined to 42.8 percent for thirty-one countries in 2018 and to 39.8 percent for thirty countries in 2021. Majorities met this standard in only thirteen countries in 2013, and this number declined to ten in 2018 and seven in 2021. Only three countries tallied majorities in all three surveys: Guinea, Niger, and Tanzania. In 2021, citizen identification with the South African state stood at 15.5 percent, Nigeria's at 15.5 percent, and Uganda's at 14.3 percent, the lowest levels among the surveyed countries.

Table 2.13. Percent Identifying with Nation Totally or More Than
with Ethnic Group

	2021	2018	2013	Change 2018–21	Change 2013–18
Angola	37.5				
Benin	29.0	25.7	**58.1**	**3.3**	−32.4
Botswana	26.2	29.3	22.8	−3.1	**6.5**
Burkina Faso	47.8	47.1	48.7	**0.7**	−1.6
Cabo Verde	44.5	**72.6**	33.0	−28.1	**39.6**
Cameroon	35.9	43.9	45.5	−8.0	−1.6
Côte d'Ivoire	46.3	42.2	48.2	**4.1**	−6.0
Eswatini	**68.2**	**74.7**		−6.5	
Gabon	**51.9**	**63.6**		−11.7	
The Gambia	48.5	**53.4**		−4.9	
Ghana	34.6	36.5	44.3	−1.9	−7.8
Guinea	**80.7**	**82.8**	**74.0**	−2.1	**8.8**
Kenya	38.1	**53.8**	**55.8**	−15.7	−2.0
Lesotho	32.2	27.5	**52.5**	**4.7**	−25.0
Liberia	19.6	23.5	27.8	−3.9	−4.3
Madagascar		45.7	**70.5**		−24.8
Malawi	32.6	26.2	41.5	**6.4**	−15.3
Mali	**50.9**	47.4	**50.9**	**3.5**	−3.5
Mauritius	32.1	25.2	30.5	**6.9**	−5.3
Mozambique	20.8	28.2	47.7	−7.4	−19.5
Namibia	25.7	33.1	44.1	−7.4	−11.0
Niger	**62.3**	**53.0**	**70.3**	**9.3**	−17.3
Nigeria	15.5	18.1	14.4	−2.6	**3.7**
São Tomé and Príncipe		**56.7**			
Senegal	**74.1**	42.6	**52.9**	**31.5**	−10.3
Sierra Leone	47.4	23.9	**58.2**	**23.5**	−34.3

Table 2.13. *(continued)*

	2021	2018	2013	Change 2018–21	Change 2013–18
South Africa	15.5	32.1	**70.3**	−16.6	−38.2
Tanzania	**51.7**	**57.0**	**67.7**	−5.3	−10.7
Togo	39.5	**52.9**	**54.2**	−13.4	−1.3
Uganda	14.3	24.0	20.3	−9.7	**3.7**
Zambia	44.2	39.6	33.9	**4.6**	**5.7**
Zimbabwe	26.9	43.7	**53.0**	−16.8	−9.3
Average	39.8	42.8	47.8	−3.0	−5.0
Std dev	16.7	16.3	15.7	11.7	15.5

Note: Bold signifies majorities and positive change.
Source: Afrobarometer.com.

Conclusion

This chapter has documented the gradual decline in democracy in sub-Saharan Africa from several perspectives since the beginning of the twenty-first century. This decline during the first two decades has, on balance, signaled a failure of practice both to sustainably expand and deepen democracy itself and to begin to accomplish the companion objective of strengthening and reforming chronically weak, fragile sub-Saharan African states.

Nonetheless, African citizens have continually sustained a preference for democracy at fairly high levels over the familiar authoritarian alternatives. They have begun to betray some uncertainty and skepticism concerning the efficacy of multiparty, competitive elections. However, more recently, they have appeared to renew their support for core individual democratic liberties, including the ability to speak their minds, join any organization they choose, and experience untrammeled media freedom.

At the threshold of a fourth decade of sub-Saharan African democratization, the degree to which a fundamental challenge Crawford Young recognized at its birth will ultimately be met remains to be determined. He wrote: "For many in Africa, a remoralization of the public realm and relegitimation of the state required political opening" (Young 2012, 196). The viability of that opening in sub-Saharan Africa remains at risk, undermined by pervasive corruption: specifically, (1) perceived very poor governmental performance in combatting corruption, and (2) significant risk to individuals who report corruption. Plausibly, pervasive corruption has contributed to weakening citizen trust in core democratic institutions, specifically presidencies and parliaments. Perhaps still more profoundly, weaknesses in democratic practice may also be an important factor in diminished levels of citizen identification with their nation-states over identification with their residual ethnic identities.

Post–Cold War democratization has posed existential challenges to received wisdom and practice. Presumed sequential requirements for state formation and a certain level of economic development prior to democratization have yielded to the existential priority of attempting simultaneous strengthening and reform of fragile states and promoting equitable and steady economic development as well as democratization. However, improved levels of economic development early in the new century have not appeared to prompt either strengthened democratic development or state reform and legitimation.

Since about 2005, sub-Saharan Africa has experienced gradual democratic regression. A modest correlation between changing levels of democratization and those of state fragility suggests that diminishing democratization may equally have influenced and been influenced by persistent, pervasive state fragility. But it also suggests that democratic political renewal may remain possible. Favorable circumstances, reformed democratic political leadership, and emergent, shared commitment to rein in rampant corruption may yet help to strengthen trust in democratic institutions and increase citizen identification with their nation-states, preserving the possibility that they may one day become fully democratic African states.

Notes

An earlier version of this essay was published as "Third Wave Democracy and the State in Sub-Saharan Africa," in *Africa in World Politics: Sustaining Reform in a Turbulent World Order*, edited by John W. Harbeson and Donald Rothchild (New York: Routledge, 2023), reprinted by permission of the publisher.

1. An underlying issue in all this was the extent to which colonially constructed states were even states at all. The late Crawford Young addressed this issue authoritatively in 1994. He concluded that, while not possessing all the properties of genuine states, they possessed enough to qualify as such.

2. Full disclosure: I was a Freedom House consultant on Africa for three years early in this century.

3. Freedom House has included Western Sahara and Somaliland with all independent countries only for 2018–2021. South Sudan has been an independent country only
since 2011.

4. Afrobarometer has steadily expanded its surveys to include thirty-two SSA countries in its eighth round of surveys, leaving seventeen for future surveys, including Burundi, Central African Republic, Chad, Comoros, Congo, Democratic Republic of the
Congo, Djibouti, Equatorial Guinea, Eritrea, Guinea-Bissau, Madagascar, Mauritania,
Rwanda, São Tomé and Príncipe, Seychelles, Somalia, and South Sudan. Collectively,
they averaged twenty-eight in Freedom House's 2021 scores, compared to forty-one for
all SSA countries. Two were free (Seychelles and São Tomé and Príncipe). Four were
partly free (Comoros, Guinea-Bissau, Madagascar, and Mauritania). The remaining
eleven were all unfree.

References

Alfonso, Felipe B., and David C. Korten, eds. 1983. *Bureaucracy and the Poor: Closing the Gap.*
West Hartford, CT: Kumarian Press.

Bratton, Michael, and Nicholas Van de Walle. 1997. *Democratic Experiments in Africa: Regime Transitions in Comparative Perspective.* New York: Cambridge University Press.

Bratton, Michael, Robert Mattes, and Emmanuel Gyimah-Boadi. 2005. *Public Opinion,
Democracy, and Market Reform in Africa.* New York: Cambridge University Press.

Chenery, Hollis, Montek S. Ahluwalia, John H. Duloy, C.L.G. Bell, and Richard Jolly.
1974. *Redistribution with Growth: Policies to Improve Income Distribution in Developing Countries in the Context of Economic Growth.* New York: Oxford University Press.

Harbeson, John W., and Donald Rothchild, eds. 2023. *Africa in World Politics: Sustaining
Reform in a Turbulent World Order.* 7th ed. London: Routledge.

Harbeson, John W., Donald S. Rothchild, and Naomi Chazan, eds. 1994. *Civil Society and
the State in Africa.* Boulder, CO: Lynne Rienner.

Huntington, Samuel. 1991. *The Third Wave: Democratization in the Late Twentieth Century.*
Norman: University of Oklahoma Press.

Lewis, William Arthur. 1965. *Politics in West Africa.* New York: Praeger.

Linz, Juan J., and Alfred Stepan. 1996. *Problems of Democratic Transition and Consolidation:
Southern Europe, South America, and Post-communist Europe.* Baltimore: Johns Hopkins
University Press.

Wing, Susanna. 2008. *Constructing Democracy in Transitioning Societies of Africa: Constitutionalism and Deliberation in Mali.* New York: Springer.

Young, Crawford. 1994. *The African Colonial State in Comparative Perspective.* New Haven,
CT: Yale University Press.

Young, Crawford. 2012. *The Postcolonial State in Africa: Fifty Years of Independence, 1960–2010.*
Madison: University of Wisconsin Press.

3

The Colonial Legacy of Policing as State Building

Kaden Paulson-Smith

Between 2019 and 2021, individuals in thirty-four African countries viewed the police as the most corrupt of state institutions and "more predatory than protective," with many reporting violent encounters, especially the most vulnerable (Logan 2022). Police corruption, extortion, violence, and political manipulation across the African continent have been broadcast by media outlets, investigated by humanitarian organizations, scrutinized by international leaders, and increasingly studied by scholars (Beek et al. 2017; Sakpa 2020; SABC News 2021; *Al Jazeera* 2022). Much of this came to the fore with global uprisings against police violence in the summer of 2020 (Cave, Albeck-Ripka, and Magra 2020) and increased vulnerability to state violence throughout the COVID-19 pandemic (Hayden et al. 2021). Others have documented a longer trajectory of these views and systematic experiences (Agbiboa 2015).

Even when violent experiences with the police are contextualized within longer histories of state violence, issues with policing today are commonly framed as deviations from otherwise protective institutions. For instance, when tracing the roots of one of the most infamous cases of a corrupt and violent police force to the apartheid regime (Egwu 2021), journalists claim that the

South African Police Service's violence has caused "an inherent disconnect between the mandate of law enforcement and the perception of the execution of their duties" (Feltham and Rupiah 2021). Police violence, in this case, is considered contrary to the role of the police, leading people to fear and oppose the police instead of going to them for protection, which is implied as the police's purpose. Furthermore, the claim that contemporary violence conflicts with the police's mandate implies that the police's function as a coercive arm of government is a new development despite prior colonial histories that established the police as such (e.g., Steinberg 2014).

Around the world, this framing has fueled recommendations for legal reforms, combating impunity, implementing punitive measures against violence and corruption, separating the police from the executive branch, demilitarizing police forces, offering legal training for police officers and citizens, emphasizing compliance with human rights principles, improving reporting mechanisms, and providing greater funds to professionalize forces and prevent bribery and extortion (Transparency International 2016; "Panel of Experts Report On Policing and Crowd Management" 2018; Dalton 2020; Burger 2021; Talane 2021; Edwards 2022). However, the logic of reform rests on certain assumptions about the purpose of the modern police and its relationship to the state and society. These assumptions are rooted in the fabled origin story of the modern police and its founding principles. A historical examination of the development of the police and the state within a broader history of colonization problematizes reform as a solution.

The most well-known story is that of Britain's 1829 Metropolitan Police Act, which created the world's first professionalized police force (Novak et al. 2019). Sir Robert Peel, known as the father of the modern police, characterized the new uniquely civilian nature of his "bobbies" with the motto "The police are the public and the public are the people." Modern police forces were supposed to be seen as civilian, not military; they were to be separate from the state, not controlled by it; and they were to operate domestically, not internationally—three principles that do the work of legitimizing police around the world to this day (Seigel 2018, 2019). However, before bringing "the bobbies" to London, Peel led the Royal Irish Constabulary not as a public "service" to the Irish but as "an imposer of force on the people" (Sinclair 2008, 174). The first Metropolitan Police Force was actually the successor to this imperial force.

Before reaching London, Britain had trained colonial police forces in Ireland and spread them from Palestine to India and Ceylon to British-colonized

West and East Africa as early as 1780 (Sinclair 2008). Prior to this, slave patrols operated in the Carolina and Virginia colonies in the early eighteenth century, originating from legislation that deputized slave catchers as agents of the state in the Barbados colony in the seventeenth (Hadden 2003). Frantz Fanon described how imperial powers used "agents of law and order" for "frequent, direct intervention" to "ensure the colonized are kept under close scrutiny" (2004, 4). Contrary to Peel's portrayal of police officers as civilian servants rather than occupying soldiers, Fanon argued that the police did not mask their oppressive nature and brought "violence into the homes and minds of the colonized subject" with "the clear conscience of the law enforcer" (4). The public and policymakers often neglect the foundational role of enslavement and imperialism in the police's development. This may be why the myth of a civilian–military divide still persists and continues to reinforce the legitimacy of police around the world today (Seigel 2019, 523).

The main reason the colonial police were tasked with maintaining order was to facilitate the extraction of taxes and labor to finance colonial administrations and to profit European metropoles (Killingray 1986, 411). Walter Rodney has translated colonial governments' emphasis on "the maintenance of law and order" to "the maintenance of conditions most favorable to the expansion of capitalism and the plunder of Africa" (2018, 196). In this sense, extortion and political control were not signs of a broken police force but suggested a functioning one. Furthermore, incidents of colonial police officers wielding and threatening violent force were not symptoms of policing gone awry. They were strategies that made the colonial state possible. What is cast as the "corruption" of police forces across the African continent and a defect of the postcolonial state can be more accurately understood as the design of the modern police and a persistent leftover from colonialism. These issues are not a defect of the state but an essential component that allowed for the repression of indigenous resistance, the ruthless extraction of labor and resources, the theft and settlement of land, and the establishment of a state apparatus.

In this chapter, I focus on the centrality of policing under British colonialism by applying Crawford Young's state-building framework to a dockworkers' strike in the former Tanganyika Territory, where the police arrived after World War I in 1919 when the British took the colony from Germany. This analysis illustrates how colonial police forces were not a civilian force tasked with preventing or detecting crime, as Peel alleged, but one charged with taking on the military's responsibility of maintaining order and suppressing resistance, the defining imperatives of the colonial state.

Young's Framework of Colonial State Building

State Building

According to Young's framework, there are two stages of European domination: conquest and statecraft. Conquest was associated with the partition of territories (e.g., the "Scramble for Africa") and is often described as a single act, whereas creating states out of these territories was an extended series of acts that sought to establish "permanent domination" of European powers (Young 1994, 95). While these stages were, in reality, far less distinct or complete, this analysis focuses on the second stage, during which colonial police forces were spread throughout the world. The second stage, which Young refers to as "constructing Bula Matari," aimed to assert European sovereignty through diplomacy and/or force so as to convey superior power that would "congeal into enduring forms of dominance" (95).[1] Long-lasting dominance was pursued through the establishment of states.

The imperial sovereignty doctrine of European international law allowed for the creation of states, based not on consent but on whoever came out as a victor in conquest and domination, as established by the Berlin Conference (1884–85) and the Doctrine of Discovery (Miller and Stitz 2022). Sovereignty would hold only if "effective occupation" was achieved. This occupation, according to Young, required "prescriptive force by the creation of a visible infrastructure on the ground of garrisons [armed forces] that affirmed imperial presence and served as an embryonic framework for assertion of rule" (Young 1994, 96). In other words, European domination relied on the framework of states with borders to lay claim to territories and to establish rule, order, and revenue (100). A shift in colonial bureaucratic strategy followed World War I: colonial administrators became increasingly professionalized instead of just being enlisted from military forces and increasingly autonomous from central administrators and the metropole (101).

Local security forces were subsequently mandated to establish hegemonic rule over colonies, but there were not enough European military troops to cover such wide swaths of land. The British rotated military officers among colonies, recruited soldiers within colonies, and "augmented" troops with "sizable armed police forces" (Young 1994, 105). European powers that failed to establish coercive administrative apparatuses during this state-construction phase also risked rival colonial powers' encroachment, as the Portuguese experienced in Angola.

Establishing hegemonic rule was fundamental to colonizing territories, but so was financing these governing structures, which led to more formalized agencies and extractive institutions to get indigenous populations to pay for the governing apparatuses being imposed on them (Young 1994, 78). Attempts to control African labor through taxation "became the very core of colonial state construction, the hinge on which its logic turned" (79). Establishing hegemony and generating revenue through controlling labor and taxing local populations were the principal imperatives that the state sought to achieve.

The Police in Young's Imperatives of the State

While he did not discuss this extensively, Young left traces of how he thought the police and broader security forces featured in the project of state building. Most evidently, on the cover of *The African Colonial State in Comparative Perspective* (1994) is a painting of the Congo Free State,[2] which Belgian King Leopold II brutally seized and operated as his personal possession, ultimately killing between ten and fifteen million people. This painting depicts African security officers being directed by a white Belgian authority who is overseeing their execution of violence. This image illustrates how Young conceptualized the colonial state. One might expect professionalized security forces that wield coercive force to play a strong role in Young's theorizing of the colonial state. However, in his six imperatives of the state, police and policing explicitly feature in only two: hegemony and security: "hegemony is sustained through the policing apparatus whose professionalization is one of the hallmarks of the modern state" (Young 1994, 35–36, citing Bayley 1975), and hegemony required a local security force to "underwrite" it and serve as its "coercive arm" (Young 1994, 105).

I build on and depart from Young's understanding of the role of professionalized local security forces. I argue that the police were central to achieving or attempting to achieve all six state imperatives. I focus on the police because they were the most important security force in carrying out day-to-day counterinsurgency campaigns to prevent challenges to the state ("Global Counterinsurgency and the Police-Military Continuum" 2022). Resistance to the colonial state often arose in situations when Africans refused to be subject to economic exploitation and colonial law and order that was enforced by the police (Paulson-Smith 2022). This is not to suggest that colonial police forces were separate from the military or not militarized forces themselves. The League of Nations prohibited military bases and forces in colonial territories, except for the purposes of policing and defense (for example, see the "British Mandate for East Africa" 1923). Police forces were built as military organizations, and police constables were drawn from military regiments (Burton 2003, 68), illustrating Micol Seigel's (2019) incisive argument that the police were "always already" military.

Contrary to Young, I contend that the police forces were not *part of* the state's "harsher realities of daily hegemony" (Young 1994, 166) because there was no preexisting state that they served. The police did not just expand the state's reach and capacity of control, as Young observed (1994, 73–74); the police were the state's essential manifestation of power (Seigel 2018, 10). They *created* the state by enacting daily hegemony to effectively occupy indigenous peoples and their land, especially urbanizing areas where economic and political power was concentrated (Burton 2003). It is unclear how the creation of a colonial state could have been possible without the colonial police.

Alternative Explanations

Instead of viewing the police as necessary to the success of colonial domination and state building, one alternative but not necessarily contrary view considers the colonial state and police as failures. According to this argument, the police were not a significant force during colonization because Europeans were limited in their attempts to consolidate power and assert authority over populations by the same factors as precolonial leaders, which is the position taken by Jeffrey Herbst (2000). Herbst points to the disproportionate police-to-civilian ratio and the limited reach of the British throughout their vast territories to make the claim that colonial policing, like state building, was a failure (2000, 79). Killingray's archival evidence from multiple contexts does paint a picture of the colonial police and the Native Authority as small, inadequate, incompetent, weak, underfunded, ill equipped, inefficient, illegitimate, and sometimes nonexistent (1986).[3]

The theory of policing as state building that I develop in this chapter by drawing from Young would help explain Herbst's and others' assessment of the colonial state as a failure. Where the state was weak and nonexistent, so were the police. Furthermore, by examining specific instances where the police and state failed, we can gain insight into the local resistance behind these failures, following James C. Scott (1998, 2009). Studying the police as an entry point to anticolonial resistance may also reveal the "infrastructural frontiers" or "the material edge of states" marking the limits of colonial power (Schouten and Bachmann 2022, 2).

Analysis: Policing as State Building

I start with Young's imperatives of the colonial state, but where he deems the state central to achieving these imperatives essential to colonization, I argue that the police were central to this endeavor. For this theory to be accurate, we would expect the police to carry out the defining objectives of the state. If they do, particularly in contexts that do not use states in their political organization, it can be said that the police are bringing the state into being. It is most important that we observe the police carrying out the core twin imperatives of the state: creating hegemony and ensuring revenue generation. As Young implies, and as Fanon and Rodney observe, these imperatives come together most clearly in attempts to control labor.

I evaluate my theory of policing as state building using archival data on colonial attempts to control African labor in Dar es Salaam, the former colonial capital of Tanganyika, which is now known as mainland Tanzania. This chapter describes a dockworker strike that took place in 1950 and the series of events that unfolded in its aftermath using British colonial correspondences, propaganda films, parliamentary Hansards, police annual reports, and news reports. Many of the official British government sources used for this analysis were not disclosed to the public until recently and were therefore excluded from previous historical work on labor organizing and policing in Tanganyika. For instance, C.S.L. Chachage noted in his description of this strike, "One of the strikers claimed that the strike had taken place because of oppression. Otherwise, besides this reason, nothing is known about the cause of the 1950 strike" (1986, 283–84). This chapter examines resistance to policing through the actions and words of everyday workers as much as possible, as well as through police actions and discourse that circulated among British officials about the role of the police in suppressing uprisings.

I use this case to evaluate whether the police can be said to be responsible for Young's six imperatives of the state: hegemony, autonomy, security, legitimacy, revenue, and accumulation. These imperatives cannot be measured separately because they are always interacting and usually competing (Young 1994, 40), so I also describe how they are connected, overlapping, and/or in tension with each other. I find evidence of the police attempting to achieve the main imperatives of the state, but at every turn the people subjected to colonial rule mounted challenges to these imperatives. This leads me to conclude that the police were a main tool of colonization but also an entry point for resisting colonization: the British built the colonial state through the police, but Africans also fought colonialism through the police. This dynamic would continue to shape the relationship between the police, the state, and society after the end of formal colonial rule.

A Dockworker Strike in Dar es Salaam

Dockworkers in Dar es Salaam staged a strike in 1950 that was violently suppressed by the police, leading to a week of demonstrations throughout town. Workers were striking against three proposed policies from the port authorities and the colonial administration: more systematic surveillance through the addition of a gate to the entrance of the harbor to improve monitoring and control over workers' movements; a change in status from daily paid "casual" workers to monthly paid permanent workers, which would lead to less reliable and lower wages; and a new registration scheme requiring everyone to get registered and carry an identification card ("Tanganyika: Strikes and Riots" 1950).

On that morning, when the strike was supposed to take place, the police arrived. According to the deputy governor's report, the workers made the first move and allegedly attacked an officer from behind (Fletcher-Cooke 1950). One correspondent described what happened next with the headline "Africans attack patrol" and said that "rioting broke out . . . when a crowd of several hundred Africans attacked a police patrol with heavy pangas, sticks, and stones . . . police officers opened fire with revolvers, killing one African and wounding seven other rioters" ("Tanganyika: Strikes and Riots" 1950). This incident led to a series of demonstrations over the week throughout the area, and the police mobilized to crack down on what were called "violent mobs" and "African riots" (for more details about the subsequent demonstrations and police mobilization, see Paulson-Smith 2022, 9–13).

This 1950 strike and union had a long history of challenging labor exploitation and the colonial state in Tanganyika, including past successes with overturning these same proposed policies. The Stevedores and Dockworkers Union initially emerged out of the 1943 General Strike, which had started with dockworkers and spread throughout Tanganyika (Chachage 1986, 276–77). The 1950 strike also built on a decade of labor organizing across industries in the territory, taking off in 1939 when strikes occurred every day and then spreading to almost every region by 1948 (Chachage 1986, 276–77, 283). Throughout 1950, there would be fifty strikes involving at least 7,444 workers and resulting in 11,006 working days lost, according to the *Tanganyika Annual Report of the Labour Department* (Jackson and Manktelow 2015, 220). These strikes resulted in

major wins for workers, as well as intensified legal restrictions and violent policing strategies coordinated by the colonial administration to systematically suppress future labor disturbances.

Ports, along with plantations and mines, "formed the backbone of the colonial economy," and this particular strike resulted in the "worst forms of violence the town had ever experienced" (Chachage 1986, 283–84). The colonial
government was more anxious about industrial disputes than any other issue
during this time, and this strike illustrates why "it was in the towns where the
colonial government lost control first in Tanganyika" (Chachage 1986, 286, citing Iliffe 1970 and Coulson 1979). By examining labor organizing and the police's attempted suppression of it, we can better see how everyday policing and
state building worked—and broke down. I next describe the six imperatives of
the state with an examination of the police's role in carrying out those imperatives in the context of the dockworker strike.

Hegemony

Establishing hegemony involves establishing domination through discipline
and punishment according to a created rule of law (Young 1994, 36, borrowing
from Foucault 1995). If the police were carrying out the hegemonic objective of
the state, they would be involved in a continuous "struggle to ensure the supremacy of their authority" and would counter refusals to that authority with
force (Young 1994, 35). As stated earlier, hegemony is one of the two imperatives that Young explicitly identifies with policing.

When the Dockworkers Union threatened to strike, this was perceived as a
challenge to colonial supremacy and authority, so the police preemptively intervened and tried to eliminate the threat. They used force by opening fire on a
crowd of civilians who were armed with sticks, stones, and farm tools because
this strike was seen to present such a threat to colonial domination that it was
not enough to simply arrest and imprison the workers later. This strike was not
only a refusal to work but "a refusal to acknowledge the domination of the
state," which called for force (Young 1994, 35). In his report to the secretary of
state for the colonies, the deputy governor condemned the strike as "irresponsible" and proclaimed that the union's actions "constituted a challenge to law
and order" (Fletcher-Cooke 1950, 2). This collective refusal was perceived as a
major challenge because it was a rejection of the legitimacy of the imposed law
and order and a threat to the economic extraction that law and order were supposed to maintain (Rodney 2018, 196).

The police were the main agents responsible for the "continuous struggle to ensure the supremacy of their [colonial] authority" (Young 1994, 35). Because this strike challenged colonial hegemony, London concluded that the only way to reinforce British rule was by increasing the police's capacity for violence to subdue future "disturbances" like the strike and following demonstrations. The legitimacy of the police's use of force was never questioned by officials in London, as evidenced by their insistence that a "formal enquiry" into the "disturbance" was unnecessary ("Tanganyika: Strikes and Riots" 1950).

Autonomy

Autonomy, in the context of a colonized territory, is the degree of that territory's independence and sovereignty in relation to the metropole. Colonial authorities were increasingly constrained only by settler communities and corporate interests (Young 1994, 159). If the police were responsible for increasing the autonomy of the colonial administration, they would aim to consolidate power and professionalize and institutionalize the "apparatus of rule" (36). The police would allow for high-level colonial officials to be increasingly independent in interpreting their own territory's interests and managing the territory accordingly (122).

The police advanced the autonomy of the Tanganyika colonial administration by becoming an increasingly professionalized force, especially after World War II, and increasingly independent from command at the London Colonial Office. Colonial police forces had their own hierarchical administrations in each territory and responded directly to the governor, as evidenced by the Tanganyika governor's authorization of arrests of striking dockworkers and banning of strikes altogether in 1943 (Iliffe 1970, 132) and the banning of the dockworkers' union and confiscation of property after 1950 (Chachage 1986, 283–84).

Reports filed by the deputy governor and messages between London officials suggest that they wanted to preserve this independence of the police. They blocked an official inquiry into the demonstrations and were primarily concerned with better equipping the police to prevent future so-called disturbances. The workers were challenging this autonomy by challenging the police, those who were entrusted with carrying out British colonial policies. The deputy governor sought to impress upon his higher-ups in London that the threat these workers posed had been eliminated. The strikers were cast as a "small irresponsible element" of "hooligans" who were believed to "have left town," and "at no time was the situation out of hand" (Fletcher-Cooke 1950; "Tanganyika: Strikes and Riots" 1950).

Security

While conventional contract theory holds that a state agrees to provide safety for its citizens in exchange for their sacrifice of some freedoms, this does not apply to colonial states because they did not necessarily rely on the consent of colonized populations to govern. Instead, "no social contract other than conquest bound its subjects to its rule" (Young 1994, 139). As previously mentioned, Young illustrates this relationship using the symbol of Bula Matari. So, while ensuring public safety is theoretically at the heart of a state's reason for being, in colonial contexts security is instead associated with "the hegemonic apparatus" of coercion (Young 1994, 117). In this sense, securing the colonial enterprise is perhaps the most obvious state imperative for which the police are responsible, and Young does acknowledge the police and military as "the institutional core of the state" (37).

The strikers and the protesters they inspired constituted a direct threat to the internal security of the territory in the eyes of the police. They viewed the demonstrators as violent before they acted and considered their concealed weapons to be further evidence of the threat they posed to security (Fletcher-Cooke 1950). According to the deputy governor, "it was found that in *every case* the arrested persons were carrying concealed weapons such as knives, axes, iron bars, bottles and clubs" (emphasis in original). The strike and actions of the protesters were characterized by one journalist as the "attempted murder" of a British police officer (Reuters 1950). These protestors were perhaps depicted as such a threat because they challenged the security of those tasked with providing the security of the state.

The state imperative of achieving security for the colonial enterprise was threatened by workers organizing to protect their own security by protesting new policies that would reduce their wages, job security, and safety through increased surveillance and more frequent interactions with the police. The colony's financial security relied on workers showing up and operating the docks, and the colonizers' physical security relied on workers falling in line and not acting collectively, since they outnumbered the British. Even though military troops were called in to stand by and navy ships circled the harbor, it was the police who intervened and who were in charge of suppressing the subsequent demonstrations throughout town ("Tanganyika: Strikes and Riots" 1950). More so than the military and the navy, the police seemed to be what Young (1994, 37) terms the main "national security council" of the state through their daily policing duties in commercial centers like Dar es Salaam.

As the institutional core of the state, the aftermath of the strike led the police to further arm and equip themselves to suppress future "disturbances" to the state's security. The police's struggle to put down the strike and the subsequent demonstrations were attributed to the police force's not being sufficiently well equipped with tear gas and communications technology: "It seems to me that if a little of this had been used on the mob at the right moment it would have had the desired effect but I doubt whether any tear gas bombs were available!" and "The disturbance in question clearly shows the weakness of Police equipment," in the words of the assistant police adviser in London, who had previously worked for the London Metropolitan Police (Abbiss 1950).

Legitimacy

Legitimacy is the core of the Weberian state because hegemonic rule rests on its own credibility. If the police were responsible for producing legitimacy for British colonization, they would visibly possess superior force to demonstrate their monopoly on violence and thus credibility (Young 1994, 37). According to Fanon, every police officer and soldier served as "the official, legitimate agent, the spokesperson for the colonizer and the regime of oppression" (2004, 3). However, coercion is like a gold reserve that underpins this power: if coercion is used too much, it loses value (Young 1994, 37, citing Parsons 1964). Therefore, we would expect the police to attempt to render colonial rule legitimate not solely through using violence, but through maintaining the threat and possibility of using violence at any time (Seigel 2018).

There are two angles from which to evaluate the state imperative of legitimacy: from the inside of a colony (e.g., as perceived by populations subject to colonial rule or European colonial settlers) and from the outside of a colony (e.g., as perceived by European metropoles or the United Nations). The police feature prominently in attempts to create a sense of a legitimate state from both angles.

Young believes that the colonial administration's "battle for legitimation on the European front was won, but colonial agents were well aware that its command over its subjects relied ultimately on force" (1994, 139). This made establishing hegemony precarious, so the police sought to create the appearance of legitimacy to suppress challenges to colonial rule, which was potentially one reason they were used instead of the military to ensure daily hegemony from within the territory. During the strike, the police sought to preserve colonial authority and to maintain the right to enforce these policies by demonstrating that they possessed "superior force" to the workers (Young 1994, 37). As previously mentioned, this duty lies at the heart of the Weberian state, which has a monopoly over violence. The police sought to visibly demonstrate their capacity for violence as a way to uphold their claim to the legitimate use of this violence and, therefore, their legitimate domination over the territory.

The strike challenged the state's legitimacy that the police attempted to create. The Dockworkers Union sent "threatening" letters with its demands to the port manager, the labor commissioner, the chief secretariat, and the private secretary (Stevedores and Dockworkers Union 1950). When those demands were not met, the dockworkers withheld their labor. This signifies not only a questioning of increased monitoring, regulation, and control but also a questioning of the authority behind these policies. By withholding their labor, the workers were challenging the port authority's and the colonial administration's power to make them work.

Revenue and Accumulation

Revenue generation was central to colonization because resources were, at a minimum, required to finance the administration of colonies, and resources were also expected to stimulate the Western European economy, especially in the period of postwar reconstruction. If the police were central to ensuring revenue generation, they would "engage in a ceaseless struggle with civil society to extract the resources necessary" (Young 1994, 38). The police would do this while attempting to balance acting as a predator and maintaining legitimacy, which is the challenge that Young identifies with achieving this imperative (1994, 39) and a tension that is contested today (Logan 2022).

Accumulation is the amassing of wealth through an expanding economic base that generates revenue. African labor was the primary factor of production during colonization, because "virtually all operations" were labor intensive (Young 1994, 137). Across all colonial powers, public infrastructure was financed by "what amounted to a labor tax" (174). Especially after World War II, colonization required steady labor "under the direction of a property owner and the supervision of the state" and also required that "laborers be made to learn and internalize new values and attitudes" (Young 1994, 138, quoting Cooper 1997, 2–3). Young says colonial administrators and African chiefs oversaw labor, but he does not name the police here. If the police were responsible for carrying out the imperative of accumulation, they would be at the forefront of attempts to establish an expanding economic base through controlling labor and ensuring revenue generation over time.

Financing and profiting off colonial territories were the main priorities and motivations of the British Empire, and the pressure to achieve these priorities only intensified throughout the twentieth century. The police were central to extracting resources for the colonial project, most straightforwardly through tax collection but also, less noticeably, through surveilling and controlling colonial workers, especially in urban areas, where capital was concentrated. It follows that in labor disputes between African workers and colonial industries, the police took the side of commercial interests.

However, the Dockworkers Union tested the role of the police and asked a police officer patrolling the docks on the morning of the strike if he would help prevent others from working. The officer refused, even though, as the dockworkers pointed out, police used the dock area to "get a hold of people," preventing them from working on a regular basis (Fletcher-Cooke 1950). The workers' attempt to subvert the role of the police and their resulting observation highlights the conflictual nature of the police's duties. The police attempted to achieve the state imperatives of revenue generation and accumulation, which involved not only the use of threats but also the use of force, as was the case in suppressing the strike and the subsequent demonstrations. Simultaneously, however, the police attempted to secure legitimate hegemonic rule, which was undermined by the use of force against subjected populations.

Conclusions and Implications: Postcolonial Legacies of Resisting Police and State

A definitive insight that Young leaves us with is that "the colonial state lives, absorbed into the structures of the independent polity," which allows for the state's "formidable capacity for its own reproduction across time and in the face of systematic efforts by new regimes to uproot prior forms and build new blueprints" (1994, 2). I argue that the police were essential to this production and reproduction of the state, so much so that the police should be central in Young's conceptualization of Bula Matari, the symbol of "white domination that was the energizing force in the superstructure of imperial hegemony" (2). If we conceptualize the police as a distinctive feature of the nineteenth-century European state superimposed on African polities, this might help explain the persistent institutions of the colonial state and the police's place in it. Despite reforms and resistance to the police after independence, colonial policing institutions continued to shape state practices and ideologies of racialized, sexualized, gendered, and classed control in the territory that would become Tanzania in 1964 (Kamau 2006; Kapinga 2014; Shivji and Yahya-Othman 2014). Because of these connections, many contemporary issues are derived from the colonial legacies of the police and state.

Essential to addressing these issues is the takeaway that the colonial police system, as the primary weapon of state building, never went unchallenged. Strikes and, more broadly, collective organizing that challenged colonial imperatives were deeply connected to resistance to the colonial police. These dynamics shaped postcolonial practices, ideas, and the materiality of policing and the state.

First, throughout formal colonial rule and during the transition to independence, anticolonial efforts to dismantle the British Empire were bound up with resistance to the police. Challenging the police was central to liberatory self-governance strategies. Anticolonial resistance to the police helped bring about the end of the British Empire. This resistance involved attempts to physically interrupt and overthrow, bureaucratically weaken, and fundamentally delegitimize the police as a daily manifestation of the colonial state. These forms of resistance demonstrated that "the Territory could do without that force," as stated by one African representative in the Legislative Council (Tanganyika Legislative Council 1959). I find that there was a rise in collective organizing to challenge colonial authority, especially following World War II, as reflected by a wave of strikes, which resemble the one described here, across West and East Africa (Cooper 1996). These tactics often targeted or came head to head with the police. One potential explanation for this is that the police were the main way people came into contact with the state, so the police became an important avenue of resistance to colonialism. Collective organizing, like the dockworker strike, was resistance not only to economic exploitation but also to forms of state surveillance, policing, and violence that were being ramped up during this pivotal time.

Second, the challenge of policing institutions in the transition to self-governance shaped the postcolonial police system and its relationship with the newly independent state, partly by disrupting its operations and partly by accelerating its growth and connections to London. We can see how efforts to disrupt colonial policing and to Africanize the inherited state accelerated the growth of policing leading up to independence by spurring the development of innovative strategies and the stockpiling of weapons for controlling riots, strikes, and forms of protest that continued through the end of formal British colonial rule. The broader security and intelligence system remained in place, and British officials sought to protect their power "by transforming formal empire into informal influence," such as by fortifying the system with security assistance for decades to come (Maguire and Franklin 2020, 2). We can also see this through efforts to pass legal and bureaucratic measures aimed at legitimizing and empowering the police, such as cross-national arrangements between governors aimed at expanding police power beyond state lines and provisions to protect police power in Tanganyika's first constitution (Smith 1961). Overall, the falling British Empire was reluctant to concede control over the police and used the police to institutionalize British influence over the postcolonial state into independence.

This analysis raises many questions, such as: how do these legacies of coloniality, policing, and resistance inform state practices and ideas today? Why does this matter for contemporary politics in Tanzania and other postcolonial contexts? What role might social movements for police and prison abolition play in dismantling systems of state violence? If we understand that the mandate of the first police forces in most African contexts was to carry out the imperatives of the colonial state and bring the state into being, we may then see issues like violence and extortion not as flaws in executing that purpose but as continuations of it. In this sense, the police are not broken but are working exactly as designed. This calls into question the logic of reforming the police, as expressed in recent uprisings such as the #EndSARS protests across Nigeria (Dayo 2020; Jones 2020). By putting this analysis in conversation with resistance in other postcolonial and settler colonial contexts, we may enable new insights to emerge about the continued and remaining work of decolonization.

Notes

1. Bula Matari, which means "he who crushes rocks," was a nickname for Henry Morton Stanley. This name went on to symbolize "intrusive alien authority more generally" and was a metaphor for the "crushing, relentless force of the emerging colonial state in Africa" (Young 1994, 1–2).

2. I appreciate Scott Straus pointing out this connection.

3. The Native Authority was established as part of the system of British indirect rule (see Burton 2002).

References

Abbiss, George. 1950. "Letter from Abbiss." CO 691/209/8. The National Archives, Kew.

Agbiboa, Daniel Egiegba. 2015. "Protectors or Predators? The Embedded Problem of Police Corruption and Deviance in Nigeria." *Administration & Society* 47 (3): 244–81.

Al Jazeera. 2022. "US Issues Sanctions on Sudan's Police over Protest Crackdown." March 21. https://www.aljazeera.com/news/2022/3/21/update-3-u-s-places-sanctions-on-sudans-central-reserve-police-over-protest-crackdown.

Bayley, David. 1975. "The Police and Political Development in Europe." In *The Formation of National States in Western Europe*, edited by Charles Tilly, 328–79. Princeton, NJ: Princeton University Press.

Beek, Jan, Mirco Göpfert, Olly Owen, and Jonny Steinberg. 2017. *Police in Africa: The Street Level View*. New York: Oxford University Press.

"British Mandate for East Africa." 1923. *American Journal of International Law* 17 (3): 153–57. https://doi.org/10.2307/2212953.

Burger, Johan. 2021. "South Africa's Police Need Urgent and Fundamental Reform." ISS Africa, June 28. https://issafrica.org/crimehub/iss-today/south-africas-police-need-urgent-and-fundamental-reform.

Burton, Andrew. 2002. "Adjutants, Agents, Intermediaries: The Native Administration in Dar Es Salaam Township, 1919–1961." In *The Urban Experience in Eastern Africa, c. 1750–2000*, edited by Andrew Burton, 98–118. Nairobi, Kenya: British Institute in Eastern Africa.

Burton, Andrew. 2003. "'Brothers by Day': Colonial Policing in Dar Es Salaam under British Rule, 1919–61." *Urban History* 30 (1): 63–91. https://doi.org/10.1017/S0963926803001044.

Cave, Damien, Livia Albeck-Ripka, and Iliana Magra. 2020. "Huge Crowds around the Globe March in Solidarity against Police Brutality." *New York Times*, June 6, sec. World.

Chachage, Chachage Seithy Loth. 1986. "Socialist Ideology and the Reality of Tanzania." PhD diss., Glasgow University, Glasglow, Scotland.

Cooper, Frederick. 1996. "'Our Strike': Equality, Anticolonial Politics and the 1947–48 Railway Strike in French West Africa." *Journal of African History* 37 (1): 81–118.

Cooper, Frederick. 1997. *From Slaves to Squatters: Plantation Labor & Agriculture in Zanzibar & Coastal Kenya, 1890–1925*. Portsmouth, NH: Heinemann.

Coulson, Andrew. 1979. *African Socialism in Practice: The Tanzanian Experience*. Nottingham: Spokesman.

Dalton, Melissa. 2020. "Conduct Is the Key: Improving Civilian Protection in Nigeria." Center for Strategic and International Studies, July 9. https://www.csis.org/analysis/conduct-key-improving-civilian-protection-nigeria.

Dayo, Bernard. 2020. "Can Nigeria's #EndSARS Protests Lead to Police Abolition?" *Al Jazeera*, October 23. https://www.aljazeera.com/features/2020/10/23/can-nigerias-endsars-protests-lead-to-abolishing-the-police.

Edwards, Louise. 2022. "Model Law Promotes Rights-Based Police Reform across Africa." Association for the Prevention of Torture, January 3. https://www.apt.ch/en/blog/model-law-promotes-rights-based-police-reform-across-africa.

Egwu, Patrick. 2021. "South African Police Are Undertrained, Uncontrolled, and Deadly." *Foreign Policy*, May. https://foreignpolicy.com/2021/05/31/southafrica-police-brutality-julies/.

Fanon, Frantz. 2004. *The Wretched of the Earth*. Translated by Richard Philcox. New York: Grove.

Feltham, Luke, and Kiri Rupiah. 2021. "When Violence Is Policy: How Do We Curb Police Brutality?" *Mail and Guardian*, April 25. https://mg.co.za/politics/2021 -04-25-when-violence-is-policy-how-do-we-curb-police-brutality/.

Fletcher-Cooke, John. 1950. "Confidential Telegram from Fletcher-Cooke to Jones, with Memorandum on 'Industrial Dispute: Dar Es Salaam Docks February, 1950.'" Dar es Salaam. CO 691/209/8. The National Archives, Kew.

Foucault, Michel. 1995. *Discipline & Punish: The Birth of the Prison*. Translated by Alan Sheridan. 2nd ed. New York: Vintage Books.

"Global Counterinsurgency and the Police-Military Continuum." 2022. Special issue, *Small Wars & Insurgencies* 33 (4–5).

Hadden, Sally E. 2003. *Slave Patrols: Law and Violence in Virginia and the Carolinas.* Cambridge, MA: Harvard University Press.

Hayden, Sally, Maurice Oniang'o, Linus Unah, and Patrick Egwu. 2021. "Africa's Hidden Victims: Pandemic Prompted Surge in Police Brutality." *100Reporters* (blog), June 28. https://100r.org/2021/06/africas-hidden-victims-pandemic-prompts-surge -in-police-brutality-blacklivesmatter/.

Herbst, Jeffrey. 2000. *States and Power in Africa: Comparative Lessons in Authority and Control.* Princeton, NJ: Princeton University Press.

Iliffe, John. 1970. "A History of the Dockworkers of Dar Es Salaam." *Tanzania Notes and Records* 71:119–48.

Jackson, Will, and Emily Manktelow. 2015. *Subverting Empire: Deviance and Disorder in the British Colonial World.* New York: Springer.

Jones, Mayeni. 2020. "End Swat: Nigerians Reject Police Unit Replacing Hated Sars." BBC News, October 14, sec. Africa. https://www.bbc.com/news/world-africa -54531449.

Kamau, Evelyn. 2006. "The Police, the People, the Politics: Police Accountability in Tanzania." Commonwealth Human Rights Initiative and Kenya Human Rights Commission. https://www.humanrightsinitiative.org/publications/police/tanza nia_country_report_2006.pdf.

Kapinga, Wilbert B. L. 2014. "Organs of State Violence: The Police Force." In *Escalating State Violence and Impunity: A Reader*, edited by Issa G. Shivji and Saida Yahya-Othman, 13–23. Dar es Salaam: Media Council of Tanzania.

Killingray, David. 1986. "The Maintenance of Law and Order in British Colonial Africa." *African Affairs* 85 (340): 411–37.

Logan, Carolyn. 2022. "Africans across 34 Countries See the Police as Predatory, Not Protective." *Washington Post*, March 19.

Maguire, Thomas J., and Hannah Franklin. 2020. "Creating a Commonwealth Security Culture? State-Building and the International Politics of Security Assistance in Tanzania." *International History Review* (April): 1–22.

Miller, Robert, and Olivia Stitz. 2022. "The International Law of Colonialism in East Africa: Germany, England, and the Doctrine of Discovery." *Duke Journal of Comparative & International Law* 32 (1): 1–59.

Novak, Kenneth, Gary Cordner, Bradley Smith, and Roy Roberg. 2019. *Police & Society.* 8th ed. New York: Oxford University Press.

"Panel of Experts Report on Policing and Crowd Management." 2018. South African Police Service. https://www.scribd.com/document/504368279/Panel-of-experts -report-on-policing-and-crowd-management.

Parsons, Talcott. 1964. "Some Reflections on the Place of Force in Social Process." In *Internal War: Problems and Approaches*, edited by Harry Eckstein, 33–70. New York: Free Press of Glencoe.

Paulson-Smith, Kaden. 2022. "'Police Fire on Rioters': Everyday Counterinsurgency in a Colonial Capital." *Small Wars & Insurgencies* 33 (4–5): 633–53.

Reuter. 1950. "Attempted Murder." 42540/50. Dar es Salaam. CO 691/209/8. The National Archives, Kew.

Rodney, Walter. 2018. *How Europe Underdeveloped Africa*. Brooklyn, NY: Verso.

SABC News. 2021. "Police Corruption Tops List of Complaints Received by Corruption Watch." September 23, sec. South Africa. https://www.sabcnews.com/sabc news/police-corruption-tops-list-of-complaints-received-by-corruption-watch/.

Sakpa, Delali. 2020. "In Africa, Concerns over Rising Police Brutality." *Deutsche Welle*, September 7. https://www.dw.com/en/in-africa-concerns-over-rising-police -brutality/a-54845922.

Schouten, Peer, and Jan Bachmann. 2022. "Infrastructural Frontiers: Terrains of Resistance at the Material Edge of the State." *Geoforum* (June).

Scott, James C. 1998. *Seeing like a State: How Certain Schemes to Improve the Human Condition Have Failed*. New Haven, CT: Yale University Press.

Scott, James C. 2009. *The Art of Not Being Governed: An Anarchist History of Upland Southeast Asia*. New Haven, CT: Yale University Press.

Seigel, Micol. 2018. *Violence Work: State Power and the Limits of Police*. Durham, NC: Duke University Press.

Seigel, Micol. 2019. "Always Already Military: Police, Public Safety, and State Violence." *American Quarterly* 71 (2): 519–39.

Shivji, Issa G., and Saida Yahya-Othman. 2014. *Escalating State Violence and Impunity: A Reader*. Dar es Salaam: Media Council of Tanzania.

Sinclair, Georgina. 2008. "The 'Irish' Policeman and the Empire: Influencing the Policing of the British Empire—Commonwealth." *Irish Historical Studies* 36 (142): 173–87.

Smith, Armitage. 1961. "The Establishment of Service Commissions with Functions Relating to the Appointment and Disciplinary Control of Police Officers." Tanganyika Constitutional Conference Paper no. 3. Dar es Salaam. CO 1037/149. The National Archives, Kew.

Steinberg, Jonny. 2014. "Policing, State Power, and the Transition from Apartheid to Democracy: A New Perspective." *African Affairs* 113 (451): 173–91.

Stevedores and Dockworkers Union. 1950. "Letter from The Stevedores and Dockworkers Union to The Chief Secretariat to the Government." Ref. no. DU/2/91. Dar es Salaam. CO 691/209/8. The National Archives, Kew.

Talane, Moepeng Valencia. 2021. "Our Police Can Do Better, Why Aren't They?" *Transparency International* (blog), February 4. https://www.transparency.org/en /blog/cpi-2020-police-brutality-south-africa.

Tanganyika Legislative Council. 1959. "No. 78 Use of Police beyond Tanganyika Border." Extracts from Legislative Council debates, vol. 3, sessions 58/59. Dar es Salaam. CO 822/1321. The National Archives, Kew.

"Tanganyika: Strikes and Riots." 1950. CO 691/209/8. The National Archives, Kew.

Transparency International. 2016. "How to Put an End to Police Corruption in Africa." Transparency.Org, July 7. https://www.transparency.org/en/news/corruption-of -police-in-africa-must-end-now.

Young, Crawford. 1994. *The African Colonial State in Comparative Perspective*. New Haven, CT: Yale University Press.

Rethinking the Politics of Identity

Part II

4

Religion as Cultural Pluralism

One Identity among Many

Rachel Beatty Riedl

C‍rawford Young's pathbreaking work on cultural pluralism (1976) taught us about the impacts of cultural diversity on political life. It was a vital correction to primordial views of identity in general and African sociopolitical organization in particular, demonstrating the creation of new categories produced by "specific processes of modernizing change" (Sklar 1977, 517). The book paved the way for later instrumental and constructivist interpretations of the relative creation of identity as an evolving result of different conjunctions of historical forces and contemporary phenomena (Young 1993). Young's work provided a foundation for thinking about situational logics of multifaceted identity categories—for identity pluralism within a single individual and how particular categories become politicized as a defining cleavage within complex societies: "Cultural pluralism in operation is contingent upon its immediate environment. The historical trajectory of a given polity provides one set of defining parameters" (Young 1993, 27). Building on this pluralistic and context-specific understanding of identity, scholars sought to define the influence of the state and institutions on cultural pluralism (Posner 2005; Singh and vom Hau 2016), ways to conceptualize ethnicity (Chandra

2006), and the consequences of such pluralism for a variety of political outcomes (Horowitz 1985; Singh 2015).

Across the social sciences today, the recognition of pluralist identities and their relative significance in society as rooted in sociopolitical logics is a definitive domain of scholarly progress. Young taught us to take seriously myriad forms of identity—nationalism, ethnicity, and religion. And his research and teaching pushed us to distinguish among these categories on the basis of their defining logics and in relation to state power. To do so requires going beyond treating religion as one form of ethnic identity. It requires recognizing when and why religious identities are similar to ethnicity and when and why religious identity, thought, and practice have the potential for different logics. This is where Young's legacy may lead us today.

Religion and Politics in Africa:
A Holistic and Disaggregated View

What is the relationship between religion and politics in Africa, and what are the future questions of interest in this field? The topic is central to our understanding of cultural pluralism because (1) religion reflects a diversity of ideas, practices, and social structures that surrounds every person on the planet in an interwoven historical and contemporary landscape; (2) at the micro level, religiosity and the importance of religion in one's daily life are self-reported to be at very high levels across the continent; (3) understanding such variation in *how* religions impact politics and *under what conditions* is essential work for fuller understandings of significant outcomes related to human well-being such as peace and security, socioeconomic development, and equity and justice within and across communities. Building on Young, scholars of African politics have long recognized that "religion matters," but how and why remain important, open questions.

This chapter starts with the premise that the defining characteristic of religion is belief in the supernatural, the divine. From that definitional starting point, religion *shares* characteristics with other types of social identities, such as ethnicity, but religion also encompasses multiple other characteristics that *differentiate* religious identities from other types of social identity categories. Variation across religions' denominational, spatial, and temporal instances demonstrate distinct characteristics that have causal power in understanding the relation to political and socioeconomic outcomes. To take Young's foundations of cultural pluralism to the fullest extent today, the study of religion and politics should further explore these divergences between religious identity and other types of social identity. Our analyses should seek to disaggregate and isolate the importance of (and variations in) a set of relevant dimensions of religions: beliefs in the supernatural, organizational structure, transnational networks, hierarchies of authority, spiritual connections to land and other natural resources, and modes of praxis, among other issues.

Religions' Characteristics and Relation to Other Identity Categories

Religious identity is often conceived as one type of ethnicity, alongside other possibilities, such as nation, ancestral language, region, or tribe, that are used to explain political action (Kasfir 1979; Horowitz 1985; Rothchild 1997; Varshney 2003; Posner 2005; Birnir 2006; Chandra 2006; Wilkinson 2006; Bellin 2008; McCauley and Posner 2019). Examples abound across the world, including the Hindu–Muslim cleavage in India, the Christian–Muslim conflict in Nigeria, and Buddhist nationalism in Sri Lanka; these are but a few of the examples that portray religion in ethnic terms.

Kanchan Chandra (2006) identifies ethnic identities as a subset of identity categories in which eligibility for membership is determined by attributes associated with or believed to be associated with descent. Religious identity *could* be descent-based, inherited at birth, and viewed by a community and individual as unalterable. At the other end of the spectrum, religious identity could be a product of conversion within a pluralistic and fluid religious environment. Therefore, the variations within religion itself are significant, offering more or less overlap with ethnic identity according to the form of religion itself and features of religious affiliation. Religion is not a descent-based attribute by definition, although some religious identities may overlap in practice on this specific characteristic.

This elision between religion and ethnicity may be empirically and conceptually proximate in some cases when religious identification overlaps with group representation goals and networks of trust and monitoring that are often attributed to (politically salient) ethnicity. Like other group identities, religious identity is often accompanied by notions of what the prototypical member looks like and behaves like, which shapes members' self-presentation and visibility to others. Therefore, religious identity is often connected to role and behavioral prescriptions in ways that mirror ethnic identity.

Yet these prescriptions also vary across religious subgroups and geographic zones. Religious variations are significant even within world religion or denominational categories, due to syncretic evolution in tandem with local societies and histories, which offer a distinct potential for very heterogeneous communities of co-believers.

Like other group-based identities, religion also implies a certain density of social ties. These shared characteristics between religious identity and ethnic identity suggest that theories of monitoring and co-identity strategy selection for public goods provision (Habyarimana et al. 2007) may overlap for both categories.

Yet, in many cases, religious and ethnic identities do not overlap exactly. In these cases, we have much to understand about interaction effects. Do overlapping ethnic affiliations and/or language networks but contrasting religious affiliations change the kinds of reciprocity norms that inform the potential for co-ethnic cooperation and investment? And/or do cross-cutting cleavages of ethnicity and religion provide for greater public service provision and feelings of community *because* the density of social ties are conceptually and practically equivalent *or because* the density of social ties offers different types of opportunities across ethnic rather than religious group affiliates? If the density of social ties is based on conceptually distinct connections, through different types of activities, then dense social ties may shape different kinds of behavioral expectations and norms of reciprocity.

John McCauley and Daniel Posner (2019), for example, present religious identification and ethnic identification as equivalent alternatives for potential salient social cleavages and argue that the political environment shapes the weight that people attach to one or the other in Burkina Faso and Côte d'Ivoire. This is an effective strategy for understanding this question: under which conditions does membership in a religious group become socially salient *instead of* an ethnic group? However, a rich conceptual understanding of the ways in which religious identities are and are not similar to ethnic identities is imperative to interrogate the causal mechanisms where we might assume they are operating as functional equivalents.

This attention to a potential range of differences between religious and ethnic identities also presents a challenge. Religion is not a coherent or static category (Hurd 2017). Religion is not *one* thing. Religion has many components, which do not all exist simultaneously and which vary across and within religious categories and across time and space. And while in many cases religious identity is often perceived as if it were "assigned at birth," there are potential shifts over time.

Religions themselves vary in the degree to which they share Donald Horowitz's (1985) defining ethnic characteristic, a "myth of common ancestry." Some religions rely on conversion. Others demand matrilineal descent. Even within the individual, religion is not static. Religious identity itself can shift over the course of one's lifetime. Conversion is possible, with higher and lower barriers that are context-dependent. And while one exists within a web of religiously interpretive schemas and cultural reference points that attempt to give meaning and order to the world (McClendon and Riedl 2015, 2019), one can, to a greater or lesser degree, opt in or out of religious identification and exposures.

Treating religion, therefore, as one among many possible types of ethnic identities is insufficient. It can overlap in specific ways, functioning as a group network and providing certain behavioral prescriptions. But there are also good theoretical reasons to consider the potential for religiosity to function somewhat distinctly as a marker of individual and collective identity (Grzymala-Busse 2012). Like ideational identity categories but not definitionally ethnic ones, religious identity is accompanied by broad philosophies about social life and the ways the world works. Religious identities offer elements of "common culture"—including shared doctrine about right behavior and right thought—that solely descent-based attributes may not necessarily entail. Further, ethnic identity as a descent-based attribute implies constrained change and visibility (Chandra 2006). Attributes associated with descent are, on average, difficult to change in the short term. And descent-based attributes are often visible in a sticky way—evident to others through one's name and physical features—that are available for (mis)interpretation to other observers. Religious affiliations vary in the degree to which they may be visible and sticky in similar ways: some may be evident in surnames or given names, and some may be locally associated with particular physical features. While religious praxis and behavioral codes of dress, gender interactions, or lifestyle may create visibility, the potential fluidity of behavior makes it more possible to disguise or adapt such characteristics across different settings.

In sum, claims as to why and how ethnic or religious identities matter for certain outcomes are based on assumptions of particular properties (Chandra 2006), so whether or not these properties are indeed shared and how they vary is important for a deeper understanding of the role that religion can play in politics. A productive way forward is to disaggregate from definitional categories to the set of specific characteristics that hold distinct properties and connect these properties to the mechanisms through which each impacts political outcomes.

Religions' Variations

Religion can productively be disaggregated and tied to specific implications for social organization and political action (Menchik 2017; McClendon and Riedl 2021). Among these, religion can serve as systems of spiritual belief and ideational content that provide frameworks for how to think about the world and one's place within it; instructions about what to value and how to act; social identities and networks that generate communal dynamics including relational opportunities for cooperation or animosity, competition, and monitoring; transnational networks that provide for potential authority, community, and resource foci beyond local and national borders; institutional embodiment of group identity and interest-group mobilization, including strategies for leadership and relative gains; organization and infrastructure to provide opportunities for service distribution, targeting, and social engagement; patron linkages and power hierarchies that create opportunities for status categories, clientelistic exchange, and leadership hierarchies; intra- and intergroup competition markets for followers and resources; practices of performance, ritual, and participation; and spiritual meaning associated with specific land, water, and other natural resources that may regulate behavior and create visibility and opportunities for (or limits to) participation within and across group membership (McClendon and Riedl 2021).

The actual characteristics of religious groups matter whether they apply to all members of that group by definition, the degree to which they apply across different types of religious groups, and how and when they overlap with other types of identity groups such as ethnicity. These variations should inform our approach to studying identity groups more generally—disaggregating by characteristic and its theoretical implications, recognizing the differential forms of "groupness," and recognizing religiosity as individual belief and practice without groupness (Brubaker 2004). Scholars of Africa have a head start in this domain, with experts long recognizing that beliefs about the supernatural do not neatly divide into world religion categories, so-called believers and nonbelievers, the public and private realm, or even the secular and the sacred (Ilesanmi 1995; Chitando 1997; Ellis and Haar 2004; Galvan 2004; Kalu 2008; Knighton 2009; Sperber and Hern 2018). This approach should guide conceptual foundations, research design, empirical observation, and theoretical understandings of religion and politics in the world today.

All variation proceeds from the shared definition of a belief in the divine, the supernatural, and the spiritual realm. For the vast majority of believers, this is interwoven with what might be considered the secular realm; a holistic approach includes the sacred and secular in one organic reality (Ilesanmi 1995, 54). Religion is a mode of apprehending reality: "a conviction that the material and immaterial aspects of life cannot be separated, although they can be distinguished from each other" (Ellis and Haar 2007, 387). What forms religion takes vary within this holistic approach to spiritual life. What counts as a religion

Table 4.1. Religion Disaggregated and Compared to Ethnicity: As Similar Concepts within Cultural Pluralism

Potential components of religions	Relation/contrast to ethnicity	Implication for politics and theory	Example
Descent-based social identity category.	One and the same; remaining question of whether functional equivalents in interaction.	Theories of ethnic politics (e.g., monitoring, norms of reciprocity, in-group versus out-group competition) apply. Question the degree to which "cross-cuttingness" across ethnically and religiously pluralistic societies are more or less deeply divided and to what end.	Religious cleavage overlaps or cuts across broad categories of regional, ethnic, and/or linguistic divisions, and the legacies of historical political, economic, and social advantage impact the degree to which society is divided (multidimensional characteristics of social structure—cross-cuttingness, cross-fractionalization, and subgroup fractionalization in relation to economic growth (Selway 2011). Whether religion or ethnicity is politically salient is driven by identity frames intimately tied to the policies and strategies that elites pursue, owing to the manner in which their followers respond to ethnic and religious cues (ethnic and religious conflict in Cote d'Ivoire: Miran-Guyon 2012; McCauley 2017).
Social networks that generate communal dynamics.	Similar to ethnicity, the depth and breadth of social networks could vary by type and frequency of religious practice, the extent of religious transnational networks, and so on.	Religiosity is positively related to civic engagement and helping behavior through dense religious social networks.	Religious networks have a stronger impact on civic engagement than general social networks in the US (Lewis, MacGregor, and Putnam 2013).

continues

Table 4.1. (*continued*)

Potential components of religions	Relation/contrast to ethnicity	Implication for politics and theory	Example
Transnational networks.	Like nationalism, religion can be an imagined community—"a process of expanding oneself by transcending our time and space and creating new images of the world and ourselves" (Anderson 1983, 76).	· Create connections and feelings of belonging on a potentially global scale to people with different political environments, socioeconomic class status, ethnic identities, and beyond. Can be harnessed to undermine state sovereignty and/or authoritarian governments.	Growth of transnational religious communities, facilitated by new forms of intergroup communication, has undermined authoritarian governments in particular cases, such as Vatican II publicly expressing concern with human rights and democracy issues, but is not a generalized threat (Haynes 2001).
Group identity; interest-group mobilization; intra- and intergroup competition markets for followers and resources.	Group identity and mobilization similar to ethnicity. The possibility of conversion creates a competitive marketplace in some religious landscapes while not available in others; fluidity in scale of ethnic affiliation likewise varies over time and political institutional environment (Posner 2005).	Religious mobilization, like ethnic group mobilization, can be a force for status quo or opposition, but the possibility of religious competition creates incentives for new forms of sociopolitical incorporation, expanding membership to enlarged constituencies and aligning religious elite interests with "followers." When conditions of religious monopoly prevail, religious elites are more likely to align with political elites and ignore the religious and social needs of marginalized followers.	Theories of monitoring and co-identity strategy selection for public goods provision (Habyarimana et al. 2007).

Table 4.2. Religion Disaggregated and Compared to Ethnicity: As Distinct from Ethnicity, Cultural Pluralism with Cultural Content

Potential components of religions	Relation/contrast to ethnicity	Implication for politics and theory	Example
Systems of spiritual belief and ideational content that provide frameworks for how to think about the world and one's place within it.	Provides individual level cues and causal mechanisms based on beliefs. Exposure and effect are possible to nonmembers (through media and social contexts). Conversion (rapid change) and belief evolution (gradual change) are both possible.	Priming and persuasion through message exposure provide distinct interpretative maps that diagnose political problems and varied solutions.	Pluralism of sermons influence political participation and the longevity of that impact (sermon content influences political behavior in Kenya: McClendon and Riedl 2015).
Explicit instructions about what to value and how to act.	Potential parallel in informal norms regulating private domains such as family code, gender interactions, social values, mannerisms, and so on; shared expectation that ethnic groups are heterogeneous in these instructions, as are religious groups. Religion has the potential to be more explicit, dogmatic, and rigid and to govern different domains.	Expectations of conflicting preferences between members of different groups; visible indicators may mark behavior but vary in degree of observables, making mobilization of one's own group against another group more or less possible; specific instructions may provide rules and regulations to shape group and individual behavior.	A set of received values or moral positions may shape vote choice (religion and redistributive voting in Western Europe: Stegmueller 2013). Religious teachings raise sensitivities, shape preferences that inspire and motivate forms of political action (Arab Spring religious participation in Tunisia and Egypt: Hoffman and Jamal 2014); religious injunctions given in Senegal and regularly invoked at election time as voting instructions to the faithful (Villalón 2015).

continues

Table 4.2. (*continued*)

Potential components of religions	Relation/contrast to ethnicity	Implication for politics and theory	Example
Possibility of eternal rewards, afterlife, and so on.	Extends time horizons and preference ordering to calculations beyond this world/individual life span.	Influence of religion can shape Maslow's Hierarchy of Needs: eternal salvation may rank above all other needs, e.g., peace and security; love and belonging; production, consumption, and distribution decisions.	If conflicting issues are seen as indivisible and hierarchy of needs prioritizes eternal salvation, conflict intensity and duration can be higher for religious-affiliated rebel groups and government (religion and conflict resolution in civil wars: Svensson 2007).
Hierarchical leadership positions.	Religious authorities have the potential to transcend and compete with political authority structures. At the local level, this may parallel ethnicity (it may actually be one and the same in traditional leaders). Similar to ethnicity in frequent patriarchal structure, although variation in gendered leadership across religions and ethnicities.	Creates potential for patron–client relations, "big-man rule." But, variation in hierarchical institutionalization (e.g., high levels in Protestant and Catholic, low levels in Evangelical and Pentecostal) creates varied rules for leadership ascent and heterogeneity in who leadership is open to (including, e.g., women, members of marginalized ethnic communities).	Religious leaders emerge as alternatives to traditional clientelism, encouraging members to break from their past, to trust leadership, and to commit exclusively to their religious social network. The religious movement creates payoff structures that replicate the exchange of resources for loyalty central to big-man rule, filling voids left by the state and providing new vertical social networks (increasing political role of new Pentecostalism in Ghana: McCauley 2013).

| Organizational infrastructure. | At the local level, organizational infrastructure provides varying degrees of institutionalized leadership selection and formalized mechanisms of member engagement. This may be similar to ethnicity depending on practices within ethnic identity groups and across religious groups. At the global level, world religions offer the possibility of alternative power centers (e.g., Vatican, for Catholics; Dalai Lama for Buddhists) that have autonomous resources and authority/decision making in determining elite status within any given locality (e.g., bishops, cardinals). Significant variation within and across religious types, from highly decentralized and localized to highly centralized and global. | Local religious authorities use organizational infrastructure to uphold distinct forms of power and moral authority, separate from political and economic elite realms, which can be tools to support, counter, or remain autonomous from state and economic elites. Domestic political agendas can be countered or supported with international religious organizational resources and authority structures. External locus of decision making in hierarchy in some cases creates more autonomy from the state and possibility for opposition, dissent. | Religious leaders serving as pro-democracy activists, challenging authoritarian political elites (Anglican Bishop challenging Moi's authoritarianism in Kenya: Sabar 2009). Religious authorities serving as "neutral" transitional figureheads, peace negotiators, relying on their moral authority and organizational leadership roles to serve the public (Archbishop of Cotonou presided over the National Conference in Benin: Gifford 1994; Nwajiaku 1994). |

continues

Table 4.2. (*continued*)

Potential components of religions	Relation/contrast to ethnicity	Implication for politics and theory	Example
Social service provision and distribution systems.	Potential for conversion and/or value orientation may mean incentives to distribute to current nonmembers; significant variation in extent and type of social services provided, with frequent focus on (religious) education as a core service, and visibility of social service provision to political elites and state.	Religious public service provision can function as a parallel to the state (propping it up), or a rival, and/or the domain of a particular religious-partisan section of the population, or a site of political competition to claim credit, affiliation. Offers potential for religious institutional direct access to state ministries, policymaking.	Religious organizations may use domains of service provision in exchange for political access and policymaking authority in state ministries (health policy, education policy, in Eastern Europe, Canada, and the United States: Grzymala-Busse 2015); service provision conveys to voters a politically valuable image of provider organization's competence and probity, which can transfer to political support as a political party or affiliated candidates (Muslim Brotherhood as service provider created reputational and then partisan advantage: Brooke 2017). The political economy of conversion also shapes service provision: Catholic religious leaders ignored poor rural indigenous parishioners in Latin America, but, when confronted by an expanding Protestantism, they became major institutional promoters of social service provision, ecclesiastic decentralization, and the practice of religion in their own language (Trejo 2009).

Practices of performance, ritual, and participation.	Potential for regularized meeting times and spaces, creating a focal point for reinforcing "groupness," the opportunity for sociopolitical organization and/or resource distribution.	Basis for political mobilization and collective action; basis for identifying "in-group" versus "out-group" on the basis of right practice, attendance, interaction; hub for creating alternatives to state resource distribution and ideologies.	Creates networks of mobilization, organizational hubs, opportunity structure for protest or other political agendas (Ardic 2012; Lynch 2012).
Spiritual connections to land and other natural resources.	Potential for a similar basis for geographic and regionally based claims for nation, autonomy, self-determination. Different potential for civic mobilization around governing the commons and environmental protections.	Potential to drive social and economic investment patterns at the group and individual level; potential for collective action around land and resource claims. Also potential site for exclusion.	Land maintenance and production strategies, social investments, and political engagement may be oriented around prioritizing land and natural resource protections, including individuals' rights to burial in a given location (Onoma 2019). This can also shape the nature of rural–urban linkages, where citizens vote and what issues they prioritize, and prioritization of geographic or regional affiliations in social identity alongside spiritual beliefs that tie them to land (Riedl and Robinson 2018).

then includes relationships to land (place as in geography as well as material resources such as the soil, water, and minerals within it), well-being and health, community relations, and social status.

From this holistic starting point, we can make progress on the variations within and across religions by identifying component parts and the mechanisms through which they connect to political outcomes. Disaggregated components demonstrate that religion cannot and should not fit within a Parsonsian conception of culture, whereby culture is a unitary and internally coherent set of attributes that characterizes a group. Instead, religion refers to the "webs of significance" that are constructed as cultural customs, social interactions, attitudes and behaviors (Geertz 1973). These pluralistic meaning systems provide channels through which human beings perceive, understand, and respond to the world around them. Depending upon the disaggregated component of the study, religion can be usefully approached as a set of cultural frames, as repertoires, as narratives, as cultural capital, as symbolic boundaries, as habitus, and as institutions. The disaggregation of religions' characteristics allows us to focus on what can be empirically observed and how people connect their religious beliefs, praxis, institutions, or social networks to particular political ends (tables 4.1. 4.2).

In sum, existing conceptions of religion are diffuse and multifaceted. This heterogeneity accounts for diversity *between* religious groups, *within* religious groups, and *within an individual*. Future literature on religion and social identity categories, such as ethnicity in general, should take care to identify the specific components of interest and the mechanisms through which they function. Additionally, given the important variation along a spectrum and sets of conceptual categories, scholars working on religion and politics must take care to specify the degree to which the analysis pertains to "religion" writ large or the specific, disaggregated dimension of religion observed in a given place and time. Certainly, religion *matters* for our understanding of politics, but the interesting questions are how and under what conditions.

Religion and Ethnicity as Similar and Distinct Bases for Politically Salient Cleavages and Forms of Political Action

To demonstrate the utility of a holistic and disaggregated view of religion and politics in Africa, I address the question of when and where religious identities are mobilized as politically salient cleavages (in addition to or as an alternative to other identities such as class, nationalism, language, race, ethnicity, or region) and how religion shapes varied forms of political action, with a brief empirical examination of Senegal. Two overarching descriptions summarize the case. First, in Senegal, as in most countries across the continent, religious identity has not been politicized into a relevant political cleavage, partisan affiliation, or the basis of conflict.[1] Significantly, religious groups were not institutionalized as particularistic state categories in Senegal (Lieberman and Singh 2012), in part as a colonial legacy and an independence-era manifestation of laïcité.

Second, as in other parts of the world, religious groups' organizational structure, hierarchical relation to public policy domains, and political elite formation create opportunities for inclusion or exclusion at particular historical moments (Grzymala-Busse 2015). The political project in Senegal has sought accommodation across heterogeneity since its colonial inception. With the nationalist era leader and postindependence president Leopold Senghor came a legacy of complementarity: combining the rational, secular state with the spiritual dimensions of religions (Smith 2013, 158). Senghor saw the combination of reason with faith and state republican nationalism with the cultural celebration of local territories and their moral communities. The model of unity with diversity is one that served him well as a double minority (Catholic and Serer) but was also a part of the political project of the newly born nation. This founding narrative of republican national unity with ethnic, linguistic, and religious diversity has also acted as a restraint, for example, in limiting mass violence in the long war in the Casamance (Straus 2015).

Transnational Networks and Group Identities

In Senegal, the pluralistic Muslim brotherhoods—comprising more than 95 percent of the population—play an important social, political, and economic role as intermediaries between the state elite and the masses (Villalón 1995). The religious leaders, *marabouts*, have long served as brokers—helping the state to extract from and control the population while distributing state resources to their followers through material aid. Religious leaders have served as regulators, helping the state to negotiate moments of social and economic upheaval and to bolster the regime's governance while maximizing the *marabout*'s direct access to political power.

Despite vigorous political competition in recent decades (Riedl and Sylla 2019) and the multiplicity of Muslim brotherhoods alongside a small Christian population, the religious groups' organizational structure and hierarchical relation to political elite formation have maintained strong channels of elite religious incorporation into the central state apparatus. The integration of the religious elite as allies and mediators between the state and the population began in the colonial period and carried through the early postindependence era. The ideational frames, social service provision, and hierarchical authority structure of the Muslim brotherhoods were well suited to serving in an alliance role as the providers of goods, legitimacy, and authority to the population—with the political elite a step removed. Hence, the political elite have sought to maximize their support among all religious leaders rather than to divide and politicize the brotherhoods in a relation of mutual accommodation and intervention (Cruise O'Brien 1971; Copans 1980; Coulon 1981; Diop 1981, 1992; Diop and Diouf 1992; Villalón 1995; Robinson 2000; Searing 2002; Babou 2007; Diouf and Leichtman 2009; Smith 2013, 152).

The nonpoliticization of religious differentiation in Senegal, as in Yorubaland (Laitin and Watkins 1986), is not the result of an equivalent lack of socioeconomic differentiation between different religious affiliations. The Senegalese brotherhoods control significantly different economic resources and political inroads, with the Mourides involved in economic sectors such as the historic groundnut trade (Cruise O'Brien 2003). The ethnic and religious pluralism, including the heterogeneity of religious brotherhoods, has evolved along with a republican model of state and citizenship to create a tripartite sense of belonging: each individual has a community of "believers" (co-religionists), a community of "citizens" (as loyalty to the state and republican constitutionalism), and a community of "kin" (co-ethnics and local patriotism as loyalty to the land of the region) (Smith 2013, 149). These three spheres of socialization and practices are critical in the imagination of the Senegalese community, the crafting of its political culture, and the sharing of a social ethos of hospitality that cuts across linguistic and religious divides.

Islam has deeply influenced ethnic identities and affiliations, reformulating the relationship between kin group and territory and serving as a tool in "delocalizing imaginations of community and ethnohistorical landscapes" (Smith 2013, 152). Islam itself is not a homogenizing force but a tool used to distinguish long-standing Muslim communities (Tukulor, Soninke, Wolof, and Mandinka) from more recent Muslims (Serer, Joola) and hence to *differentiate* between ethnicities according to different religious credentials. This speaks directly to the importance of the varied interaction between ethnic and religious identities. Cross-cuttingness alone is an insufficient concept to explain how Islam in Senegal works to *expand notions of shared Islamic connectivity while creating hierarchies of ethnic affiliates* in their status as partially to fully "Islamized." The religious and cultural pluralism in Senegal includes hierarchies of believers, from newcomers to long-established ethnic groups, creating a patterned relationship of tolerance between the state and the spheres of ethnicity and religion, which can be described as "proportional equidistance," combining equal respect by principle and actual acknowledge of the different weights of the different communities (Smith 2013, 147).

Social Networks and
Organizational Infrastructure

In addressing the question of what forms of politics religious actors take up, there are many possible outcomes. In general terms, religious actors can attempt to form religious parties (de jure and de facto), develop partisan alliances with secular parties, offer support for specific candidates, advocate for particular policy positions and legislation, attempt to seize and transform the state in line with religious beliefs, engage in democratization reforms as agents of transition, advocate for good governance and anticorruption, provide social services as an alternative to state engagement, or use violence to challenge status quo. There is variation in how religious actors engage as groups in the political realm and which factions and religious organizations pursue which particular actions. Religious activists can build upon institutional forms of organization to engage successfully in the political realm (Kalyvas 1996; Altinordu 2009). Religious organizations can influence policy and politics through covert, internal access or by forming political parties to represent their interests indirectly (Grzymala-Busse 2015). Social service distribution networks among religious groups provide varied organizational infrastructures that contribute to a group's politicization and competition with other groups. A religious group's particular connection to land, territory, or other resources might lead it toward certain political goals, such as autonomous control.

There is certainly a social network component to Senegalese mosques, both in solidifying horizontal relationships among followers and in the hierarchical, vertical relations between religious authorities and followers.

For the vast majority of Senegalese Muslims, affiliation with one of the Sufi orders is central to their identity and to participation in social networks. Allegiance to one of the orders is mediated by an attachment to a *cheikh* or guide, known as a *marabout* in Francophone Africa. For most Senegalese, the relationship to a *marabout* is a centrally important component of all aspects of life. A unique aspect of the Senegalese Sufi model is its organizational infrastructure. This is based on an institution known as the *daaira*, which unites followers of a particular *marabout* in a well-organized local cell and, in turn, links through hierarchical networks to other such cells (Villalón 1995, 149–99). This system has placed *marabouts* at the center of very highly structured and dynamic social networks, with clear implications for social, political, and economic action (Villalón 2015).

This social foundation created an infrastructure and mobilizational potential that successive governments—from colonial to postindependence—have sought to accommodate and benefit from. The powerful and cohesive forms of social organization of the Sufi orders created opportunities for a type of embedded autonomy with the state—religious orders are capable of both engaging with the state and maintaining an important degree of autonomy (Villalón 2015). The ultimate consequence of this social network has been to contribute to the country's political stability through a deep integration of religion and politics, with a significant degree of religious mobilizational potential for political engagement, and a strategy of maintaining moral authority of the religious realm simultaneous with direct political influence.

Explicit Instructions and
Hierarchical Leadership Positions

In Senegal, religious leaders have historically endorsed certain candidates through a direct proclamation, but they have not formed religious parties or mobilized religious followers around explicit political goals (Villalón 2015). Instead, religious leaders have used direct influence at the heart of the political establishment to maintain the accommodation relationship and promote their political interests.

With the rising tide of religious pluralism, due to generational factions within the religious brotherhood leadership and general political liberalization, the marketplace of religious competition also has become more acute. This has led some members of maraboutic families to encourage different forms of political mobilization, moving beyond supporting the dominant ruling party since independence, and led others to mobilize youth voter drives and encourage their followers to "vote their conscience." The marketplace of religious competition also has increased between religious authorities and the state over issues such as which institution would retain the greatest social influence and authority over the people during increasingly challenging socioeconomic conditions and increasing dissatisfaction with the ruling regime and the accommodation of the religious elites to it. Religious elites have consistently acted with strategic self-interest, supporting the ruling party while its dominance was clear and then moving to establish more independence from the political realm as the government and regime increasingly came under critique in order to protect themselves from losing religious legitimacy by being overly implicated in the political sphere. Crucially, religious elites have sought to balance the tensions between rising demands for political reform from within their own set of followers and their continuing courtship with political power for direct influence.

Conclusion

The multiple dimensions of religion raised in this chapter present a starting point for researchers grappling with the complexity of religious importance, building upon Young's critical focus on the complexity of pluralistic identity. One key step is to recognize the disaggregated nature of religion *and* ethnicity, to identify when, where, and why religion becomes politicized as a relevant social cleavage, and to what ends. This builds on Young's key legacy in *The Politics of Cultural Pluralism* and following work such as *The Rising Tide of Cultural Pluralism: The Nation-State at Bay?*, which give great weight to explicitly political factors. Young called attention to the dynamic nature of cultural identifications, emphasized the political arena, and wrote about the interaction between state power, institutions, ideas, material resources, and politically salient groups. New research building on Young's tradition will continue to push his work along these lines to further disaggregate the attributes of identity categories themselves (Menchik 2017; McClendon and Riedl 2019) and to identify the when, where, and how of particular forms of cultural politics that arise in contextualized circumstances and sequences (e.g., Arriola 2013; Brubaker 2013; Singh and vom Hau 2015).

Young recognized the continual potential for caste, race, ethnicity, religion, language, and nationalism to overlap and combine or reside in tension and conflict. While his deep empirical expertise in Africa and the task of nation building shaped his approach and informed his analysis, the questions he asks, the conceptual contributions, and the theoretical lens he provides have continued to resonate across world regions and time. Leading scholarship on the exclusivity and inclusivity of nationalism and its potential for incorporation or exclusion (Mylonas 2013; Tudor and Slater 2020; Mylonas and Tudor 2023) extends Young's postcolonial concerns into the present era of state and nation making with remarkably similar inquiries. This chapter seeks to extend Young's framework to recognize more explicitly the potentially unique factors associated with religion, as opposed to other forms of cultural pluralism, and how that maps to the potential Young identifies for fluid identities to combine and compete in different contexts. In which ways can the various characteristics of religion differentially shape social mobilization, interest representation, and political participation? These are questions Young anticipated and set the agenda for in his pathbreaking work on cultural pluralism. For those of us fortunate enough to learn from and with him, these questions were at the heart of his teaching on ethnicity, religion, and nationalism—a course that formed me as a hopeful political scientist (but yet a naive and eager undergraduate) in his final graduate seminar in Madison, Wisconsin, in 1999.

Religious affiliations will continue to increasingly vary in the nature of their ideational frames, hierarchical authority structures, organizational features, and social service provisions. Many theories of African politics have not sufficiently grappled with these core features of citizens' lives. The spiritual relation to land and resources remains an important open question for understanding political, economic, and social investments, ultimately connecting the spiritual and the secular in ways that average citizens live out on a daily basis. To continue Young's tradition in expanding our understanding of cultural pluralism, its determinants, and its consequences, the future for research on religion is ripe for exploration.

Note

1. Where it has been politicized, however, such as in nearby Nigeria and Côte d'Ivoire, the conflict has been particularly enduring and overlapping with political competitions surrounding representation, state resource distribution, and claims over inclusion and exclusion from the nation.

References

Altinordu, A. 2009. "The Incorporation of Religious Politics: Political Catholicism and Political Islam in Comparison." ASA Comparative Historical Section Mini-› Conference, Berkeley, CA, 2009.

Anderson, Benedict. 1983. *Imagined Communities: Reflections on the Origins and Spread of Nationalism*. New York: Verso.

Ardıc, Nurullah. 2012. "Understanding the Arab Spring: Justice, Dignity, Religion and International Politics." *Afro Eurasian Studies* 1 (1): 8–52.

Arriola, L. R. 2013. "Capital and Opposition in Africa: Coalition Building in Multiethnic Societies." *World Politics* 65 (2): 233–72.

Babou, Cheikh Anta. 20007. *Fighting the Greater Jihad: Amadu Bamba and the Founding of the Muridiyya of Senegal, 1853–1913*. Athens: Ohio University Press.

Bellin, Eva, 2008. "Faith in Politics: New Trends in the Study of Religion and Politics." *World Politics* 60 (2): 315–47.

Birnir, Jóhanna Kristín. 2006. *Ethnicity and Electoral Politics.* New York: Cambridge University Press.

Brooke, Steven. 2017. "From Medicine to Mobilization: Social Service Provision and the Islamist Reputational Advantage." *Perspectives on Politics* 15 (1): 42–61.

Brubaker, Rogers. 2004. *Ethnicity without Groups.* Cambridge, MA: Harvard University Press.

Brubaker, Rogers. 2013. "Language, Religion and the Politics of Difference." *Nations and Nationalism* 19 (1): 1–20.

Chandra, Kanchan. 2006. "What Is Ethnic Identity and Does It Matter?" *Annual Review of Political Science* 9:397–424.

Chitando, Ezra. 1997. "A Curse of the Western Heritage? Imagining Religion in an African Context." *Journal for the Study of Religion* 10 (2): 75–98.

Copans, Jean. 1980. *Les marabouts de l'arachide: La confrérie mouride et les paysans du Sénégal.* Paris: Le Sycomore.

Coulon, Christian. 1981. *Le Marabout et le Prince: Islam et pouvoir au Sénégal.* Paris: Pedone.

Cruise O'Brien, D. B. 1971. *The Mourides of Senegal: The Political and Economic Organisation of an Islamic Brotherhood.* Oxford: Clarendon.

Cruise O'Brien, Donal B. 2003. *Symbolic Confrontations: Muslims Imagining the State in Africa.* London: Hurst.

Diop, Abdoulaye Bara. 1981. *La société Wolof: Les systèmes d'inégalité et de domination.* Paris: Karthala.

Diop, Abdoulaye Bara. 1992. "Les paysans du bassin arachidier: Conditions de vie et comportements de survie." *Politique africaine* 45:39–61.

Diop, M. C. 1981. "Fonctions et activités des dahiras mourides urbains." *Cahiers d'études africaines* 21 (81–83): 79–91.

Diop, Momar Coumba, and Mamadou Diouf. 1992. "L'administration sénégalaise: Les confréries réligieuses et les paysanneries." *Africa Development/Afrique et développement* 17 (2): 65–87.

Diouf, Mamadou, and Mara Leichtman, eds. 2009. *New Perspectives on Islam in Senegal: Conversion, Migration, Wealth, Power, and Femininity.* New York: Springer.

Ellis, Stephen, and Gerrie Ter Haar. 2004. *Worlds of Power: Religious Thought and Political Practice in Africa.* Vol. 1. New York: Oxford University Press.

Ellis, Stephen, and Gerrie Ter Haar. 2007. "Religion and Politics: Taking African Epistemologies Seriously." *Journal of Modern African Studies* 45 (3): 385–401.

Galvan, Dennis. 2004. *The State Must Be Our Master of Fire: How Peasants Craft Culturally Sustainable Development in Senegal.* Berkeley: University of California Press.

Geertz, Clifford. 1973. *The Interpretation of Cultures.* New York: Basic Books.

Gifford, Paul. 1994. "Some Recent Developments in African Christianity." *African Affairs* 93 (373): 513–34.

Grzymala-Busse, Anna. 2012. "Why Comparative Politics Should Take Religion (More) Seriously." *Annual Review of Political Science* 15:421–42.

Grzymała-Busse, Anna. 2015. *Nations under God: How Churches Use Moral Authority to Influence Policy.* Princeton, NJ: Princeton University Press.

Habyarimana, James, et al. 2007. "Why Does Ethnic Diversity Undermine Public Goods Provision?" *American Political Science Review* 101 (4): 709–25.

Haynes, Jeff. 2001. "Transnational Religious Actors and International Politics." *Third World Quarterly* 22 (2): 143–58.

Hoffman, Michael, and Amaney Jamal. 2014. "Religion in the Arab Spring: Between Two Competing Narratives." *Journal of Politics* 76 (3): 593–606.

Horowitz, Donald L. 1985. *Ethnic Groups in Conflict*. Berkeley: University of California Press.

Hurd, Elizabeth Shakman. 2017. *Beyond Religious Freedom: The New Global Politics of Religion*. Princeton, NJ: Princeton University Press.

Ilesanmi, S. 1995. "Inculturation and Liberation: Christian Social Ethics and the African Theology Project." *Annual of the Society of Christian Ethics* 15:49–73.

Kalu, Ogbu. 2008. *African Pentecostalism: An Introduction*. New York: Oxford University Press.

Kalyvas, Stathis, 1996. *The Rise of Christian Democracy in Europe*. Ithaca, NY: Cornell University Press.

Kasfir, Nelson. 1979. "Explaining Ethnic Political Participation." *World Politics* 31 (3): 365–88.

Knighton, Ben, ed. 2009. *Religion and Politics in Kenya: Essays in Honor of a Meddlesome Priest*. New York: Palgrave Macmillan.

Laitin, David D., and James T. Watkins IV. 1986. *Hegemony and Culture: Politics and Change among the Yoruba*. Chicago: University of Chicago Press.

Lewis, Valerie A., Carol Ann MacGregor, and Robert D. Putnam. 2013. "Religion, Networks, and Neighborliness: The Impact of Religious Social Networks on Civic Engagement." *Social Science Research* 42 (2): 331–46.

Lieberman, Evan S., and Prerna Singh. 2012. "Conceptualizing and Measuring Ethnic Politics: An Institutional Complement to Demographic, Behavioral, and Cognitive Approaches." *Studies in Comparative International Development* 47 (3): 255–86.

Lynch, Marc. 2012. *The Arab Uprising: The Unfinished Revolutions of the New Middle East*. New York: Public Affairs.

McCauley, John F. 2013. "Africa's New Big Man Rule? Pentecostalism and Patronage in Ghana." *African Affairs* 112 (446): 1–21.

McCauley, John F. 2017. "Ethnic and Religious Identity in Côte d'Ivoire's Conflict." Chap. 6 in *The Logic of Ethnic and Religious Conflict in Africa*. Cambridge: Cambridge University Press.

McCauley, John F., and Daniel N. Posner. 2019. "The Political Sources of Religious Identification: Evidence from the Burkina Faso–Côte d'Ivoire Border." *British Journal of Political Science* 49 (2): 421–41.

McClendon, Gwyneth, and Rachel Beatty Riedl. 2015. "Religion as a Stimulant of Political Participation: Experimental Evidence from Nairobi, Kenya." *Journal of Politics* 277 (4): 1045–57.

McClendon, Gwyneth H., and Rachel Beatty Riedl. 2019. *From Pews to Politics: Religious Sermons and Political Participation in Africa*. Cambridge: Cambridge University Press.

McClendon, Gwyneth, and Rachel Beatty Riedl. 2021. "Using Sermons to Study Religions' Influence on Political Behavior." *Comparative Political Studies* 54 (5): 779–822.

Menchik, Jeremy. 2017. "The Constructivist Approach to Religion and World Politics." *Comparative Politics* 49 (4): 561–81.

Miran-Guyon, Marie. 2012. "Native Conversion to Islam in Southern Côte d'Ivoire." *Journal of Religion in Africa* 42 (2): 95–117.

Mylonas, Harris. 2013. *The Politics of Nation Building: Making Co-Nationals, Refugees, and Minorities.* New York: Cambridge University Press.

Mylonas, Harris, and Maya Tudor. 2023. *Varieties of Nationalism.* Cambridge: Cambridge University Press.

Nwajiaku, Kathryn. 1994. "The National Conferences in Benin and Togo Revisited." *Journal of Modern African Studies* 32 (3): 429–47.

Onoma, Ato Kwame. 2019. "Should Christians and Muslims Co-habit after Death: Diverging Views in a Senegalese Commune." *Africa Today* 66 (1): 29–50.

Posner, Daniel N. 2005. *Institutions and Ethnic Politics in Africa.* Cambridge: Cambridge University Press.

Riedl, Rachel Beatty, and Amanda Lea Robinson. 2019. "Shifting Allegiances? Urban/Rural Linkages, Ethnic Orientation, and Political Behavior in Kenya." Working Paper.

Riedl, Rachel Beatty, and Ndongo Samba Sylla. 2019. "Senegal's Vigorous but Constrained Election." *Journal of Democracy* 30 (July): 94–108.

Robinson, David. 2000. *Paths of Accommodation: Muslim Societies and French Colonial Authorities in Senegal and Mauritania, 1880–1920.* Athens: Ohio University Press.

Rothchild, Donald S. 1997. *Managing Ethnic Conflict in Africa: Pressures and Incentives for Cooperation.* Washington, DC: Brookings Institution Press.

Sabar, Galia. 2009. "'Was There No Naboth to Say No?' Using the Pulpit in the Struggle for Democracy: The Anglican Church, Bishop Gitari, and Kenyan Politics." In *Religion and Politics in Kenya*, edited by Ben Knighton, 123–42. New York: Palgrave Macmillan.

Searing, James F. 2002. *"God Alone Is King": Islam and Emancipation in Senegal: The Wolof Kingdoms of Kajoor and Bawol 1859–1914.* Oxford: James Currey.

Selway, Joel. 2011. "The Measurement of Cross-Cutting Cleavages and Other Multidimensional Cleavage Structures." *Political Analysis* 19 (1): 48–65.

Singh, Prerna. 2015. *How Solidarity Works for Welfare: Subnationalism and Social Development in India.* Cambridge: Cambridge University Press.

Singh, Prerna, and Matthias vom Hau. 2016. "Ethnicity in Time: Politics, History, and the Relationship between Ethnic Diversity and Public Goods Provision." *Comparative Political Studies* 49 (10): 1303–40.

Sklar, Richard. 1977. "Reviewed Work: *The Politics of Cultural Pluralism.* By Crawford Young." *American Journal of Sociology* 83 (2): 516–20.

Smith, Etienne. 2013. "Religious and Cultural Pluralism in Senegal: Accommodation through 'Proportional Equidistance'?" In *Tolerance, Democracy, and Sufis in Senegal*, edited by Mamadou Diouf, 147–79. New York: Columbia University Press.

Sperber, Elizabeth, and Erin Hern. 2018. "Pentecostal Identity and Citizen Engagement in Sub-Saharan Africa: New Evidence from Zambia." *Politics & Religion* 11 (4): 830–62.

Stegmueller, Daniel. 2013. "Religion and Redistributive Voting in Western Europe." *Journal of Politics* 75 (4): 1064–76.

Straus, Scott. 2015. *Making and Unmaking Nations: War, Leadership, and Genocide in Modern Africa*. Ithaca, NY: Cornell University Press.

Svensson, Isak. 2007. "Fighting with Faith." *Journal of Conflict Resolution* 51 (6): 930–49.

Trejo, Guillermo. 2009. "Religious Competition and Ethnic Mobilization in Latin America: Why the Catholic Church Promotes Indigenous Movements in Mexico." *American Political Science Review* 103 (3): 323–42.

Tudor, Maya, and Dan Slater. 2020. "Nationalism, Authoritarianism, and Democracy: Historical Lessons from South and Southeast Asia." *Perspectives on Politics* 19 (3): 1–17.

Varshney, Ashutosh. 2003. *Ethnic Conflict and Civic Life: Hindus and Muslims in India*. New Haven, CT: Yale University Press.

Villalón, Leonardo Alfonso. 1995. *Islamic Society and State Power in Senegal: Disciples and Citizens in Fatick*. Cambridge: Cambridge University Press.

Villalón, Leonardo A. 2015. "Cautious Democrats: Religious Actors and Democratization Processes in Senegal." *Politics & Religion* 8 (2): 305–33.

Wilkinson, Steven. 2006. *Votes and Violence: Electoral Competition and Ethnic Riots in India*. Cambridge University Press.

Young, Crawford. 1976. *The Politics of Cultural Pluralism*. Madison: University of Wisconsin Press.

Young, Crawford, ed. 1993. *The Rising Tide of Cultural Pluralism: The Nation-State at Bay?* Madison: University of Wisconsin Press.

5

Sectarian Identity Formation and the Future of the African Postcolonial State

Lessons from Nigeria

Dauda Abubakar

The African postcolonial state has been at the center of Africanist scholarship for the past six decades, and the literature has focused on not only the nature, sociopolitical dynamics, and character of the state (Young 1994, 2002, 2004, 2012; Zartman 1996; Mamdani 1996, 2002; Tripp 2010; Straus 2015) but also the drivers of violent conflicts that undermine democratization and nation-building projects (Reno 2011; Bratton and van de Walle 1997). Using Nigeria as a case study, this chapter examines how sectarianism and doctrinal schisms within and between various Islamic groups exacerbate social and political violence as well as state fragility. With a population of more than two hundred million people and approximately five hundred diverse ethnic nationalities with different religious practices, Nigeria is one of the largest multicultural societies in Africa. Although Islam and Christianity are the two dominant religious faiths, there are, nevertheless, different sects within these religious communities. For example, within Islam in northern Nigeria, there are several sects, including Qadiriyya, Tijaniyya, Shi'ites, the Izala Movement, Maitatsine, and, more recently, Boko Haram (Mustapha 2014; Mohammed 2018). Since the return to democratic rule in 1999, Nigeria has witnessed the resurgence of ethnoreligious conflicts, terrorism, and insurgency. Understanding the crisis of the Nigerian state and the dilemmas of democratization, I contend, requires unpacking the central role of sectarian identity formation and its implications for nation building. In developing this argument, I begin by examining the nineteenth-century Sokoto Jihad as a historical background for understanding the contemporary rise of sectarianism in northern Nigeria, specifically the emergence of the jihadi-Salafist group known as Boko Haram. I also draw comparative illustrations from other African countries to show how the weaponization of ethnoreligious identity by predatory elites exacerbates violent insurgency and state fragility in the postcolony. A brief review of the debates in the literature on the African postcolonial state and religious violence is in order.

There are two dominant theoretical orientations in the literature on the sources of violent conflict and state fragility in Africa. The first is Crawford Young's cultural pluralism framework (Young 1976, 2012; Young and Turner 1985), which argues that ethnic, linguistic, racial, and religious identities are instrumentalized by elites and political entrepreneurs to secure political power. The competitive mobilization of ethnoreligious identities, according to this perspective, exacerbates communal violence and undermines state legitimacy. Elites who capture power in the zero-sum electoral process entrench neopatrimonial networks that deepen autocracy, predatory rule, and corruption. In his cogent analyses of the legacies of the colonial state in Africa, Young (1994, 2) reminds us that "in metamorphosis, the caterpillar becomes butterfly without losing its inner essences." Although political independence in the 1960s meant relative autonomy for the African postcolonial state and its citizenry, Young alerts us that the colonial state and its practices remain "absorbed into the structures of the independent polity" and that "a state, once institutionalized, has a formidable capacity for its own reproduction across time and in the face of systematic efforts by new regimes to uproot prior forms and build new blueprints." While I concede that Young's prescient conceptual paradigm of "cultural pluralism" and colonial state logic of autocracy constitutes an important lens in the analyses and understanding of the genealogies of violent conflicts in Africa, the framework elides the central role of religion and sectarian identities as a crucial frame in comprehending the complex drivers of conflicts in the postcolonial realm. As Sebastian Elischer (2021, 227) reminds us that, while the role of religion in African social life is often acknowledged, the precise relationship between the postcolonial state and specific religious communities has rarely been explored in depth. The issue of religious identity, sectarianism, and its relation to politics and violence in postcolonial Africa has also not been given much attention (Ellis and Ter Haar 2007). Although major civil wars, as Scott Straus (2012, 180) reports, have declined in postcolonial Africa, there still remain low-intensity religious conflicts, including the Boko Haram crisis in northeastern Nigeria; jihadi Salafist warfare in Mali; Al Qaeda in the Islamic Maghreb and its insurgency against Algeria; the lingering Al-Shabaab violence in Somalia and northeastern Kenya; and the violent conflict in the Central African Republic between the Balaka and anti-Balaka forces. An important connecting thread in these crises is the element of religious identity and sectarianism, where specific religious communities insist that the postcolonial state should reflect the core values of their theology and doctrines as the premise for governance and state policy formulation.

The second orientation in the literature on political violence in the African postcolonial state is the greed and grievance paradigm (Richards 1996; Chabal and Daloz 1999; Reno 2002, 2009; Collier and Hoeffler 2004), which asserts that civil wars emerge in societies when rebel groups are driven by greed to extract commodities such as diamonds, gold, copper, coltan, and other high-value minerals through predation for profiteering and that this process may generate further grievances and induce diasporas to finance further conflict (Collier and Hoeffler 2004, 27). The civil wars in Sierra Leone and Liberia in the 1990s, the rebellion by minority ethnic groups in Nigeria's oil-rich Niger Delta, and the continuing rebel insurgencies in Eastern DR-Congo seem to indicate the explanatory power of the greed and grievance framework in our understanding of African postcolonial state crises.

While these two state-centric epistemologies certainly provide some analytical purchase in understanding the dilemmas of political violence and state fragility in postcolonial Africa, they do not seriously interrogate the phenomenon of religious identity and sectarianism as important analytical frames in the entangled histories of violence and insurgencies in Africa. As Daniel Philpott (2007) reminds us, although the nexus between religion, state, and society may not explain every episode of political violence, nevertheless, religion still matters in deeply divided societies such as Nigeria, Sudan, Mali, Kenya, Chad, Niger, Burkina Faso, Mauritania, and the Central African Republic, where there are significant Muslim populations.

Epochal events, including the 1979 Iranian Revolution, which led to the establishment of a theocratic Islamic republic, and the events of September 11, 2001, which led to the invasion of Afghanistan and the "Global War on

Terror," contributed to the resurgence of religion and sectarianism as central sociocultural and political phenomena that impact national and global affairs (Ibrahim 1991; Fox 2002, 2004; Mamdani 2004; Toft 2006, 2007; Montclos 2014, 2015; Kassim 2015, 2018; Mustapha and Meagher 2020). According to Monica Duffy Toft (2007), from 1940 to 2000, 42 out of 133 civil wars, or 32 percent, involved religion. Specifically, in the 1940s, religious conflicts made up 19 percent of civil wars; this figure increased to 29 percent in the 1950s but dropped to 21 percent in the 1960s. However, by the 1970s, violent conflicts that centered on religious identity rose to 36 percent of all civil wars and then to 39 percent in the 1980s, reaching 43 percent in the 1990s. By the 2000s, civil wars with religious dimensions increased to 50 percent of all civil wars (Toft 2006, 9). For more than a decade, the Nigerian government and its neighbors in the Lake Chad Basin have been fighting the terror group Boko Haram in an intractable insurgency conflict.

The purpose of this chapter, therefore, is to fill the gap in the literature on the centrality of religion and sectarian identity formation in explaining the crises of the African postcolonial state. I argue that while state-centric paradigms may provide some analytical purchase in explaining the dilemmas of political violence in postcolonial Africa, they nevertheless fall short in incorporating sectarianism and doctrinal schisms as important variables in understanding the dynamics of violence and insurgencies in the continent.

The chapter is divided into three interrelated sections. The section that follows examines the history of nineteenth-century Islamic reform movements with emphasis on the Sokoto jihad of Sheikh Uthman dan Fodio that overthrew the Habe (Hausa) rulers on the grounds that they were mixing Islam with syncretism. For the Sokoto jihadists, the purification of Islam and the establishment of the Caliphate were cardinal objectives of the reform movement. As I show later in the chapter, Boko Haram, a radical Salafi Islamist group that emerged in northeastern Nigeria in 2002, taps into the ideology of religious purity in its war against the Nigerian state and Western modernity (including liberal democracy and education), in general. The second section highlights the rise of sectarian identities in northern Nigeria's Islamic marketplace, particularly the Salafist strand of Islam, and its implications for the state and society. Specifically, I describe how the emergence of Sheikh Abubakar Gumi along with the Izala Movement (known as Jama'at izalat al-bid'a wa iqamat al-sunnah, or JIBWIS, that is, the group for removing religious innovation and establishing Sunnah) intensified sectarianism and the politicization of religious purity (Østebø 2015). I also discuss the use of *takfirism* (ex-communication of fellow Muslims from the faith) as a strategy for mobilizing followership, attacking

Sufi-oriented Muslim Brotherhoods, and condemning Christians as infidels (*Kafir*) in Nigeria's entangled religious marketplace. The third section examines the rise of Salafi radical extremism in the form of Boko Haram (also known as Jama'at Ahl al-Sunnah Lidda'awat wa-l-Jihad, that is, people committed to the propagation of the Prophet's teachings and jihad), its ideological orientation and critique of the Nigerian state, and the response of the federal government toward the insurgency. In the final section, I postulate on the possible trajectories of Boko Haram insurgency and proffer some policy solutions that may facilitate the restoration of peace and social order in a turbulent Nigeria.

Sectarian Identity Formation and the Politicization of Religious Purity: Islamic Reform Movements in Historical Perspective

Islam was introduced into precolonial West Africa through three major social and economic processes. First was the trans-Saharan trade, through which Islam reached the ancient Kanem-Bornu Empire in the Lake Chad Basin around the tenth century. A second stream was the role of Muhammad al-Maghili (1463–99), a renowned Islamic scholar from North Africa "who visited several cities in Sub-Saharan Africa including Kano and Katsina" and is credited with advising Muhammad Rumfa (1463–99), the then ruler of Kano, and with introducing the Shari'a legal system along with the Shura (advisory council) as the institutional mechanisms of Islamic governance (Mustapha, 2014, 2). A third and more critical trend in the spread of Islam in West Africa can be traced to the influence of indigenous Muslim scholars such as the Wangarawa, Fulbe (Fulani), and Kunta, who were central to the initiation of the jihad movements of the eighteenth and nineteenth centuries in West Africa.

Thus, the contemporary call to arms against alleged elite corruption, moral decadence, and the decline of Islamic virtues of justice and equity is not new to the West African subregion. As far back as the early eighteenth century, Fulani reformers waged violent jihad against incumbent rulers in the name of purifying Islam and establishing the Caliphate. For example, between 1727 and 1728, Fulani Muslims rose up against rulers in Futa Jallon in the Upper Guinea region and established an Imamate. In 1775, al-Hajj Umar Tall led a revolt in the Futa Toro region of Senegambia and established the Tukulor Empire, in which Islam became the dominant religion. The trend of Islamic reform continued with the 1818 revolution by Sekou Ahmadu, which gave rise to the Macina Caliphate in the inner Niger River bend in West Africa.

However, the most dominant Islamic revolutionary movement that initi-ated the program of reform and purification of Islam in West Africa is the jihad of Uthman dan Fodio, which overthrew the Habe rulers in northern Ni-geria. The Sokoto Caliphate, which emerged from dan Fodio's jihad of 1804, was anchored in Shari'a Islamic law, and it survived for about a century, until its defeat by the British colonialists, in 1903. Even after its defeat and the impo-sition of colonial rule, the Sokoto Caliphate has remained a symbolic and ideo-logical reference point for various Islamic sects in Nigeria's religious marketplace. Several clerics (revered Islamic scholars, also called *ulama*) in post-colonial Nigeria have made reference to the Sokoto Caliphate and the Shari'a system as the glorious days of Islam in the precolonial territory that became northern Nigeria. Muslim clerics assert that Muslims have an obligation to struggle for the restoration of Shari'a at the national level in Nigeria's legal system (Mustapha 2014; Thurston 2016a). It is pertinent to note that although the British colonial state defeated the Sokoto Caliphate, it nevertheless an-chored the imperial machinery of indirect rule in traditional rulers and en-cased Islam along with Shari'a (customary) law as legal practice in northern Nigeria. The autocratic colonial machinery of indirect rule, along with the emirate system, provided the institutional foundations of neopatrimonialism in postcolonial Nigeria. As Young would put it, although the caterpillar may transform into a butterfly through political independence, it, nevertheless, re-tains its inner essence.

Indeed, as I show later in the chapter, Mohammed Yusuf, the founder and leader of the Boko Haram jihadi Salafist group, appropriated dan Fodio's jihad as a strategic model to legitimize the use of violence against the Nigerian state to "purify Islam" and enthrone a Caliphate based on Shari'a law (Mustapha 2014; Kassim 2015; Mustapha and Meager 2020). According to Abdulbasit Kassim (2015, 197), "Boko Haram is the first Islamic group in northern Nigeria to carry out an ideological hybridization of the religious philosophy of global jihadi-Salafism and the cultural framing of Islamic traditions of Uthman dan Fodio." To be sure, it is equally important to indicate that while dan Fodio's Is-lamic doctrine and theology fall within the Sufi Qadriyya order, Boko Haram's eclectic ideological orientation reflects more Salafi doctrines, especially in the use of *takfirism*, martyrdom, and extremist violence against all those who op-pose their strand of Islam.

The lingering debate in Nigeria around the establishment of Shari'a law and the declaration of jihad against "infidels" (and the differing sectarian/ theological interpretations by clerics) have remained major sources of reli-gious/sectarian violence in Nigeria. Since the end of the civil war, in 1970, political entrepreneurs as well as clerics have, more often than not, weaponized religion, especially around the Shari'a issue, for mobilizing followers who are subsequently used as a "vote bank" during elections. As Abdul Raufu Mustapha (2014, 5) puts it, "such a followership was critical for the individual Muslim ruler or the economic and political influence of the individual cleric within the 'prayer economy'" that enhances access to political and economic elites in government. Herein lies the centrality of religion and the related processes of sectarian identity formation as a crucial element for deciphering the sources of extremism and violent insurgency in an African postcolonial state such as Nigeria. The Islamic religious landscape in northern Nigeria has diverse sects that have different doctrinal orientations, including the Sunni, Sufi, and Shi'ite orders that I describe here.

The Sufi order has two main sects. First, there is the Qadriyya sect, which emerged as the dominant strand of Islam in the expansive Sokoto Caliphate. According to Mustapha, the death of Sheikh dan Fodio, in 1817, "saw the gradual restoration of many pre-jihad practices," as well as the erosion of moral integrity in the governance of the emirates, excessive taxation of the poor, enslavement, and state corruption; all these elicited further agitations for reform and revivalism (Mustapha 2014, 2). The gradual erosion of the social and political virtues of the Qadriyya sect, which undergirded the Sokoto Caliphate and provided it with some measure of legitimacy, eventually gave way to the fragmentation of sacred authority and the emergence of competing sects that engendered hostility, sectarianism, and violence in northern Nigeria. As sectarianism intensified, some clerics weaponized minor doctrinal and interpretative discourses of the Qur'an into a strategy for radicalization (Umar 2012, 2020; Thurston 2015, 2016a, 2016b; Kassim 2018). By the 1830s, the second sect, the Tijaniyya Sufi order, was introduced into northern Nigeria and attracted significant followership, especially in Kano, a sprawling metropolitan city of more than seven million, which is predominantly Muslim.

A third important sect in northern Nigeria's Islamic marketplace is called the Islamic Movement of Nigeria (IMN), which has its roots in the Muslim Student Society (MSS) in Nigerian universities and is led by Sheikh Ibrahim El-Zakzaky. IMN is inspired by the Shi'ite 1979 Islamic revolution in Iran, from where it draws significant financial support. The centerpiece of El-Zakzaky's critique is directed not only against the corruption of the Nigerian state but also against other Islamic clerics and traditional rulers in northern Nigeria. According to El-Zakzaky, agitations for the implementation of Shari'a in Nigeria by Muslims are a diversion because a genuine and pristine Islamic legal system can be established only in the context of a Caliphate.

A fourth sect that emerged in northern Nigeria around the early 1970s is Sheikh Abubakar Gumi's Izala movement, which identifies itself as part of the Sunni sect and is closely aligned with Saudi Arabia's Wahhabi practices. According to Muhammad Sani Umar (2020), Gumi, in his 1972 treatise *al-aqida al-sahiha*, charged that "followers of Sufi orders [Qadriyya and Tijaniyya] hold beliefs and practices contrary to Islam," thereby effectively declaring them apostates, for which they could legitimately be killed. Sufi leaders responded with their own salvo accusing Gumi of "being deceitful, a liar and an opportunist" (Umar 2020, 57).

In the early 1980s, the Izala movement relocated its headquarters to Jos in the Middle Belt—a predominantly Christian part of Nigeria—under the leadership of Sheikh Ismaila Idris. Meanwhile, young northern Nigerian clerics who went to Saudi Arabia's Medina University had begun returning home with erudite knowledge of the Qur'an, as well as of the Arabic language. As these Medina returnees began their teachings and leading prayers at mosques, a theological schism erupted within the Izala movement, leading to its split into two sectarian camps—Izala A based in Jos, and Izala B, based in Kaduna. It is from this internal Izala schism that a radical Salafist sect called Ahls-al-sunnah emerged (Brigaglia 2012; Thurston 2015; Umar 2015; Montclos 2016), and it is from within the Ahls-al-sunnah that Mohammed Yusuf would eventually carve out the jihadi-Salafist sect called Boko Haram (Thurston 2011, 2018; Umar 2012; Kassim 2018). According to Umar (2012), while "mainstream Salafists focused on capturing and Islamizing the [Nigerian] state, *Boko Haram* saw obedience to a secular [democratic] state as idolatry and was intent on destroying it." The narrative presented here shows how the process of sectarian schism within northern Nigeria Islam provided a fertile ground for the emergence of Boko Haram as a radical Salafist movement that would threaten the foundations of democratic rule and security in postcolonial Nigeria.

In the section that follows, I briefly examine the emergence of radical Salafism in northern Nigeria, focusing on the rise of Boko Haram and its implications for the democratization project and nation building. I also speculate on the implications of the Nigerian experience for other deeply divided postcolonial African states, including Mali, Kenya, and Sudan, to mention a few.

Salafi Radicalism and the Rise of Boko Haram in Northeastern Nigeria

The third wave of democratization (Huntington 1991) that swept across the African continent in the 1980s and 1990s reinvigorated civil society in the contestations for power at local and national levels; in addition, the diverse Islamic sects in Nigeria took the opportunity to propagate their ideologies, theology, and philosophies of governance. During Nigeria's return to democratic rule in 1999, Olusegun Obasanjo, a former military head of state (1976–79), emerged as the president.

The election of Obasanjo to the presidency provided northern Nigeria's ethnoreligious entrepreneurs with the ammunition to resurrect agitation for the implementation of *Shari'a* law. This triggered violent conflicts, especially in Kaduna and Plateau states, where there are a significant number of Christians and Muslims. Also in 1999, Ahmed Sani Yerima, the governor of Zamfara state, in northwestern Nigeria, unilaterally declared Shari'a Islamic law as the legal system. During the 2003 general elections, several candidates contesting for the office of governor at the state level made the implementation of Shari'a law the cornerstone of their campaign promises. By 2004, twelve of the nineteen states in northern Nigeria had declared Shari'a law as the legal system in their states. This exacerbated fear and anxiety among Christian minority groups in northern Nigeria.

While Muslims, along with Islamic civil society organizations, such as Jama'tul Nasril Islam (JNI) and the Supreme Council of Islamic Affairs (SCIA), rejoiced over this success, the Christian Association of Nigeria (CAN), an umbrella civil society entity composed of Catholics, Protestants, and Pentecostal churches, urged President Obasanjo to condemn the twelve governors who had declared Shari'a the legal system in their states. Furthermore, CAN leadership advised the federal government to declare such actions unconstitutional and to state that it violates the principle of secularity of the Nigerian state as enshrined in the 1999 Constitution (Harnischfeger 2008, 78). While Muslims saw the implementation of Shari'a in Nigeria as essential to the practice of their faith, Christians saw it as a hegemonic agenda for the "Islamization" of the country and the marginalization of Christian communities. Furthermore, Christian minorities in northern Nigeria were apprehensive that the implementation of Shari'a might lead to injustice and abuse of judicial power. However, President Obasanjo, knowing the sensitive and potentially explosive nature of the Shari'a controversy, remained silent. The National Assembly was also deadlocked on the issue and could not provide any clear path forward.

In 2005, political thugs (known as ECOMOG, after the West African regional peacekeeping unit of the same name) affiliated with the then governor of Borno state, Senator Ali Modu Sheriff (SAS), unleashed violence against Christian communities in Maiduguri, the Borno state capital. Several churches and properties were destroyed, and many Christians were killed during worship

(International Crisis Group 2014; Montclos 2014). Governor Modu Sheriff had earlier promised his predominantly Muslim constituency that he would fully implement Shari'a if elected governor. Mohammed Yusuf, who had established himself as the leader of the Yusufiyya sect, encouraged thousands of his followers to cast their votes for Modu Sheriff in the 2003 elections. Media reports indicate that some of the ECOMOG thugs are committed supporters of Yusuf, and they would later constitute the foot soldiers of the Boko Haram insurgency (International Crisis Group 2014, 12). Thus, an important material benefit that elites, such as Ali Modu Sheriff and the northern governors, derive from the manipulation of sectarian identity in Nigeria's politics is that it facilitates the securing votes during elections. Following his election in 2003, Sheriff created the Ministry of Religious Affairs, which was charged with the implementation of Shari'a. The ministry became an avenue for rewarding political thugs and cronies with jobs in the public service and a channel for patronage and air flight tickets during the annual Hajj to Mecca. Religious identity became an important element in the practice of neopatrimonialism.

At a broader level, two important questions remain: how did Mohammed Yusuf, who is not even a grounded cleric in Islam, command a significant followership that would eventually unleash violent sectarian insurgency in Nigeria? Second, in what ways did the internal sectarian fractionalization in northern Nigeria's Islam provide an opening for Boko Haram to spread its ideology of radicalization into Salafi terrorism? The answer to the first question can be traced to Yusuf's membership of the Muhammed Indimi Mosque in Maiduguri and his subsequent mentorship by Sheikh Ja'afar Adam, a Medina Salafi returnee cleric, who provided Yusuf access to the broader Ahls-al-sunnah Salafi sect in northern Nigeria. Mohammed Yusuf would exploit this religious network and not only develop social relationships with other clerics but also gain access to elites in power at local and national levels. The neopatrimonial network that characterizes Nigeria's social and political landscape provided Yusuf with the enabling environment to cultivate acquaintances at higher levels of power. Thus, as his influence continued to expand within Salafi sectarian circles, Yusuf leveraged his access to elites in state power to garner wealth and economic capital. He established his mosque at Unguwan Doki in Maiduguri and named it Marqaz Ibn Taymiyya after the renowned fourteenth-century Salafi theologian Sheikh Ahmad Ibn Taymiyya (1268–1328).

As for the second question, on sectarian fractionalization, Yusuf strategically aligned his doctrinal discourses not only along the lines of violent jihadi Salafism but also with the symbolism of the nineteenth-century dan Fodio jihad. Furthermore, the Shari'a controversy that began with the democratization process in 1999 provided Yusuf with the perfect ammunition to insist that Muslims in Nigeria deserve a caliphate and that jihad is a legitimate obligation to realize such an objective. In his book *Hadhihi Aqidatuna wa Minhaju Da'awatuna* (This Is Our Creed and the Methodology of Our Preaching), Yusuf provides an overview of the theology and philosophy of Boko Haram:

> Our religion is Islam, our creed is the creed of the *al-salaf al-salih Ahlul Sunnah Wal Jama'ah*, and our *manhaj* [religious obligation] is jihad. We believe that the Shari'a is the only truth. The Constitution is a lie; it is *Kufr* (infidel). Democracy is a lie; it is *Kufr*. Working with a government that does not rule by the Shari'a is a lie; it is *Kufr*. For those who are ignorant, let them be aware that it is important for a Muslim to make *hijrah* [relocating away from the land/community of unbelief] from the institutions established by the *tawagit* [idolatry]." (Kassim, 2015, 189)

By making conscious reference to *al-salaf al-salih* (i.e., the pious predecessors) as well as jihad, Yusuf aligns his sectarian agenda not only with that of Ibn Taymiyya but also with that espoused by dan Fodio and the Sokoto jihadists. His goal was to tap into the historical memory of the Caliphate and to mobilize his audience into action against liberal democracy, constitutionalism, and the Nigerian state. In 2003, Yusuf's supporters embarked on the *hijrah* by relocating to Kanamma area in Yobe state, where they called themselves the "Nigerian Taliban" and began attacking police stations, banks, and government institutions in Damaturu, the capital of Yobe state (Mohammed 2015, 6–7). Security agencies crushed the Kanamma commune, and the remnants of the Yusufiyya movement retreated to the Mandara mountains in Gwoza local government area. However, the Nigerian military and security forces dislodged them from the Gwoza hills, and many of them returned to Maiduguri to regroup.

In 2005, Yusuf returned from self-exile in Saudi Arabia and advocated the use of violence against the army, the police, and all security agencies. In one of his sermons, Yusuf began to prepare their minds for jihad by stating that:

> In the process, they will abuse you, call you names, and some of you may even die. They will shoot some of you, and we will just pray, "may Allah give you *aljanna*" [Paradise] and proceed without any qualms. Can we endure? We ought to endure. May Allah give us the will to endure. . . . We are not yet primed for victory, but we are working towards getting ready for victory. This is what we are looking for, brothers. This is an incipient *dawah* [proselytization], but it cannot be crushed. It cannot be killed. If we stand by what the Prophet said, we should stand by, even if we die in the process, this *dawah* will continue—even after a hundred years. Once the truth comes out, you are in trouble. (Yusuf 2006, audio tape, quoted in Mohammed 2015, 10–11)

Yusuf's mentor, Sheikh Ja'afar Adam, criticized Yusuf for lack of moral integrity and inadequate knowledge of Islam. The sectarian schism between Sheikh Adam and his former mentee, Yusuf, began to grow. In 2007, Adam was assassinated in his Dorayi Mosque in Kano. Another Salafi cleric, Sheik Auwal Albani Zaria, was also assassinated, and Boko Haram is believed to be behind these assassinations (International Crisis Group 2014). Furthermore, traditional rulers of the Gwoza, Kano, and Fika Emirates, who are adherents of the Tijaniyya and Shi'ite sects, were also targeted. The emir of Gwoza ended up being ambushed and killed by Boko Haram in 2012. In addition, in 2009, Boko Haram targeted telecommunication facilities, journalists, schools, churches, army and police barracks, precincts, and personnel in Borno and Yobe states (Montclos 2014; Mustapha 2014; Mustapha and Ehrhardt 2018; Thurston 2018).

The federal government under President Yar'Adua responded with ferocious military force that led to the destruction of Mohammed Yusuf's mosque and killed hundreds of his supporters. Yusuf was arrested and subsequently executed by the military without recourse to any legal proceedings. The extrajudicial murder of Mohammed Yusuf only fueled the radicalization of his followership not only in northeastern Nigeria but also across the Muslim community in the Lake Chad Basin, including Cameroon, Chad, and Niger. Using both repression and forced conscription, Boko Haram expanded its fighting force from four thousand members in 2009 to approximately six thousand to eight thousand in 2014. The federal government deployed about fifteen thousand soldiers in the war against Boko Haram.

Between 2009 and 2015, Boko Haram transitioned into a full-blown terror group led by Abu Bakr Shekau, who was brutal in prosecuting the jihad. According to Montclos (2016, 882), in September 2010 Boko Haram operatives attacked a prison in Bauchi, releasing about 721 of the 759 inmates, including 150 members of the sect. About 506 of the released inmates joined Boko Haram. In 2014, the group attacked Giwa Barracks in Maiduguri, releasing between 800 and 1,600 inmates, who were given the option to join the insurgency. Boko Haram also expanded its operations to cover all six states in northeastern Nigeria and set up cells in major northern Nigerian cities, such as Kano, Kaduna, Jos, Abuja, and Yola. On Christmas day in 2011, a Boko Haram cell attacked the St. Theresa Catholic Church in Madalla near Abuja (Nigeria's federal capital), killing forty-three Christians and injuring dozens of worshippers. In 2012, an underground cell in Kano targeted police stations, state security services, and prisons, killing about 186 people. Similarly, in 2014, a Boko Haram lone wolf called Aminu Sadiq Ogwuche detonated a suicide bomb in the Nyanya neighborhood in Abuja, killing more than 250 civilians.

Boko Haram has also been notorious for targeting schools in northeastern Nigeria. For example, in April 2014, its operatives attacked the government girls' secondary school in the town of Chibok, abducting 276 girls who were preparing for their final exams. Although about one hundred of these girls have been rescued, many of them remain in captivity. It is also reported that between 2013 and 2015, Boko Haram attacked the schools of agriculture in Gujba, Mamudo; government secondary schools in Potiskum and Buni Yadi in Yobe state, where they killed more than a hundred male students. According to a UNICEF report, Boko Haram violence has forced about 952 school-age children to flee, and more than six hundred thousand students have lost access to learning because of the conflict (Human Rights Watch 2016, 18). In May 2013, Boko Haram fighters attacked the fishing towns of Gamboru-Ngala and Baga, killing more than three hundred and two hundred civilians, respectively. After securing a large swathe of territory in northern Borno state, Boko Haram leaders declared a "caliphate" with its headquarters in Gwoza.

Between 2003 and 2016, Boko Haram and the Nigerian military are estimated to have killed more than 32,292 civilians (Montclos 2016, 884) and displaced another 2.5 million who are living in internally displaced persons (IDP) camps around Maiduguri. The abduction of schoolgirls in Chibok, the attack on the United Nations Offices in Abuja, and Shekau's declarations of fealty (*baya*) to the leader of the Islamic State (Deash), Abu Bakr al-Baghdadi, in 2015 spurred the international community as well as regional actors to provide military support for Nigeria in the war against terror. Furthermore, the countries of the Lake Chad Basin Commission, including Nigeria, Chad, Niger, and Cameroon, set up the Multinational Joint Task Force (MNJTF) to fight Boko Haram in the region. Chadian armed forces, which have been involved for several years in warfare against insurgency in the Sahara Desert, began to rout Boko Haram fighters in the Lake Chad area, while within Nigeria the Civilian Joint Task Force (CJTF or Yan Gora) in conjunction with the armed forces successfully flushed out Boko Haram fighters from Maiduguri city into the Sambisa forest. The Nigerian Air Force targeted the group in their hideouts in the forest as well as in surrounding villages, leading to the decimation of a significant number of its foot soldiers.

Deeply divided African postcolonial states such as Sudan, Kenya, Egypt, Algeria, Uganda, the Democratic Republic of Congo, and the Central African Republic have experienced internal violent conflicts centered around ethnic, religious, or sectarian identity. They have also witnessed struggles over resources, including land, water, pasture, or minerals, that have led to the killing of innocent civilians and the decimation of livelihoods. In Algeria and Kenya, as Nigeria, religious identity, citizenship rights, and sectarianism have been conflictual fault lines. In Sudan, although the secession of South Sudan may have enhanced some measure of peace between the Muslim North and the Christian South, the lingering racial divide between the "Arabs" and "Africans" in Darfur continues to fester through state-sponsored ethnic cleansing (Mamdani 2002). Civil society mobilization against continuing military autocracy, repression of democracy activists, and the absence of a clear path to peace and national reconciliation highlight the persistent challenges of identity politics in Sudan and other postcolonial African states.

Furthermore, within the Republic of South Sudan, the inability of the ruling Sudan People's Liberation Movement (SPLM) under President Salva Kiir to close ranks and transcend ethnic divisions undermines the cohesion of the country. Mali, which at one point was described as the model of democracy and the "donor darling" of the World Bank and the International Monetary Fund, descended into a violent insurgency after the 2012 coup d'état that overthrew the Amadou Toumani Touré regime. The Tuareg insurgency in the north opened a window of opportunity for jihadi Salafi groups such as Al Qaeda in the Maghrib (AQIM), the Movement for Justice and Oneness in West Africa (MUJAO), and the Islamic State in the Greater Sahara (ISGS) to expand their influence in Mali, thereby disrupting the democratization process (Villalón, 2021).

It is important to note that, like the Boko Haram insurgency in northern Nigeria, where jihadi Salafists tap into dan Fodio's jihad to legitimate their violent agenda, jihadi Salafists in Mali similarly tap into the history of the nineteenth-century reform movement of Sheikh Sekou Ahmadu to justify the agenda of "purifying Islam" in the country through the overthrow of democratic rule. In the case of Uganda, Aili Mari Tripp (2004, 16) reports that there have been historic sectarian identity conflicts between Roman Catholics and Protestants affiliated with different political parties and that President Yoweri Museveni has exploited these divisions to entrench semi-authoritarian rule. In North Africa, Algeria and Egypt are two countries where religion and sectarianism constitute persistent sources of violence. For example, during the "Arab Spring" insurrections in Egypt, the Islamic Brotherhood allied itself with democracy activists to overthrow the Mubarak regime and eventually installed an Islamist regime under President Morsi. Coptic Christians in Egypt have frequently been targeted by Islamist extremists and their places of worship destroyed. Also, during the 1992 elections in Algeria, the Islamic Salvation Front (FIS) mobilized its teaming followers and was on the verge of winning a parliamentary victory before the military intervened and suspended the process.

Consequently, the transition process was truncated as FIS withdrew into the countryside and began attacking security agencies.

The ensuing violence turned into civil war as the Armed Islamic Group (GIA; the military wing of FIS) expanded its attacks into major cities. Al Qaeda in the Islamic Maghreb (AQIM) took advantage of the turmoil in Algeria and expanded its operations through the Salafi Group for Preaching and Combat (GSPC), the splinter group of the GIA. The foregoing narrative suggests that religious and sectarian identities certainly constitute an important analytical lens through which we can productively decipher the drivers of sociopolitical violence and state fragility in postcolonial Africa.

Conclusion

Crawford Young's intellectual legacy in terms of his theoretical contributions to our understanding of the African postcolonial state is certainly immense. Specifically, his analytical framework of cultural pluralism and the enduring legacies of the colonial state structures and autocracy in African postcolonial states provide us with a crucial lens for understanding the dilemmas of nation building and democracy in Africa. However, as I have demonstrated, issues of religious identity and the processes of sectarian identity formation are equally crucial conceptual frames that further deepen our knowledge and understanding of the drivers of political violence in Africa. As described in this chapter, in northern Nigeria's religious marketplace, the political weaponization of Islam and "sectarian purity" are relevant in understanding the trajectories of the Boko Haram insurgency and state fragility. Although Boko Haram has splintered and most of its top commanders decimated, the security threat has not abated. What are the possible solutions to sectarianism and religiously inspired violent conflicts in postcolonial Africa? How can the nation-state building project in postcolonial Africa be reformed to ensure that the interests and core values of all citizens are reflected in the democratization process?

In terms of addressing sectarianism, it is essential for the Nigerian government to ensure that clerics and religious leaders are held accountable for any form of provocative acts of violence emanating from their members or places of worship. Specific laws should be incorporated in Nigeria's Constitution that clearly indicate legal penalties for acts of religious or sectarian violence that cause harm to citizens, property, and society. In addition, central organizations such as the Ja'matul Nasril Islam (JNI) and the Christian Association of Nigeria (CAN), which are responsible for promoting and protecting the interests of Muslim and Christian communities, should be required to vet or monitor the various religious clerics that teach followers within their respective faith communities.

It is also imperative to note that violence is fundamentally a political phenomenon, and its solution has to be explored in the political realm. This calls for decolonizing the political space (Mamdani 2020, 18), which should involve a reimagination and a redefinition of the political community that productively addresses the question of belonging, as well as the rights and obligations of the citizenry. Specifically, as I have shown in the case of Nigeria, it is not religious differences per se that drive violence; rather, it is the politicization of such differences by predatory entrepreneurs such as Yusuf, Governor Ali Sheriff, and their supporters that drives violence. Thus, decolonizing the political does not mean that Nigerians, and, indeed, Africans, should give up their cultural or religious identities and reject diversity. Rather, my argument is that what Africans ought to reject is the weaponization of diversity, especially in the religious marketplace. As I have demonstrated in this chapter, Mohammed Yusuf and his followers exploited sectarian diversity in Nigeria's religious marketplace to unleash violence. In terms of reconstituting the nation-building project, it is equally imperative that all segments of society, including youth, women groups, professional associations, community-based organizations, and "majority" and "minority" communities, be brought on board in the democratization project. Constitutional designs should take on board ethnic and religious diversities through conscious mechanisms of proportional representation. Furthermore, in decolonizing the political landscape, African policymakers should rethink the Eurocentric notion that the nation-building project necessarily requires that society be homogenized and centralized through the monopoly of the instruments of violence and that it reflect a majoritarian identity. As history has repeatedly shown, such approaches more often than not lead to genocidal violence and ethnic cleansing, thereby unmaking the nation (Straus 2015). Sectarian entrepreneurs, as this chapter has shown, are the avatars of a new homogenizing ideology that undermines social cohesion rather than building the nation.

References

Bratton, Michael, and Nicholas Van de Walle. 1997. *Democratic Experiments in Africa: Regime Transitions in Comparative Perspective.* Cambridge: Cambridge University Press.

Brigaglia, Andrea. 2012. "A Contribution to the History of the Wahhabi Daʻwa in West Africa: The Career and the Murder of Shaykh Jaʻfar Mahmoud Adam (Daura, ca. 1961/1962–Kano 2007) 1." *Islamic Africa* 3 (1): 1–23.

Chabal, Patrick, and Jean-Pascal Daloz. 1999. *African Works: Disorder as Political Instrument.* Bloomington: Indiana University Press.

Collier, Paul, and Anke Hoeffler. 2004. "Greed and Grievance in Civil War." *Oxford Economic Papers* 4:563–95.

Elischer, Sebastian. 2021. *Salafism and Political Order in Africa.* Cambridge: Cambridge University Press.

Ellis, Stephen, and Gerrie Ter Haar. 2007. "Religion and Politics: Taking African Epistemologies Seriously." *Journal of Modern African Studies* 45 (3): 385–401.

Fox, Jonathan. 2002. *Ethnoreligious Conflict in the Late 20th Century: A General Theory.* Lanham, MD: Lexington Books.

Fox, Jonathan. 2004. *Religion, Civilization and Civil War: 1945 through the New Millennium.* Lanham, MD: Lexington Books.

Harnischfeger, Johannes. 2008. *Democratization and Islamic Law: The Shari'a Conflict in Nigeria.* Chicago: University of Chicago Press.

Human Rights Watch. 2016. "They Set the Classrooms on Fire: Attacks on Education in Northeast Nigeria." Human Rights Watch Report. Washington, DC.

Huntington, Samuel P. 1991. *The Third Wave: Democratization in the Late Twentieth Century.* Norman: University of Oklahoma Press.

Ibrahim, Jibrin. 1991. "Religion and Political Turbulence in Nigeria." *Journal of Modern African Studies* 29 (1): 115–36.

International Crisis Group. 2014. "Curbing Violence in Nigeria: The Boko Haram Insurgency." *Africa Report*, no. 216. Brussels: International Crisis Group.

Kassim, Abdulbasit. 2015. "Defining and Understanding the Religious Philosophy of Jihādī-Salafism and the Ideology of Boko Haram." *Politics, Religion & Ideology* 16 (2–3): 173–200.

Kassim, Abdulbasit. 2018. "Boko Haram's Internal Civil War: Stealth Takfir and Jihad as Recipes for Schism." In *Boko Haram beyond the Headlines: Analyses of Africa's Enduring Insurgency*, edited by Jacob Zenn, 3–32. West Point, NY: Combating Terrorism Center.

Mamdani, Mahmood. 1996. *Citizens and Subjects: Contemporary Africa and the Legacy of Late Colonialism.* Princeton, NJ: Princeton University Press.

Mamdani, Mahmood. 2002. "Making Sense of Political Violence in Postcolonial Africa." *Identity, Culture and Politics* 3 (2): 1–24.

Mamdani, Mahmood. 2004. *Good Muslim, Bad Muslim: America, the Cold War and the Roots of Terror.* New York: Pantheon.

Mamdani, Mahmood. 2020. *Neither Settler nor Native: The Making and Unmaking of Permanent Minorities.* Cambridge, MA: Harvard University Press.

Mohammed, Kyari. 2015. "The Message and Methods of Boko Haram." In *Boko Haram: Islamism, Politics, Security and the State in Nigeria*, edited by Marc-Antoine de Montclos, 3–32. Los Angeles: African Academic Press.

Mohammed, Kyari. 2018. "The Origins of Boko Haram." In *The Oxford Handbook of Nigerian Politics*, edited by Carl Levan and Patrick Utaka, 1–23. London: Oxford University Press.

Montclos, Marc-Antoine Perouse. 2014. *Nigeria's Interminable Insurgency: Addressing the Boko Haram Crisis.* Africa Program Research Paper. London: Chatham House.

Montclos, Marc-Antoine Perouse, ed. 2015. *Boko Haram: Islamism, Politics, Security and the State in Nigeria.* Los Angeles: African Academic Press.

Montclos, Marc-Antoine Pérouse. 2016. "A Sectarian Jihad in Nigeria: The Case of Boko Haram." *Small Wars & Insurgencies* 27 (5): 878–95.

Mustapha, Abdul Raufu, ed. 2014. *Sects and Social Disorder: Muslim Identities and Conflict in Northern Nigeria*. London: James Curry.

Mustapha, Abdul Raufu, and David Ehrhardt, eds. 2018. *Creed and Grievance: Muslim–Christian Relations and Conflict Resolution in Northern Nigeria*. London: James Curry.

Mustapha, Abdul Raufu, and Kate Meagher, eds. 2020. *Overcoming Boko Haram: Faith, Society and Islamic Radicalization in Northern Nigeria*. London: James Curry.

Østebø, Terje. 2015. "African Salafism: Religious Purity and the Politicization of Purity." *Islamic Africa* 6:1–29.

Philpott, Daniel. 2007. "Explaining the Political Ambivalence of Religion." *American Political Science Review* 101 (3): 505–25.

Reno, William. 2002. "The Politics of Insurgency in Collapsing States." *Development and Change* 33 (5): 837–58.

Reno, William. 2009. "Explaining Patterns of Violence in Collapsed States." *Contemporary Security Policy* 30 (2): 356–74.

Reno, William. 2011. *Warfare in Independent Africa*. New York: Cambridge University Press.

Richards, Paul. 1996. *Fighting for the Rainforest: War, Youth and Resources in Sierra Leone*. London: James Curry.

Straus, Scott. 2012. "Wars Do End! Changing Patterns of Political Violence in Sub-Saharan Africa." *African Affairs* 111 (443): 179–201.

Straus, Scott. 2015. *Making and Unmaking Nations: War, Leadership and Genocide in Modern Africa*. Ithaca, NY: Cornell University Press.

Thurston, Alexander. 2011. "Abubakar Gumi's Global Salafism and Locally Oriented Polemics in a Northern Nigerian Text." *Islamic Africa* 2 (2): 9–21.

Thurston, Alexander. 2015. "Nigeria's Mainstream Salafis between Boko Haram and the State." *Islamic Africa* 6 (1–2): 109–34.

Thurston, Alexander. 2016a. "The Disease Is Unbelief: Boko Haram's Religious and Political Worldview." Analysis Paper no. 22. Brookings Institution Project.

Thurston, Alexander. 2016b. *Salafism in Nigeria: Islam, Preaching and Politics*. Cambridge: Cambridge University Press.

Thurston, Alexander. 2018. *Boko Haram: The History of an African Jihadist Movement*. Princeton, NJ: Princeton University Press.

Toft, Monica Duffy. 2006. "Religion, Civil War and International Order." Discussion Paper 2006-03. Belfer Center for International Affairs (BCIA).

Toft, Monica Duffy. 2007. "Getting Religion? The Puzzling Case of Islam and Civil War." *International Security* 31 (4): 97–131.

Tripp, Aili Mari. 2004. "The Changing Face of Authoritarianism in Africa: The Case of Uganda." *Africa Today* 50 (3): 3–26.

Tripp, Aili Mari. 2010. *Museveni's Uganda: Paradoxes of Power in a Hybrid Regime*. Boulder, CO: Lynne Rienner.

Umar, Muhammad Sani. 2012. "The Popular Discourses of Salafi Radicalism and Salafi Counter-Radicalism in Nigeria: A Case Study of Boko Haram." *Journal of Religion in Africa* 42 (2): 118–44.

Umar, Muhammad Sani. 2015. "Salafi Narratives against Violent Extremism in Nigeria." Monograph. Abuja: Center for Democracy and Development.

Umar, Muhammad Sani. 2020. "The Role of the Ulama in Radicalization and Counter-radicalization." In *Overcoming Boko Haram: Faith, Society and Islamic Radicalization in Northern Nigeria*, edited by Mustapha, A. R and Kate Meagher, 33–63. London: James Curry.

Villalón, Leonardo A. 2021. *The Oxford Handbook of the African Sahel*. London: Oxford University Press.

Young, Crawford. 1976. *The Politics of Cultural Pluralism*. Madison: University of Wisconsin Press.

Young, Crawford. 1994. *The African Colonial State in Comparative Perspective*. New Haven, CT: Yale University Press.

Young, Crawford. 2002. "Deciphering Disorder in Africa: Is Identity the Key?" *World Politics* 54 (4): 532–57.

Young, Crawford. 2004. "The End of the Postcolonial State in Africa? Reflections on Changing African Political Dynamics." *African Affairs* 103 (410): 23–49.

Young, Crawford. 2012. *The Postcolonial State in Africa: Fifty Years of Independence, 1960–2010*. Madison: University of Wisconsin Press.

Young, Crawford, and Thomas Turner. 1985. *The Rise and Decline of the Zairian State*. Madison: University of Wisconsin Press.

Yusuf, Muhammad. 2006. "Tafsir" [Teaching]. Audio tape. https://www.youtube.com /watch?v=fmZoQxjIj4E.

Yusuf, Muhammad. 2009. "Hadhihi Aqidatuna wa Minhaju Da'awatuna" [This Is Our Creed and the Methodology of Our Preaching]. Unpublished manuscript in author's possession.

Zartman, I. William, ed. 1996. *Collapsed States: The Disintegration and Restoration of Legitimate Authority*. Boulder, CO: Lynne Rienner.

6

The Politics of Identity in the Democratic Republic of Congo

The Enduring Power of Crawford Young's Analysis and Its Limits

Timothy Longman

Are you Mubala or Mupende?

Question asked of Crawford Young in Idiofa, the Democratic Republic of Congo, 1962 (Young 1976, 3)

But, if you all speak the same language, how do you know who's in which ethnic group?

Congolese human rights activist, Mbarara, Uganda, 1995

We don't have ethnic conflict. We're Congolese!

Civil society activist, Bukavu, 2000 (field notes, Bukavu, March 2000)

Two areas of expertise for which Crawford Young is best known, the politics of the Democratic Republic of Congo (DRC) and the politics of identity, were deeply connected in his thinking and writing. Young begins his influential book *The Politics of Cultural Pluralism* (1976) with the story of his being challenged to situate himself ethnically in the midst of the Democratic Republic of Congo's political strife in the early 1960s. His experience of being forced to identify himself as either Mbala or Pende, as reported in the epigraph, serves as the basis for his reflection on the shifting nature of identities that is the focus of the book. By the time he was writing *The Politics of Cultural Pluralism*, a decade later, the salience of Mbale and Pende identities had largely dissipated (Young 1976, 3–5).[1] A chapter on the DRC, or Zaire as it was then known, serves as the first case study that Young uses to demonstrate his theories about the flexible and contextual nature of identity (Young 1976, 163–215). Young also included chapters on ethnicity in both of his books on the DRC, *Politics in the Congo*, published in 1965, and his 1985 book with Thomas Turner, *The Rise and Decline of the Zairian State*.

Young continued his interest in the politics of identity, sponsoring at least two NEH seminars on the topic in the 1980s and early 1990s and editing a collected volume, *The Rising Tide of Cultural Pluralism* (1992). In the introduction to that book, Young notes developments in academic thinking on identity politics, acknowledging responses to his instrumentalist approach that emphasizes the limits to the flexibility of identity—the primordial approach from some anthropologists and the constructivist approach from authors such as Benedict Anderson (1983). While he indicated the evolution in his own thinking spurred by these responses, Young never revisited the topic of identity politics in the DRC in his writings.

In this chapter, I explore identity politics in the DRC to reflect on how the Congolese case shaped Young's understanding of identity and to assess developments that have taken place since he last wrote on the topic, in 1985. This chapter draws on the abundance of scholarly works published on the DRC in the past thirty years, including a number focused specifically on identity politics and on my own research visits to the DRC in 2000, 2007, 2012, and 2020. I review the major ethnic conflicts that have occurred throughout the country since 1985. On the basis of this review, I contend that Young's analysis of the highly flexible nature of identity and the degree to which political engagement shapes ethnic salience remains insightful, though the limits to the flexibility of identity that he noted later in his career also prove important, as a few groups in the DRC, like the Banyamulenge, the Luba-Kasai, and the Mbuti, have remained targets of scorn and exclusion. In particular, exploring the language that people use to talk about ethnic groups, I argue that when group identities become racialized—that is, viewed as biological rather than cultural—differences become less malleable and more rigid, making identity-based conflict more persistent.

Crawford Young on Ethnicity in the DRC

According to Young and Turner (1985, 193) in their chapter on identity, "Ethnicity, in contrast to class, is defined by consciousness. It is rooted in a collective recognition of affinity, to which social and emotional meanings are attached. Its imputation of intimacy finds reflection in the frequency with which kinship metaphors are used to express it; a co-ethnic is a brother, not a mere friend." In other words, an ethnic group is a collection of people who are connected to one another, like an extended family. Members of an ethnic group share an inherent personal relationship, a type of brotherhood, but, in contrast to the connections implied by family or lineage, that connection is "social and emotional" rather than primarily biological.

Young's ideas on identity were profoundly shaped by the particular circumstances of the DRC. Home to as many as three hundred ethnic groups, the DRC has no single group that dominates at the national level. At the same time, competition for power at the local level has been extremely important in shaping ethnic identities. In his works, Young emphasized the role of political competition in heightening the salience of ethnic identities and noted that shifting political circumstances could lead to a lessening of ethnic identification and a reduction in ethnic tensions. He labeled this approach instrumentalism because of the ways in which political elites used identity as an instrument to gain political power (Young 1976).

In his first book, *Politics in the Congo*, Young explores the emergence of ethnic identities in the colonial period and the ways in which the struggles for political power in the late colonial and early independence period heightened ethnic identification—but only for certain groups, in certain contexts. (He revisits this period in both *The Politics of Cultural Pluralism* and *The Rise and Decline of the Zairian State*.) He notes that, although much of Congo's precolonial population had little sense of ethnic identity, living in decentralized communities without sharp cultural boundaries, Europeans approached the Congo with a belief in the innate tribalism of Africa's people. This understanding shaped European interactions with the Congolese and helped to construct relatively fixed identities from previously disparate peoples. The system of indirect rule needed "traditional" authorities through whom to rule, so chiefs were named for groups that had previously lacked clear rulers, while identity cards and other official paperwork required individuals to list their ethnicity, forcing individuals to identify officially with a group. Missionaries played an important role in standardizing languages, often melding diverse dialects into languages that came to be recognized as distinguishing coherent ethnic groups, as the second epigraph suggests. Young notes that the definition of groups was less purposeful in the Belgian Congo than in many of Britain's African colonies but that the cumulative effect of colonialism was to push Congolese into ethnic communities, even if the definition of these communities remained somewhat flexible (Young 1965, 235–40).

In addition to colonial policy, Young identified urbanization as a major driver of ethnic consciousness, as individuals became more aware of their similarities to those from their home area as they encountered people from other areas with different languages and customs (Young 1965, 240–53). Young further noted that, despite the recent emergence of most of the Congo's ethnic identities, the political activism around independence heightened ethnic identities in many places. Two factors were key—a sense of relative deprivation, as some groups viewed others as unfairly advantaged, and the development of an ethnic ideology that helped group members recognize their identity and come to understand and share their group's sense of grievance. In the DRC, these factors were not uniform across groups or across the country as, for example, neither of the two major groups in Kinshasa, the Bakongo and Bangala, had an obvious advantage, while the Luba-Kasai not only had a clear ethnic ideology but also were regarded as privileged by both the Lulua around Kananga and among the Luba-Kat around Katanga (Young and Turner 1985).

Just prior to independence and particularly in the years immediately after, armed conflict took place in a number of locations in the Congo. Most of the DRC's disturbances were not primarily ethnic in nature, but ethnicity was usually a factor, and explicitly ethnic conflicts—like the ones between the Mbale and the Pende that Young encountered in Idiofa in the early 1960s or the attacks that displaced nearly one million Luba-Kasai from Kananga in 1959 and from Katanga during the secessionist movement of 1960–63—added to a general sense of political chaos and undermined the appeal of ethnic politics as a central principle for political organization. As Young and Turner explained, "The peculiar pathology of the First Republic [the period from 1960 to 1965] utterly discredited the pluralist formula, and set the stage for the powerful reassertion of the unitary nation-state model as New Regime ideology. . . . Above all, First Republic politics at all levels were saturated with ethnicity. While it was generally not the sole or even the major factor in particular events, ethnicity was nearly always present in the perceptions of the actors and in the understandings of the spectators as well" (1985, 41).

The central debate at the time of independence was over whether the Congo should be a decentralized federal state where ethnic groups would be empowered or a unitary state where national identity would trump ethnic identities. The first president, Joseph Kasavubu, rose to power as leader of the Bakongo ethnic association Alliance of the Bakongo (ABAKO) and advocated for regional power, while the first prime minister, Patrice Lumumba, embraced an anti-imperialist ideology that emphasized the need for unity. Even though Lumumba was arrested and assassinated shortly after independence, his idea of a unified national identity and centralized state ultimately won the day. The chaos of the first five years of independence created strong support for military leader Mobutu's promise to establish a unified state when he took power in a 1965 coup (Young 1976, 167–74, 211–15). Young notes the degree to which the ethnic sentiments that were mobilized with relative ease in the late 1950s and 1960s dissipated as even previous advocates for a more decentralized or federalist model, including Kasavubu and Moïse Tshombe, leader of the Katanga separatist movement, came to embrace an emphasis on national unity over regional and ethnic identities. Young's later work notes how Mobutu Sese Sekou's policies of promoting a unified national identity while ensuring ethnic representation helped to diminish the salience of ethnicity nearly everywhere. He writes that in the DRC, "The dramatic contrasts in the perception of ethnic conflict in the various historical phases through which it has passed, even in the brief period since independence, effectively demonstrate the force of the political arena in structuring conceptions of cultural pluralism. The fluid and situational character of ethnicity in Africa is illustrated through its complex permutations in the last two decades of Zaire's history. The interaction between ideologies of national integration, oriented to a Zaire-wide loyalty, and mobilized ethnic solidarities stands out" (Young 1976, 164).

In *The Rise and Decline of the Zairian State*, Young and Turner note that as president, Mobutu not only promoted national unity as necessary for security but also ensured that each ethnic group felt connected to the state. Mobutu incorporated ethnicity into the patron–client system that secured his power, distributing patronage posts (governorships, cabinet ministries, and judicial and parastatal positions) so that each ethnic community had a patron who could distribute a share of the spoils of the state, thereby tying every group to the regime and allowing each group to feel that it had access to the state's resources. To gain access to state resources, such as scholarships, development projects, or land, Congolese had to go through their ethnic patron, which reinforced identities even as it linked groups in a common national project. Young and Turner argue that "the state itself is the most decisive single factor in the complex pattern of mutations and reformulations of social consciousness within civil society. . . . Social consciousness is not—or not yet—congealed into permanent, structured categories" (Young and Turner 1985, 138–63).

In sum, Young observed in the DRC that ethnicity could be very important for politics but that ethnic identities were flexible and contextual rather than fixed and determinative. He noted that political competition and state policies were the primary drivers helping to consolidate or weaken group identities and to enflame or cool ethnic tensions. The case of the DRC influenced his thinking as he developed his ideas on the instrumentalization of identity that he explored comparatively in *The Politics of Cultural Pluralism*. The Congo thus became the empirical foundation for understanding how politics shapes ethnicity.

The Politics of Identity in the DRC since 1985

When I first traveled to the DRC for research in 2000 in the midst of the Second Congo War, a number of people in North and South Kivu insisted that ethnic conflict was not something typically Congolese but was rather something imposed on the country by Rwanda, as reflected in the third epigraph at the beginning of the chapter. Yet, even as they claimed that ethnic conflict was not typical for the DRC, the Congolese I interviewed often used ethnic identifications to talk about the ongoing violence, identifying Tutsi or Banyamulenge soldiers or Nande and Hunde chiefs. In the two decades since that initial fieldwork trip, ethnic conflict has remained a major feature of Congolese politics. Yet, the idea that ethnic politics is not something deeply rooted in Congolese society but rather something that comes and goes depending upon the situation remains widespread among Congolese themselves.

In this section, I review the ethnic dimension of Congolese politics since Young last published on the topic, in 1985. As Young and Turner correctly noted, in contrast to the late 1950s and early 1960s, when ethnic conflicts were widespread in many parts of the country, the Mobutu regime kept ethnic conflict to a minimum for several decades. In his last years in office, however, the period after the publication of Young and Turner's book, Mobutu's rule became increasingly unpopular, and he turned to ethnic scapegoating to help build his power. At the same time, the movement for democratic governance also provoked stronger ethnic identifications. Since Mobutu's fall in 1997, ethnic conflict has become even more common. Both the First and Second Congo Wars and the subsequent shift toward elected government have inspired ethnic clashes. Reviewing the main ethnic conflicts that have taken place in the DRC over the past several decades, I note that while some conflicts have proven temporary, with some identities increasing in salience while others have diminished—in much the fashion that Young observed—a few ethnic groups have faced more consistent social exclusion, raising questions about the extent to which ethnic identities can be seen as merely contextual. In the final section of the chapter, analyzing the language that Congolese use to discuss various groups, I argue that racism and the racialization of identity help to explain the persistence of some conflicts.

The Local Dynamics of Ethnic Conflict

In this subsection, I provide a quick overview of ethnic conflict in the context of the DRC's changing political landscape since 1985, demonstrating that Young's ideas about the flexibility of identity remain useful for explaining the majority of ethnic conflicts. Ethnic politics in the DRC are shaped by the presence of as many as three hundred ethnic groups, many of them quite small. Four national languages—Kikongo, Kiswahili, Lingala, and Tshiluba—bring together diverse groups in regions where they are spoken as second languages (Turner 2013). The diversity of groups, with no single group making up more than 20 percent of the population, has helped prevent large-scale ethnic conflicts.[2] At the same time, small-scale conflicts have taken place periodically in many parts of the country since the colonial era in response to struggles over land and natural resources, political access and power, and armed conflict. Young noted how the 1957–58 municipal and 1959 legislative elections created competition that crystallized local-level identities (Young 1976), while Mobutu's ethnic management policies served to diminish ethnic tensions (Young 1985, 138–63).

Since Young last published on Congolese identity politics, in 1985, most ethnic conflict in the DRC has continued to reflect the flexible and contextual nature of group identities. In Mobutu's last decade in office, both changes in official policy and a shifting political context led to increasing ethnic mobilization. As the power and reach of the central state declined and economic conditions deteriorated in the 1980s, Congolese relied more and more on ethnic associations as one means of support (Emizet 1999). Facing sharply declining popularity, Mobutu began exploiting ethnic differences in an effort to secure his power through a divide-and-rule strategy, particularly seeking to divert popular anger against Luba-Kasai and Banyarwanda and away from his regime.

The return to competitive politics also fostered ethnic competition. Once Mobutu announced, in 1990, that opposition political parties would be allowed, several hundred new parties were created, most of them associated with a single ethnic group or subgroup. The Sovereign National Conference that began in August 1991 to discuss the DRC's political future involved 2,842 delegates "representing all classes and strata of Congolese society," including 204 political parties (Nzongola-Ntalaja 2002). As Kisangani Emizet (1999, 188) notes, "the democratization process, which from 1991 to 1996 opened the political system, has increased political demands along ethnic lines even from minority groups." Contention over who should be represented in the Sovereign National Conference heightened ethnic tensions, particularly in the eastern DRC, and some groups began to form local militias, ostensibly to defend their ethnic interests. Jason Stearns (2022) notes that in the early 1990s, ethnic groups struggled over control of the land, with some groups claiming to be autochthonous, that is, the original inhabitants of the territory, holding special claims to the land. These struggles created the conditions for the ethnic violence that took place in the region a few years later. As he writes, "In the 1990s, *autochtonie* became the central focus of armed groups, but ethnicity was still expressed in very local terms, motivated by concrete communal grievances" (Stearns 2022, 31).

The two wars that ravaged Congo from 1996 to 2003 further heightened ethnic tensions. The Alliance of Democratic Forces for the Liberation of Congo-Zaire (Alliance des forces démocratique pour la liberation du Congo-Zaïre, ADFL) was a Congolese rebel group led by former Mulelist rebel leader Laurent Kabila and initially composed primarily of members of the Banyamulenge ethnic group, trained by Rwanda. In October 1996, the ADFL and troops from Rwanda and Uganda launched attacks on the eastern DRC, initially claiming the need to protect Banyamulenge civilians from attacks, then adding as a second justification the security threat posed by the presence just across the border of Rwandan troops and militia that had carried out the genocide against the Tutsi in Rwanda in 1994, and finally arguing that security could be guaranteed only by ousting President Mobutu. The war came to focus largely on the goal of removing Mobutu, and many local ethnic militia groups, which came to be known as Mai-Mai, joined in support, helping to bring Kabila to power as president (Turner 2007, 3–5; Reyntjens 2009; Stearns 2022).[3]

Once the ADFL drove Mobutu from power and Kabila became president, he named a government of his own supporters, largely excluding civil society and opposition political parties, even though the pro-democracy movement had helped create the conditions that allowed the ADFL victory. Many Rwandan troops remained in the DRC, and a number of Banyamulenge assumed prominent positions, particularly within the military, which some Congolese came to resent. In the face of growing anti-Tutsi resentment (discussed later), a year after taking office, Kabila asked the Rwandan troops to return home. A few attacks on Tutsi both in Kinshasa and in the east served as a pretext for Rwanda and Uganda to sponsor a new Congolese rebel group, the Congolese Rally for Democracy (Rassemblement congolais pour la démocratie, RCD), again with troops composed mostly of Banyamulenge, many of whom were soldiers who had left Kabila's army. In August 1998, troops mutinied in Goma, and fighters from the RCD, Rwanda, and Uganda invaded, quickly occupying a large swath of the eastern DRC. A dramatic airlift of Rwandan troops across the country nearly led to the capture of Kinshasa, but the intervention of Angola, Zimbabwe, and Namibia on Kabila's behalf thwarted the attack in the west. The war soon broke down into a stalemate, with the rebel groups fracturing into a couple of factions backed by Uganda occupying much of the north of the DRC, the Rwandan-backed RCD occupying much of the east, and progovernment troops and their international allies occupying the rest of the country (Turner 2007, 5–8; Reyntjens 2009, 194–230).

The Second Congo War served to intensify ethnic community identification in the eastern DRC. This time, most local people regarded the war not as a liberation but as a foreign occupation. Even though the rebel groups set up ethnically diverse governments in the regions they controlled, the local populations viewed these regimes as mere lackeys for Rwanda and Uganda. The Mai-Mai groups, many receiving support from the government in Kinshasa, launched guerrilla operations against the rebels and their foreign backers, and some targeted local Rwandan-speaking populations. Mai-Mai groups sometimes also came into conflict with one another as they competed for territory and supporters (Stearns 2022, 33–35). Séverine Autesserre (2010) argues that the failure to understand the local-level nature of much of the violence in the eastern DRC is a key reason that the international community, approaching the conflict in global terms, failed to bring the violence effectively to an end. As she writes, "Local agendas have held tremendous influence throughout modern Congolese history, and they have often been intertwined with macro-level dimensions" (Autesserre 2010, 38).

Since the postwar transition in 2006, violence has remained endemic in the eastern DRC. The persistence of Rwandan-backed Tutsi militias, the National Congress for the Defense of the People (Congrès national pour la défense du people, CNDP) from 2004 to 2009 and then M-23 since 2012, has justified the continued arming of the Mai-Mai groups. Yet while the Mai-Mai groups claim to represent the interests of particular ethnic communities, in practice, many have become self-sustaining through pillage and exploitation of local populations, often the very people they claim to be protecting. The abundance of natural resources in the region has funded weapons purchases that allow armed groups to maintain themselves even without popular support (Stearns 2022). In short, although ethnic conflict appears at first to be a major source of violence in the region, in fact, most conflicts have little to do with ethnicity—with the exception of violence involving the Tutsi- or Nilotic-identified groups such as the Banyamulenge and Hema.

Elections held in 2006, 2011, and 2018 highlighted ethnic differences, as elites founded parties based largely on a single ethnic group. In the eastern DRC, some politicians formed alliances with local militia groups. As Stearns (2022, 48) explains, "Politicians who had previously obtained power through networking and patronage now had to prove themselves at the ballot box. For some, armed mobilization was an easy way to curry favor, play to ethnic stereotypes, and intimidate opponents. Elections also created losers, some of whom then resorted to violence."

While local-level ethnic violence has been concentrated in the east, electoral competition has sparked violence in a few other places. Among the most serious cases took place in Mai-Ndombe Province in western DRC in December 2018. Members of the Batende and Banunu ethnic communities had been in conflict over land, with limited violence taking place several times in the past, as far back as 1963. In the run-up to the 2018 elections, Batende attacked Banunu in several villages, killing several hundred, supposedly at the behest of two Batende candidates for parliament. The electoral commission delayed the vote for three months, but these two candidates ultimately won their seats and then subsequently faced charges for inciting the violence (Deutsche-Welle 2021).

These examples of local-level ethnic violence demonstrate the continuing relevance of Young's observation about the flexibility of identity. Contextual factors such as wars and elections have heightened ethnic identities. The salience of identities has risen and fallen and interacts closely with factors such as access to state resources. As wars and insurgencies have repeatedly swept across the east, alliances have shifted and been reconfigured; new militia groups have formed while others have disappeared, indicating a degree of fluidity that belies the idea of ethnicity as fixed and primordial. The idea of the importance of local context in explaining the nature of violence has been popularized in recent years by Stathis Kalyvas' (2006) work on civil wars and adapted to Congo by Autesserre (2010), though neither scholar acknowledges the resonance of this concept with Young's focus on instrumentalism.[4]

The Bakongo

While most ethnic conflicts in the DRC since 1985 have reinforced the flexible and contextual nature of identity, a few group identities and conflicts have proven more persistent. The Bakongo, the DRC's largest ethnic group, have been among the most persistent in retaining their identity, yet their experience demonstrates the continuing importance of context. The Bakongo are the descendants of the Kongo Kingdom, a large political community centered in what is today Angola and stretching into modern-day DRC and Republic of Congo. In the DRC, the Bakongo live primarily in the provinces of Kongo-Central, Kwilu, Kwango, and Kinshasa. Young writes extensively about political mobilization by the Bakongo in both *Politics in the Congo* and *The Politics of Cultural Pluralism*. The Bakongo were the first to face colonial intervention, first by the Portuguese in the 1500s, then, in the 1880s, by Belgians as Henry Morton Stanley forced compulsory labor to build a railroad from the coast to the interior. Not surprisingly, they were also among the first to mount forms of resistance, including the Kimbanguist religious movement in the 1920s and riots in the 1940s.

Young argues that urban centers serve to highlight ethnic identities as members of various groups encounter one another. As the capital, called Leopoldville in the colonial era, developed, it was populated largely by Bakongo migrants from downriver and migrants from upriver who came to be known as the Bangala. The interaction of the two groups pushed Bakongo elite to organize themselves, with ABAKO founded in 1950 in Kinshasa. Several of the cities where Bakongo live—especially Matadi and Boma—remain overwhelmingly Bakongo even today, along with a small number of migrants from other parts of the country, but in the cities of Kikwit and Bandundu, much of the population came to speak Kikongo as a lingua franca during the colonial era, even though most had not identified historically as Bakongo. ABAKO sought to mobilize all Kikongo speakers, and ties to the historic Kongo Kingdom, which had broken apart by the time the Belgians arrived, provided a mythic framework for Bakongo identity (Young 1965, 1976).

Although President Kasavubu rose to prominence as the leader of ABAKO, Young noted that after Mobutu took power, Bakongo identities seemed less pronounced. ABAKO was banned, and Mobutu's policies of simultaneously

incorporating ethnic groups and suppressing ethnic mobilization helped reduce the salience of Bakongo identity. As Young (1976, 186) writes, "In the late
1950s, Kongo identity seemed on the verge of acquiring an institutionalized
ideology; a decade later, the trend toward affirmative identity seemed arrested." The institution of elections in 2006 led to only a moderate remobiliza-
tion of Bakongo identity. In the first round of the 2006 presidential election,
Antoine Gizenga, a native of Kwilu and a Kikongo speaker, won overwhelmingly in Bandundu Province (which then included Kwilu and Kwango), while
Jean-Pierre Bemba, from far northern DRC, won Kongo-Central. In the second round of voting, both regions voted for Bemba over the ultimate victor,
Joseph Kabila.[5] When the provincial legislature named a supporter of President Kabila as governor of Kongo-Central (then called Bas-Congo), in January
2007, violent clashes between Bemba supporters and government troops led to
several dozen deaths, but this violence had little to do with ethnicity, as the man
named governor was himself Mukongo (Bavier 2007).

My own research among Kikongo speakers reinforces Young's observation
about the contextual nature of identity. When I conducted interviews in Boma
and Matadi a year after the 2006 election, many people I spoke with complained about the imposition of "outsiders" in the provincial administration
and other state offices. Many also complained that Kongo-Central, because of
its ports and the petroleum industry, was a major source of state revenues but
that they got little back from the state and instead were subsidizing other parts
of the country, which contributed to a sense that the local population was being
exploited (field notes, Bas-Congo, December 6–9, 2007). In Bandundu, in contrast, no one spoke about "outsiders" or expressed concern about his or her region being exploited. As in Kongo-Central, in Bandundu, Kikongo is the main
language, and many people identify as Bakongo. Yet ethnically and regionally
based tensions were much less pronounced, perhaps because of a context of
ethnic diversity and the relative economic neglect of Bandundu (field notes,
Bandundu and Kongo-Central [then Bas-Congo], December 1–8, 2007).

The Luba-Kasai

The experience of the Luba-Kasai presents two divergent cases, one that seems
to affirm Young's instrumentalist approach and another that challenges it.
Young provides considerable detail about ethnic conflicts in the southern provinces of Katanga and Kasai in the years around independence. Although the
descendants of the Luba Kingdom spread out through much of these provinces and the use of the Tshiluba language was widespread, divergent ethnic

identities emerged as two distinct Tshiluba-speaking groups emerged in Kasai. In the late precolonial period, Lulua in the north participated in slave raiding, while Luba-Kasai in the south became targets of those raids, weakening their community. The vulnerability of the Luba made them more receptive to early Christian missionary efforts, while many also migrated to Katanga in the colonial era, seeking employment in the mineral sector. As a result of both factors, as the colonial state developed, the Luba-Kasai were better positioned to take on administrative posts and otherwise prosper in the new economy. This turned the tables on the Lulua, who organized an effective ethnic association in 1952 that articulated grievances against the Luba, whom they portrayed as privileged and exploiting them (dia Mwembu 1999). In October 1959, Lulua attacked Luba living in the city of Kananga, killing hundreds, and over the next year, nearly one million Luba fled into South Kasai (Young 1965, 263–72). As Young (1976, 187) argues, while there had initially been an attempt to create a pan-Luba identity, "a territorialization of ethnic self-concept came only under the cultural shock of the enforced exodus."

Despite the seriousness of the 1959 wave of anti-Luba-Kasai violence in Kananga, "it never had a successor event," as Young noted in 2002 (554). In Kasai, the differences between the Luba and the Lulua largely disappeared over time. All parts of Kasai supported Etienne Tshisekedi's candidacy for the presidency in 2011 and Felix Tshisekedi's candidacy in 2018. In 2016, interference by the Kabila government in the naming of a Lulua clan leader known as Kamwina Nsapu led him to organize a short-lived uprising. The Kamwina Nsapu militia brought together both Lulua and Luba-Kasai, who fought government troops and targeted non-Luba civilians, including Chokwe and Pende (Africa Research Bulletin 2017; International Federation for Human Rights [FIDH] 2017).[6] When I visited Mbuji-Mayi in 2020, I found that the Luba-Kasai took pride in having one of their own, Tshisekedi, as president, but they were disappointed that he had not yet turned around their dire economic circumstances. The approach that people took was not the ethnic antagonism I encountered in Katanga (discussed later) but rather the sort of patrimonial expectations familiar to the Mobutu era (field notes, Mbuji-Mayi, March 2020).

In contrast, anti-Luba-Kasai sentiments in Katanga have been much more persistent. In the region known as the Copper Belt, which includes the cities of Lubumbashi, Likasi, and Kolwezi, Tshiluba is widely spoken, but Kiswahili is more common. Many Luba-Kasai migrated to the area for economic opportunity during the colonial era, both working in the mines and engaging in trade and other economic activities, coming to dominate much of the economic life in Katanga's urban centers. In 1960, Belgian expatriates in Katanga, seeking to maintain control of the region's rich mining economy, pushed local leaders to declare independence just days after the DRC itself gained independence. While the primary motivation for secession was economic, the local populations, often known as Luba-Katanga, expelled thousands of Luba-Kasai (Gérard-Libois 1966; dia Mwembu 1999).

The Katanga secession had a lasting impact on identity in the region. In 1977 and 1978, former Katangese soldiers who had been living in Angola since the 1960s launched attacks on Katanga that required foreign intervention to contain (Young and Turner 1985, 255–58; Kennes and Larmer 2016), and the idea of Katangese independence has never been fully put to rest. In fieldwork in 2011 and 2012, Sandrine Vinckel (2015) heard many Katangese speak favorably about the idea of secession as a way of protecting their interests against supposed exploitation by other Congolese. The Bakata Katanga militia group, with roots in the earlier Katanga secession efforts, has continued to push for independence. During my fieldwork in Katanga in 2020, local people claimed that Bakata Katanga received support from high officials in the armed forces with close ties to former President Kabila (interviews in Lubumbashi and Likasi, February and March 2020).

Anti-Luba-Kasai rhetoric has been a tool that leaders both inside and outside Katanga have used to build political power. In the face of secessionist sentiments and his own declining popularity, Mobutu sought to appeal to the Luba-Katanga by scapegoating the Luba-Kasai. From the early 1980s, Etienne Tshisekedi, a native of Kasai, was an outspoken opponent of Mobutu and was the recognized leader of the democracy movement in the 1990s. Mobutu appointed Nguza Karl-i-Bond as prime minister in 1991 in a move to undercut Tshisekedi's appeal. Both Nguza and the governor of Katanga stoked anti-Luba-Kasai sentiments in Katanga that led to a series of ethnic attacks from 1991 to 1996 that drove thousands of Luba-Kasai out of jobs in the mining industry and civil service, killed as many as five thousand, and pushed thousands more to flee to Kasai for safety (dia Mwembu 1999; Vinckel 2015).

ADFL leader Laurent Kabila was a native of the Kiswahili-speaking areas of western Katanga. When he became president, Kabila ignored established democratic leaders like Tshisekedi and instead named to office many people from Katanga, a group that came to be known as the "Katanga Mafia," while Tshisekedi emerged as one of Kabila's most outspoken critics. When Joseph Kabila succeeded his father, in 2001, he continued a policy of punishing Kasai for its opposition to his government, excluding the province from government investment and plunging it into poverty (International Crisis Group 2006). Elections in 2006, 2011, and 2018 reignited anti-Luba-Kasai tensions in

Katanga (International Crisis Group 2006; Vinckel 2015). In 2018, unable to run for another term and failing to garner enough support for his hand-picked candidate, President Joseph Kabila manipulated the election results to name Etienne Tshisekedi's son, Felix, as president, hoping that Tshisekedi would prove a mere figurehead, with Kabila retaining real power behind the scenes by naming a parliament dominated with his supporters and using his personal wealth to buy support (Englebert 2019). In Haut-Katanga, the province that includes Lubumbashi and Likasi, Kabila arranged for a close personal ally to become governor after Tshisekedi's selection, despite popular objections.[7] Like the governor in the 1990s, the governor who took office in 2019 stoked anti-Luba-Kasai sentiments. In the recent iteration of ethnic scapegoating, Luba-Katanga elites have accused the Kasaians, most of whom have fled the poverty in their home region seeking opportunity in the Copper Belt, of bringing crime and insecurity to Katanga, while also stealing jobs from the Luba-Kat. In my 2020 visit to Lubumbashi and Likasi, I was startled by the degree to which even human rights activists and other ostensibly progressive Katangese bought into the idea that the Kasaian migrants were a major social problem. The language used by Luba-Kat to discuss the Kasaians (which I discuss further later) was explicitly racial, treating the Kasaians as fundamentally different from locals and more problematic. The contrast was sharp between the Luba-Kat's view of Luba-Kasai as inherent outsiders and the Luba-Kasai's self-perception of Kasai as simply one of a range of Congolese groups (field notes, Lubumbashi and Likasi, February 29–March 4, 2020).

Banyamulenge and Other Tutsi Groups

The most intense recent ethnic conflicts in the DRC have involved speakers of the Rwandan language, Kinyarwanda, particularly members of the Tutsi group. Kinyarwanda is a Bantu language spoken today throughout Rwanda and in parts of the DRC and Uganda (Nassenstein 2019). Populations speaking Kinyarwanda emerged in the Congo in a variety of ways. The borders of the Kingdom of Rwanda fluctuated in the precolonial period, and the borders drawn by the colonial powers did not coincide exactly with the boundaries of the Kinyarwanda linguistic area, leaving a native Kinyarwanda-speaking population within the DRC (Vansina 2004).

Immigration was also a major source of Kinyarwanda speakers in the DRC. The Banyamulenge, literally the people of the Mulenge hills, are a Kinyarwanda-speaking group that has been in the DRC since prior to colonial conquest. The exact date when the Banyamulenge migrated from Rwanda remains in contention, but "there is agreement [among scholars] that a large group of Tutsi pastoralists had put down roots in South Kivu by the end of the 19th century" (Vlassenroot 2002, 502). After Belgium took control of Rwanda in World War I, it established a policy to encourage migration from Rwanda to lightly populated parts of North Kivu to provide labor on plantations (Tegera 1995). Anti-Tutsi violence in Rwanda from 1959 to 1965 and again in 1973 drove thousands of additional Rwandans to flee into the DRC, the largest portion settling in North Kivu, though some settled in other parts of the country, including South Kivu (Turner 2013, 100–103).

Because of these factors, by the early 1990s Rwandaphones made up about half of the population of North Kivu, including both Hutu (who had been the main participants in the colonial migration program) and Tutsi (some of whom had migrated in the colonial era seeking grazing land but most of whom fled ethnic violence in Rwanda around independence). Congolese generally considered the two groups a single Banyarwanda community, with Tutsi associated with pastoralism and Hutu with farming. Colonial administrative and land control policies disadvantaged the Banyarwanda, as Hunde, Nyanga, and other groups with claims to autochthony were given chieftaincies and control over the land despite constituting a much smaller portion of the population. After Mobutu took power, he revived these colonial policies that preserved political power for "original inhabitants." At the same time, Rwandans constituted a large portion of the economic elite of North Kivu, since some of the Tutsi who fled Rwanda were from wealthy families, including chiefs and other royals (Turner 2013).

The divide between Banyarwanda economic and demographic importance and the political power of other groups became a source of tension in the context of political competition. In the early 1990s, groups in North and South Kivu pushed to exclude Banyarwanda and Banyamulenge from representation in the Sovereign National Conference, claiming that they were Rwandan rather than Congolese, while local officials sought to exclude Rwandaphone populations from voting in potential future elections by refusing to register them as Congolese citizens. The fact that some Banyarwanda arrived in the DRC after independence was used to justify the exclusion of all Rwandans, including those like some Banyarwanda around Goma who had no roots in Rwanda or Banyamulenge who had been in the DRC for more than a century. After the governor of North Kivu pledged in March 1993 that government forces would back Hunde and Nyanga efforts to "exterminate" Banyarwanda, local militia in Masisi and Walikale attacked Banyarwanda, killing from seven thousand to forty thousand and displacing more than a quarter million (UNHCR 1996).

The 1993 attacks targeted both Hutu and Tutsi, but the 1994 genocide against the Tutsi in Rwanda transformed the understandings of the Rwandaphone population, creating a sharp divide between Hutu and Tutsi in Congo.[8] As the largely Tutsi rebel group the Rwandan Patriotic Front (RPF) took control of Rwanda in July 1994, the Hutu army and militias that had carried out the genocide fled into the DRC, mixing in with a million Hutu refugees. The genocide was justified through an ideology that treated Tutsi as a non-Bantu racial group that had conquered Rwanda a few centuries earlier and had exploited the Bantu ever since, an idea developed during the colonial era that had continued to shape Rwandan self-understandings (Mamdani 2001). After the RPF came to power, many of the Tutsi who had been living in the DRC for decades returned to Rwanda, while Hutu from Rwanda integrated with Congolese Hutu and spread their ideology that regarded the Tutsi as a separate racial group. The consciousness of a distinction between Hutu and Tutsi spread to other Congolese groups, which increasingly targeted Tutsi.

Interethnic skirmishes involving Rwandan Hutu militias took place in North Kivu as early as July 1994 but became more systematic in late 1995 and early 1996. On the basis of April 1996 interviews with Tutsi refugees from the DRC, I wrote in a human rights report at the time that, "Because of the fighting, communities in Masisi and Rutshuru that formerly enjoyed ethnic diversity have become increasingly monoethnic as the dominant ethnic group in each community forces others to flee. Villages in the area are increasingly identified as 'Hutu' or 'Hunde' or 'Nande.' As such, they become the targets of the militia from rival groups" (Longman 1996). Meanwhile, militia from all groups targeted Tutsi, including Tutsi with historic Congolese roots. As one woman from Rutshuru told me, "Before the arrival of the Interahamwe, there were no problems for Tutsi in our area. After the Interahamwe came, problems started with the Bahunde. The Bahunde said, 'What are you doing still here when others are returning to their country?'" (Longman 1996).

The September 1996 ADFL incursion into the DRC, organized and backed by Rwanda and Uganda, was justified as a response to both the presence of armed groups in refugee camps just across the Rwandan border and attacks on Tutsi in Congo, which they characterized as a continuation of the genocide. The invasion started a process that solidified the sharp social exclusion of Congolese Tutsi. While headed by an ethnic Luba-Kat (Kabila), Banyamulenge served as the core of ADFL forces, and both Banyamulenge and Congolese Tutsi were the core fighters in the RCD that launched the Second Congo War as well (Turner 2007; Reyntjens 2009). Since the conclusion of that war, Banyamulenge and Banyarwanda have regularly supported uprisings, like the

CNDP and M-23, demanding greater social inclusion, yet because these uprisings have been supported by Rwanda, they have served to further alienate the Tutsi from other Congolese (Verweijen and Vlassenroot 2015; Verweijen 2016). One Banyamulenge leader explained to me in 2012 the untenable situation their community was caught in. As he told me, "If the Rwandans leave, we will be slaughtered. But as long as we're associated with the Rwandans, we'll never be accepted as Congolese" (interview in Kigali, August 10, 2012). As I discuss later, however, increasingly, the targeting of Congolese Tutsi arises not simply from their association with Rwanda but also because they are identified in racial terms that separate them from other Congolese groups.

Hema

Conflict has persisted in the Ituri district in northeastern DRC for two decades between the Hema and the Lendu peoples. Throughout a large section of the Great Lakes Region of Central Africa, an important social division exists in a number of groups between populations identified as pastoralists and others identified as farmers. Among some groups, such as the Bahaya in Tanzania and the Banyoro and Banyankole in Uganda, this remains a social division within a single ethnic group, while in Rwanda and Burundi, the division is treated as an ethnic division itself. In nearly all these groups, the pastoralists have been politically dominant. In Ituri, this distinction appears to have emerged through the migration of pastoralists from Uganda over several centuries into a region occupied by Lendu and Nande farmers. The pastoralist group known as Hema maintained the Kinyoro language in some areas but adopted Kilendu elsewhere. Treated as intellectually superior by colonial administrators and missionaries, Hema managed to gain both political and economic power, and under the Mobutu regime they not only gained political power but also came to control much of the land in parts of Ituri, taking over plantations set up in colonial times. Conflicts over land arose periodically in the Mobutu era but were suppressed (International Crisis Group 2003).

The Second Congo War heightened the Hema–Lendu conflict, as the central state lost control over the region, and conflicts over land ignited. As Johan Pottier explores, colonial concepts of Hema superiority and Lendu savagery have continued to shape the conflict. Although violence has taken place on both sides, with Hema and Lendu armed groups attacking one another and targeting civilians, the conflict is widely portrayed exclusively as savage Lendu committing genocide against the Hema. Uganda, which controlled the region throughout the Second Congo War, strongly favored the Hema, presumably because Ugandan president Yoweri Museveni is himself a Hima Munyankole (Pottier 2010). Violence between the Hema and the Lendu was at a peak from 1999 to 2003 and then broke out again in 2017 and has persisted since (International Crisis Group 2020).

Mbuti, Twa, and Other Pygmy Groups

Although the term "pygmy" is now generally considered a pejorative term, it is still widely used to describe several groups identified as short in stature and considered the original inhabitants of Central Africa prior to the Bantu migrations. Two main groups are found in the DRC: the Mbuti, who live mostly in the rainforests of the far northeast, and the Twa (also known as Cwa), who live in parts of the Kivus, Orientale, Katanga, and Equateur. These groups were long characterized as primitive and backward peoples and have faced regular prejudice and social exclusion. Colonial-era racial hierarchies regarded the Mbuti and the Twa as the least evolved racial groups in Central Africa, with the lowest intelligence and least capacity, and they were excluded from education and employment opportunities (Duffy 1984). Colonial policies denied Mbuti and Twa groups their own chiefs in the system of indirect rule and the control of land that would entail, making them dependent on other groups, which "barely tolerated them and used them as cheap labor for agricultural chores" (Autesserre 2010, 146–47).

While today many ecologists, anthropologists, and others regard these groups romantically as simple people living in harmony with nature (Turnbull 1961), general Congolese public opinion continues to view the Mbuti and the Twa as backward, savage, and dirty people.[9] They live largely in isolated rural communities with little access to social services. According to a Minority Rights (2004) report, "Discrimination by other ethnic groups is ingrained, and the Bambuti are often stereotyped as beggars and thieves. Despite the visible poverty and marginalization of the Bambuti, DRC authorities have denied that they suffer discrimination." The pygmy groups have been targeted in the ongoing conflicts in the eastern DRC, particularly as they live in areas with valuable resources that rebel groups and business interests hope to exploit. Official policy has also marginalized the Mbuti and the Twa, expelling them from their homes inside national parks in the name of conservation. In the best-documented case, the government expelled Twa when making Kahuzi-Biega National Park in North Kivu to create a preserve for lowland gorillas. The Twa lived around the margins of the park, denied legal access to the hunting and gathering from the forest that had historically sustained them. Although a change in policy in 2018 officially allowed their return, soldiers and park guards have attacked villages and killed Twa community members (Rugiriza and Sengenya 2021; Flummerfelt 2022).

Race as a Confounding Factor

As this review of the DRC demonstrates, Crawford Young's analysis of the contextual and flexible nature of identity has remained useful for explaining the role of ethnic politics in the country. Shifting contexts created by armed conflict, economic competition, elections, and official policies have heightened or diminished the salience of various ethnic identities. While group boundaries have not proven as flexible as Young's original characterization might have suggested, the significance of various identities has waxed and waned, and alliances between groups have shifted precipitously over time. Yet the cases of the Luba-Kasai, Tutsi, Hema, Mbuti, and Twa indicate that some identities seem more fixed than others and have remained more consistent targets for violence. In *The Rising Tide of Cultural Pluralism*, Young himself noted that his instrumentalist approach failed to account sufficiently for the "affective tie" of communitarian identities that can make identity-based conflict so volatile (1992, 3–35).

While Young claimed that primordial and constructivist approaches complemented his instrumentalist approach by explaining the durability of some ethnic animosities in the DRC, I contend that an alternative factor helps to explain, at least in part, why some groups have been targeted more consistently than others: race. While Young discusses race in *The Politics of Cultural Pluralism*, he limits his analysis to the conventional Western divides, such as the division between whites and blacks in South Africa. Yet I would contend that racist ideas have had a much wider impact on identity than Young's work acknowledges. As Young discusses, colonial administrators and Christian missionaries categorized populations to make them legible, but they did so according to then-popular ideas about race shaped by concepts of social Darwinism. The Europeans categorized the vast majority of Congolese groups as sharing a common heritage as Bantu, while a few groups were characterized as non-Bantu. This categorization was regarded as not merely linguistic but racial, as a fundamental biological difference. While ethnicity refers to cultural traditions among an imagined extended family grouping that shares a common history, race refers to physical differences that also manifest themselves in behavioral differences, such as laziness or cunning.[10] Turner notes that the accounts of Congolese culture based on missionary writings and taught in schools well after independence emphasized that Congolese groups were distinguished not just by their languages but also by their physical appearance and their ways of life: "from there to the identification of the Congo as a 'Bantu' country, where Sudanese and Nilotics are outsiders, is a short step" (2013, 76).

The lasting effects of this racist thinking are seen most obviously in ongoing attitudes toward the Twa and the Mbuti. Labeled as Pygmy by Europeans, these groups were regarded as the original inhabitants of the area and considered the least evolved and, therefore, least civilized peoples. Ironically, even missionaries who rejected the theory of evolution nevertheless adopted the idea of a racial hierarchy from social Darwinism. The racist stereotypes of Pygmies as backward, lazy, dirty, and dishonest have persisted into the present. Autesserre reports that one of the Bantu Congolese she interviewed said that Mbuti were "somewhere between animals and men" (2010, 147).

Racist thinking has increasingly shaped attitudes toward other excluded groups. In an exploration of the rhetoric that drove the anti-Kasaian violence of the early 1990s, Dibwe dia Mwembu (1999) finds that leaders evoked a history of exploitation. But they also used language that treated Kasaians as a racial other, calling them "liars, deceitful, wicked, superstitious, despicable, egotistical, cheats, hegemons, traitors, cobalt thieves, saboteurs of the Katangese economy, and the accomplices, or even better, the authors of the underdevelopment of the province" (492). The attitudes that people expressed in my interviews suggested that the Kasaians were fundamentally different from the Katangese in ways that were not simply cultural. People I interviewed in Katanga in 2020 attributed many of the problems in the region to immigrants from Kasai and used derogatory terms to talk about them, describing them as dirty, criminal, untrustworthy, and troublesome (field notes, Lubumbashi and Likasi, February 29–March 4, 2020).

The role of racism in antipathy for Tutsi in the DRC is more complex, as Rwanda's repeated incursions into the country have played the central role in inspiring anti-Tutsi sentiment. At one level, anti-Tutsi attitudes are clearly driven by nationalism and the anger at Rwanda's meddling inside the DRC. Yet racial stereotypes have also reinforced the identification of Tutsi as outsiders who do not belong in the DRC. Few Congolese made a sharp distinction between Hutu and Tutsi until the Hutu militia who had organized the genocide in Rwanda began to target Tutsi in the DRC in 1994, and local Congolese ethnic militia soon followed suit. When the RPF invaded in 1996, Congolese leaders warned of Rwandan expansionism, which they attributed to the racial characteristics of Tutsi. As Lars-Christopher Huening explains, "with the start of what was later termed the first Congo war, identities crystallised around racist stereotypes of belligerent, powerful, devious and conspiratorial Tutsi" (2013, 27).

Organizers of the 1994 genocide in Rwanda promulgated an ideology that portrayed Tutsi as an outside Nilotic group that sought to dominate Bantu peoples such as the Hutu because of their very nature. This anti-Tutsi ideology was imported into the DRC after 1994 and interacted with Congolese ideas about Rwandan expansionism (Prunier 1997; Longman 1999). A 2008 study of violent rhetoric in the Great Lakes Region noted that "Rwanda is always identified as a potential, current and permanent aggressor of the Greater Congo. According to rumours, Tutsis worldwide are networking, like the Jews under Zionism, to expand Rwandan borders and build a Hima/Tutsi empire in the Great Lakes Region" (Mugangu et al. 2008, 21). In denouncing Rwandan incursions into the DRC, leaders have characterized the Tutsi as a threat, using racist language. During the Second Congo War, Kabila's foreign minister called for the Congolese to exterminate the Tutsi "vermin" (Ndahinda and Mugabe 2022, 7). A recent analysis of social media found that Congolese on YouTube, Twitter, and elsewhere claim that Tutsi are manipulative, deceitful, greedy, power hungry, and violent. One YouTube video claimed, "Tutsi is synonymous with 'killer'" (Ndahinda and Mugabe 2022, 19). These sorts of racist characterizations are coupled with claims that no Rwandaphones can make a legitimate claim to Congolese citizenship and that all should be sent "back to Rwanda."

The Hema have suffered in part by comparison to the Tutsi, another group regarded as a racially superior outsider group that exploited local populations. Although the Toro are themselves a Bantu group, the Hema—who are believed to have immigrated from Butoro—have come to be regarded as Nilotic, in part because many speak the Nilotic language Kilendu. Ironically, this allows the Lendu, a Nilotic group, to claim legitimate membership in Congolese society while excluding the Hema. The association of the Hema with Uganda reinforces their outsider status, while their economic dominance is used to reinforce ideas about their racial superiority. Hema are treated as part of the supposed Tutsi–Hima project to conquer the entire region.

In sum, while identity remains largely contextual and flexible in the DRC, much as Crawford Young first noted nearly sixty years ago, the racialization of some identities impedes that flexibility. I am not suggesting that racism alone explains persistent social exclusion, but when it interacts with and reinforces other factors, such as conflicts over land, economic inequality, and nationalism, racial prejudice is a powerful wedge between groups. While ethnicity is the idea of a common history, race rests on the idea of biological difference. The more groups are identified not simply as different ethnicities but as different races, the more they are viewed as irreconcilably separate. In the DRC, Mbuti and Twa are regarded as intrinsically inferior, incapable, and unworthy of modern development in a context where they occupy desirable land and resources. Banyamulenge, Tutsi, and Hema are portrayed as not simply foreign occupiers in Congo but as racial others, fundamentally different from Congolese. This racist logic drove the genocide against the Tutsi in Rwanda in 1994, and it continues to drive harassment, discrimination, and violence against groups within the DRC today.

Notes

This chapter's second epigraph is from a conversation with human rights activists at a regional human rights conference sponsored by Human Rights Watch, Mbarara, Uganda, 1995. All translations from French by the author.

1. The Mbale were one of the more local groups in Idiofa, while the Pende were from another part of Kwilu Province, near the city of Kikwit. As Young (1976) points out, they were not historic enemies, but growing struggles over political power and resources heightened tensions between the groups after independence.

2. Horowitz (2000) has argued that the particular ethnic constitution of a country has a profound impact on the occurrence of conflict, with a limited number of groups or a large group fostering conflict and a proliferation of groups discouraging conflicts.

3. The term "Mai-Mai" is drawn from the Swahili word for water, based on the belief that, through purity and ritual practice, the fighters could turn bullets into raindrops. At the beginning of the conflict, the term was used by a few specific groups, but during the course of the war it became the general term to refer to all the non-Kinyarwanda-speaking ethnic militia groups. See also my report on the beginning of the first war (Longman and Des Forges 1997).

4. Autesserre (2010) references Young but not his works on identity. Kalyvas (2006) does not reference Young at all.

5. In a 2015 administrative reorganization, the province of Bandundu was split into three provinces: Kwilu, Kwango, and Mai-Ndombe. The name of the province, previously known as Bas-Congo, was changed to Kongo-Central.

6. Although this conflict was relatively small and short-lived, it gained considerable international attention because it led to the death of two UN experts in March 2017.

7. In the 2015 administrative reorganization, Katanga was divided into five new provinces.

8. The best source on the genocide in Rwanda is Alison Des Forges (1999), for which I served as a researcher and contributing author.

9. Colin Turnbull wrote several books on the Mbuti, including famously the *Forest People* (1961), that popularized the image of the Mbuti as simple and respectful people. See also Ahmed (2004), Peterson (2000), and Duffy (1984).

10. The literature on the conceptualization of race and its impact on society is vast, going back to works like Eric Voegelin's (1997) *Race and State*, originally published in 1933, and continuing in important recent works like Marx (1998) and Kendi (2017). Key ideas in much of this work are the degree to which race, in many contexts, is viewed as inflexible and the ways in which it is believed to shape individual character.

References

African Research Bulletin. 2017. "DRCongo: Kasai Violence." *African Research Bulletin.* May 12. https://doi-org.ezproxy.bu.edu/10.1111/j.1467-825X.2017.07627.x.

Ahmed, Syed Z. 2004. *Bambuti: The Mysterious Inhabitants of the Rain Forest.* Conshohocken, PA: Infinity.

Anderson, Benedict. 1983. *Imagined Communities: Reflections on the Origins and Spread of Nationalism.* New York: Verso.

Autesserre, Séverine. 2010. *The Trouble with the Congo: Local Violence and the Failure of International Peacebuilding.* New York: Cambridge University Press.

Bavier, Joe. 2007. "At Least 37 Killed in West Congo Violence." Reuters, February 1.

Des Forges, Alison. 1999. *Leave None to Tell the Story: Genocide in Rwanda.* New York: Human Rights Watch.

Deutsche-Welle. 2021. "Hope for Justice in the Democratic Republic of Congo 2018 Yumbi Massacre." December 17. https://www.dw.com/en/hope-for-justice-in-the-democratic-republic-of-congo-2018-yumbi-massacre-tribunal/a-60149024.

Dia Mwembu, Dibwe. 1999. "L'épuration ethnique au Katanga et léthique du redressment des torts passé." *Canadian Journal of African Studies* 33 (2/3): 483–99.

Duffy, Kevin. 1984. *Children of the Forest.* New York: Dodd, Mead.

Emizet, Kisangani N. 1999. "Political Cleavages in a Democratising Society: The Case of the Congo (Formerly Zaire)." *Comparative Political Studies* 32 (2): 185–228.

Englebert, Pierre. 2019. "Aspirations and Realities in Africa: The DRC's Electoral Sideshow." *Journal of Democracy* 30 (3): 124–38.

Flummerfelt, Robert. 2022. "To Purge the Forest by Force: Organized Violence against Batwa in Kahuzi-Biega National Park." April. London: Minority Rights.

Gérard-Libois, Jules. 1966. *Katanga Secession.* Madison: University of Wisconsin Press.

Horowitz, Donald L. 2000. *Ethnic Groups in Conflict.* Berkeley: University of California Press.

Huening, Lars-Christopher. 2013. "Making Use of the Past: The Rwandophone Question and the 'Balkanisation of the Congo.'" *Review of African Political Economy* 40 (135): 13–31.

International Crisis Group. 2003. "Congo Crisis: Military Intervention in Ituri." June 13. Brussels: ICG.

International Crisis Group. 2006. "Katanga: Congo's Forgotten Crisis." *Africa Report*, no. 103, January. Brussels: ICG.

International Crisis Group. 2020. "DRCongo: Ending the Cycle of Violence in Ituri."
    Brussels: ICG.
International Federation for Human Rights (FIDH). 2017. *Massacres au Kasaï*. Paris:
    FIDH.
Kalyvas, Stathis N. 2006. *The Logic of Violence in Civil War*. Cambridge: Cambridge Uni-
    versity Press.
Kendi, Ibram X. 2017. *Stamped from the Beginning: The Definitive History of Racist Ideas in
    America*. New York: Bold Type Books.
Kennes, Erik, and Miles Larmer. 2016. *The Katangese Gendarmes and War in Central Africa:
    Fighting Their Way Home*. Bloomington: Indiana University Press.
Longman, Timothy. 1996. "Forced to Flee: Violence against Tutsi in Zaire." New York:
    Human Rights Watch; Paris: FIDH.
Longman, Timothy. 1999. "Nation, Race, or Class: Defining the Hutu and Tutsi of East
    Africa." In *The Global Color Line: Racial and Ethnic Inequality and Struggle from a Global
    Perspective*, edited by Joseph Feagin and Pinar Batur-Vanderlippe, 103–30. Bradford,
    UK: JAI Press.
Longman, Timothy, and Alison Des Forges. (1997) 2017. "Attacked by All Sides: Civilians
    and the War in Eastern Zaire." New York: Human Rights Watch.
Mamdani, Mahmood. 2001. *When Victims Become Killers: Colonialism, Nativism, and the Geno-
    cide in Rwanda*. Princeton, NJ: Princeton University Press.
Marx, Anthony W. 1998. *Making Race and Nation: A Comparison of South Africa, the United
    States, and Brazil*. Cambridge Studies in Comparative Politics. New York: Cambridge
    University Press.
Minority Rights. 2004. "'Erasing the Board:' Report of the International Research Mis-
    sion into Crimes under International Law Committed against the Bambuti in the
    Eastern Democratic Republic of the Congo." London: Minority Rights.
Mugangu, Séverin, Paulin Bapolisi, Vincent Mukwege, Elly Habibu, and Augustin
    Chabwine. 2008. "Intercommunity Rumours, Stereotypes, and Suspicions in South
    Kivu." In *Words That Kill: Rumours, Prejudice, Stereotypes, and Myths amongst the Peoples of
    the Great Lakes Region of Africa*, 17–27. Nairobi: International Alert.
Nassenstein, Nico. 2019. "Kinyarwanda and Kirundi: On Colonial Divisions, Dis-
    courses of National Belonging, and Language Boundaries." *Modern Africa: Politics,
    History, Society* 7 (1): 11–40.
Ndahinda, Felix Mukwiza, and Aggée Shyaka Mugabe. 2022. "Streaming Hate: Explor-
    ing the Harm of Anti-Banyamulenge and Anti-Tutsi Hate Speech on Congolese
    Social Media." *Journal of Genocide Research*. https://doi.org/10.1080/14623528.2022
    .2078578.
Nzongola-Ntalaja, Georges. 2002. *The Congo, from Leopold to Kabila: A People's History*. Lon-
    don: Zed Books.
Peterson, Richard. 2000. *Conversations in the Rainforest: Culture, Values, and the Environment in
    Central Africa*. Boulder, CO: Westview Press.
Pottier, Johan. 2010. "Representations of Ethnicity in the Search for Peace: Ituri, Demo-
    cratic Republic of Congo." *African Affairs* 109 (434): 23–50.
Prunier, Gerard. 1997. *The Rwanda Crisis: History of a Genocide*. New York: Columbia Uni-
    versity Press.

Reyntjens, Filip. 2009. *The Great African War: Congo and Regional Geopolitics, 1996–2006.* Cambridge: Cambridge University Press.

Rugiriza, Ephraim, and Claude Sengenya. 2021. "DRC: Indigenous Twa Are Free but Still Landless." JusticeInfo.net, September 6. https://www.justiceinfo.net/en /81604-drc-indigenous-twa-freed-still-landless.html.

Stearns, Jason. 2022. *The War That Doesn't Say Its Name: The Unending Conflict in the Congo.* Princeton, NJ: Princeton University Press.

Tegera, Aloys. 1995. "La réconciliation communautaire: Le cas des massacres au Nord-Kivu." In *Les crises politiques au Burundi et au Rwanda (1993–1994)*, edited by Andre Guichaoua, 395–402. Université des Sciences et Technologies de Lille.

Turnbull, Colin. 1961. *The Forest People.* London: Chatto and Windus.

Turner, Thomas. 2007. *The Congo Wars: Conflict, Myth, and Reality.* London: Zed Books.

Turner, Thomas. 2013. *Congo.* Malden, MA: Polity Press.

UNHCR. 1996. "Repatriation of Rwandan Refugees from Eastern Zaire." March.

Vansina, Jan. 2004. *Antecedents to Modern Rwanda: The Nyiginya Kingdom.* Madison: University of Wisconsin Press.

Verweijen, Judith. 2016. "Stable Instability: Political Settlements and Armed Groups in the Congo." Nairobi: Rift Valley Institute.

Verweijen, Judith, and Koen Vlassenroot. 2015. "Armed Mobilisation and the Nexus of Territory, Identity, and Authority: The Contested Territorial Aspirations Banyamulenge in Eastern Congo." *Journal of Contemporary African Studies* 33 (2): 199–212.

Vinckel, Sandrine. 2015. "Violence and Everyday Interactions between Katangese and Kasaians: Memory and Elections in Two Katanga Cities." *Africa* 85 (1): 78–102.

Vlassenroot, Koen. 2002. "Citizenship, Identity Formation and Conflict in South Kivu: The Case of the Banyamulenge." *Review of African Political Economy* 29 (93): 499–516.

Voegelin, Eric. 1997. *Race and State.* Vol. 2 of *The Collected Works of Eric Voegelin.* Edited by Klaus Vondung. Columbia: University of Missouri Press. Originally published as Eric Voegelin, *Rasse Und Staat* (Tübingen: Mohr, 1933).

Young, Crawford. 1965. *Politics in the Congo: Decolonization and Independence.* Princeton, NJ: Princeton University Press.

Young, Crawford. 1976. *The Politics of Cultural Pluralism.* Madison: University of Wisconsin Press.

Young, Crawford, ed. 1992. *The Rising Tide of Cultural Pluralism: The Nation-State at Bay?* Madison: University of Wisconsin Press.

Young, Crawford. 2002. "Deciphering Disorder in Africa: Is Ethnicity the Key?" *World Politics* 54:532–57.

Young, Crawford, and Thomas Turner. 1985. *The Rise and Decline of the Zairian State.* Madison: University of Wisconsin Press.

7

Ethnicity, Interests, and Class in Tanzania

Constructing Explanations

Joel Samoff

Identities matter. Sometimes. But which identities? In what circumstances?

For Africa, over many years, cultural identities have been offered as an explanation. For the 2022 Kenya election: "ethnicity has shaped Kenyan politics for decades, leading to rampant corruption and disenfranchisement, and sometimes, around elections, full blown violence" (Dahir 2022; also Lynch 2014; Egbejule 2022).

Yet, offering cultural identity as an explanation poses two immediate problems. First, identities can be neither simply observed nor assumed but rather are complex constructions and relationships and negotiated understandings that require analytic unpacking. And second, where ethnicity matters, its salience cannot be explained by ethnicity.

My concern here is to explore three proffered explanations for political behavior in contemporary Africa, beginning with *ethnicity*, followed by *interests* and *class*. My approach to exploring these perspectives is to start at the bottom.

170

How can the ordinary events of local communities help us understand ethnicity, interests, and class as explanations for political behavior? The impetus for this analysis is the continuing quick reach to ethnicity to explain Africans' and Africa's behavior. Both everyday discussions and academic research regularly assume and then insist that ethnic identity has deep roots and a long history and that, most often, ethnic identity prevails over other motivations for behavior.[1] To address the pervasiveness, the content, and the consequences of that asserted essential link between Africa and ethnicity, I shall begin with attention to local experiences in Tanzania.

The most visible threads of political analysis have changed with the times. In the early European writing on Africa, the widespread assumption was that it was culture that mattered, especially race.[2] The historic framing is clear. Europeans differentiated between the civilized and the barbarians, us and them, both creating a self-reassuring self-identification (not the Other) and a justification for intrusion and exploitation. Subsequently, decolonization reinforced that framing, generating notions of development and modernization, which provided the theoretical underpinnings for interpreting human progress as more or less linear, characterized by a fundamental distinction between the more and the less modern.[3] Scholars refined the distinction between barbarian and civilized into traditional and modern. By clothing the traditional-versus-modern distinction in scientific language and credibility, social science provided a foundation for the notions that backward is a property of Africa—that is, a cause, not an effect; a condition, not a process—and that the humane task of colonialism and postcolonial tutelage was to overcome that backwardness. A moral rationale for immoral practices. Cultural divisions were assumed to be basic, installed at birth, and reinforced by patterns of social organization. Race, deemed primordial, justified racism, the association of particular behaviors with sets of people defined by their racial identity. Those associations persist.

As its scholarship developed, modernization was increasingly presented as postracial. That claim was embedded in Parsons's pattern variables; for example, status and privilege could be secured by ascription (traditional) or achievement (modern). The process of modernization, it was widely assumed, would modify the nature of interactions within Africa. Groupings based on association would succeed those based on birth.

That transition need not be smooth. Tribes might appear in modern guise as ethnic associations. There might be conflict between the traditionalists and the modernizers, perhaps as the latter used ethnic associations to generate capital for new businesses. And even as the pluralism of interest groups displaced the pluralism of tribes, the older patterns would persist. Personnel officers and landlords might show ethnic favoritism. Ethnic ties might remain important in forming companies, unions, and football teams. Appeals to ethnic solidarity ("tribalism") might occasionally disrupt coalition building among interest groups. The transition might be halting and spasmodic, with temporary reverses. But the process was inexorable: just as industry would replace agriculture, cultural ties would recede in importance as associational groupings were constructed, as individual replaced collective orientation, and as achievement and universal replaced ascriptive and particularistic norms. The modernization perspective thus expected the explanatory role of cultural pluralism to be displaced by interest-group pluralism.

Another challenge to the primacy of race emerged, nurtured by the turbulent global politics of most of the twentieth century. For authors who found Marx instructive, the analytic framework was quite different, but the assessment of the declining importance of cultural divisions was similar. As Africa was incorporated into an expanding capitalist world system, the small-scale self-sufficient precapitalist societies would be overwhelmed, the bulk of the rural population would be detached from the land, and ties of class would supersede those of culture.[4] In this view, the process was expected to be quite traumatic—a revolutionary transformation in the mode of production and a sharp tearing of the social fabric. Prevailing values, customs, authority structures, sex roles, and family relationships would all change as production, and thus stratification and power, were reorganized. Here, too, there was an inexorable quality to the process of change. Some romantics might bemoan the transformation, but the peasantry was an anachronism and, even more so, the tribe.

Perhaps reflecting a global political economy in which socialism is deemed to have failed, both as a political and an economic transformation and as an alternative analytic perspective, journalists and scholars once again look to cultural identity to explain political behavior. Regular are the articles and studies that report confirmation that people across Africa agree with, prefer to do business with, and vote for those termed "co-ethnics" (Fearon and Laitin 2003; Habyarimana et al. 2009; E. Green 2011, 223). The more recent attention to ethnicity as explanation recognizes its social construction, often locates its origins more in politics and history than in biology, but retains the idea that it is primordial, with deep roots (Fearon 2008).

Crawford Young has been a perceptive and critical analyst of those trends, regularly highlighting their limitations and insisting on attention to context and complexities. His early recognition of the situational construction of identity

(Anderson, Von der Mehden, and Young 1967) was extended and elaborated in his masterful study of the politics of cultural pluralism (Young 1976) and subsequently updated and insightfully revised (Young 1993). His perspective combined the social construction of ethnicity with the situational specificity of its salience. That narrowed the settings in which ethnicity can be an explanation and highlighted the ways in which ethnic identities are shaped and corroded by nationalism, state action, and other forces. Particularly compelling in his encyclopedic review of major social science strains was his argument that identity is conjunctural, not primordial (Young 1986). He challenges us to develop explanations for those conjunctions. With his encouragement, the analysis that follows is a response.

Notwithstanding the confidence with which much of the scholarship on Africa assumed the incompatibility of ties of culture and ties of interest and class, ethnic groups, interest associations, and classes exist simultaneously and interact. Though their relative importance may vary from one place to another, none has eliminated the others. That suggests we need an explanatory framework that addresses this complexity. At the same time, in recognizing the importance of ethnicity, interests, and classes, our explanatory framework must not become an eclectic grab bag into which we put everything we observe and in which there are no discernible patterns. Nor must that explanatory framework be a cover for the claim that since life is complex and since the relevant factors are many, the researcher can simply pick and choose what is to be emphasized.

To develop an inclusive explanatory framework, it is productive to review very briefly the evolution of the political economy of Tanzania, especially in the period following its independence, when both the country and scholars sought to move beyond tribe.[5] Unpacking common assertions about ethnicity in Tanzania provides a foundation for, first, recognizing the limitations of ethnic identity as an explanation for political behavior; second, exploring the interactions of ethnicity, interests, and class; and, third, understanding that explanations organized around ethnicity, interests, and class are not alternatives but rather address different questions.

The Creation and Shifting Salience of Ethnicity

The image of tribal Africa is ubiquitous. Africans were organized into groups called tribes, which combined physiological (physical type), economic (e.g., herders or farmers), political (clan-based, centralized), social (patrilineal, matrilocal, exogamous), and other characteristics. Those tribes were then used as a basic unit of analysis in studying Africa (Magubane 1976).

Not infrequently, the name assigned to those groupings was derived from terms used by outsiders and may not have existed in the language of the named people themselves. That externally imposed labeling reflects two more general points made by contemporary observers: (1) organizational patterns in Africa were varied and changing, and, although some arrangements had deeper roots than others, all began somewhere, and all could change, and (2) individuals had multiple identities, each of whose importance was more a response to situational factors than a function of the identity itself. Indeed, the word "tribe" must be understood as part of a European language for differentiating and deprecating the African experience. What were nations and states, even empires, in Europe become tribes in Africa, just as kings and emperors become chiefs, and lords, dukes, knights, marquis, viceroys, and the like become headmen. As Mafeje has shown, the literature has been so encumbered with an ideology of tribalism that there may be little remaining viable use for the term "tribe" (Mafeje 1971).[6]

Yet ethnic identities do exist, and they do matter. Attentive visitors to Tanzania quickly encounter references to progressive Chagga people, to superstitious Ha, and to Hehe, quick to anger and violence. These ethnic explanations, which are asserted by some observers as firmly as they are rejected by others, do have a concrete basis, and it is worth exploring those roots, very briefly, for two areas of Tanzania.

Modernization in Kilimanjaro

In the popular imaginary, Kilimanjaro is modernization in Tanzania, or at least a modernization model to be emulated.[7] Nineteenth-century long-distance caravan traders rested and provisioned in Kilimanjaro, bringing broader recognition of Kilimanjaro and its residents and inserting them into international trade.[8] As those exchanges unfolded, Kilimanjaro leaders sought to use them to advantage. In the twentieth century, Kilimanjaro became the site for a link between Tanganyika and the world economy. Coffee was brought to the mountain's well-watered hillsides by European missionaries. At first controlled by chiefs, coffee planting was quickly undertaken by commoners. In part because Tanganyika was a League of Nations Mandatory territory, in part because of the earlier experience of peasant unrest (Maji-Maji), in part because of the small size of the settler community, and in part because of the British Colonial Office's preoccupation with its Kenyan interests in East Africa, the guiding principles of Tanganyika's administration were to restrain the settlers, encourage the smallholders, and limit its capital investment. The residents of Kilimanjaro, with education and other assistance from the missionaries, adapted well to those principles.

The coffee growers, however, have never been content with what they regarded as their unjustly small share of coffee revenues. Commoners were able to use coffee production to organize and finance a challenge to their chiefs, ultimately unseating them in the energized nationalism after World War II. Subsequently, having gained control of the coffee cooperatives, the growers drew on the ethos of ujamaa, African socialism, and allied with the independent Tanzanian government to oust most of the remaining European coffee farmers.

By the 1970s, the combination of high population density, the security of plantain production (the local staple crop), the economic returns even from small coffee plots, and the importance of social networks and cultural practices of owning land on the mountain all combined to slow the amalgamation of large land holdings. Almost everyone farmed some coffee. Over time, however, there developed increasing differentiation among the coffee growers. Farmers who inherited or accumulated some wealth purchased land, planted higher-quality seedlings, used fertilizers, pesticides, and piped irrigation, employed labor, added dairy cows, and ultimately diversified their marketed harvest.

Although the differentiation among the coffee growers is clear, class conflict within Kilimanjaro has been muted. Where the major tension that commanded local attention pitted Kilimanjaro residents against the European settlers, or against the British administration, or against the Tanzanian government, the prosperous growers could mobilize ethnic and regional ties and claim to represent the interests of all of Kilimanjaro. The continuing existence of economic opportunities, both within and outside Kilimanjaro, has meant that there are few local citizens with no land at all, which in turn has delayed a challenge to the more prosperous by the landless. The assistance of the churches, especially in education, has largely enabled the dominant local class to maintain its control over key positions, to ensure that it is succeeded by its children, to extend the hegemony of its values and orientations, and at the same time to claim that development in Kilimanjaro compared to that in the rest of the country reduces the importance of inequality within the region.

Kilimanjaro was thus a link between the world market and Tanganyika. Coffee went out, and ideas, institutions, and some money came. Because of the importance of coffee revenue to the Tanzanian economy and because Kilimanjaro's education advantages enabled its citizens to have substantial national influence, the values and orientations consonant with capitalist development spread beyond the region's borders. Kilimanjaro's local dominant class was able to oppose socialist development strategies largely by redefining them so they were not at odds with their own interests. At the same time, the continuing importance of coffee exports to the Tanzanian economy has prevented the national leadership from challenging more directly those in power within Kilimanjaro (Samoff 1979a).[9]

This very abbreviated discussion of a series of important events in Tanzania's political history shows clearly that what is often discussed as a distinctively ethnic (Chagga) role in Tanzanian politics has a base that is more regional than cultural. As well, what are taken to be particularly Chagga characteristics—whether advanced education, or aggressive entrepreneurship, or contemporary marriage and childbirth practices—all must be understood in terms of the role of Kilimanjaro in the incorporation of Tanganyika and Tanzania into an expanding world economy. There is a sense of ethnic identification and solidarity among the inhabitants of Kilimanjaro, but that sense is a function of particular societal circumstances and not of the ethnicity itself.

A similar insight can be drawn from a review of the experiences of Tanzanians who were much less able to take advantage of the incorporation process.

Underdevelopment in Kigoma

Where the image of Chagga ethnicity in contemporary Tanzania emphasizes progressive, educated, modern, western, and entrepreneurial, the parallel image of Ha ethnicity focuses on superstitious, resistant to change, short-tempered, and unreliable. Yet the two images, despite their sharp contrasts, stem from a single source: the process of incorporation.

"Structured incapacity" captures well the modern history of the Kigoma region on Lake Tanganyika on Tanzania's western border.[10] Prior to the imposition of European rule, the local peoples in Kigoma had created a relatively strong local state based on a client relationship between earlier resident farmers and later arriving herders, able to protect itself, to engage in short- and long-distance trade, and even on occasion to impose its will on its neighbors. The slave trade went through Kigoma, but for the most part sought its captives across the lake in the Congo. The foreign merchants, largely Arab and Asian, settled in Ujiji town, and were not disruptive challenges to the local political system. At the turn of the twentieth century, the Germans claimed control, but were unable to establish an administration outside the urban area.

British rule, imposed after World War I, was much more destructive to Kigoma society. The collection of taxes and the maintenance of the role of local chiefs against structural counterweights within Kigoma society led to the erosion of the territorially based clan system and undermined the broader social organization. The increasing importance of political boundaries cut Kigoma off from its natural trading partners around the lake. That the administrative capital of Tanganyika was on the opposite edge of the country distanced Kigoma from both British decision-making and nationalist agitation. The high costs of transporting produce on the cross-country railway line effectively precluded Kigoma's participation in the emerging national and export markets.

With limited income from their major economic activities and needing cash to pay taxes, the people of Kigoma turned to selling their labor. The same factors that made Kigoma peasants into laborers meant that there was little employment opportunity locally. The search for work outside Kigoma was facilitated by the arrival of labor recruiters, especially for coastal sisal estates.

The disruptions of Kigoma society also produced a culture of conservatism. Peasants were less oriented toward seizing opportunities than toward minimizing risks. New economic opportunities were infrequent, but when they occurred, Kigoma residents were generally unable or unwilling to take advantage of them.

As Kigoma society disintegrated, ethnic awareness intensified and ethnically based social networks expanded. The assertion of ethnicity and of the importance of ethnicity was a survival mechanism. To the extent that ethnic ties could reduce insecurity and provide support, ethnic identity was strengthened. At the same time, the decay of the older social structures and the exclusion from the newer economic and political arrangements provided an active terrain for those who offered remedies to society's (and individuals') ills. Superstition and witchcraft flourished.

In short, the incorporation of Kigoma into the expanding world system involved the destruction of economic opportunities, political organization, and social networks. What had been a regional power became a labor reservoir. Backwardness—low productivity, rudimentary technology, weak political structures, superstition and witchcraft, and an ethos of conservatism—had been induced. Those with the greatest motive for challenging the system imposed on them were rendered less and less capable of mounting the challenge.

Creation of Ethnicity

How, then, are we to understand ethnic identity?[11] Although the term "tribe," or "ethnic group," suggests historical depth and persistence, many students of

Africa have noted the creation of ethnicity. Banton found widespread self-identification as Temne in Sierra Leone when the British administrative arrangements for Freetown made that advantageous (Banton 1956). Young recounts an extraordinary story of the manufacture of the Bangala in the colonial Congo, more by outsiders than by Africans (Young 1967, 31–33; Young 1976, 171–73.). My own research on elections in Zambia in the 1970s found candidates who asserted new ethnic identities to organize support and seek votes. Yoruba and Ibo owe their ethnic solidarity to external threats. Both fission and fusion are ongoing. It is useful to return briefly to the peoples of Kilimanjaro to explore the malleability of ethnicity.

During the early missionary expansion, Kilimanjaro was divided into more than thirty small chiefdoms and two major religions.[12] When the primary lines of conflict were drawn between the small states, the two major religious groups, each largely unchallenged in its own area, could reach across warring parties and play an integrative role by enabling people to broaden the scale of their basic allegiance. As conflicts between the (former) small states became less significant and conflicts between the two major religious groups intensified, the recognition of Chagganess, spurred by tension between Kilimanjaro people and an external opponent (settlers, British administration, national government), was integrative in that it tended to moderate religious conflict and permit people to recognize a broader community. In national politics, Chagganess could be, and was, divisive rather than integrative. Each broader identity expanded the political community, but it did so by sharpening the divisions within the still larger setting.

Events of the late 1960s sharply posed the issue of who was a Chagga. Kilimanjaro residents were encouraged to move to new lands to relieve land shortage, with financial support from the Chagga Land Fund, originally established to compensate the Chagga for land alienated to Europeans. Only Chagga were eligible for support from the Chagga Land Fund. But who was a Chagga? The Regional Development Committee considered that question when an individual who had been born and raised in Kilimanjaro but whose father was not Chagga sought financial assistance. After a good deal of discussion, there was clear agreement on a proposal advanced by the party district chairman (the senior locally elected party official) that all those who had lived their lives in Kilimanjaro and who considered themselves Chagga confronted the same land shortage and should therefore be officially considered Chagga in the allocation of relocation assistance.

Ethnicity was determined by consensus at a public meeting. Common experience was accepted, in this situation, as a more important determinant of ethnicity than lineage. That we find this surprising is evidence of the power of the ideology of tribalism. After all, ethnic identities have been created, molded, and destroyed throughout human history, though perhaps a bit less formally and consciously than in this example. That some Kilimanjaro residents may regard this individual as "not really a Chagga," and that he himself may manifest some confusion about his ethnic identity, are less important than the malleability of the identity patterns.

Ethnicity Becomes Salient

Some areas in Tanganyika, like Kilimanjaro, were incorporated into the world system in a way that generated local classes that saw their own interests as tied to those of capitalist expansion. In other areas of Tanganyika, like Kigoma, the incorporation process generated local classes that provided labor and discouraged them, especially through their understanding of the world and of themselves, from challenging capitalist expansion. Put somewhat differently, what was regarded as the backwardness of west-central Tanzania was not a natural state that the local residents had not yet transcended. Rather, it was the outcome of the organization of production in Kigoma, which both undermined local economic opportunities and, at the same time, required cash payments. The culture of conservatism that emerged in Kigoma and the caricature of the Ha people in the rest of Tanzania as slow thinkers, socially awkward, and prone to violence are not traditional or rooted in an idealized peasant morality. Rather, the worldview of Kigoma residents has been shaped by their life chances.

In contemporary Tanzania, entrepreneurship may well be a Chagga ethnic characteristic (in the commonsense meaning that people who come from Kilimanjaro are more likely than other Tanzanians to exhibit entrepreneurial behavior), and, similarly, superstitiousness may well be a Ha ethnic characteristic. But that the Ha rank security over progress is not eternal, nor rural, nor Ha, nor even African, but rather capitalist, just as capitalist as the entrepreneurship of the Kilimanjaro smallholders.

Ethnicity matters in Tanzania. But what ethnicity is and when and how it matters are not determined by ethnicity.

The Limits of Ethnicity as Explanation

That ethnicity is so prominent in discussions of Africa requires that we address critically its uses. Ethnicity enters Africa literature along two paths. One is in the effort to explain observed behavior, for example, voting. The other is in the persisting insistence on the traditional/modern distinction.

For the first, the brief comparison of Kilimanjaro and Kigoma provides dramatic evidence of the creation of ethnicity. People living in the vicinity of the mountain became known by a name, Chagga, that they did not use. Responding to the imposition of European rule moved small mountain-side states from conflict to alliance. As the label "Chagga" became useful locally, it was domesticated and internalized. No longer largely an external designation, it became local culture. As it evolved, the identity entered local politics as an interest, for example, rallying support for opposition to the dominant party. As we have seen, ethnicity was created at the small scale as well. By a community vote, someone born on the mountain and raised amid land shortage was Chagga, independent of ancestry and descent. As in Sierra Leone, the Congo, Nigeria, and elsewhere, ethnicity was created.

The compelling evidence from across the continent requires us to take seriously the understanding that identities are socially constructed, even identities as deeply felt and as passionately asserted as tribe, however primordial they may seem to particular people and particular moments. That evidence also requires us to recognize the situational specificity of the mobilization of identities. Yes, identities matter. Yes, identities can move people and influence their behavior. Yes, deeply felt identities can be associated with voting, or conflict, or cooperation. But which identities matter—everyone carries many—is necessarily circumstantial and cannot be explained by identity. Together, the social construction and situational specificity of identity mean that identity must always be understood in context. Decontextualized assertions of or claims about identity have, at best very limited and partial explanatory utility.

Those observations about identities are relevant in many societies. For Africa, ethnicity carries additional baggage. Trenchant critiques over many years have not disencumbered academic research and public discourse from the association of Africa with traditional, that is, the antithesis of modern—crudely, backward, or more politely, risk averse, reluctant to innovate, resistant to change, farther back on the development continuum. The durability of the distinction between traditional and modern reinforces among researchers a frame for studying Africa that incorporates notions of improvement and social engineering. That framing shapes the public discourse as well, captured in the US president's ugly and revealing reference to "shithole countries" (Dawsey 2018). Yes, ugly, but widely shared.

The ideology of "traditional" is more problematic than the ideology of "tribe." More problematic for Africa's development and, indeed, more frightening, than an angry mob motivated by calls for ethnic solidarity are academics who assume that Africa is backward (an original condition that appears, like ethnicity, to require no explanation) and who seek to explain why Africa is poor rather than why and how Africa has been impoverished (the result of a process that demands explanation). Less visible and, when questioned, defended as science, scholars' assumptions about "tradition" and "traditional versus modern" are more widely influential and more difficult to challenge than bigots' or heads of state's pronouncements about racial purity. For research on Africa, far from an independent variable, ethnicity is a quagmire from which scholars must struggle to escape.

Interests and the Institutional Setting of Class Conflict

Just as much of the scholarship on Africa began with the assumption that the social divisions that mattered were those based on primordial identities, so it assumed that over time, groupings based on ascriptive characteristics would be superseded by organizations based on associational ties. That process would be neither instantaneous nor smooth. Indeed, the exigencies of urban life might produce a new tribalism fueled by efforts to draw on ethnic identities. But, in this view, the general process was clear: modernization was corrosive to the ethnic ties of the past. Common interest would be the focal point for political organization. Ethnic associations would become interest groups.

The assumed universality of this transition from cultural to interest-group pluralism meant that African politics could be understood as interest-group competition. Groups were formed to articulate, advocate, and defend common interests. Organizations emerged to aggregate these interests. Coalitions could then use electoral and other mechanisms to influence policy. In this view, ethnic ties might remain important, but their political significance was through interest-group activity. Divisions along class lines might also exist, but because associational groups were usually cross-cutting, there was no inexorable and irreconcilable conflict between classes.

It is instructive to explore this transition in thinking about African politics— that political outcomes can be better understood in terms of interest-group formation, coalition, and competition—through the lens of local government in Kilimanjaro.

Local Government in Kilimanjaro

At independence, Tanzania's local government reflected a mix of British heritage and one-party state. Local councils were largely dominated by their executive officers. The single-party state added both local party institutions and an appointed Area Commissioner with both government and party authority. Thus, there was extensive interpenetration of party and government institutions. Often, it was unclear whether an official was acting in a government or party capacity.

Extended fieldwork in Kilimanjaro permitted intensive study of several heavily contested local issues. Interest-group politics were clear, as was the government's dominant role. The local party organization was influential, but it did not govern, most often legitimizing the bureaucracy's role and decisions. Expertise and administration generally prevailed over politics and mobilization.

Subsequent changes in the structure of Tanzania's local government reinforced that tilt. Through the 1970s, district-level participatory institutions were weakened in favor of a strengthened region-focused development administration.[13]

Politics within this local government institutional arena can be understood in terms of interest-group competition, our concern here. The actors varied, depending on the issue. Not infrequently, tension arose between the local party and national party headquarters. The civil service mediated among these interests, often more partisan than neutral. Thus, for any given issue, a combination of careful interest-group analysis and a clear understanding of the imperatives of organizational behavior would seem to provide a relatively full explanation for specific outcomes.

But to stop there would not yield a complete explanation at all. To explain outcomes in terms of institutions and interests is to leave major questions unanswered. Why were particular institutional arrangements adopted, here favoring expertise over participation? And why were some interests, but not others, articulated and respected? Here, we see the limits of the explanatory power of the focus on interests and organizations. To answer those questions requires a broader perspective: local institutions as arenas for class conflict.

In Kilimanjaro, during this period, the locally dominant class alliance included prosperous farmers, salaried urban employees, and merchants, the three often related.[14] Their class enemy and, because classes are defined by opposition as well as by role in production, their nature changed over time. During British rule, the major opposition was between European settlers and an aspirant African agricultural and salaried petty bourgeoisie. Since local government was still an externally imposed and dominated institution, the institutional framework then centered on the coffee cooperatives, created by the nascent petty bourgeoisie to challenge the settlers and the colonial administration. Subsequently, with the British civil service now an ally, the cooperatives constrained the settlers. Opposition then turned to the local chiefs, who, with British assistance, were emerging as agricultural capitalists. In independent Tanzania, class opposition was between the locally based Kilimanjaro petty bourgeoisie and nationally based classes: the merchants, the bureaucracy, and a nascent socialist impulse based on the defensive radicalism of segments of the national leadership.

During much of the 1960s the Kilimanjaro petty bourgeoisie allied with the local bureaucracy to dominate outcomes. Local institutions provided an arena not only for the resolution of intraclass conflicts among the partners of the dominant class alliance but also for the construction of that alliance itself. Those institutions also provided a mechanism for generalizing the values and perspective of the locally dominant classes. Efforts to challenge them could be portrayed as an attack on regional and ethnic interests so that local peasants and workers came to see their interests as best protected by siding with the local petty bourgeoisie rather than with national commercial or bureaucratic classes or with peasants and workers elsewhere.

Thus, interest-group pluralism provides a useful but partial explanation for observed behavior. The transformations in the structure of local government over the late 1960s and early 1970s favored expertise over participation, administration over politics. Those transformations suited a nationally dominant bureaucratic ruling class as it institutionalized the legitimacy of the bureaucracy's rule. Those transformations also suited the national party leadership by reducing the role of institutions responsive to locally based opposition.

Intersecting Explanations

My argument thus far is that there was pluralism in Tanzania's first decades and that ethnicity and interests did matter. Tanzanians recognized communities based on ascriptive characteristics and reinforced by social networks and customs, and they acted in terms of those communities. Tanzanians also recognized shared interests, and they formed groups to assert, secure, and protect those interests.

The process of political institutionalization, however, was not a neutral evolution toward greater functional specificity and rationalization but rather a modification of specific institutions to suit distinctly class interests. The institutions of local government were not simply the managers of interest-group competition but were as well both settings and outcomes of class conflict. The trajectory was not toward universal modernization and interest-group politics but toward bureaucratic class rule.

Classes and Crises

The Marxist perspective articulated by twentieth-century anticolonial movements and the president Julius Nyerere's efforts to define African socialism
sparked critical and insightful analyses of class and class conflict in independent Tanzania; space permits no more than an overview of its major outlines
here.[15] First, however, it is important to comment on my use of class.

Class is understood as a relationship here—two sorts of relationship simultaneously. Class is defined by role in production, as production is organized at
any particular moment. At the same time, class is defined by opposition to
other classes. That is, class is defined by both structure and process. Neither is adequate by itself. And both are constantly changing.

In this usage, it is essential to distinguish class from stratification. A population can be studied by stratifying it. The ordering principle may be complex,
say, the combination of income, education, occupation, and status. While stratification has to do with the hierarchical ordering of society, class refers to a
necessarily conflictual relationship that revolves around the creation and ap-
propriation of wealth (organization of production). Classes may be stratified,
and there may be patterns of stratification that cut across classes, but class and
stratum are very different analytic constructs, each with its own intellectual origins, theoretical underpinnings, and empirical utility. I use class here, then, in
the search for structural sources for change in contemporary Africa.

A Bureaucratic Governing Class in Tanzania

Tanzania's incorporation into a changing world system involved an initial competition between rival European states followed by a half-century of relative
inattention under British oversight. At independence in 1961, with no significant set of African owners able to assert itself as a capitalist class, a petty-
bourgeois leadership, drawn from civil servants and teachers on one hand and
from merchants on the other, assumed office (Samoff 1979a, 1981). The new
arrangement of power was an alliance of classes. The dominant ally, still able
to control major decisions about the direction of the economy and to impose
(though incompletely) its values and worldview, was external. Internally, there
was competition between the commercial and bureaucratic elements of the
ruling class alliance.

As the Europeans departed, the largely Asian merchants could take economic and political advantage of their assumption of control over export-
import trade and their strengthened position in retail commerce.[16] But Asians

in Tanzania had survived British rule by strengthening the internal ties of their separate community. Their norms emphasized communal, and therefore racial, solidarity. Unable to secure acceptance as Europeans, they avoided being treated as Africans. Though their economic situation was for the moment relatively secure, they had failed to develop a mass political base. Nor, given their intermediary position and the discriminatory nature of their communal ties, could they then create one. At first, this commercial class prospered in independent Tanzania. Tanzanian leaders insisted that citizenship mattered, not race. When the major economic enterprises were nationalized in 1967, many Asians found their skills in demand.

Nevertheless, the largely Asian commercial class was effectively eliminated from the ruling-class alliance. It simply had no mass power base on which to draw. As its political position weakened, its economic role began to disintegrate. The African petty bourgeoisie could muster its nationalist and socialist rhetoric to replace private trading firms with public corporations. Ejected from the ruling-class alliance, severely restricted in its ability to accumulate, and constrained in its lifestyle by the elimination of most private schools and health care, many Asians simply left. Related crises of power and accumulation had undermined the Asian commercial class.[17]

The major internal element in the ruling alliance became the bureaucracy. Administrators increasingly acted on behalf of the owners of production. As major economic enterprises were nationalized and as new ventures most often involved joint private–public ownership, civil servants became managers and directors. Over time, the bureaucracy recognized that its corporate interests coincided with a class role. That is, the bureaucracy was not a class because it was the bureaucracy, but because as the bureaucracy it assumed a specific role in the organization of production: that of manager, and in limited areas, owner of the means of production. As the major internal partner in the ruling class alliance, the bureaucracy became the governing class in Tanzania.

This brief outline of organization and reorganization within the ruling class alliance portrays the transitions far too mechanically, understates the importance of ongoing conflict, and obscures the discontinuous and spasmodic process of change. To deepen this discussion of class in Tanzania, therefore, it is helpful to use a notion of crisis to periodize the Tanzanian political economy.

Crises in Tanzania

Several major traumas for the Tanzanian political economy stimulated a reorganization of social forces and a realignment of classes, which in turn created the setting for and conditioned the response to the succeeding crisis. I use crisis loosely here to characterize significant disruptions in political life. I am concerned with traumas that are sufficiently severe to threaten the political order or at least the political, economic, social, and ideological bases of those who hold power. This notion of crisis focuses on moments in Tanzania's political history that make more clearly visible underlying structural relationships and tensions.

One crisis was that which led to the definition of the contemporary Tanzanian state: incorporation into an expanding world economy. That incorporation led to the demise of a political order that revolved around independent and interdependent agriculturally based societies and commercial city-states. The new leadership, rooted in the civil service and commerce, negotiated the British departure and crafted a liberal development strategy: emphasis on export production, active search for foreign assistance, nonalignment in foreign policy, expanded political participation, rapid increase in social services, and vague generalizations about self-reliance. The talk about socialism reflected an ideology of defensive radicalism that sought to avoid the evils of capitalism (Ake 1979).

By the mid-1960s, a new crisis. Prices for the major export, sisal, had fallen precipitously. The union with Zanzibar and the challenge to Britain over settler rule in Rhodesia led to disruptions in foreign relations and the loss of expected aid. Tanzania's leaders concluded that the liberal development strategy was fundamentally flawed. Tanzania was not developing but still underdeveloping (Nyerere 1968b). In the efforts to reorganize production and restructure power, parastatal corporations became the preferred vehicle for accumulating capital and the path for the African petty bourgeoisie toward large-scale ownership.

At the same time, part of the national leadership sought to constrain the nascent Tanzanian bourgeoisie by reaching out to a mass base. A new leadership code restricted opportunities for private accumulation and consumption.[18] The countryside was to be organized into socialist villages and cooperatives. Ostensible changes could be manipulative. Unenforced leadership restrictions might win popular support without undermining the nascent bourgeoisie. Participatory mechanisms might leave control unchanged. The socialism in socialist villages might not extend beyond the label.

Thus, the crisis of the mid-1960s, the failure of the liberal development strategy, enabled one part of the national leadership to use nationalism to eliminate its major opponents, while another part sought to create an institutional framework for a socialist transformation. The new development strategy was distinctly radical: nationalization of major economic institutions, restrictions on consumption by the most affluent, progressive taxation, decolonization of the curriculum, strengthened rural health services, greater attention to economic diversification and industrialization, and a well-publicized commitment to self-reliance.

In some respects, there was substantial progress toward both self-reliance and socialist transformation. By the late 1970s, much of large-scale economic activity and capital formation were in the public sector. Inequality was reduced. Expanded access to clean water improved rural health. Self-reliance and socialism seemed desirable and achievable. "The transition to socialism in Tanzania could be said to be nearly accomplished" (R. Green 1977, 24; see also R. Green 1975, 1976).

A third crisis. By the end of the 1970s, the radical development strategy also seemed seriously flawed. Mass participation in important decisions remained limited. Socialist villages had little communal production, and cooperatives became obstacles to socialist progress. Foreign partners dominated the parastatals. Inequalities were increasingly visible. Problems in food production and slow economic growth were poorly managed. Critics, within and outside the country, insisted that Tanzanian socialism had failed. Perhaps. Too much socialism? Or too little?

In this understanding of policies and institutions as outcomes of and arenas for class conflict, this agricultural crisis of the mid-1970s fostered both political continuity and political realignment. Administrative rule (the bureaucracy as the governing class) was consolidated, accompanied by increased reliance on state institutions for economic production. At the same time, a continued commitment to socialist transformation reformed institutions of popular participation and governance.

Though Nyerere held off external pressures into the 1980s, the intermediary position that permitted alliances with transnational capital on the one side and with Tanzanian peasants and workers on the other—a seemingly erratic shift from comprador to populist policies—was structurally unstable. Externally specified structural adjustment and its consequences followed soon after Nyerere's retirement.

Ethnicity, Interests, and Class

This brief review permits more general observations on ethnicity, interests, and class in Tanzania and in Africa more generally. First, as explanations, ethnicity and interests are both visible and partial. Neither can explain its own significance.

Second, ethnicity, interests, and class are not competing explanations for observed political behavior. Those perspectives are not only guided by different assumptions but also stimulated by different questions and a different sense of the problems to which research (and political action) should be addressed.

Most often, the writing on ethnic pluralism in Africa, identity politics, is concerned with how people organize themselves in specified circumstances, why, and with what consequences. The starting assumption is that ethnicity is a, or the, driving force of African social structure and thereby of individual and collective behavior. Can the mobilization of ethnic identity explain voting outcomes? Yes and no. Politicians' appeals to ethnic identity can motivate behavior and thereby provide a first explanation of voting outcomes. So, too, can appeals to women or Christians. The politicization of identities can also help us understand the generational transmission of perspectives on society. But beyond the assumption that ethnicity is primordial rather than constructed, ethnicity cannot explain why political leaders seek votes by appealing to ethnic identity rather than to group interests (winning the teachers' or nurses' votes) or to classes (workers, peasants). Nor can ethnicity explain the electoral consequences of the tension between owners and laborers.

The writing on interest-group pluralism in Africa has largely been concerned with governance and with conflict management and resolution. What are the major interests expressed in society, how are those interests manifested in institutional arrangements, and how can the necessary interplay of interests be maintained without threatening the political order? The starting assumptions here, drawn from notions of modernization and development and including some insights from Marx and Weber, are that there will be conflicts of interest, that those conflicts will supersede conflicts between groups defined by religion, race, ethnicity, and region, and that those conflicts are both the strength and the weakness of the polity. They permit innovation and progress, but, if not adequately managed and channeled, they also jeopardize the relative stability and continuity necessary for progress. Can notions of interest and rational self-interested behavior explain voting outcomes? Yes and no. Collectively, groups organize to secure a school, or to expand access to free medical care, or to change licensing rules. Individually, people enter the voting station with their calculation of which candidate is more likely to respond to their interests as, say, laborer, or teacher, or driver. To return to a Tanzania example, the combination of identity and interests can help us understand the political marginalization of Asian merchants. But that combination cannot fully capture the consequences, including voting, of the declining role of merchant capital in its competition with industrialists, bankers, and bureaucrats.

The writing on class and class conflict is largely concerned with social change at a broad scale. Why is (a particular) society the way it is, and what are the (inherent and contradictory) pressures for change? The starting assumptions here are that there are necessarily antagonistic conflicts between owners and producers in capitalist society, that those conflicts are structurally rooted in the organization of production, and that the study of the contending classes will reveal the dynamism of the system as a whole. Since in this view significant improvement in the quality of life for the mass of the population is inconsistent with the maintenance of capitalism, progress will necessarily be discontinuous, conflictual, and traumatic rather than incremental and orderly.

Consider a South Africa example. Do identity or interests or class explain neighborhood attacks on Somali shopkeepers? Well, they all do, but in different ways. Recognizing the political mobilization of identity—South Africans versus foreigners—is essential to understanding how people were organized to burn shops. Recognizing the combination of identity and interest is essential to understanding Somalis and their shops as the target, rather than mine owners or bankers. Focusing on the organization of production is essential to understanding the anomie, anger, and volatility of a class that is deeply conscious of its persisting high unemployment and limited life chances.

Put simply, studies of ethnicity, interests, and class are responsive to different questions and operate at different levels of analysis. Each perspective is incomplete without attention to the concerns of the others, and the best of each incorporates the insights of the others.

A third observation is that the common thread that is woven through these perspectives is conflict. All people have multiple identities. Which identity is salient cannot be explained by identity but depends on the situation. The most important of the situations are those of conflict, since at times of conflict, people are stimulated to organize, and in organizing, people draw on relevant identity patterns to sort out expected allies and enemies. But which identity patterns are most available for that will be determined, or at least constrained, by the situation itself.

A fourth observation from this research is that each starting point incorporates and situates the others. That embedding highlights the explanatory utility of what Ollman has termed internal relations (Ollman 1990, 1993, 2003). Explanatory power is enhanced not by dissecting an element of interest—the most common social science approach—but rather by addressing their interconnections and context. Just as the politics of ethnicity can be more fully understood by nesting them within a study of interests, so can the politics of interest be more fully understood by nesting them within a study of class. The analytic challenge is not to ask whether ethnic identity or union membership matters more to voters but to explore how they interact, often each shaping the other, in a concrete situation.

Fifth, the objective situation can be understood at many different levels, demonstrating again that attention to interactions and to context and complexity has more explanatory power than approaches that insist on the dissection and controls of the laboratory experiment. Consider the nineteenth-century antislaving patrols of the British navy. Why did a Royal Navy captain intercept a slave ship and land its captives on the African coast? Well, because he had instructions from the Admiralty, though in any specific case his own values, technical considerations, private profiteering, his psyche, and even chance may have modified those instructions. But why did the Admiralty issue those instructions? Well, that has to do with power in the British Parliament and the orientation of the British government at the time. But why did the British government turn from encouraging slaving to opposing it, not only in British colonies and on British ships but everywhere? Well, that has to do with a transition in the dominant interests within the British government from merchants and planters who benefited from the slave trade to industrialists and bankers for whom slave production was an obstacle to their accumulation of capital. In other words, the specific actions of a particular British naval officer can be understood at several levels, from the direction of the wind to class conflicts in the metropole. An explanation adequate for the behavior of specific individuals at a specific time (the captain and his crew) falls short as an explanation for broader social phenomena (the end of the slave trade). The narrower levels are neither wholly determined by nor wholly independent of the broader levels. Indeed, those levels are nested within each other. A nested reality requires a nested explanatory structure.

In this understanding, ethnicity, interests, and class are not alternative and exclusive patterns of human organization but rather interconnected patterns. As explanations, each is appropriate to a different set of questions and to a different level of analysis. The situations that energize these patterns are those of conflict, and, in our contemporary era, especially conflicts over what is produced, over how that is produced, over the distribution of that produce, and, most important, over how the decisions on those issues are made.

Notes

An earlier version of this chapter was published as Joel Samoff, "Pluralism and Conflict in Africa: Ethnicity, Interests, and Class in Tanzania." *Civilisations* 32, no. 1–33, no. 2 (1982/83): 97–134.

    1. Identity politics are of interest but not a primary focus here. I am concerned with how and why ethnicity matters but not with whether or not ethnicity matters more than religion, region, gender, socioeconomic status, or some other asserted identity. Intrigu-

ing, certainly, but critical attention to identity politics is beyond the scope of this analysis (Tripp 1999; Young 1999).

2. For many authors, both academic and nonacademic, the *culture* in *cultural pluralism* is a large tent that refers to ties that are deeply rooted and reinforced by language, affinity, and custom. For Africa, race (both observed and legislated), tribe (still common usage notwithstanding efforts to retire the term), and ethnicity (successor to "tribe," especially in academia, with similar definitions) cohabit in that tent.

3. Parsons's (1963) pattern variables provided scientific legitimacy for that differentiation. Mudimbe (1988, 1994) explores how those who saw themselves as modern required an "other" to define themselves, inventing it as necessary.

4. Many Marxian scholars explain the persisting importance of culturally defined divisions in terms of the maintenance of noncapitalist modes of production within and subordinated to the capitalist mode of production as a relatively low investment strategy for exploiting peasant production. For an overview and references, see Foster-Carter (1978).

5. I do not consider the existence of a plurality of social identities in and of itself a societal problem. Indeed, in the broadest sense, that plurality of identities is a rich cultural resource.

6. After the 1967 census, Tanzania removed tribe and race from its periodic data collection.

7. For this analysis, I focus on the period following Tanzania's (Tanganyika until 1964) independence, and I draw on fieldwork from the late 1960s through the 1980s. I use the term Kilimanjaro to refer to the area around the mountain, particularly Moshi town and its surrounding rural district. Subsequently, that area was subdivided among additional districts created in Kilimanjaro Region. This brief summary is drawn from Samoff (1974, 1979a, 1979b, 1979c, 1981, 1982); Samoff and Samoff (1976).

8. The terms for the mountain, Kilimanjaro, and the people, Chagga, were external labels. Organized into competing states whose languages were not fully mutually intelligible, the local people did not formally recognize a common identity until they confronted the European colonial empires, first German, then British. For an overview of that identity formation, Samoff (1974, chapter 1), and Bender (2013).

9. The analysis here is focused on the decades following Tanzania's independence. When party competition developed in the 1990s, Kilimanjaro became a strong base for a major, but thus far electorally unsuccessful, challenge to the ruling party (by then, Chama Cha Mapinduzi).

10. The characterization and this brief summary are drawn especially from Wayne (1973, 1975). While my focus here is the first two decades of Tanzania's independence, more recent research confirms the persistence of Kigoma's relative disadvantage, especially in education: Rubakula, Wang, and Chao (2019). See also Scherer (1960); McHenry (1980); Sago (1983); Weiskopf (2011); Msanya (2015).

11. Just as "cultural pluralism" creates space for many terms and meanings, so too does "ethnicity." Horowitz captures the range: "groups differentiated by color, language,

and religion; [ethnicity] covers 'tribes,' 'races,' 'nationalities,' and castes" (1985, 53). Chandra reviews the sources and highlights the analytic problems (2006).

12. Catholic and Lutheran. During this period, Islam was important in Moshi town but was not deeply entrenched on the hillsides.

13. Reviewing the subsequent evolution of local government in Tanzania is beyond the scope of this analysis. For an introduction, see Samoff (1989, 1–18); Tidemand (2015, 69–84). For a participant's overview, see Max (1991).

14. I find "class" the appropriate term here, notwithstanding the different productive roles of direct producers, government functionaries, and traders. The overall organization of production situated them similarly, as did their common enemy. Their common class interests overrode their potentially divergent corporate (interest-group) interests.

15. The debates on class and class conflict in Tanzania and on class as an analytic construct were intense. Alongside and regularly stimulating the intellectual vitality of the academic arena were Nyerere's and TANU's efforts to elaborate and implement their notions of African socialism. For an introduction and references, see Pratt (1976); Shivji (1976); Saul (1979); Resnick (1981); Coulson (1982); McHenry (1994).

16. I adopt here common Tanzanian usage: "Asian" to refer to earlier and more recent immigrants from the Indian subcontinent.

17. There were exceptions. Ismailis, with economic and political support from the Aga Khan, managed the transition more successfully than others. A few Asians were influential in this period, including within the ruling party, but as individuals, not as a class.

18. Elaborated in the Arusha Declaration (1967; included in Nyerere 1968a, 1968b), the leadership code was incorporated into Tanzania's constitution in a 1967 amendment.

References

Ake, Claude. 1979. "Ideology and Objective Conditions." In *Politics and Public Policy in Kenya and Tanzania*, edited by Joel D. Barkan, 117–28. New York: Praeger.

Anderson, Charles W., Fred R. Von der Mehden, and Crawford Young. 1967. *Issues of Political Development*. Englewood Cliffs, NJ: Prentice-Hall.

Arusha Declaration and TANU's Policy on Socialism and Self Reliance. 1967. https://library.fes.de/fulltext/bibliothek/2-tanzania-s0019634.pdf.

Banton, M. 1956. "Adaptation and Integration in the Social System of Temne Immigrants in Freetown." *Africa* 26 (4): 354–67.

Bender, Matthew V. 2013. "Being 'Chagga': Natural Resources, Political Activism, and Identity on Kilimanjaro." *Journal of African History* 54 (2): 199–220.

Chandra, Kanchan. 2006. "What Is Ethnic Identity and Does It Matter?" *Annual Review of Political Science* 9:397–424.

Coulson, Andrew. 1982. *Tanzania: A Political Economy*. Oxford: Clarendon Press.

Dahir, Abdi Latif. 2022. "How a Kenyan Power Broker Lost His Stronghold, Then the Presidency." *New York Times*, August 20.

Dawsey, Josh. 2018. "Trump Derides Protections for Immigrants from 'Shithole' Countries." *Washington Post*, January 12.

Egbejule, Eromo. 2022. "Courting the Kikuyu: Kenyan Politicians Split Biggest Voting Bloc." *Al Jazeera*, August 6. https://www.aljazeera.com/features/2022/8/6/courtng-the-kikuyu-kenyan-politicians-split-biggest-voting-bloc.

Fearon, James D. 2008. "Ethnic Mobilization and Ethnic Violence." In *Oxford Handbook of Political Economy*, edited by Barry R. Weingast and Donald A. Wittman, 852–68. Oxford: Oxford University Press.

Fearon, James D., and David D. Laitin. 2003. "Ethnicity, Insurgency, and Civil War." *American Political Science Review* 97 (1): 75–90.

Foster-Carter, Aidan. 1978. "The Modes of Production Controversy." *New Left Review* 107 (January–February): 47–77.

Green, Elliott. 2011. "The Political Economy of Nation Formation in Modern Tanzania: Explaining Stability in the Face of Diversity." *Commonwealth and Comparative Politics* 48: 223–44.

Green, Reginald Herbold. 1975. "Relevance, Efficiency, Romanticism and Confusion in Tanzanian Planning and Management." *African Review* 5 (2): 209–34.

Green, Reginald Herbold. 1976. *Tanzanian Goals, Strategies, Results: Notes toward an Interim Assessment*. Toronto: Conference on Socialist Development in Tanzania.

Green, Reginald Herbold. 1977. *Toward Socialism and Self Reliance: Tanzania's Striving for Sustained Transition Projected*. Research Report, no. 38. Uppsala: Scandinavian Institute of African Studies.

Habyarimana, James, Macartan Humphreys, Daniel N. Posner, and Jeremy M. Weinstein. 2009. *Coethnicity: Diversity and the Dilemmas of Collective Action*. New York: Russell Sage.

Horowitz, Donald L. 1985. *Ethnic Groups in Conflict*. Berkeley: University of California Press.

Lynch, Gabrielle. 2014. "Electing the 'Alliance of the Accused': The Success of the Jubilee Alliance in Kenya's Rift Valley." *Journal of Eastern African Studies* 8 (1): 93–114.

Mafeje, Archie. 1971. "The Ideology of Tribalism." *Journal of Modern African Studies* 9 (2): 253–61.

Magubane, Bernard. 1976. "The Evolution of the Class Structure in Africa." In *The Political Economy of Contemporary Africa*, edited by Peter C. W. Gutkind and Immanuel Wallerstein, 169–97. Beverly Hills: SAGE.

Max, John A. O. 1991. *The Development of Local Government in Tanzania*. Dar es Salaam: Tanzania: Educational Publishers and Distributors.

McHenry, Dean E. 1980. "Reorganization: An Administrative History of Kigoma District in Western Tanzania." *Tanzania Notes and Records* 84–85:65–76.

McHenry, Dean E., Jr. 1994. *Limited Choices: The Political Struggle for Socialism in Tanzania*. Boulder, CO: Lynne Rienner.

Msanya, Bernard Dismas. 2015. "Effects of Corruption on Economic Development in Tanzania: Case Study of Kigoma-Ujiji Municipality." Master's thesis, Universitat Jaume I, Castellón, Spain.

Mudimbe, Valentin Y. 1988. *The Invention of Africa: Gnosis, Philosophy, and the Order of Knowledge*. Bloomington: Indiana University Press.

Mudimbe, Valentin Y. 1994. *The Idea of Africa.* Bloomington: Indiana University Press.

Nyerere, Julius K. 1968a. *Freedom and Socialism / Uhuru na Ujamaa.* Dar es Salaam: Oxford University Press.

Nyerere, Julius K. 1968b. *Ujamaa: Essays on Socialism.* Dar es Salaam: Oxford University Press.

Ollman, Bertell. 1990. "Putting Dialectics to Work: The Process of Abstraction in Marx's Method." *Rethinking Marxism* 3 (Spring): 26–74.

Ollman, Bertell. 1993. *Dialectical Investigations.* New York: Routledge, Chapman and Hall.

Ollman, Bertell. 2003. *Dance of the Dialectic: Steps in Marx's Method.* Urbana: University of Illinois Press.

Parsons, Talcott. 1963. *Structure and Process in Modern Societies.* New York: Free Press, 1963.

Pratt, Cranford. 1976. *The Critical Phase in Tanzania, 1945–1968: Nyerere and the Emergence of a Socialist Strategy.* Cambridge: Cambridge University Press.

Resnick, Idrian N. 1981. *The Long Transition: Building Socialism in Tanzania.* New York: Monthly Review Press.

Rubakula, Gelas, Zhanqi Wang, and Wei Chao. 2019. "Land Conflict Management through the Implementation of the National Land Policy in Tanzania: Evidence from Kigoma Region." *Sustainability* 11 (22): 6315.

Sago, Laurent. 1983. "Labor Reservoir." In *Migrant Labour in Tanzania*, edited by Walter Rodney, Kapepwa Tambila, and Laurent Sago, 29–57. Hamburg: Institut für Afrika-Kunde.

Samoff, Joel. 1974. *Tanzania: Local Politics and the Structure of Power.* Madison: University of Wisconsin Press.

Samoff, Joel. 1979a. "The Bureaucracy and The Bourgeoisie: Decentralization and Class Structure in Tanzania." *Comparative Studies in Society and History* 21 (1): 30–62.

Samoff, Joel. 1979b. *Bureaucrats, Politicians, and Power in Tanzania: The Institutional Context of Class Struggle.* Los Angeles: African Studies Association Annual Meeting.

Samoff, Joel. 1979c. "Education in Tanzania: Class Formation and Reproduction." *Journal of Modern African Studies* 17 (1): 47–69.

Samoff, Joel. 1981. "Crises and Socialism in Tanzania." *Journal of Modern African Studies* 19 (2): 279–306.

Samoff, Joel. 1982. "Class, Class Conflict, and the State in Africa." *Political Science Quarterly* 97 (1): 105–27.

Samoff, Joel. 1989. "Popular Initiatives and Local Government in Tanzania." *Journal of Developing Areas* 24 (October): 1–18.

Samoff, Joel, and Rachel Samoff. 1976. "The Local Politics of Underdevelopment." *Politics and Society* 6 (4): 397–432.

Saul, John S. 1979. *The State and Revolution in Eastern Africa.* New York: Monthly Review Press.

Scherer, Johan Herman. 1960. "The Ha of Tanganyika." *Anthropos* 54:841–904.

Shivji, Issa G. 1976. *Class Struggles in Tanzania.* New York: Monthly Review Press.

Tidemand, Per. 2015. "The Political Economy of Local Government Reforms in Tanzania." In *Perspectives on Politics, Production, and Public Administration in Africa: Essays in Honor of Ole Therkildsen*, edited by Anne Mette Kjær, Lars Engberg-Pedersen, and Lars Buur, 69–85. Copenhagen: Danish Institute of International Studies.

Tripp, Aili Mari. 1999. "The Political Mediation of Ethnic and Religious Diversity in Tanzania." In *The Accommodation of Cultural Diversity: Case Studies*, edited by Crawford Young, 37–71. New York: St. Martin's.

Wayne, Jack. 1973. *Some Notes on the Sociology of Dependency: The Underdevelopment of Kigoma Region, Tanzania*. Dar es Salaam: Annual Social Science Conference of the East African Universities.

Wayne, Jack. 1975. "The Development of Backwardness in Kigoma Region." In *Rural Cooperation in Tanzania*, edited by Lionel Cliffe et al., 131–44. Dar es Salaam: Tanzania Publishing House.

Weiskopf, Julie E. 2011. "Resettling Buha: A Social History of Resettled Communities in Kigoma Region, Tanzania, 1933–1975." PhD diss., University of Minnesota, Minneapolis.

Young, Crawford. 1976. *The Politics of Cultural Pluralism*. Madison: University of Wisconsin Press.

Young, Crawford. 1986. "Nationalism, Ethnicity, and Class in Africa: A Retrospective." *Cahiers d'études africaines* 26 (3): 421–95.

Young, Crawford. 1993. "The Dialectics of Cultural Pluralism: Concept and Reality." In *The Rising Tide of Cultural Pluralism: The Nation-State at Bay?*, edited by Crawford Young, 3–35. Madison: University of Wisconsin Press.

Young, Crawford, ed. 1999. *The Accommodation of Cultural Diversity: Case Studies*. New York: St. Martin's.

8

State Construction, Ethnicity, and Social Status

The Bifurcated Trajectories of Haalpulaaren in the Mauritania–Senegal Borderland

Cédric Jourde

Reflecting on the politics of ethnicity in his 2012 *Postcolonial State in Africa*, Crawford Young wrote that "ethnic and territorial maps of the continent do not overlap, yet the state system imposed bounded arenas within which active competition and cooperation occur" (314). As a student of Young, I was led by a reflection akin to this one to work on my doctoral dissertation on the politics of ethnicity in the Mauritania–Senegal borderland. This region, locally known as Fuuta Tooro, is split into two countries along the Senegal River Valley. There, at the end of the nineteenth century, French colonizers used the river to draw an administrative boundary, partitioning the Pulaar-speaking community (or Haalpulaar; pl. Haalpulaaren) and other groups (Soninke and Wolof mainly) into two different colonial polities, Mauritania and Senegal. In 1960, they became independent states. Though Pulaar-speakers formed a majority in Fuuta Tooro itself, they were a minority in both countries.

The chapter has two objectives. First, it uses Young's scholarly contributions on the construction of states and political regimes to analyze how they shaped ethnic politics in the Mauritania–Senegal borderland. In effect, as time passed, from the late colonial era up to the current postcolonial period, Haalpulaaren were to participate in two very distinct political arenas, depending on which side of the border they found themselves on. But state construction as a process is closely linked to another central pillar of Crawford Young's research agenda: political regimes.[1] We can see this interaction between states and regime dynamics when Young, looking at the onset of the postcolonial era, argued that "Ghostly residues of Bula Matari [the colonial state] were concealed within the apparently triumphant civil society" (1994, 218). In colonial and postcolonial Mauritania, state construction took on a decidedly authoritarian direction, which translated into the ethnic marginalization and eventually the oppression of Pulaar-speakers and other non-Arabic-speaking minorities. By contrast, in Senegal, state construction followed a more pluralist path, much less prone to violence and the exclusion of different communities.

The second objective of this chapter is closely intertwined with the previous one. It follows Young's careful attention to history and how the *longue durée* (long haul) is ingrained in current political events. In doing so, we are better equipped to recognize the significance of a local caste system with deep historical roots and its impact on intraethnic tensions. Interestingly, if interethnic relations in the two countries increasingly traveled on a different orbit, intraethnic tensions did not diverge significantly. The colonial state, as well as Mauritania's authoritarian state and Senegal's more democratic state, all relied on, reproduced, and partially consolidated a descent-based social status (or "caste") hierarchy within the Pulaar-speaking community that has its origins in the eighteenth century and even before. In his 1976 book on cultural pluralism, Young shed light on social status and caste in West Africa, "a rigid, ranked system of social strata, endogamous and ascriptive" (1976, 60). His observation applies to Fuuta Tooro: on both shores of the Senegal River, people from "noble" (or "free") lineages, who exerted much political and economic power in the precolonial era, were able to monopolize most positions of authority in the colonial and postcolonial era, whereas those of "slave" or "artisan" status have been kept at the periphery of political affairs and face major hurdles in their attempt to own land. Overall, this dual pattern, by which the state system impacted *inter*ethnic politics without significantly altering *intra*ethnic politics, will be the focus of this essay.

The Bifurcation of Interethnic Politics
in Mauritania and Senegal

To understand how state construction and ethnic politics mutually nurtured each other, we can begin with another of Crawford Young's wonderful metaphoric formulations: "the elixir of sovereignty hardened the map lines of the colonial partition into a permanent array of containers" (2012, 89). In the aftermath of World War II, the introduction of electoral politics and the growth of the bureaucracy contributed to the politicization of ethnicity. But it did so in different ways. In Mauritania, ethnicity became a salient identity marker, almost an existential one. Most political actors saw that the colonial territory and, when independence became a foreseeable possibility, the country would be dominated by the Biḍān (or "White Moors"). The French had named this colony after what they believed was its most important community, the "Maures." This left the status of non-Moor ethnic minorities from the South (the Haalpulaaren being the largest) rather uncertain.[2] In Senegal, by contrast, ethnicity was much less salient. There was, to be sure, the unresolved issue surrounding the status of Casamance (Dalberto 2020), south of Senegal.[3] But overall, ethnicity did not raise existential questions as it did in Mauritania. The "elixir of sovereignty," to use Young's apt metaphor, revealed "the complicated historical role of the Senegal River as a social force that both unites the Haalpulaar'en but now demarcates their experiences in profound ways" (Hames 2017a, 105).

At the end of the 1940s, Haalpulaar cultural entrepreneurs from both sides of the river created an organization to defend the interests of their communities in the two colonies: the Union générale des originaires de la vallée du fleuve, or UGOVF (General Union of Senegal River Valley Natives). They aimed at defending the interest of Haalpulaaren in the two colonies where, they believed, two ethnic groups dominated them: the Moors in Mauritania and the Wolof in Senegal. UGOVF activists' frame of mind, however, was still embedded in a larger French West Africa where administrative boundaries had not yet congealed into "a permanent array of containers," as Young said. But by the end of the 1950s, when the advent of independence was becoming tangible, Haalpulaar cultural entrepreneurs on both sides of the river began debating the future of Fuuta Tooro. What would happen, they wondered, once the French left? They discussed three options: (1) the status quo, which meant that the Senegal River would remain a boundary separating two independent countries; (2) the whole Valley, both its northern and southern shores, would join Senegal, following a kind of imagined "racial" divide whereby Mauritania would be the country of white Moors and Senegal would integrate all "Black African" communities; or (3) Fuuta Tooro would become a state of its own, independent from Senegal and Mauritania, along the territorial lines of the Imamate of Fuuta Tooro, the Haalpulaar-dominated Muslim polity that existed from 1776 to 1881 (Jourde 2002, chap. 5). The last two options shared one fundamental feature: the Senegal River would *not* be used to partition Haalpulaar communities, as captured by the expression "The river is not a boundary" (*maayo wonaa keerol*), to quote a Senegalese poet interviewed by John Hames in his fascinating doctoral dissertation (2017a, 105).

Of course, in the end, *Uti Possidetis* prevailed, as it did across most of the colonial/postcolonial world, enshrined in the Organization of African Unity (OAU), according to which the newly formed sovereign states should retain their colonial border. Thus, the boundary the French had drawn separating the two banks of the Senegal River became an international boundary separating and splitting ethnic communities. As Young explained in his *Politics of Cultural Pluralism* (1976), the state became "this cast-iron grid superimposed upon the culturally diverse populace of the third world." It became "the authoritative arena which defines the framework for cultural pluralism" (67). This helps us understand the bifurcated trajectories of Haalpulaaren in Mauritania and Senegal. With the creation of two separate states, each with political dynamics of its own, the political saliency and intensity of ethnic identities followed two distinct paths. Each postcolonial state, with its "reality-shaping power," as Young rightly said (1976, 66), became a hegemonic political arena, distinct from its neighbor, shaping in its own specific ways how people experienced ethnicity, how they lived their "Haalpulaar-ness." In simple terms, Mauritanian Haalpulaaren faced dynamics of exclusion based on their ethnic identity, something their Senegalese co-ethnic never experienced.

In effect, since independence, Mauritanian Haalpulaaren, as well as Wolof and Soninke, would be increasingly excluded from top positions in the one-party state (1960–78) and the military-led state (1978–91). This process was accompanied by regular episodes of violence targeting Haalpulaaren (1966, 1986, 1987), which eventually culminated in the great wave of violence of 1989–91. During this period, hundreds of civilians and military were killed and around 100,000 were violently expelled from Mauritania to Senegal (N'Diaye 2022). The global "Third Wave" of democratization in the early 1990s contributed to the transformation of the Mauritanian military regime into a competitive authoritarian regime. After 1991, the level of violence decreased, but the actual marginalization of Haalpulaaren and other ethnic minorities did not decline significantly. The key institutions of the state continue to be controlled

primarily by individuals of White Moor (Biḍān) background. Few Haalpulaaren can be counted at the top of central institutions such as the ministries of
Defense, Interior, and Justice, while most of the higher echelons of the military
hierarchy, which continues to dominate the state, are staffed by officers of
Biḍān origin (N'Diaye 2017).

During these various historical phases, Haalpulaar cultural and political
entrepreneurs created various associations, political parties, or social movements to defend their community. As I explained, UGOVR, the first major organization in Fuuta Tooro, was created in 1948 by political actors from both
sides of the river. But as the prospect of independence became more plausible,
the bifurcated experience of "Haalpulaarness" became more tangible. This led
Haalpulaar politicians of the Mauritanian shore to create a Mauritania-only
organization, the Union des originaires de la Mauritanie du Sud (UOMS,
Union of Natives of Southern Mauritania), in 1957. The name itself reified the
territorialization of politics. The "elixir of sovereignty," as Young nicely said,
was starting to disseminate into the body politics of each territory. Once Mauritania became independent, Haalpulaar cultural and political entrepreneurs
organized various movements in response to the growing exclusion of Haalpulaaren from the state apparatus. A short-lived but nevertheless significant form
of protest erupted in 1966 with the Manifesto of the 19, which opposed the
Arabization of the education system. Briefly analyzing the Mauritanian case in
his *Politics of Cultural Pluralism*, Young predicted quite accurately what was to
happen in Mauritania. Looking at the first fifteen years of independence (1960–
75), he saw that "it is very clear that Moors will continue to dominate politically
and that their commitment to the gradual implementation of Arabic as a national language is unlikely to weaken. . . . Arabism seems a highly probable response to this situation" (1976, 411). Young was right. In the 1980s, Haalpulaaren
felt the same apprehensions, this time reinforced by the 1983 Land Reform,
which was used by cronies connected to the president's inner circle to grab land
in Fuuta Tooro. It is in this context that in 1986 a group of young political activists created the Forces de libération africaines de Mauritanie (FLAM; African Liberation Forces of Mauritania). The Ould Taya regime responded by
cracking down on many Haalpulaar activists suspected of being members of
the FLAM. Two of the historical figures who had been arrested, Teeñ Yous-
souf Gueye and Tapsirou Djigo, died in jail, while many others flew to Senegal. Following the state-sponsored violence of 1989–91 and the liberalization of
the political scene in 1991, many Haalpulaaren joined opposition parties as a
way to protest the *Biḍān* military leaders, now dressed in civilian clothing
(Jourde 2002). The territorialization of Haalpulaar citizens' experience in the

Mauritanian polity, its "Mauritanization" so to speak, was further demonstrated in 2011, when cultural entrepreneurs created the *Touche pas à ma nationalité* movement (TPMN; Don't touch my nationality). This movement emerged when the government sought to use biometric technologies to register the population.[4] As Zekeria Ould Ahmed Salem (2018) explained, the new agency in charge of biometric enrollment seemed to be purposefully imposing hurdles on citizens originating from Fuuta Tooro. More recently, new cases of land grabbing in the Valley also contributed to this persistent sentiment of marginalization among Haalpulaaren (Ahmedou 2019; Le Calame 2022). In sum, the construction of the Mauritanian state, this "cast-iron grid," as Young called it (1976, 67), impacted how Haalpulaaren experienced ethnicity in Mauritania. This contrasted with how Haalpulaaren on the Senegalese shore experienced their "Haalpulaarness" throughout the construction of the Senegalese state.

In effect, in Senegal, the construction of the state followed a more pluralist direction than that of Mauritania, and ethnicity did not become a defining criterion of political and economic inclusion and exclusion. This is not to say that ethnic identities had no political significance. To be sure, since the early 1960s Haalpulaar cultural entrepreneurs in Senegal mobilized the community to defend their "linguistic citizenship" (Hames 2017b), fighting against what they described as the assimilation of their language and culture into a hegemonic "Wolofization" of the Senegalese society (McLaughlin 1995; Humery-Dieng 2001; Hames 2017a). This could be seen in the creation of ethnolinguistic associations such as Fedde Bamtaare Pulaar (Association for the Progress of Pulaar, or APR) in the 1960s and the production of widely popular radio shows in Pulaar language, as well as in the implementation of alphabetization classes in Pulaar (Schmitz 2008; Hames 2017a). But the battle for cultural autonomy was not, as seen in Mauritania, in reaction to harsh state-led exclusionary mechanisms in the political and economic spheres. Cultural and political entrepreneurs were much freer to create organizations and invest in the public sphere.

However, and this is more speculative, since the election of Macky Sall as president in 2012, the politicization of ethnicity may have taken a more disturbing turn than in the past. For the first time in Senegal's history, a Haalpulaar was elected president. After his election, an anti-Haapulaar discourse that had barely been heard before began to surface. The idea of a "Pulaar lobby" was used to criticize the president.[5] To be sure, all Senegalese presidents have been accused of nepotism in public discourses; this in itself is not new. But it is probably the first time the ethnic identity of a president was used explicitly to make these accusations. The fact that it was directed against a Haalpulaar politician, one who did not originate from the "Wolof" heartland, seems significant. To illustrate with one of the many comments that can be found online, one reader of the most popular news site called for Sall's removal from power by emphasizing specifically his ethnic identity: "Halpoularization [*sic*] of power, Halpoular [*sic*] president, Halpoular prime minister, Halpoular president AN, so goes the regime of dirty Macky. *We can't wait until 2024 to get rid of this ethnic clan management of power.*"[6] The potential crystallization of an ethnicized discourse is something to watch in the years to come in Senegal.[7]

Dembacracy in Fuuta: Intraethnic Politics

The preceding discussion on the bifurcated construction of ethnicity in the two neighboring states purposefully left aside an important piece of historical and sociological information: since (at least) the eighteenth century, the Haalpulaar society, like many other ethnic communities of the Sahel (such as the Moors, Soninke, Wolof, Bamana, and Manding), has been structured along "status" (or "caste") lines. The "free" (or "nobles") lineages dominate the social status stratification, exercising political, economic, and religious power, while those of "artisans" and "slave" status are situated at the bottom of the pyramid (Jourde 2021). "Free" lineages were in control of both political leadership positions (e.g., village chief, chief of the land, grand electors of the Imamate) and religious positions (e.g., imam, *qadi*, Sufi shaykh). Meanwhile, their economic power rested on their ownership of agricultural land along the shores of the Senegal River and its tributaries. As I will explain further, noble lineages adapted well to the colonial and postcolonial periods mainly through their integration into the structure of the state and of the ruling parties in both countries. In contrast, people who bear the stigma of "slave," called *maccuɓe* (sing. *maccuɗo*), were generally denied access to land ownership and to positions of power and religious authority (Kamara 2000; N'Gaïde 2003; Leservoisier 2008; Schmitz 2009).

The extent to which social status inequalities *within* the Haalpulaar community intersect with ethnic politics on both shores of the Senegal River has not been studied closely by specialists of ethnic politics in the region. To better grasp these intraethnic dynamics, I want to refer to Crawford Young's research once again. First, as Young pertinently noted with respect to West Africa, "A clear correlation is discernible between upper-caste origin and representation in the modern elite" (1976, 60). Second, in his last book, *The Postcolonial State in Africa*, Young added some nuances to the already very refined and subtle understanding of ethnicity of his 1976 book. Young drew from John Lonsdale's notions of "political tribalism" and "moral ethnicity" (Lonsdale 1994). "Political tribalism" is what the previous section of this chapter analyzed, that is, the extent to which political actors and the institutions they build frame dynamics of domination, exclusion, or resistance in the name of ethnicity. For its part, "moral ethnicity" is a "matrix of social responsibility" (Young 2012, 326), where members of a given community debate notions of status, privilege, access to and redistribution of wealth and power, and the moral foundations that justify these practices. This matrix can be stable over time, but it can also be disputed, transformed entirely, or partly reproduced and altered, depending on the context.

To grasp the political ramifications of this social status hierarchy, the sociologist Yaya Wane (himself a Haalpulaar from a well-known noble "religious" lineage) shed light on a fascinating concept: *Dembacracy* (Wane 1969). This portmanteau concept plays with the given name Demba, which, in Haalpulaar communities, is generally attributed by parents to their third boy. By extension, Demba refers to the person who cannot aspire to any grand political, economic, or social role, unlike the eldest son or even the second son. It is the "average person." Interestingly, of course, there is a gender dimension to this. The name of the third daughter in Haalpulaar society is Penda, but I have not found any trace of the notion of Pendacracy. *Dembacracy*, according to Wane, was coined by Haalpulaar political elites to characterize the new era (post–World War II) when elected assemblies were established. The fact that (almost) anybody could vote and that anybody could become a candidate meant, for these noble Haalpulaar elites, that the "Dembas" could suddenly become political, social, or economic leaders. As the Senegalese political scientist Alioune Badara Diop further explains, the noble elite resented *Dembacracy*, for it was "suspected of wanting to upset the sacred hierarchy of the elites by 'accidentally' favoring the election of a Demba: a man who does not have the social extraction and the patronymic required to 'legitimately' claim power" (2009, 20).[8]

I do not have the space to elaborate on the origins and transformations of this social status hierarchy prior to the colonial era (Schmitz 1994; Kane 2004), but for the purpose of this chapter, let me simply say that this stratification is significant in light of how the French colonizers integrated it into the structure of the colonial state and, later, into the postcolonial state construction. Once again, Young provides us with a useful grid to better decipher how the colonial state shaped the status hierarchy. As he explained in his 1994 book on the African colonial state, French colonial authorities on the ground, in Fuuta Tooro as well as in many other locations across the empire, quickly abandoned the theoretical notion of "direct rule," recognizing the "pragmatic virtues of precolonial structuration of domination in molding societies for subjugation" (108).

Thus, they relied on a form of indirect rule, seeking "intermediaries of hege-mony'" (Young 1994, 107). In Fuuta Tooro, as in many other places, *chefs de can-ton* (local district chiefs) "were recruited from ruling families" (Young 1994, 150). In doing so, French colonialists injected into local societies a substantial dose of authoritarian rule backed by the power of Bula Matari, the colonial state, thereby undermining mechanisms of checks and balances that previously ex-isted. Young noted "the irony of indirect rule as creating, in reality, a transla-tion into local African society of the authoritarian principle *so deeply imprinted on Bula Matari*" (1994, 224).[9] This led to what we could call the Bula Matari-ization of local ruling groups, reinforcing the power of lineages with noble (or "free") status, while subaltern individuals and groups, especially non-noble ones, were even more excluded from positions of power across Fuuta Tooro during the colonial era.

When the French introduced electoral politics, after World War II, the sem-blance of democratic spirit it displayed quickly dissolved: elections and party politics were not meant to make the local political scene more democratic, eq-uitable, or fair in any sense. Local colonial officers, at least in Fuuta, were not willing to let Bula Matari be challenged by Fuutanke elected representatives. In concrete terms, this meant that soon after some moderate anticolonial figures rose to prominence in the first elections in 1946, they were quickly pushed aside by the colonial administration, which made sure to guarantee the electoral suc-cess of trustworthy individuals belonging to ruling families with a "stake" in the colonial architecture. These intersecting "politico-administrative dynasties," as Ibrahima Sall calls them (2007, 53), held firm on their authority on both sides of the river against the threat of *Dembacracy*.

When both countries became independent, political dynamics at the national level and at the local level were clearly not favorable to *Dembacracy*, to the rise of "Dembas" in political affairs, and even less of "Pendas." As I ex-plained in the previous section, the national political scene in both countries was eventually led by de facto and then de jure single-party regimes in the 1960s and parts of the 1970s. The two countries parted ways when Senegal re-introduced a degree of multipartyism in the 1970s, which eventually led to democratic alternations in power in the 2000s, while Mauritania plunged into military politics in 1978–91, followed by the establishment of a competitive au-thoritarian regime with military officers in civilian clothing (1991 to today). But how did the local social status hierarchy fare among Haalpulaar commu-nities on the two shores of the river? In other words, did *Dembacracy* flourish in some parts, maybe on the southern bank, or did noble groups prevent its growth?

Table 8.1. Share of the Ruling Socialist Party's
Candidate (Abdou Diouf) in Presidential Elections,
1983–93 and 2000, Fuuta Tooro vs. National

Year	Matam Department (Fuuta Tooro)	National
1983	93%	83%
1988	94%	73%
1993	89%	58%
2000 (second round)	71%	42%

Source: Data for the 1983, 1988, and 1993 elections are from Beck (1996, 161). Data for 2000 are the score of the second round of the presidential election, held on March 19, 2000 (Diop 2009, 222).

On the Senegalese shore of the river, in the first decades of the postcolonial era, most Haalpulaaren elected officials and members of Léopold Senghor's ruling UPS (and, after 1978, the Parti Socialiste, or PS) came from noble families. *Rimbe* ("free"/noble) politicians found a way to consolidate their political hegemony over the southern shore despite the official socialist and progressist discourses of the time (Diop 2009, 45). In her doctoral dissertation, Linda Beck, a student of Crawford Young, demonstrated how these ruling families successfully integrated the local and national neopatrimonial networks of the Socialist party-state, capturing political positions (elected seats and administrative positions) and resources while delivering the votes to the ruling party (Beck 1996). For many Senegalese Haalpulaar noble families, letting *Dembacracy* grow in Fuuta Tooro was not thinkable. To illustrate this point, Beck quotes one of her informants, who said that "The equation of democracy with equality, nevertheless, disturbed a young toorodo [noble], who expressed his exasperation with this 'misinterpretation' of democracy, fearing that members of the lower castes would 'take their equality as a basis for revenge . . . [such that] if I were a candidate, they would not vote for me because I am a toorodo [noble religious status]'" (1996, 208). The hold of the Socialist Party in Fuuta Tooro can be seen in earlier data retrieved by Beck (1996, 61) and Diop (2009), which I have combined in table 8.1: in the 1980s and 1990s, the PS secured a higher percentage of votes in Fuuta than in the rest of Senegal, thanks to the hegemonic role of ruling lineages. Looking at the heartland of Fuuta, the Matam Department, the PS won 93 percent of the votes in 1983 (vs. 83 percent nationally), 94 percent in 1988 (vs. 73 percent nationally), and 89 percent in 1993 (vs. 58 percent nationally).

Political and economic capital intersected, which in the context of Fuuta, a heavily agricultural region, meant that noble families maintained their control over land in spite of various land tenure reforms. "Dembas" have a hard time securing access to land. Beck offers a magistral perspective on this: despite the progressive spirit of the 1964 Land Reform, "The PS state took no action against these [noble] individuals who served as their political intermediaries with the population; nor did the state seek to break the 'conspiracy of silence' of interested noble-politicians by educating the population as to their new rights" (1996, 187). The 1972 reform, which added a more democratic feature to the system (through the elections of rural councils), followed the same path: "Despite the potential for radically altering local power structures, the reforms, once again, served more as political rhetoric than reform" (Beck 1996, 187). Bloch describes the power dynamic at stake: rural councils were "a modern means for traditional elites to maintain their dominance, legitimized by the trappings of democratic processes" (Bloch 1988, 2, quoted in Beck 1996, 188). What did all of this do to the status hierarchy and the possibility for lower-caste people to improve their condition and change sociopolitical power relations? According to Beck, the failed land reforms point to the "disadvantaged position of the lower castes and landless *tooroo∫e* who do not even benefit from a trickle down of patronage when their interests contradict those of the elites" (Beck 1996, 188). Jean Schmitz, Abdoul Sow, and Sonja Fagerberg-Diallo further explain how noble families maneuvered: rural councils have "consolidated rather than weakened the power of traditional elites, who invested the councils in the name of 'decentralization,' thereby restoring the power of the 'old turbans'" (2021, 7). The construction of huge dams on the Senegal River and other important irrigation schemes across the Valley in the 1980s to the 1990s had the potential to favor low-caste families. But ruling families once again mobilized their political and economic capital and prevented any significant change to land ownership (Beck 1996, 197).

The post-1990s wave of democratization had the potential to bring about the establishment of *Dembacracy*, as it injected, at least officially, more freedom into the political system while enlarging the political field. But political scientist Alioune Badara Diop observes that despite the alternations in power at the national level, which led the ruling PS to lose power in 2000 (which was followed by a second alternation in 2012 and a third alternation in the National Assembly in 2022), the anti-*Dembacracy* forces are still quite strong at the local level in Fuuta. As he explains, all political parties in Fuuta continue to rely on "the 'natural'

leadership of a single social group: the *toorobbe*. In fact, the identity of the political actors evolving within these parties reveals an overwhelming predominance
of politicians from the top of the social stratification" (Diop 2009, 225).

On the Mauritanian shore of Fuuta, as I demonstrated, those who had
opposed colonial authorities and their allies among the local ruling chiefs were
either relegated to the margins of political life or eventually co-opted into what
would become the de facto, and soon de jure, single party (Jourde 2002, chap. 5).
Members of the Territorial Assembly and government ministers in the 1950s all
came from noble families. The same was true once Mauritania became independent in 1960. From the 1960s to the 1980s, as Marchesin shows in his work on
Mauritania, Fuutanke political leaders were almost all nobles (Marchesin 1992).
There was one deputy in the National Assembly at the time of the PPM single
party (1960–78) who actually was from the "slave" community (not a Haalpulaar,
however, but a Soninke). Informants used to tell me this story about him: he was
famous for having said to President Ould Daddah (1960–78), "You may have created a parliament and everything, but you have not brought democracy over
here. Me, even if I am a *député*, I am still your captive."[10]

The "Third Wave" of democratization did not have much of an impact in
Mauritania either, at least in terms of noble families' control over political positions and land. *Dembacracy* had a hard time flourishing on the Mauritanian
shore of the river. The continuing domination of Arabic-speaking elites over
Fuutanke rested on a kind of asymmetric alliance with "noble" Fuutanke political actors that left little space for "Dembas" (Jourde 2002). As the Haalpulaar
mayor of an important town of the Valley (on the Mauritanian shore) told me
back in 1999, "Nobles continue to hold on the highest positions, be it amongst
Moors, Haalpulaaren or Sooninke. For instance, take this person [gives me the
name], he's from my town, he's an engineer and the Project manager of [a
major international organization present in Mauritania]. But when he organized a [political] committee [for the ruling party], he said he could not be the
Chair, because he would not be able to summon people, to talk in front of people, because of his [slave] origin. We just can't change people's mentality." In
addition, similar to Senegal, ruling Fuutanke families also derived much of
their power from the control they exerted over land. When irrigated schemes
began to appear, noble lineages successfully captured these new economic opportunities, which they could then use to buttress their political influence (Leservoisier 1994).

With the help of my research assistant, M. L. Sakho, we have identified and
collected the social status of Haalpulaar mayors in the recent local elections in
both Mauritania (2013 and 2018) and Senegal (2014 and 2022). These data

Table 8.2. Haalpulaar Mayors' Social Status in the Senegal River
Valley (Senegal and Mauritania)

Location and date	Noble	Artisan	Former slave	Former slave (other ethnic groups)
Senegal Fuuta, 2014	43	1	3	0
Senegal Fuuta, 2022	41	2	4	0
Mauritania Fuuta, 2013	21	1	0	5
Mauritania Fuuta, 2018	21	1	0	5

Source: Information gathered by M. L. Sakho and the author.

provide an interesting window into the continuing control noble lineages exert
over local politics in Fuuta on both sides of the river. Of course, a more systematic study still needs to be done, taking into account a much larger number of
political and economic positions of authority. But for the sake of this chapter,
the social status of mayors still provides a revealing indication of the "conditions of entry" into the local political competition on the northern and southern shores of the Senegal River Valley. As we can see in table 8.2, in Senegal,
out of forty-seven mayors, forty-three were noble in 2013 (91 percent), and
forty-one were noble in 2018 (87 percent). There were only three *maccuɗo* (slave
status) mayors in 2014 and four in 2022. In Mauritania, in the past two local
elections, in 2013 and 2018, all Haalpulaaren mayors were noble, with the exception of one "artisan." The only mayors of "former slave" status are not
Haalpulaaren, ruling over from localities with large non-Haalpulaaren communities (Haratin [Moors] and Soninke). This echoes the epigraph that I included (2002), which was a quote from a Fuutanke mayor, who in 1999 said the
following: "I did not want to be mayor. We wanted somebody who is not from
a ruling family. However, this is not possible yet."[11] The one exception on
the Mauritanian shore, which confirmed the rule enunciated by the mayor I
quoted, was the then mayor of Boghe (1994–2001), whom I had also interviewed several times. But this was an exception indeed (after him, the two mayors who succeeded him were from ruling noble families). More than twenty
years later, it appears things have not changed significantly.

Normative factors combined with political and economic factors could pos-
sibly explain the continuing domination of mayors of noble backgrounds at the
local level regardless of the type of regime (more democratic in Senegal and

more authoritarian in Mauritania). For Mauritania, the hypothesis I made back in 2002 still stands, I believe. After the violence of the 1986–91 era, the authoritarian regime relied on dominant ruling families in Fuuta and, together, staged their mutual understanding that politics was not for *Dembas*. Furthermore, one could hypothesize that the tensions surrounding ethnic relations make it particularly harder for anticaste activists to thrive among Haalpulaar communities. When facing a solid authoritarian regime that perpetuates the marginalization of their ethnic group, Haalpulaar activists may have a difficult time shedding light on *intra*ethnic problems such as social status inequalities. Indeed, doing so can be strategically framed by Haalpulaar elites as a form of betrayal of one's own ethnic group, spreading intraethnic disunity at a time when people should regroup to defend the entire community.

In Senegal, however, one could have expected a different outcome thanks to the country's democratic success. But we must remember that the institutionalization of fair elections and the ensuing possibility for opponents to win elections and beat incumbents at the national level does not necessarily mean that the sociological profile of leaders has become more diverse. This is perhaps even more so at the local level, where norms delineating who ought to be a leader of the community are salient. This is, after all, what Diop's study suggested (2009, 44): the institutionalization of democratic elections has not significantly eroded the symbolic capital of noble political actors locally. The competition *among* "nobles" may be more open and fairer than in Mauritania, but the normative attributes about who gets to run for office in the first place have not truly changed. This normative dimension is undoubtedly coupled with a political-economic one. The analysis of Linda Beck mentioned earlier made clear how noble families were able to use their political and economic power to consolidate their control over land despite all the land reforms adopted since independence. Meanwhile, they have also been incorporated in the neopatrimonial networks of the state and the ruling party of the moment. This economic capital has proven to be useful in electoral campaigns, contributing to their success in winning mayoral elections. As Beck concluded, "patronage politics of the Senegalese state has permitted the nobles access to the necessary economic resources to remain in power and maintain their status in society" (1996, 206). This could explain why little change has been seen at the local level despite a more democratic national arena.

This is not to say that *Dembacracy* can never flourish on one or both shores of the river. Although the numbers are very low, it is important to notice that in Senegal, there were three (2013) and then four (2018) mayors of slave status following the past two elections, compared to none in Mauritania. This could indicate that the significantly higher democratic quality of Senegal's political life

could incrementally bring some changes in Fuuta. If we look beyond local elections, we notice that in Senegal, there are serious attempts at challenging the
social status stratification and its political, economic, and social consequences.
Though I lack the space to elaborate here, I will provide a short example. In
2004, individuals of "slave" status in the Senegalese Fuuta created an organization called Endam Bilali (the descendants of Bilal, the Black companion of the
Prophet) to mobilize their community and confront the status hierarchy.[12] They
established cells in different towns and villages of the Valley.[13] Very tellingly,
members of Endam Bilali do not seek to erase their slave status or hide it.
Rather, they seek to proudly celebrate who they are, their history, and their culture. Their demands are mainly directed at the state and at local political elites,
calling for equitable access to land, formal education, religious education, and
social recognition more generally. They are active locally, organizing many social and religious celebrations and mobilizing quite a large number of people.
Their recent annual meetings have been sponsored by a very popular Sufi
shaykh, one of the few who has been able to overcome the status hierarchy as
someone who is not "noble."[14] It is too soon to measure the effect Endam Bilali
will have on social stratification on the Senegalese shore of the river and
whether this movement, along with others, embodies the gradual development
of *Dembacracy* in Fuuta, but it is undoubtedly a movement that will need to be
followed closely.

Conclusion

Crawford Young has given us immensely valuable and heuristic analytical tools
to decipher processes of state construction, political regime dynamics, and trajectories of identities. In addition, he possessed an extensive empirical knowledge of the historical and political realities of many different societies and
countries. These two forms of knowledge nurtured each other. These were the
lessons I wanted to apply when I first left to undertake fieldwork in Mauritania
in 1999. I have kept them with me ever since, as I sought to illustrate in this
chapter. In this chapter, I wanted to draw from some of the many lessons Young
taught us, including how to analyze the bifurcated trajectories of Haalpulaar
communities in two neighboring states, Senegal and Mauritania. To do so, it
required that we envision both how the divergent dynamics of state construction impacted this partitioned ethnic community and how "being a Haalpulaar" on one side of the Senegal River would eventually differ a lot from being
similarly situated on the other side. But it also meant that we should pay atten-

tion to historical dynamics and explore internal debates and practices that sustained acute inequalities among the members of these communities.

Crawford Young was a wonderful *passeur de savoir*, a transmitter of knowledge. He was an incomparable *enseignant-chercheur*, this French title that captures more than the word "professor" the essence of who he was: both a teacher (*enseignant*) and a researcher (*chercheur*). It refers to one who transmits both the motivation and the compulsion to know more, to be a perpetual student, one whose quest to learn can never be satiated. As I went back to his books and scholarly articles to write this chapter, I was once again amazed by how much I could learn again and again, both analytically and empirically. This, I hope, is a legacy of Crawford Young that we need to pass on to future generations of students and scholars.

Notes

1. See Young's chapter 6 in his *Postcolonial State* (2012), devoted to "Democratization and Its Limits." As Young's research assistant in my first year in Madison in 1995, I was tasked with a simple mission: writing research briefs on the status of democratization/authoritarianism in every single African country! There was no better way for me to learn about countries other than the one I wanted to work on for my dissertation.

2. In 1903, the French created the Protectorate of the Land of the Moors of the Lower Senegal (Protectorat des pays maures du Bas-Sénégal). In 1904, this protectorate became the Territory of Mauritania and was fully integrated into French West Africa.

3. At the end of the colonial era, Casamance regionalism was driven neither by ethnicity nor by religion, even if some ethnic communities, such as the Diola, formed a majority and Islam was a minority religion. This regionalism originated from its distinct historical and territorial integration in Senegal, as an enclave stuck between then British Gambia, (Portuguese) Guinea-Bissau, and French Guinea. See Dalberto (2020).

4. See their 2011 memorandum here: http://haratine.blogspot.co.uk/2012/04/mauritanie-memorandum-du-mouvement.html.

5. For instance, see the comments made by this politician: https://senegal7.com/oumar-sarr-denonce-un-lobby-toucouleur-autour-de-macky-sall/.

6. https://www.seneweb.com/news/Politique/amadou-ba-la-face-cachee-de-lsquo-rsquo-_n_388254.html

7. Hames (2017a, 118) also noted this ethnicization of criticisms against Macky Sall.

8. On *Dembacracy*, see also Schmitz (2000, 40) and Beck (1996, 207).

9. On the role of local ruling lineages during the colonial period in Fuuta, see also Beck (1996, 182) and Kane (1987).

10. Interview, Nouakchott, July 18, 1999.

11. Interview with a then young mayor from a ruling family from Fuuta, Nouak-chott, November 4, 1999.

12. Interview with a member of the association, Dakar, June 2, 2017.

13. For a fascinating account of one of Endam Bilali's meetings, see this enlighten-ing article: Abderrahmane Ngaide, "Le feccere Fuuta de 1776 en question? Mathioubé et alors!," September 14, 2012, http://www.avomm.com/Le-feccere-Fuuta-de-1776-en -question-Mathioube-et-alors-_a15230.html.

14. Interview with a member of the association, Dakar, June 2, 2017.

References

Ahmedou, Hamdi. 2019. "Mobilisations citoyennes contre les accaparements fonciers en Mauritanie." *Revue internationale des études du développement* 238 (2): 61–88.

Beck, Linda. 1996. "'Patrimonial Democrats' in a Culturally Plural Society: Democrati-zation and Political Accommodation in the Patronage Politics of Senegal." PhD diss., University of Wisconsin–Madison.

Bloch, Peter. 1988. "An Egalitarian Development Project in a Stratified Society: Who Ends up with the Land." Madison, WI: Land Tenure Center.

Dalberto, Séverine Awenengo. 2020. "Hidden Debates over the Status of the Casa-mance during the Decolonization Process in Senegal: Regionalism, Territorialism, and Federalism at a Crossroads, 1946–62." *Journal of African History* 61 (1): 67–88. https://doi.org/10.1017/S0021853720000043.

Diop, Alioune Badara. 2009. *Le Sénégal, une démocratie du phénix?* Dakar: Karthala.

Hames, John. 2017a. "'A River Is Not a Boundary': Interplays of National and Linguis-tic Citizenship in Pulaar Language Activism." *Canadian Journal of African Studies* 51 (1): 103–22.

Hames, John. 2017b. "Language Activism on the Airwaves: Pulaar Radio Broadcasting in the Senegal River Valley." *Communication, Culture and Critique* 10 (4): 657–74.

Humery-Dieng, Marie-Ève. 2001. "Le paradis, le mariage et la terre: Des langues de l'écrit en milieu fuutanke (arabe, français et pulaar)." *Cahiers d'études africaines* 41 (163–64): 565–94.

Jourde, Cédric. 2002. "Dramas of Ethnic Elites Accommodation: The Authoritarian Restoration in Mauritania." PhD diss., University of Wisconsin–Madison.

Jourde, Cédric. 2021. "Social Stratification in the Sahel." In *The Oxford Handbook of the Afri-can Sahel*, edited by Leonardo A. Villalón, 632–49. Oxford: Oxford University Press.

Kamara, Ousmane. 2000. "Les divisions statutaires des descendants d'esclaves au Fuuta Tooro mauritanien." *Journal des africanistes* 70 (1): 265–89.

Kane, Mouhamed Moustapha. 1987. "A History of Fuuta Tooro, 1890s–1920s: Senegal under Colonial Rule. The Protectorate." 2 vols. PhD diss., Michigan State Univer-sity, East Lansing.

Kane, Oumar. 2004. *La première hégémonie peule: Le Fuuta Tooro de Koli Teṇṇella à Almaami Abdul.* Paris: Karthala.

Le Calame. 2022. "Nouvelle histoire d'accaparement des terres à Boghé." http://www .lecalame.info/?q=node%2F13173.

Leservoisier, Olivier. 1994. *La question foncière en Mauritanie: Terres et pouvoirs dans la région du Gorgol*. Paris: L'Harmattan.

Leservoisier, Olivier. 2008. "Les héritages de l'esclavage dans la société haalpulaar de Mauritanie." *Journal des africanistes* 78 (1–2) (March): 247–67.

Lonsdale, John. 1994. "Moral Ethnicity and Political Tribalism." In *Inventions and Boundaries: Historical and Anthropological Approaches to the Study of Ethnicity and Nationalism*, edited by Preben Kaarsholm and Jan Hultin, 11:131–50. Occasional Papers. Roskilde.

Marchesin, Philippe. 1992. *Tribus, ethnies et pouvoir en Mauritanie*. Paris: Karthala.

Mc Laughlin, Fiona. 1995. "Haalpulaar Identity as a Response to Wolofization." *African Languages and Cultures* 8 (2): 153–68.

N'Diaye, Boubacar. 2017. *Mauritania's Colonels: Political Leadership, Civil-Military Relations and Democratization*. London: Routledge.

N'Diaye, Sidi. 2022. "'Ce que nous voulons, c'est une Commission vérité et réconciliation': La justice transitionnelle en Mauritanie: Un modèle, sa promotion et des évitements politiques." *L'année du Maghreb* (26): 97–118.

N'Gaïde, Abderrahmane. 2003. "Stéréotypes et imaginaires sociaux en milieu Haalpulaar: Classer, stigmatiser et toiser." *Cahiers d'études Africaines* 43 (172): 707–38.

Salem, Zekeria Ould Ahmed. 2018. "'Touche pas à ma nationalité': Enrôlement biométrique et controverses sur l'identification en Mauritanie." *Politique africaine* 152 (4): 77–99.

Sall, Ibrahima. 2007. *Mauritanie du sud: Conquêtes et administration coloniales françaises, 1890–1945*. Paris: Karthala.

Schmitz, Jean. 1994. "Cités noires: Les républiques villageoises du Fuuta Tooro (Vallée du fleuve Sénégal)." *Cahiers d'études africaines* 34 (133–35): 419–60.

Schmitz, Jean. 2000. "'L'élection divise': La politique au village dans la vallée du Sénégal." *Afrique contemporaine* (194): 34–46.

Schmitz, Jean. 2008. "La vallée du Sénégal entre (co)développement et transnationalisme." *Politique africaine* 109 (1): 56–72.

Schmitz, Jean. 2009. "Islamic Patronage and Republican Emancipation: The Slaves of the Almaami in the Senegal River Valley." In *Reconfiguring Slavery: West African Trajectories*, by Benedetta Rossi, 86–111. Liverpool: Liverpool University Press.

Schmitz, Jean, Abdoul Sow, and Sonja Fagerberg-Diallo. 2021. "Atlas et archives de la moyenne vallée du fleuve Sénégal." IRD.

Wane, Yaya. 1969. *Les toucouleur du Fouta Tooro (Sénégal): Stratification sociale et structure familiale*. Dakar: Université de Dakar/IFAN.

Young, Crawford. 1976. *The Politics of Cultural Pluralism*. Madison: University of Wisconsin Press.

Young, Crawford. 1994. *The African Colonial State in Comparative Perspective*. New Haven, CT: Yale University Press.

Young, Crawford. 2012. *The Postcolonial State in Africa: Fifty Years of Independence, 1960–2010*. Madison: University of Wisconsin Press.

9

Crawford Young's Cultural Politics Analytic Paradigm Applied to Ukraine-Russia

Joshua B. Forrest

The goal of this chapter is to argue that Crawford Young's conceptual insights within the field of comparative politics regarding the study of ethnicity, ethnic politics, nationalism, and state behavior
provide useful analytic guideposts for understanding political change contem-
porarily as in the past. To do so, I will outline some of the key principles that
represent what I suggest may be considered to constitute a "Young-ian" analytic paradigm regarding the study of cultural politics and then proceed to explain how this paradigm enables us to better appreciate the evolution of
Ukrainian nationalism, the history of Ukraine-Russian political relations, and
the ongoing war in Ukraine. I will then conclude with some brief comparative
observations regarding the viability of this analytic paradigm for studying cultural politics in various parts of the world.

It may be noted that my construction of what I am referring to as a Young-
ian analytic paradigm is based primarily on an interpretative synthesis of central concepts in what is generally regarded as his theoretical magnum opus, *The
Politics of Cultural Pluralism* (1976), which was explicitly intended as a globally
relevant comparative study of the dynamics of cultural politics. Crawford

Young would thereafter and for the remainder of his half-century-long career become distinguished as a major contributor to research and scholarship on African politics, with enormous intellectual and academic influence on that field (which accounts for why the majority of contributions to the present volume are focused on African politics).

In the present essay, by applying his analytic paradigm on cultural pluralism to the study of Ukraine and Ukraine-Russian relations, I aim to (re)emphasize the comparative utility, timelessness, and insight of a Young-ian analytic approach to the study of the politics of culture, ethnicity, and state–ethnic relations writ large—that is, on the global stage. To do so, I outline what I take to be a two-part Young-ian conceptual paradigm, focusing on (1) the dynamics of grassroots ethnic mobilization, which can be best understood in terms of the *variability* of cultural activism, the *situational and contextual* nature of such activism, and the importance of *cultural entrepreneurship* and of *civic nationalism*; and (2) the quest by autocratic national leaders to achieve *state domination over the ethnic "other,"* here referring to the ways in which dictatorial regimes attempt to delegitimize, dominate and exploit subaltern cultural groups. I then utilize this dual analytical paradigm to explain the origin and gradual emergence of a distinctive Ukrainian identity and of a resilient Ukrainian nationalist movement; the multifaceted nature of that movement; the eventual formation of a civic, pluralistic Ukrainian nation-state; as well as the existential challenges to Ukrainian nationalism posed (in the past as at present) by Russian state repression and autocratic expansionism. I indicate that Russian leaders' regularly voiced distortions of the history of Russian–Ukrainian relations represent an effort, over the course of centuries, to justify their effort to dominate and exploit the Ukrainian "other."

Ethnic Behavior: Variable, Situational, and Entrepreneurial

Permit me to begin, then, by briefly discussing the core components of Young's paradigm, referring here to the variable, situational, and entrepreneurial nature of cultural politics and the emergence of civic nationalism, as well as the challenges posed by a hostile autocratic state.

Variability

Young's scholarship helped to more fully expose the unpredictability, adaptability, and variability of cultural political change; by doing so he meant to emphasize the many variants of grassroots ethnopolitical behavior, depending on political circumstances. Such behavior ranges from peaceable electoral engagement to mass mobilization in order to physically defend one's community from threats of violence, from intracommunity identity assertion and cultural engagement (book writing, artistic expression, ethnolinguistic education, journalism, and radio programming) to coalition building with other groups, from lobbying on behalf of one's ethnic co-members to large-scale migration to avoid the predations of a hostile state. These behaviors cannot easily be anticipated because of the fluctuating, often occluded, difficult-to-perceive challenges that arise, especially within relatively newly formed, unstable nation-states and that sometimes reflect responses to manipulative interventions by governing regimes. Because of the emotive nature of cultural mobilization (on the part of ethnic group members and those opposed to a particular group), Young emphasized the volatile nature of ethnic politics, which results in dramatic differences in types of activity within a short time frame—for example, relative apathy followed quickly by intense activism in the face of a sudden existential crisis. It is in these respects that group assertion, intercultural accommodation, and state–ethnic relations often reflect a type of politics characterized by historical variability and political unpredictability (Young 1976).

Situational/Contextual Politics

Young furthermore emphasized that the success of cultural mobilization hinges on the favorability of the broader situational context. Mobilizational success typically depends on a combination of multiple factors that may differ from one historical context to the next. Such factors may include access to economic and organizational resources, leadership capacity, a momentary window of tolerance by the state, the state's political incapacity, sustained engagement by group members, favorable alliances with other cultural groups, military capacity in the event of open hostilities, and potentially additional factors. For Young, ethnic activism is often preceded by the long-term gradual generation of deeply rooted personal attachments to particular cultural collectivities, regardless of how imprecise the historical memory of an ethnic formation may be. It is also accompanied by a favorable set of circumstances that quickly emerges. Situational opportunism may facilitate a strengthening of cultural identity and help to make it possible for political activism to produce significant mobilization by members of a cultural group. It may furthermore be noted that because of the importance of an auspicious confluence of multiple situational factors and the crucial role played by the (re)activation of emotional and cultural links, the particular timing of ethnic mobilization is inordinately challenging to predict (Young 1976, 4–5).

Here, it is important to emphasize that while always conscious of the importance of crafting a shared identity while promoting communal solidarity, Young nonetheless firmly rejected the "primordial" perspective, which prioritizes individual beliefs and sentimental attachment as the *central* determinants of ethnic behavior. Instead, Young adopted a more nuanced, multifactorial, layered approach to the study of ethnopolitical mobilization that underlines the importance of political context, historical timing, the ethnic policies of the state, economic change, nation-state integrity (or decline), changes in national and international values (such as values favoring cultural tolerance or electoral democracy), the behavior and attitude of co-national ethnic groups, and a group's historical experience with cultural activism. Thus, the emergence of a distinct cultural identity and a politically influential cultural movement depends on a combination of contextually specific opportunities and circumstances. Young made clear that as those circumstances evolve and change, the trajectory of cultural politics can become dramatically altered in a given situational instance (Young 1976).

Cultural Entrepreneurship and Civic Nationalism

Crawford Young also underlined the crucial role of "cultural entrepreneurship"—grassroots activism aiming for the social, educational, artistic, and intellectual mobilization of ethnic adherents and the crafting of a political movement capable of promoting the collective interests of the group's members (Young 1976). In certain (situationally favorable) political circumstances (such as occurred in the formation of Pakistan and Bangladesh), effective cultural entrepreneurship can help to shape the evolution of ethnic political power in such a way as to forge a de facto near convergence between the process of new nation-state formation and the process of cultural identity-strengthening (Young 1976). At the same time, Young wrote eloquently of the mutual tolerance and intercultural cooperation that may characterize successful nation building even when a predominant cultural group is able to achieve political control of most government institutions. Such cooperation often occurs when there are minority cultural groups that may populate particular localities or regions, and cultural entrepreneurs within the politically dominant group choose to pursue a strategy centered on a multigroup alliance and shared interests at multiple levels—among localities, regions, and territories—in the interest of forging mutually beneficial nation-building coalitions (rather than emphasizing ethnic exclusivism). This leads to the creation of *civic nationalism*—emphasizing loyalty to the nation-state as a whole and reflecting values of mutual respect and inclusivity, but without lessening the successful activation of per-group identity formation. In point of fact, Young asserts that such a model of nation building is more common than the creation of ethnonationalist models of nationalism (where the nation reflects uni-ethnic control of the state) (Young 1976).

State Repression of Cultural Groups

Shifting from his discussion of grassroots cultural mobilization to the topic of an autocratic state's repression of particular ethnic groups, Young emphasized the danger to cultural groups posed by power-mongering despots—such as Mobutu of the DRC—with particular regard to the carrying out of a political agenda defined by targeted social violence against ethnic minorities and the plundering of their natural resources. He analyzed with particular insight the ability of a deft autocrat to distribute state resources in ways that invoke loyalty from his kleptocratic entourage and from oligarchs within his inner circle without undermining his own leadership. Young noted that in ethnically plural societies, a ruling oligarchy can enhance its power through instrumentalist interventions that target specific cultural groups, whether by deploying patrimonial/clientelist tools of manipulation or by carrying out extensive state violence (Young 1976).

Ukrainian Nationalism and Russia's Invasions

Contemporary events make clear the heightened relevance of many of Young's insights regarding cultural politics and the importance of his multifactorial analytic paradigm for the study of cultural mobilization and state–ethnic relations. Certainly, his contextually centered, multiscalar approach and attention to historical variability and cultural entrepreneurship as well as to autocratic excess help to provide an analytical foundation for more fully appreciating the vicissitudes of present-day ethnic mobilization and the contemporary wielding of dictatorial state power against the ethnic "other" in various parts of the world today. The current catastrophic Russia-instigated war taking place in Ukraine (which began in February 2022) provides a particularly dramatic window into the role played by cultural politics in helping to determine the course of political change in the Ukrainian nation-state.

Toward State-Led Ethnic Repression

It does not take special insight to observe the extent to which Russian president Vladimir Putin has relied on a particularly expansionist approach to the wielding of autocratic power and has adopted and carried out a violent, aggressive notion of ethnonational Russophile expansionism. This has been coupled with the promulgation of a historically distorted narrative regarding Russia's purportedly "rightful" access to the territory of Ukraine, with devastating consequences for the inhabitants of that nation. Putin and his autocratic entourage instigated war on the people of Ukraine, intent on their subjugation and on the conquest and absorption into Russia of Ukrainian territory.

To be sure, the politics of Russia's military invasion of Ukraine and its attempt to institute a particularly predatory form of political overrule are exceedingly complex. Here, a Young-ian analytic prism helps to provide an explanatory overlay. Thus, it is evident that Putin and his autocratic henchmen were attempting to instrumentally galvanize the Russian populace at the grassroots; highly orchestrated Soviet-style cultural gatherings were held in stadiums in order to spread the good feeling—however artificially contrived—of shared Russian ethnic and national traditions. Military conscription was activated in February 2022 for reserve soldiers and sailors up to age forty-five and for ex-officers up through age fifty-five—with even these relatively elevated age limits subsequently removed several months later—on the pretext of a heightened need to defend the homeland against imminent Ukrainian and Western aggression. The Russian government asserted that the very preservation of the Russian cultural collectivity was at stake and that this was the rationale behind a purportedly "defensive" military mobilization ("Russian President Vladimir Putin's Full Speech," February 24, 2022; "Russia Scraps Age Limit . . . ," May 29, 2022; Stepanenko et al. 2022).

But Putin went beyond proclaiming the need for Russia to defend itself in arguing that Russia's military invasion of Ukraine is justified because, earlier in history, Ukraine once formed part of the Russian nation—indeed, it is for this reason that Putin asserted that Russia's seizure of Crimea in 2014 constituted "an act of historical justice" (Plokhy 2015, 341). Moreover, he claimed that Kyiv (the capital of Ukraine) is where the Russian people actually originated—and that, therefore, *Russian cultural identity includes the inhabitants of Ukraine*. According to this logic, those who today call themselves Ukrainians are interlopers who do not have a truly separate or independent identity—since their claim to cultural distinctiveness is based on an artificial construction of Ukrainian identity cultivated initially several hundred years ago by the Polish elite and that is encouraged today by the West, according to Putin. And so, Putin reasons, this pretension to separateness effectively means that so-called Ukrainians are, in effect, trespassing in Kyiv and throughout Ukrainian territory (Putin 2021). Putin asserted that Ukrainians are actually Russians who are falsely pretending to be a Ukrainian "other" (Shlapentokh 2021). Here, the Russian dictator Putin attempts to justify Russia's military aggression against these "Little Russians"—a demeaning term used by Russians since the mid-nineteenth century to refer to Ukrainians—by insisting, in effect, that they need to be forcibly and violently re-educated about their membership in the greater Slavic brotherhood and politically and militarily reconnected to their "Big Russian" blood relatives (Putin 2021). Indeed, as part of this effort, the Russian army in 2022 engaged in the systematic burning of Ukrainian-language books and their replacement with Russian texts and seized and removed Ukrainian art and cultural artifacts in Russia-occupied territories of Ukraine (Parsons 2022; Gettleman and Mykolyshyn 2023).

Ukraine's Historical Variability and the March toward Civic Nationalism

Notwithstanding Putin's unbalanced reinterpretation of Ukrainian history, the fact is that Ukrainians are indeed characterized by a distinctive national cultural and linguistic heritage shaped by a steady period of nation building over the past century and a half. To be sure, it is the case that their culture initially reflected an earlier Slavic origin that they share with Russians. Thus, in the tenth and eleventh centuries—long before the emergence of a vigorous Ukrainian nationalist movement in the nineteenth century—people who lived in what is today Ukraine and parts of western Russia were ruled over by an eastern Slav polity known as Kyivan Rus (Shlapentokh 2021). As a result, Ukrainians still share substantial cultural attributes with Russians, even as they now primarily identify with their own distinctive culture and celebrate their nationalist impulse, which developed steadily throughout the nineteenth and twentieth centuries. This underscores the variability and adaptability of ethnic identity throughout history. Ukrainians do not appear to perceive any particular incongruity between their own sense of cultural belonging and idiosyncratic Ukrainian identity and their simultaneous inheritance of aspects of a shared Slavic culture. Crawford Young taught us how fluid, variable, and overlapping identity can be, how it can change over time, and how ethnicities can, in the course of nation building, share multiple cultural affinities (Young 1976).

Indeed, Ukraine, while populated predominantly by ethnic Ukrainians, integrated into its national territory a number of different ethnic minorities, reflecting centuries of shifting borders, the impact of having been associated with a plurality of expansive empires, periodic waves of immigration from elsewhere in Europe, and a national tendency toward cultural tolerance. As a result, Ukraine is today characterized by a range of ethnic minorities, including Russians, Poles, Jews, Serbs, Tatars, Muslims, Armenians, Roma, Finns, and Swedes (Plokhy 2015; Panayiotou et al. 2022, 7). In point of fact, research conducted by Yu Yakymenko et al. of the Razumkov Centre (in Kyiv, Ukraine) indicates that most Ukrainians—regardless of ethnic background—have become primarily wedded to a "civic" notion of nationalism in which they feel principally attached to the Ukrainian nation-state as a whole—inclusive of its various ethnic minorities and language groups (Yakymenko et al. 2016). In a parallel study, the scholar Tatiana Zhurzhenko underlines that Ukrainians have indeed embraced a broad civic understanding of Ukrainian nationalism and a commitment to the Ukrainian nation-state writ large, most dramatically after the 2014 Russian invasion in Crimea and the Donbas region. She makes clear that those politicians who favored a uniethnic version of Ukrainian nationalism were marginalized in favor of an emphatically multiethnic, inclusive civic activism and support for democratic accountability and the rule of law amid a widespread reinvigoration of panethnic, pancultural Ukrainian national unity (Zhurzhenko 2014, 261–62). Field research conducted by the social psychologist Karina V. Korostelina in 2018 provides further support for the consolidation of a multiethnic civic nationalism characterized by strong intergroup supportive behavior (2020). Separately, a team of scholars who carried out sociological research in various regions of Ukraine between 2016 and 2021 found a high degree of tolerance for minority groups along with the intensification of an "inclusionary and pluralistic" Ukrainian identity based not on language or ethnicity but rather on a strong sense of belonging to the Ukrainian nation (Panayiotou et al. 2022). Ruslan Minich (2018), in an Atlantic Council report, Paul Pillar (2022), in an analysis for the Institute of Responsible Statecraft, and Serhiy Kudelia (2022, 256), in a study for *Current History*, all further emphasize the civic and inclusive character of contemporary Ukrainian nationalism.

Russian Autocratic Rule in Historical Context

President Vladimir Putin does not wish to admit to cultural pluralism within Ukraine, much less to the notion of an independent Ukrainian civic identity that emphasizes the unity of the various ethnicities in support of the Ukrainian nation and government. For Putin, there is no distinctive Ukrainian culture (whether civic or ethnic) but only a Russian one in Ukraine (Putin 2021). Here, Putin's attitudes and policies toward Ukrainians are reflective of the quest for hegemonic political control and expansionism that is typical of autocratic rulers. Moreover, it should be emphasized that Putin's views are consistent with and, in many respects, are a revival of the attitudes and policies put forth by leaders of historic Russian autocratic regimes and by the Russian intelligentsia, which promoted the notion of Russian cultural supremacy. Thus, the narrative of Kyiv as historically "Russian" and not Ukrainian was actively embraced by Kyiv Orthodox clergy in the seventeenth century—despite its inaccuracy (Kyiv was the origin of both the Russian and Ukrainian peoples)—because those clergy were desirous of the tsar's protection and monetary support (Plokhy 2015, 120–21). This Russo-dominant ideology became more assertively trumpeted by Tsar Catherine II (1762–96), who proclaimed the need to "Russify" Ukraine and to suppress Ukrainian culture, and indeed—throughout much of the nineteenth century—Russian government officials (under subsequent tsars) would proceed to ban the use of the Ukrainian language in Ukraine's education system (1830s), in journalism and in book publishing (1860s), all while Russian security agents sought to crush the nascent Ukrainian nationalist movement in Kyiv and elsewhere (Plokhy 2015). In the 1870s, Russian government leaders again made clear that they viewed the very existence of Ukrainian culture as a threat to the Russian empire (Plokhy 2015, 167). As a strategy to tamp down this perceived threat (as noted by Crawford Young), Russian political and cultural leaders frequently claimed throughout the nineteenth century "that there was no such thing as a Ukrainian national identity" (Young 1976, 26).

Then, in 1919 (two years after the Bolsheviks assumed power in Moscow), Soviet troops seized control of Ukraine's cities, and in 1929 Stalin proclaimed that Russians and Ukrainians are "one and the same people"—on the eve of launching a de facto military occupation of the Ukrainian countryside (Plokhy 2015, 233). That occupation would include mass executions and a forced agricultural collectivization policy (in a country in which the majority were small farmers or peasants) that resulted in the near-enslavement and starvation of the rural populace, with some four million Ukrainians perishing. In Ukraine, it is referred to as the Holodomor (or "Great Terror/Famine") (Plokhy 2015, 249–54).

Stalin's proclamation that Russo-Ukrainians are the "same people" is virtually identical to the argument regarding Russo-Ukrainian cultural contiguity that is being made by Putin today, along with the mystery—unexplained by either Putin or Stalin—as to how and why being "the same" people offers the autocrats of Russia an implied justification for the violent repression of Ukrainians who resist Russian domination and the forcible occupation of their lands.

Recalling Crawford Young's attention to the manipulative, instrumentalist narratives of expansionist autocrats, we may suggest that the cultural claims described here reflect a strategy on the part of Russian elites through which they aim to distinguish themselves as a unique and purportedly superior people—the ultimate Slav kingdom standing astride and in charge of a broader Slavic nation that includes the Ukrainians—who are somehow part of that broader Slav nation but in an inferior, dominated, and dependent position. This idealized (and historically inaccurate) imagery projecting a fantastical Russo-ethnogenesis has at least in part shaped elite Russian cultural consciousness as well as Russian foreign policy decision making intended to promote Russian state building for centuries.

Deconstructing Putin's Autocratic Perspective

Young's emphasis on the variability and contextual specificity of cultural politics in the growth of nationalism serves to facilitate our ability to underline the ways that Putin's analysis is misguided. In his public pronouncements and speeches, Putin aims to reify history into fixed events that offer clear moral equivalences: the Russians once conquered and occupied much of Ukraine, so therefore they are entitled to reconquer, reoccupy, and Russify it. But a more truthful appreciation of Ukrainian history would emphasize its variable, shifting contours, recognizing the many configurations of power and influences of empire—including lengthy periods during which (at least parts of) Ukraine were dominated by Poland, Lithuania, the Polish–Lithuanian confederation, Austria, the Austro-Hungarian empire, Sweden, Finland, and the Ottomans and Mongolians (in Crimea) (Plokhy 2015). Even if a history of successful imperial occupations were to provide some sort of moral right to perpetual occupation—which I do not believe that it does—an appreciation of the variety of forces that have shaped Ukraine would make clear that Russia would certainly not be alone in being in a position to claim rightful access to Ukrainian territory.

Putin also seeks to essentialize ethnic categories into unchanging truisms, despite the contorted logic: Ukrainians are actually Russians, but not quite fully Russian, and somehow this lesser cousin (or "Little Russian") ethnolinkage justifies the mass slaughter of those who resist Russian tutelage and overrule. A contextual interpretation of history (per Young) makes clear that Ukrainians' evolution as a diverse, distinctive culture with multiple ethnicities has taken place over the course of many centuries and in clear contradistinction from the

Russian ethnocategory. Despite their common origin—approximately one millennium ago—the cultural evolution of Russians and Ukrainians has proceeded along divergent paths, and Ukraine emerged not as a uniethnic nation
but, rather, as a Young-ian situational analysis shows, as a multiethnic nation
with a distinctive language, literature, and culture, politically oriented toward
civic values. The contemporary commitment of ethnic minorities (such as Russians, Poles, Jews, Roma, Tatars, Serbs, Swedes, and Finns) to the Ukrainian
nation-state (as noted earlier) makes this especially evident. Moreover, changing historical circumstances—such as the opportunity for Ukrainians to achieve
national independence in 1917–19 because of the collapse of the tsarist regime
and then again in 1990–91 as a consequence of the disintegration of the
USSR—provides compelling evidence of how a Young-ian approach emphasizing historical variability, contextual specificity and civic nationalism can
serve to correct Putin's ethno-essentialist narrative.

Finally, we may point out that Putin has sought to justify Russia's 2014 and
2022 aggression as defending Russia against a presumed threat posed by the
West should Ukraine continue to embrace economic, political, and security alliances with pro-Western European nations ("Russian President Vladimir Putin's Speech . . . ," May 29, 2022). Apart from the inaccurate (if not overtly false)
portrait of any such threat, Putin (and his supporters within his ruling oligarchy) ignored—in his public speeches as in his war-making policies—the 1994
Budapest Memorandum through which Ukraine agreed to destroy or give up
its nuclear weapons in return for security assurances from Russia and the 1997
Ukraine–Russia Treaty on Friendship, Cooperation, and Partnership, which
guaranteed Ukraine's territorial integrity and the inviolability of its existing
borders (Plokhy 2015, 354; Pifer 2019; Haesebrouck and Taghon 2022). Indeed,
Russia's invasion of Ukraine in 2014 and 2022 effectively upended those ac-
cords, although this remains unacknowledged by the Russian president.

It is evident that the oligarchic autocracies that have characterized the Russian state—not only at present but also throughout most of the past three centuries, from Peter I and Catherine II in the eighteenth century through to the
tsarist regimes of the nineteenth century, Stalin and Brezhnev in the twentieth
century, and Putin since he assumed power in 2000—have been marked by deep
hostility toward Ukrainian nationalism and by the ostracizing of and violent aggression against the Ukrainian people. If, as Young and Thomas Turner have
suggested, one of the hallmarks of autocratic rule, such as in the Congo, is the
attempted repression of ethnic "others" and the denial or distortion of their
grievances by the purportedly supreme leader in order to achieve domination
over them and to exploit their resources and their labor (Young and Turner

1985, 164–84), then Russia's policies toward Ukrainians, in the nineteenth to the twentieth centuries as at present, can be understood as part of the statecraft of a kleptocratic, oligarchic dictatorship. Putin's historical omissions and distortions, his denial of the legitimacy of the Ukrainian nation, and, most recently, his military invasion of that nation reflect the exploitative, violent policies and verbal manipulations of a despot above all concerned with the expansion of his regime. These are precisely the types of strategies that can be especially appreciated through the lens of a Young-ian analytic paradigm, as it underlines the role of ethnic targeting by rising autocrats in their quest to strengthen their rule while helping to enrich the oligarchic elites that support them.

Ukrainian Nationalism in Historical Context

In contrast to the distorted portrait of Ukrainian history that Putin and his predecessors aimed to artificially construct, our attention to contextual specificity, historical variability, and cultural entrepreneurship more accurately suggests that Ukrainians pursued, with considerable success, a multicentury-long path toward the establishment, elaboration, and development of their own independent culture and national identity. By the mid to late sixteenth century, territorial intrusions by Poland and by the Polish–Lithuanian Confederation helped ensure Ukraine's particular geographic identity (its contours would be depicted on maps by the 1590s). In 1618, Ukraine's paramilitary Cossack brigades, initially formed in earlier centuries to dislodge Ottoman intruders from Crimea, forced Moscow to concede much of central and western Ukraine, followed by the 1649 establishment of a Ukrainian Cossack *hetmanate* (state) in central and northeastern Ukraine (including Kyiv and Kharkiv), which lasted more than a century and which is still celebrated in Ukraine today (Plokhy 2015). Although the forces of Russian Tsar Peter I inflicted several military defeats upon these Ukrainian Cossacks between 1709 and 1721, after his death in 1725, these Cossacks—early cultural entrepreneurs of Ukrainian nationalism—continued to pursue Ukraine's political and territorial autonomy through military actions and by pursuing political alliances with a variety of nearby local power holders (Plokhy 2015, 129–30).

Subsequently, despite the ascendance of the Tsarist empire and its growing control over Ukraine, a cultural and politically nationalist movement emerged through the nineteenth century with growing vigor. A separate Ukrainian grammar was taught in elementary schools as Ukrainian literature, newspapers, and academic publications proliferated. Cultural entrepreneurs such as writers, educators, journalists, and political activists in Kyiv, Lviv, and other

cities generated widespread support for Ukrainian nationalism as of the 1830s
and 1840s, and some of them, such as the historian Mykola Kostomarov,
openly advocated Ukrainian independence and democratic governance
(Plokhy 2015). Regardless of the extent of Russian protrusion into Ukrainian
territorial space, many teachers, poets, newspaper reporters, publishers, and
members of nationalist organizations worked relentlessly to forge a Ukrainian
national identity in cultural spaces while organizing in favor of national independence on the political plane. Crawford Young himself highlighted the fact
that "even the most downtrodden nationality of all [within Europe], the Ukrainians, divided between Austria-Hungary, Poland and Russia, achieved [na-
tional] self-awareness" (Young 1976, 26).

Indeed, by 1900, a Revolutionary Ukrainian Party had been created explicitly to promote Ukraine's independence; in 1906–17, in the wake of Russia's internal political turmoil, Ukrainian activism reached new heights, with the
Ukrainian scholar and cultural entrepreneur Mykhailo Hrushevsky and thousands of his supporters demanding greater Ukrainian autonomy (Plokhy 2015,
205). The year 1918 witnessed a declaration of full Ukrainian independence by
a newly established Government of Ukraine, although it would be replaced by
USSR-approved Bolshevik officials the following year. Even after Stalin had
consolidated power (by 1929) and proceeded to unleash virulent waves of Soviet repression in Ukraine throughout the mid to late 1930s, a Ukrainian underground resistance movement remained active—and would reemerge after
World War II (especially in western Ukraine) (Plokhy 2015). Ukrainian resistance continued (at modest levels) through the 1964–82 regime of USSR Premier Leonid Brezhnev. When the Soviet Union began to collapse, in 1989,
Ukrainian cultural entrepreneurship helped ensure a full-scale nationwide mobilization of pro-democracy, pro-nationalist activists throughout Ukraine, leading to parliamentary elections and a declaration of Ukrainian independence in
1990. This was followed the next year by a referendum, in which 90 percent of
the populace approved of Ukraine's independence—including 83 percent of
voters in the Donetsk region, where nearly half the populace is of Russian ethnic origin (Zhurzhenko 2014, 251; Plokhy 2015).

Contemporary Civic Nationalism and
Cultural Entrepreneurship in Ukraine

Russia's 2014 invasion and annexation of Crimea and then of portions of Donetsk and Luhansk regions would spark a dramatic intensification of Ukrainian
national identity. Indeed, polls at the time showed that 90 percent of Ukrainians

wished to retain the country's existing territorial borders (this included most Russian speakers) as thousands of Ukrainian volunteers joined resistance units in those two occupied regions (Plokhy 2015, 343, 353; Kudelia 2022, 253). Research since then has made clear that the 2014 invasion helped to inspire cross-community collaboration and social cohesion, the proliferation of mutual aid–oriented social networks, and a dramatic rise in expressions of interpersonal trust and pro-Ukrainian civic nationalism that stretched across the country (Korostelina 2020; Kudelia 2022; Panayioutou et al. 2022; Goodwin et al. 2023, 3).

This uptick in manifestations of mutual support and civic engagement was only a prelude. Russia's full-scale invasion in February 2022 sparked a massive nationwide effort to resist the assaults, to demonstrate a determination to reinvigorate Ukrainian society even in the midst of wartime violence, and to make clear citizens' attachment to their nation even in areas under the putative control of the Russian armed forces. The cultural entrepreneurship, innovation, and resilience of ordinary local residents of bombarded Ukrainian cities and towns came to be increasingly manifested in multiple ways, as untrained volunteers joined local defense brigades, which mushroomed in each of the country's regions; residents of localities under attack defied the Russians by electing to remain on site and to assist one another, despite the existential risks; material support was provided to isolated communities in war-torn regions; wood and coal were collected and stored in hidden sheds in an attempt to ensure energy self-reliance; and electrical outlets in urban areas were provided in creative ways in order to enable residents to continue to work and to access communication networks (Alderman and Sanchez 2022; Kudelia 2022, 253–56; Specia 2023). Additional examples include the mobilization of local residents specifically in order to shield their elected local officials and mayors from capture by Russian forces; the energetic engagement of municipal councilors in helping to organize local food supplies as well as armed civil resistance units; civilians' innovative fabrication of homemade flak jackets and periscopes (made from water pipes and mirrors) for use by Ukrainian soldiers; the starting up of small businesses by internally displaced migrants in still vulnerable cities; and we may highlight the expression of heightened feelings of attachment to the Ukrainian nation in all regions of the country, including those occupied by Russian forces, as revealed in academic research interviews and surveys, social media platforms, and public statements (Alderman 2022; Brik and Murtazashvili 2022; Kudelia 2022; Kuz 2022; Schmigel 2022; Goodwin et al. 2023, 4; Husarska 2023).

Here, a Young-ian situational approach, attuned to a culture's capacity for adaptation in reflection of newly threatening contextual challenges, helps us to appreciate the extent to which the Ukrainian nationalist movement, evolving from the Cossack *hetmanate* through the subsequent four centuries, would eventually come to reflect a particularly resilient, innovative, and unifying type of civic nationalism. This evolution is central to appreciating the increasing success of cultural entrepreneurship since the nineteenth century, and dramatically as of the 2014 and 2022 invasions, with regard to the energies devoted by ordinary Ukrainians to constructing, fortifying, defending, and reinvigorating a modern Ukrainian nation-state.

Young's paradigmatic emphasis on the variability of historical outcomes and the importance of appreciating situational circumstances with respect to cultural politics was reflected in Ukrainian history through frequent alterations in the extent of territorial control held by local forces, such as Ukrainian Cossacks in earlier centuries, and by invading foreign elements. This explains why apparent political outcomes often proved temporary and shifted in dramatic fashion from one century (or even one decade) to the next. Historical variability and the importance of contextual factors can also be perceived in the flexibility of Ukrainians as they resisted, in different ways, the enormous challenges presented by a steady stream over the centuries of foreign intrusions and repressions, as well as by their tendency toward ethnic and linguistic inclusivity as they began to forge a territorial nation-state.

Finally, it is helpful to reemphasize the critical role of cultural entrepreneurship within Young's paradigm, which in the Ukrainian case reflected the persistence of activism that, over time, sought to create distinct Ukrainian social traditions and cultural expressions while engaging (if in fits and starts) in the construction and deepening of a nationalist political movement. In recent years, and especially since the 2014 and 2022 invasions, cultural entrepreneurs proved crucial to the struggle to defend and strengthen the Ukrainian nation-state—from the members of local councils and ordinary residents who organized food drives to the mayors, untrained volunteers, and civic activists who mobilized Ukrainian resistance at the grassroots level. These engaged citizens helped to ensure a reinvigoration of the meaning of Ukrainian nationalism in the wake of Russia's military onslaught.

Ukraine in Comparative Perspective

So then, Crawford Young's attention to historical variability, situational contextualism, cultural entrepreneurship, and ethnic targeting by dictatorial oligarchies have facilitated particular insights into the history of Ukrainian-Russian relations, the forging of Ukrainian identity, the eventual emergence of a

Ukrainian nation-state, and the resilience of Ukrainian nationalism. Here, we may point out that, from a comparative perspective, Young's paradigm is likely to offer similarly helpful insight into the politics of cultural pluralism currently occurring elsewhere in various parts of the globe. Thus, for example, a certain parallel may be drawn between ethnic chauvinism and aggression on the part of Russian leaders and the history of expansion into the lands of cultural minorities undertaken by Han Chinese rulers. In recent decades, this has led to the territorial displacement and cultural disenfranchisement of ethnic minorities in western China, such as the Uyghur, one million of whom have now been placed in internment camps within the Xinjiang region. Han Chinese are increasingly settling on Uyghur lands as part of the central state's policy to ensure its domination over Xinjiang territory and the exploitation of the region's natural and economic resources. Just as the Russian state aims to legitimize its forcible subjugation of Ukraine by denying that Ukrainians have a separate identity and asserting that they are part of the broader Slavic family of Russians, the Chinese dictatorship has made a point of claiming that Uyghurs are actually members of the broader Chinese family and that Xinjiang has been a part of China since ancient times (Wu 2014). This is in spite of the fact that the Uyghur, as well as the Hui, Kazakhs, Tibetans, and other cultural minorities, have relied on various efforts at cultural entrepreneurship in order to continually reinvigorate their ethnic, regional, and linguistic identities while resisting cultural subjugation within Han-dominant China (Gladney 2004).

In cases such as China and Russia, state autocrats' ethnic delegitimation of the cultural "other" and their denial of the very existence of minorities' distinctive identities serve as justification for the launching of waves of repression aimed at the forcible inclusion of minorities into the dominant national culture, but only as subordinate subjects. We find a similar process in the systematic cultural and political repression of Muslims in the Jammu and Kashmir state of India; there, local cultural groups reacted to the steady uptick in levels of state hostility over the past several decades by forming political organizations that have grown in influence and in mobilizational capacity (Chowdhary 2015). Pakistan's subjugation of its peripheralized cultural minorities in the country's Federally Administered Tribal Areas, initiated during British colonial rule, has only intensified in recent years, even as cultural movements among those minorities have spread and are deepening (Khan 2022). Parallels can also be drawn from the brutal war against the Tigrayans of Ethiopia prosecuted by President Abiy Ahmed and his oligarchic entourage, even as Tigrayans had succeeded in crafting a potent nationalist political movement and a robust, particularistic culture over the course of many decades (Záhorík and Godesso 2022).

In all these cases, autocratic leaders and regime-affiliated elites perceive the strength of their respective national governments to be most fully manifested via the hegemonic exploitation of cultural minorities, the seizure of their territories, and the extraction of their natural resources. In Russia, a zero-sum war aims to bolster the domestic base of popular support for "oligarch-in-chief" (Snyder 2018) President Vladimir Putin as he and his regime proceed to plunder the land and resources of Ukraine while repressing its citizenry. For Putin, fact-based historical analysis is exchanged for a falsified narrative that proclaims the superiority of the Russian national state and majority culture over that of the purportedly dangerous ethnic "other" (despite their supposedly shared identity). As in the additional cases briefly noted earlier, state elites ignored the evolution and consolidation of nondominant identities while attempting to repress cultural entrepreneurship and to occlude the progress of minorities' nationalistic movements. State expansionism and kleptocratic personalism on the part of the dictatorial supreme leader converged in ways that Crawford Young would have recognized as all too familiar, echoing similar processes that had been occurring (in previous decades) in the Congo, Uganda, and Nigeria. The post-Soviet and post–Cold War end of history, it seems, has today given way to an all too familiar return to the (not so distant) past—indeed, one with imperial refrains, in which Bula Matari state rulership and the violent construction of cultural hierarchies represent the essential mechanisms of twenty-first-century power politics.

Throughout this chapter, I have tried to demonstrate the explanatory utility of a Young-ian analytic paradigm that focuses not only on the role and behavior of culturally predatory autocracies but also on a fact-based analysis of the real-world history of nationalism and of state–ethnic relations in a particular setting. Such a paradigm anticipates that the accurate historicizing of cultural change is shaped by a preponderance of *contextual, situational* factors particular to a specific set of actors and time periods. A Young-ian analytic paradigm elucidates the *variability* of the extent of success of a given cultural movement in a specific epoch and explains the historical arc of changes in state–ethnic relations between one time period and the next. Moreover, a Young-ian approach appreciates that the ability of cultural identities to crystallize into successful *civic nationalistic movements* requires an explanation of the ways in which *cultural entrepreneurship* has been able to generate the kind of political momentum and organizing capacity necessary to continue to grow in an inclusive manner while circumventing and resisting the repressive policies of a violently expansionist autocracy. In all these ways, Young's analytic paradigm has proven helpful in our attempt to better understand the genesis and development of a distinctive Ukrainian identity and culture and of the relative success, however variable, of the Ukrainian nationalist movement.

References

Alderman, Liz. 2022. "Survival by Entrepreneurship." *New York Times*, September 11.

Alderman, Liz, and Diego Ibarra Sanchez. 2022. "Girding for a Hard Winter in Ukraine." *New York Times*, August 5.

Brik, Tymofee, and Jennifer Murtazashvili. 2022. "The Source of Ukraine's Resilience." *Foreign Affairs*, June 28. https://www.foreignaffairs.com/articles/ukraine/2022-06-28/source-ukraines-resilience.

Chowdhary, Rekha. 2015. *Jammu and Kashmir: Politics of Identity and Separatism*. New Delhi, India: Routledge.

Gettleman, Jeffrey, and Olekskandra Mykolyshyn. 2023. "As Russians Steal Ukraine's Art, They Attack Its Identity, Too." *New York Times*, January 14.

Gladney, Dru C. 2004. *Dislocating China: Reflections on Muslims, Minorities, and other Subaltern Subjects*. Chicago: University of Chicago Press.

Goodwin, Robin, Yaira Hamama-Raz, Elazar Leshem, and Menachem Ben-Ezra. 2023. "National Resilience in Ukraine following the 2022 Russian Invasion." *International Journal of Disaster Risk Reduction* 85 (February): 1–6.

Haesebrouck, Tim, and Servaas Taghon. 2022. "Russia's Invasion in Ukraine: What Happened Before?" Occasional Paper. Ghent Institute for International and European Studies.

Husarska, Anna. 2023. "Ukrainian Engineers, Historians and Housewives Are Keeping Putin on His Toes." *New York Times*, January 12.

Khan, Asghar. 2022. *Mainstreaming the Tribal Areas of Pakistan*. Gateway East, Singapore: Palgrave Macmillan.

Korostelina, Karina V. 2020. "National Resilience to Protracted Violence in Ukraine." *Peace and Conflict Studies* 27 (2): 1–31.

Kudelia, Serhiy. 2022. "The Ukrainian State under Russian Aggression: Resilience and Resistance." *Current History* 121 (837): 251–57.

Kuz, Martin. 2022. "Notes from a War: Resilience and Anger in a Ukraine under Siege." *Christian Science Monitor*, April 12.

Minich, Ruslan. 2018. "Nationalism Is on the Rise in Ukraine." Atlantic Council, April 5. https://www.atlanticcouncil.org/blogs/ukrainealert/nationalism-is-on-the-rise-in-ukraine-and-that-s-a-good-thing/.

Panayiotou, Orestis, Alexander Guest, Andrii Dryga, and Christoforos Pissarides. 2022. *Social Cohesion in Ukraine Part II: Towards a Tolerant, Cohesive and Inclusive Society*. UNDP/USAID/SEED.

Parsons, Robert. 2022. "In Occupied Kherson, 'the Russians Were Destroying All Books in Ukrainian.'" France 24, December 5. https://www.france24.com/en/europe/20221205-in-occupied-kherson-the-russians-were-destroying-all-books-in-ukrainian.

Pifer, Steven. 2019. "Why Care about Ukraine and the Budapest Memorandum?" Brookings Institute, December 5. https://www.brookings.edu/blog/order-from -chaos/2019/12/05/why-care-about-ukraine-and-the-budapest-memorandum/.

Pillar, Paul R. 2022. "Ukraine and the Power of Nationalism." Responsible Statecraft, May 23. https://responsiblestatecraft.org/2022/05/23/ukraine-and-the-power-of -nationalism/.

Plokhy, Serhii. 2015. *Lost Kingdom: The Quest for Empire and the Making of the Russian Nation.* New York: Basic Books.

Putin, Vladimir. 2021. "On the Historical Unity of Russians and Ukrainians." Office of the President of Russia, July 12. http://en.kremlin.ru/events/president/news/66181.

"Russia Scraps Age Limit for New Troops in Ukraine Push." 2022. BBC News, May 29. https://www.bbc.com/news/world-europe-61619638.

"Russian President Vladimir Putin's Full Speech." 2022. Barron's/Agence France-Presse, February 24. https://www.barrons.com/articles/russian-president-vladi mir-putin-s-full-speech-01645738807.

"Russian President Vladimir Putin's Speech: Victory Parade on Red Square." 2022. Office of the President of Russia, May 29. http://en.kremlin.ru/events/president/tran scripts/statements/68366.

Schmigel, Pete. 2022. "Centuries of Oppression Have Forged Ukraine's Remarkable Resilience." Atlantic Council, May 22. https://www.atlanticcouncil.org/blogs/ukrai nealert/centuries-of-russian-oppression-have-forged-ukraines-remarkable-resilience/.

Shlapentokh, Dmitry. 2021. "Putin and Ukraine: Power the Construction of History." Institute of Modern Russia, September. https://imrussia.org/en/analysis/3335 -putin-and-ukraine-power-and-the-construction-of-history.

Snyder, Timothy. 2018. *The Road to Unfreedom.* New York: Tim Duggan Books.

Specia, Marcia. 2023. "In a City Determined to Work, the Office Is Wherever There's Power." *New York Times,* January 12.

Stepanenko, Kateryna, Frederick W. Kagan, and Brian Babcock-Lumish. 2022. "Explainer on Russian Conscription, Reserve, and Mobilisation." Institute for the Study of War, Washington, DC.

Wu, Xiaohui. March 2014. "From Assimilation to Autonomy: Realizing Ethnic Minority Rights in China's Autonomous Regions." *Chinese Journal of International Law* 13 (1): 55–90.

Yakymenko, Yu., A. Bychenko, V. Zamiatin, M. Mischenko, A. Stetskev, and O. Lytvynenko. 2016. "Ukrainian Identity: Changes, Trends, Regional Aspects." *National Security & Defense* 3–4:1–134.

Young, Crawford. 1976. *The Politics of Cultural Pluralism.* Madison: University of Wisconsin Press.

Young, Crawford, and Thomas Turner. 1985. *The Rise and Decline of the Zairian State.* Madison: University of Wisconsin Press.

Záhorík, Jan, and Ameyu Godesso. 2022. "Multiple Layers of Competing Nationalisms in Contemporary Ethiopia." In *Histories of Nationalisms Beyond Europe,* edited by Jan Záhorík and Antonio M. Morone, 91–105. Cham, Switzerland: Palgrave Macmillan.

Zhurzhenko, Tatiana. 2014. "A Divided Nation? Reconsidering the Role of Identity Politics in the Ukraine Crisis." *Die Friedens-Warte* 89 (1): 249–67.

Women, Gender, and Politics

Part III

Women Do Everything except Politics

Gender Quotas in a Postconflict Society

Ladan Affi

A Somali proverb states that "the world is shaped by women, a reality that no man can dispute." Yet, the history of the Somalis is one of consistent, sustained, and ongoing denial of the place and contributions of women. From the colonial period to the present, women have been at the forefront of serving their families and their nation. Their economic and social contributions are welcomed, yet women have consistently been marginalized whenever they sought a more significant role in politics and government. Despite their long struggle to participate in the governance of their country, women have found that broad acceptance of their inclusion has yet to be attained, and the lack of women in the decision-making process has rarely been seen as an issue worth discussing. Contrary to research showing that women's "exclusion from positions of political representation and their continued underrepresentation make them and their male counterparts susceptible to a belief in women's inferiority in governing," women activists fought for greater representation at every step of the way (Alexander 2012, 439).

Women face multiple challenges in their quest for full and equal participation in politics. According to the former Puntland minister of women, Asha Gelle, one of the most important barriers to women's political participation is the clan elders, who want only men to represent the clan: "The whole culture is one of men. Women are not elders, and they are the ones who take the communal decisions, and they focus on their clan, which is a challenge for women" (Gelle n.d.).

From Somalia's independence in 1960 to the collapse of the state in 1991, a homogeneous version of Somali society was promoted, and the clan and any loyalty associated with it were viewed as antithetical to the Somali nation-state. The civil war pitted clans and subclans against each other. Multiple reconciliation conferences were held in Djibouti, Ethiopia, and Egypt that brought together the warring militia, who were claiming to protect clan interests. All these conferences failed because the faction leaders disagreed on power sharing, and none of the major clans could assert dominance over the others.

Reconstructing the state began in earnest in 2000 when the government of Djibouti organized a reconciliation conference that focused on civil society, minimizing the role of the warring groups. This conference resulted in what Crawford Young (2000) describes as cultural pluralism, which enshrined the clan "as a core of constitutional principle." The majority of Somalis claim descent from one ethnic group, although there is a sizable minority of nonethnic Somalis. After independence, the focus was on creating a single Somali identity, which sought to suppress the diversities of cultures, languages, and ethnicities that existed in Somalia (Ahmed 1995).

For most of the 1990s, major Somali clans engaged in conflict, seeking to take political control of the country and to impose their power on other clans. The idea of making the clan the foundation of the newly reconstructed state "found wholesale acceptance" among many Somalis, who believed it was the only way to end the civil war (Young 2000, 18). This was fully incorporated in the Arta Reconciliation Conference, which decreed that political representation would be based only on clan membership, which was institutionalized as the 4.5 clan power-sharing agreement. This clan power-sharing agreement was first introduced in the Ethiopian-sponsored Sodere factional meeting, but it was not adopted (Eno and Eno 2009; Osman 2015). In this agreement, the four major clans—Darood, Digil and Mirifle, Dir, and Hawiye—would receive equal numbers of political seats, and an amalgamation of minority clans would get only half of what the major clans received. This embedded the clan elders in the screening, selection, and appointment of political positions, making them the sole arbiters of who was eligible to represent the clan. For the clan elders, women, with their multiple linkages to the clans of their father, husband, and children, were suspect and were never to be chosen.

Many male politicians who view politics as a zero-sum game are a second obstacle for women seeking to participate in politics. These politicians consider the entry of women into politics as creating competition for limited seats, and they often collude with clan elders to undermine the gender quota because the clan elders determine who can occupy the political seats delegated to the clan.

The third impediment to women's pursuit of political participation is the religious actors and Islamist parties, ranging from the Muslim Brotherhood and Salafists to the extremists, that espouse a wide range of ideologies. These groups, which emerged publicly after the collapse of the state, are vocal about issues relating to women, insisting that women should remain in their homes, even though women dominate the marketplace and are the heads of the household. When women activists and politicians challenge these views, expressly demanding to know which Islamic laws forbid women from participating in politics, some of these religious actors give a variety of responses, including their opposition to the westernization of the culture, such as the mixing of genders and gender quotas (Somali Women and Human Rights Development 2020).

The fourth barrier is the international community, which is a significant actor in Somalia, yet whose activities are often driven by national interests and security concerns, which can be detrimental to Somali women's rights. The lack of a national women's organization and the limited cohesion and collaboration among women's groups hinder them from addressing the common barriers that women face. These various forces often unite to thwart women's inclusion in politics.

Women's social, economic, and peacebuilding contributions are expected when societal needs arise, and women are pushed back into the home once the crises end. From the struggle for independence until 2000, women's attempts to sit at the decision-making tables have depended on the goodwill of men. This changed in the past twenty years, when women activists became increasingly vocal about being excluded from political power and pushed for the adoption and implementation of the gender quota. This has been a slow process, with much backsliding and many failures. During the past ten years, women have sought to formalize their participation but have faced tremendous hurdles posed by the clan elders, religious groups, and male elites.

Somalia's transition into a federal system in 2012 brought with it a 30 percent gender quota for women, which was incorporated into the Somali Roadmap (Somalia Roadmap Signatories 2012). The gender quota was implemented with different levels of compliance in the federal parliamentary selections of 2012, 2016, and 2021. In each of these elections, women activists and candidates had to devise responses to overcome new challenges and met with mixed success.

This essay examines the political inclusion and exclusion of women in post-conflict Somalia through the prism of cultural pluralism as outlined by Crawford Young. It argues that the centralization of the clan, the incorporation of clan elders, and the adoption of federalism have undermined the 30 percent gender quota. It also discusses how women have responded to these challenges in seeking political participation.

Methodology

This essay is based on research conducted during two different periods, from 2016 to 2018 and in 2021. The first part was carried out in Somalia (Hargeisa, Bur'o, Garowe, and Mogadishu), in Kenya (Nairobi), and in the United States (Minneapolis) from 2016 to 2018. In-person interviews were conducted with elite Somalis, including male and female politicians at the federal, regional, and local levels; female activists; academics and researchers; and members of the international community working on Somalia. The Somalis interviewed were urbanized and educated women and men, many of whom had been part of the diaspora that moved back from Europe and North America. Some had come back to take up political positions, while others had worked with nongovernmental organizations or in the social sectors, such as education and healthcare.

The second part of this chapter draws on mixed-methods research that was conducted in the fall of 2021. The quantitative part included a survey of one thousand people in seven large urban cities across Somalia—Baidoa, Beledweyne, Bosaso, Galkayo, Garowe, Mogadishu, and Kismayo.[1]

The goal of the survey was to discern societal views on gender quotas and women's political participation. Survey participants were divided equally between women and men. Qualitative research using a mix of online and in-person one-on-one interviews in Mogadishu included sixteen women comprising women's rights and nongovernmental activists; members of current and former parliaments (both the Senate and the House of the People); MP candidates; public-sector workers at the federal, regional, and local levels; and cabinet ministers. These interviewees were a highly educated mix of local and returned diaspora, ranging in age from their thirties to sixties. Interviewees came from all regions of Somalia: Galmudug, Hirshabelle, Jubbaland, Puntland, Somaliland, Southwest, and the Benadir Regional Administration. Some of the informants had been involved in Somalia's political process for decades, including as MPs who first joined the parliament in 2000. At the same time, others were a mix of elected and unsuccessful candidates who had run for parliamentary seats in 2012, 2016, or 2021. In terms of professional experience, they worked in the financial sector, education, healthcare, humanitarian organization, and the public and private sectors.

Theoretical Framework

In his book *The Postcolonial State in Africa* (2012), Crawford Young discusses the trajectories of African states from 1960 to 2010, noting that, unlike most African states, Somalia had a distinct advantage and was "frequently celebrated as a rare African example of a genuine nation-state whose cultural coherence held promise for effective rule" (Young 2012, 3). The democratic governments (1960–69) and the military government (1969–91) promoted Somalis as being of one ethnicity, with one culture, one language, and one identity, overlooking the cultural diversity that existed in Somalia. The military government sought to erase the clan from the Somali polity, even holding public burnings of a clan effigy (Affi 2020, 129). Yet, the similarities shared by many Somalis did not eclipse their deep attachment to clan identity, which "became even more sharply divisive when political competition degenerated into armed conflict" (Young 2012, 262). The civil war that led to the collapse of the state ended this mythical narrative of homogeneity. Instead, it was replaced with cultural pluralism (Ahmed 1995).

According to Young, cultural pluralism as ethnicity plays out in three ways: primordialism, instrumentalism, and constructivism (Young 2012, 316–19). In Somalia, primordialism and instrumentalism are the common forms that clannism has taken. The former argues that clans and Islam are essential to what it means to be Somali, while the latter dominated during the war, when it was used by warlords, and does so in the present, where it is mobilized by politicians and clan elders, largely for personal gains. Bringing the clan into the political sphere was an acknowledgment of cultural diversity, bringing an end to the quagmire that arose from the war. The only way that clans could share power, or the "national cake," was to adopt federalism through the 4.5 clan power-sharing agreement (Young 2012, 317). Focusing only on the clan has resulted in the marginalization of women and minorities because of the absence of "effective accommodation of cultural diversity" (Young 2000, 4). The rest of this chapter focuses on how the mobilization of the clan has impacted women's political participation.

The traditional image of war is one of suffering, loss, and destruction, and women are often depicted simply as victims of conflict. But could war also provide opportunities to rework social relations, change societal norms, and provide different opportunities for women to enter previously male spheres? This research suggests that countries transitioning into a postconflict period might benefit from an improvement of women's rights within their societies and be able to expand women's presence in male-dominated arenas previously unavailable to them (Hughes 2009; Tripp 2015).

Like other postconflict countries, Somalia saw an increased presence of women in government and in politics. But despite these gains, primarily due to implementation of the 30 percent gender quota, women's involvement in politics continues to be challenged because the "underlying systems of oppression that perpetuate women's subordination" remain unchanged (Berry 2017, 832). However, much depends on whether women activists press for changes. This is clear in a comparison between Somalia and Somaliland. While the former has implemented a 30 percent gender quota, the latter has rejected any kind of quota, deeming it to be discriminatory and unconstitutional.[2]

Also critical is whether women can hold on to the rights gained during the conflict. Aili Mari Tripp (2015) identifies three conditions that lead to an increase in women's political equality: gender disruptions during the war, the presence of women's movements, and the inclusion of international gender norms.

First, conflict disrupts societies in unforeseen ways. During the conflicts, Somali women took on new roles, such as promoting peace through demonstrations and calling the warring groups to put down their weapons, treating the injured, and feeding the displaced. Because women can be peacemakers, they could cross conflict zones and speak with militias, calling for an end to hostilities. In Hargeisa, Bosaaso, Mogadishu, and across Somalia, women continue to push for peace. This is a role that once was the domain of men, primarily clan elders and religious leaders, but now it falls to women (Affi 2021).

Second, because of the conflict, the state was unable or unwilling to provide social services for its citizens. In these situations, women stepped up by providing humanitarian, health, educational, and other services for the community. To meet these multiple demands of the larger community, women created community organizations or nongovernmental organizations (NGOs). This creates activists who are experienced leaders and who are knowledgeable about the issues facing their communities. Once a country enters the postconflict phase, these women's groups can push for more rights for women (Tripp 2015).

Women take on the responsibility for the family, becoming heads of household and taking on the economic responsibility for feeding their families, working in male-dominated jobs such as in construction, as butchers, and as journalists, to earn a livelihood. This transforms women into important economic actors, diversifying or expanding their businesses and playing a larger, if not a dominant, role in the household economy and in their communities. These new economic resources give women a basis for demanding greater political authority in the community and beyond, especially once peace returns. According to a survey carried out by the Federal Ministry of Women and Human Rights of almost ten thousand women in south and central Somalia, 74.2 percent of survey respondents were the main person responsible for household income, and 62.4 percent were the sole breadwinner for their families. In the same survey, 92 percent of respondents wanted the opportunity to participate in decision making, and 86.6 percent believed that they would have more access if the decisionmaker was a woman (Somali Women and Human Rights Development 2020).

The final criterion leading to an increase in women's rights is the spread of new international gender norms. The presence of international organizations such as the United Nations and foreign donors who can advocate for the participation of women is critical in leading to women's presence in the political sphere. Since the beginning of the civil war in 1991, the influence of international organizations and countries over Somali affairs cannot be underestimated. For Tripp (2015), if all three criteria are present, they can lead to an increased presence of women in politics.

Women's new leadership roles in Somalia gave them increased confidence to demand more rights. As women had more control over their lives, they entered new arenas, including business, government, education, and even religious institutions. Women also worked as athletes, journalists, and in many other fields. All these changes had a domino effect, which affected existing institutions and cultural practices.

International instruments such as the Convention on the Elimination of All Forms of Discrimination against Women (CEDAW), the 1995 Beijing Declaration and Platform for Action, and UN Security Council Resolution 1325 promote the rights of women and their inclusion in politics, peace, security, and state building. Somalia has taken initial steps to ratify CEDAW, which seeks equality between women and men by ensuring that women have equal access to and equal opportunities in political and public life (Convention on the Elimination of Discrimination against Women n.d.).

Somali women have been affected by international gender norms, and the gender quota appealed to them to overcome patriarchal institutions that prevented their participation in politics. The 2012 Provisional Federal Constitution of Somalia gives women the right to participate in politics and in government (Federal Republic of Somalia, Provisional Constitution 2012). Article 3 of the

Federal Provisional Constitution states that "women must be included, in an effective way, in all national institutions, in particular all elected and appointed positions across the three branches of government and in national independent commissions." Yet women who were critical to peacebuilding, development, and the security of the nation faced considerable hurdles in participating in political and decision-making processes. Even after the adoption of the gender quota as part of the Garowe Principles, women's attainment of political seats relies on men's consent, and in each of Somalia's three most recent elections, women were forced to appeal to elders and male politicians to respect their rights. In her work on Bosnia-Herzegovina and Rwanda, Marie Berry (2017) refutes the idea that women's advancement is progressive; rather, "it is a series of fits and starts, progress and slippage" (833).

Rather than seeking to implement the 30 percent quota across all national institutions and, in particular, for all elected and appointed positions across the three branches of government and in the national independent commissions, women's groups largely focused on parliamentary and cabinet seats. But what hinders women's political advancements "is the overall lack of implementation of gender quotas [which] reveals a set of cultural and political realities that limit women's abilities to enter politics and adequately represent their constituencies" (Mohamud 2017).

For women, the gender quota is a recognition of their contribution to society and an acknowledgment that they deserve a place in governing, a say in their future, and equality in determining their lives. "While quotas have high legitimacy among female politicians, most male politicians do not consider gender quotas legitimate [because men] do not accept the basic diagnosis that women in politics face greater barriers than men" (Dahlerup 2008). Those opposed to the gender quota view it as a foreign imposition, arguing that the international community and Westernized Somali women are advancing it. Women rejected this portrayal of their wish, but in their quest for political inclusion, they have encountered "a disconnect between top-down legalistic approaches and political appointments, and rapidly transforming social and cultural phenomena that often characterize post-war societies, chief among them the rise of political Islam" (Mohamud 2017, 167).

Islamist groups, which the Barre government banned, operated freely once the state collapsed (Menkhaus 2002; Abdullahi n.d.). These groups are aligned with different ideologies, including the Muslim Brotherhood, Salafism, and Al-Qaeda. These groups also include religious scholars who are quite conservative and who adopt a stricter interpretation of Islam when it concerns women's rights. They hold differing views on how Somalia should be governed, and as they have sought to implement their vision of an Islamic society, women have not escaped their attention. These groups envision a return to true Islam, under which women are protected and respected and restrictions are welcomed by women who seek relief from clan conflicts, rape, and other violence. These Islamist groups have fought against the clan militias and against one another (Elmi and Barise 2006). They have developed significant influence in defining and interpreting Islam through their involvement in educational institutions, particularly using "Islamic texts to justify and legitimize the exclusion of women from public roles and political participation" (Mohamud 2017, 179; Abdullahi n.d., 30). Thus, women contend with "religious men who were always preaching about what women should do. They preached that everything about women is immodest. Your speech in public is, you showing your body also is. Even expressing your opinion is immodest. You should always keep your head down. You don't talk to the opposite sex; you need to be invisible" (Mohamud 2017, 177).

Despite research showing that "religion supports traditional and subordinate roles for women," Somali women have sought to push back against these interpretations (Alexander 2012, 443). But women find themselves on the defensive, referencing Islamic history and Muslim women who participated in the governing of their societies. They insist they will not go "beyond what Islam allows" (Koshin 2016). This situation is most stark in Somaliland, where women are criticized for opposing culture and religion if they insist on gender quotas. Some of the religious actors base their opposition to women's political inclusion on the argument that it is better for women to remain at home than to interact with unrelated men. These actors also recall how the Barre government executed ten religious men for opposing the 1974 Family Law, which gave women equal rights to inheritance, as further justification for their opposition to women's involvement in politics (Abdullahi 2016).

Tripp identifies key patterns that connect the transition toward a postconflict nation to changes in gender regimes, including "gender relations of power and the way power is organized hierarchically along gender lines in political institutions" (Tripp 2015, 4). Relevant to Somalia are the high death rates during the civil war, which dragged on for many years, and the fact that women were largely peacemakers (Tripp 2015, 18–19). The changes in gender norms that resulted from the civil war were expected to be temporary; after the war ended, women were once again subjected to patriarchal controls. But while society accepted women's shouldering of male responsibilities to their family, they were expected to remain out of politics and government, which some men view as the sole arena left to them (interview, December 2016, Hargeisa).

But the changes in gender roles created spaces for women to exercise leadership. During the first ten years of the civil war, women were "excluded from the all-male arena of clan-based politics. Women have directed their collective political acumen and agency into the civil society space that opened up after state collapse" (Jama 2010). Throughout the 1990s, multiple reconciliation conferences held to bring the Somali state back included only the warring factions and were "non-inclusive male-dominated and top-down peace processes"; if women were included, it was only as observers (Dini 2013).

The Arta Conference hosted by Djibouti in 2000 was the first reconciliation conference at which cultural pluralism was adopted. This conference coincided with the adoption of UN Security Council Resolution 1325 on Women, Peace, and Security and was, at the time, the largest Somali-owned peace conference that brought together representatives of civil society and business, clan elders, religious groups, intellectuals, and diaspora (Elmi and Barise 2006). Out of the 810 official delegates, 90 were women who came from across Somalia and the diaspora. Some were involved in the delivery of humanitarian and development work; others had held senior positions in the Barre government. These women seized this opportunity for a new gender regime and agreed to work together as women, advocating for their rights, regardless of clan affiliation. The women formed the sixth clan to compete with the major clans (Koshin 2016).

Two important events occurred at this meeting. For the first time, a gender quota was introduced and included under the first national charter (Heritage Institute 2017). This might have been because the leaders wanted to signal that everyone was represented at this conference and were seeking legitimacy, recognition, and foreign aid from the international community (Bush 2011). Women were allocated reserved seats in the parliament. The adoption of gender quotas was accompanied by the 4.5 clan power-sharing agreement, according to which political seats would be allocated along clan lines and clan elders would select their representatives. Unsurprisingly, "women have a limited chance of getting nominated and are always locked out" (Dini 2013, 2). The four major clans received sixty seats each, and the alliance of minority clans received thirty seats. To advocate for their rights, women created a sixth clan so that women's share would be allocated separately from the seats that fell under the clan rubric: "The women were highly organized and launched an effective lobbying strategy. Their initial goal was to gain 25 percent of the seats" (Abdullahi 2018, 213).[3] One woman member of Parliament who is serving her second term (2016 and 2021) described the 4.5 as a cancer on Somali politics, one that left women to the mercy of men. She believes that the only way out of this barrier to women's political equality is to transition to direct elections, with a

50 percent gender quota included in the constitution (interview, February 2021, Mogadishu). At Arta, women were given 10.5 percent of the seats, but less than 5 percent of these were ever filled (Abdullahi 2017, 214).[4]

A year later, in 2002, Somaliland began its democratization process, holding local elections as a precursor to parliamentary and presidential elections. In that election, 135 women competed against 1,945 male candidates for 305 seats in the local councils. Only nine women were elected, representing approximately 3 percent of seats in the local councils. All twenty-three mayors and thirteen governors and their deputies were men (Gaheir and Jama 2018). Like women in other Somali regions, women in Somaliland faced clan elders who were part of governmental institutions as the upper house of the parliament (Guurti) and who had allocated to themselves the legislative responsibilities for issues related to culture and religion and included women's issues. As Somaliland sought international recognition, activists agreed to postpone demands for women's rights (interview, January 2017, Hargeisa).

In Somalia, the Transitional National Government (TNG) could not govern because of opposition from the excluded warlords. Another conference was hosted in Kenya in 2004, which allowed Kenya and Ethiopia to design a government of their own choosing with "muscular international support" (Young 2006, 324). Faction leaders who were allied with these countries had a prominent role. Women were included under the civil society umbrella. This conference had 1,500 men and 100 women delegates. Women had one representative in each of the reconciliation committees and two in the leaders' committee. In the Transitional Federal Charter, women successfully introduced gender-neutral language and secured a 12 percent quota. However, they got only 8 percent of the seats, and their numbers continued to decline because each time a woman left, she was replaced by a man.

In Somaliland, the 2005 parliamentary election resulted in two women, Ikraan Haji Daud (elected) and Baar Saed (appointed), in the eighty-two-member lower house of the parliament and no women in the eighty-two-member Guurti. There were also five male honorary members. Thus, women constituted 1.2 percent of Somaliland's parliament (Gaheir and Jama 2018, 3).

In 2009, another reconciliation meeting sought to mediate between the Transitional Federal Government (TFG) and the opposition, the Alliance for the Re-liberation of Somalia (ARS), which included many Islamists and resulted in the parliament's expansion from 275 to 550 members. The percentage of women dropped to 3 percent (Jama 2010, 49). All three prime ministers appointed under the presidency of Sheikh Sharif appointed one woman to their cabinets as the minister of women and human rights.[5]

In 2012, Somalia embarked on ending the failed transitional period, which lasted for eight years and brought minimal governance. The transition into a federal system provided an opportunity for women to institutionalize the quota, and it also provided political leaders an opportunity to signal that they were serious about including women. The National Consultative Conference in Garowe (Garowe I and II) produced the Garowe principles that granted women 30 percent of the seats across the federal government, although women had lobbied for 50 percent (Second Somali National Consultative Constitutional Conference 2012). The provisional constitution did not include a quota, and women believed men were treating the gender quota as a "gentleman's agreement between the regional governments and the transitional federal government" (interview, July 2018, Mogadishu).

The 125 elders selected by the regions were entrusted with the sole responsibility of appointing the parliamentarians, and many refused to appoint women to represent the clans. Women encountered a great deal of difficulty and were fighting on several fronts. First, the elders insisted only men could represent the clan because women's loyalty and commitment were suspect since they were often born into one clan but married into another. What made women ideal peacemakers and peacekeepers was their ability to connect with multiple clans, but this also made them undesirable as political representatives. Women were also competing with male politicians. For example, both the prime minister and the minister of the Constitution, who seemed committed to the gender quota, grabbed seats allocated to women (interview, July 2018, Nairobi). Other barriers facing women included their lack of cohesion. The clan-based politics meant that women were divided by clan. In this process, minority clans were sometimes better for women, not because they differed from the dominant clans but because those groups were often made to give their seats to women from their clans, and if they refused, the seat would go to another minority clan (interview, July 2018, Mogadishu).

The religious groups also came out in force against the gender quota, claiming that it was the international community and its foreign ideas that were pushing Somali women out of their homes (interview, July 2018, Mogadishu). The lesson for women from the 2012 election was that their appointment to the parliament must be taken out of the hands of the clan elders and must be enshrined in the law. During this election, only 14 percent of women made it to the parliament (Dini 2013, 2).

The international community supported women's efforts to enter the parliament, although far less than women expected. For example, the United Nations secretary-general's envoy to Somalia, Augustine Mahiga, routinely asked to meet with women's groups to hear their concerns, signaling that women were important stakeholders (interview, July 2018, Mogadishu). Organizations like the New Democratic Institute (NDI) also supported women by providing leadership training. Women also benefited from the experiences of women in other countries, meeting with the Women's Caucus in the Ugandan Parliament and women MPs in Rwanda to learn about their experiences and strategies on how to enter politics and get elected to the parliament (interview, July 2018, Mogadishu).

In the government cabinet of Prime Minister Abdi Shirdon, women made up 20 percent of the cabinet and were appointed to powerful positions. Fowsiyo Yusuf Haji Aden became both the deputy prime minister and the minister of foreign affairs. This was a first not only for Somalia but also for the Horn of Africa. Dr. Maryam Qassim became the minister for social development, which combined five ministries comprising education, health, labor, youth and sports, and women and social affairs (Dini 2013, 2). Unfortunately, Shirdon's departure as prime minister a year later resulted in the replacement of these dedicated and highly competent women.

The new prime minister, Abdiweli Sheikh Ahmed, expanded his cabinet and reduced women's share of the cabinet to 5 percent (Mareeg Online 2014). The last prime minister to serve with President Hassan Sheikh Mohamud was Omar Abdirashid. He expanded his cabinet to sixty-six ministers but included only three female ministers, who held the traditionally female portfolios of women and human rights, education, and health. He also appointed two deputy ministers for justice and women and human rights. Women's share of the cabinet was 7.5 percent (Goobjoog 2015). Women did better in the five regional parliaments, with Southwest State leading the way with 21 percent female MPs, followed by Galmudug at 9 percent, Jubbaland at 4 percent, and Puntland last at 3 percent.

Women's political representation in Somaliland has continued to decline, and in 2020, women's political representation in both houses of the parliament as well as mayors and governors was negligible.[6] In 2018, attempts to introduce a 20 percent gender quota were rejected by the Somaliland parliament. There were three women councilors at the local level, two government ministers, and a deputy minister (Hassan and Abdi 2022). Similarly, the 2018 Puntland election reduced the number of women in the parliament from two to one, demonstrating that the elders are pushing back against the gender quota. The similarity between Puntland and Somaliland can be attributed only to the powerful position that elders hold in these two regions.

By 2013, women in Somalia organized around how they could attain the 30 percent allocated to them within the Garowe Principles Agreement. In the diaspora, Somalis were also discussing Vision 2016, a framework for action that was to review the provisional constitution and discuss the formation of boundaries and a federation commission that would decide the boundaries of regional states and the democratization of the electoral system, political party law, electoral management system, and other laws (Koshin 2016, 27). In two different meetings, held in Minneapolis and Toronto, only men were present, and prominent Somali politicians were in attendance. In April 2015, a group of women led by women's rights activist Zainab Mohamed Hassan discussed how they could ensure women's share in politics in the 2016 elections. A Facebook invitation to a group of two dozen women to strategize and work together on Vision 2016 led more than three hundred women to join the group within twenty-four hours as women invited one another. In June 2015, about forty women from the Somali diaspora in North America and Europe came together to mobilize for the 2016 elections. These women had different goals. Some wanted to endorse specific female candidates. Others wanted to mobilize around the provision of social services, but in the end, the group, which came to be known as the Somali Gender Equity Movement (SGEM), focused on policy and advocacy. SGEM supported any woman who wanted to run for office but refrained from endorsing candidates (interview, July 2018, Nairobi). Within a few months, SGEM had more than nine thousand members, including women from inside Somalia and women in the diaspora. SGEM's mission was to "promote social and political equity for Somali women in the public decision-making arena in 2016 and beyond" (Ahmed 2015). SGEM analyzed, through a gender lens, major documents such as the Somali Vision 2016 framework document, the provisional constitution, and other regional constitutions.

In the provisional federal constitution, SGEM identified thirty articles that could be made gender friendly. SGEM also sent letters to the regional states raising concerns over their constitutions but received no response to their letters. One of the regional presidents acknowledged the difficulties in electing women because of the clan elders' resistance to appointing women. Highlighting the challenges facing women seeking political office, when one clan elder was asked to respect the 30 percent quota and include women, he responded, "We have no women to prostitute" (interview, July 2018, Nairobi). SGEM sought all elected or appointed positions in politics and in the government to meet the 30 percent quota. SGEM engaged in awareness raising for women and held electoral education workshops for women running for office to ensure women's adequate representation. In these workshops, women were educated on how the electoral college worked as well as trained in communication and leadership (interview, July 2018, Nairobi). SGEM worked with the Federal Electoral Implementation Team (FEIT) and the state-level electoral implementation teams that handled the indirect elections.

SGEM also allied with another movement working on the same issue in Puntland. Talo-wadaag had also been formed to increase women's political participation in Puntland. The main goals of Talo-wadaag were to bring women together, to advocate for democracy and human rights, and to promote women's participation in the decision-making process (Koshin 2016, 29–30; interview, August 2017, Garowe). Fowsiyo Yusuf Haji Adan, former deputy prime minister, formed her own political party, the National Democratic Party, hoping she could compete if Somalia transitioned into one-person-one-vote (interview, July 2018, Mogadishu). Fowsiyo was motivated because "the only hope that Somali women have, if they want to get their rights, is to join political parties or create their own and to take the leadership position, this is the only way for them to obtain their rights" (interview, July 2018, Mogadishu). Women also held important positions, including as head of the Federal Independent Electoral Commission (FIET).

The religious actors were not silent, talking to the media and issuing press releases and calling for Somali women to return to their homes. Women engaged with them to discuss their concerns and to try to change their minds. However, many prominent religious actors declared they had no problem with women running for politics. Their only problem was the gender quota. In a televised debate between Batula Sheikh Ahmed Gaballe, the head of the Somali National Women's Organization, and Sheikh Nur Barud, the vice-head of a religious association, the sheikh insisted that women should compete with men on an equal plane. His objection to gender quotas stemmed from the belief that it was a foreign concept, and even though Batula explained that the effort toward a quota system was being driven by Somali women, the sheikh refused to accept it as anything other than foreigners pushing their feminist agenda on Somalia (Voice of America 2016).

Women increased their numbers to 24 percent of the parliamentary seats in the 2016 elections. Partially, this was because of the work of movements like Talo-wadaag in Puntland and SGEM in southern Somalia. But women also benefited from changes in the electoral process, whereby the elders appointed fifty-one delegates who would vote for each candidate. Rather than having 125 men deciding who would get into parliament, in this election, 14,025 people would cast votes for the 275 MPs (interview, July 2018, Mogadishu). The 30 percent quota also applied to the delegates. The elders still preferred men, but because of the enlarged electoral college, it was not entirely up to them, though they tried to control the process in different ways. For example, some elders allowed only male candidates to choose the delegates while denying that right to women candidates, thus ensuring that no one would vote for the women. In other cases, the date or the location of the election was changed (interview, July 2018, Mogadishu). Women also faced problems because the elders did not know them and their political stances. Some elders refused to meet with the women. Others met with them as a courtesy but did not want women to represent the clan (Interview July 2018, Mogadishu). Women were also disadvantaged because, during all three elections (2012, 2016, and 2021), many of the candidates were paying thousands of dollars to get elected, with most of the money given to elders and the male delegates. The funds were donated by the business community, which preferred male candidates (interview, January 2021, online).

The UNDP posed another problem for women activists. The UNDP, which was responsible for housing and feeding the delegates, was unable to secure funding in a timely manner. Candidates were then told to take care of the delegates and told they would be reimbursed later. This introduced corruption into the process, and the winners were those who could spend the most on the delegates and the clan elders. One process that was used to appear as outwardly complying with the 30 percent quota was called *Maxiis*. Some men would pay a woman to run for a parliamentary seat, understanding that the woman would vacate the seat after the election in favor of the man if she won. In other cases, a man would present a woman as a token opposition, and she would then lose the election (interview, August 2017, Garowe).

Women who could overcome these challenges and had a chance of winning were sometimes arrested or kidnapped. For example, a female candidate, Mumino Said Marsal, from Southwest, was inexplicably arrested at a checkpoint on her way to the election and held in jail until the election was over. To make her loss appear legitimate, she was told to sign a letter withdrawing her candidacy. She refused, and a letter was submitted by the regional president purporting to show that she had withdrawn from the election (interview recorded by Lul Kulmiye, October 22, 2016).

In another case, a woman from Galmudug who had met with and convinced the elders that she was the best candidate was kidnapped from her home. Unable to be present at the election hall, she lost the election (interview, July 2018, Nairobi). But there were some women who were successful. One female candidate provided housing and food and placed guards to ensure that the other candidates had no access to the delegates. She won the election.

Other women competed with men and won, but this was not the norm (interview, August 2018, Mogadishu).

The election of Mohamed Abdullahi Farmaajo as president in 2017 brought a great deal of hope, but where women were concerned, the government underdelivered. Members of SGEM and Talo-wadaag, along with other women advocates, met with Farmaajo after he appointed Hassan Ali Kheyre to ask him to honor the 30 percent gender quota (interview, July 2018, Nairobi). Out of twenty-seven ministers appointed by Kheyre, six were women, two were deputy ministers, and no women were appointed as state ministers, making women 12 percent of the cabinet. Interestingly, half of the women were from minority groups, outnumbering men from their clans (60 percent). Two of the major clans appointed no women, and a third appointed only one. Women were appointed to nontraditional positions such as Ports and Marine Transport, Commerce and Industry, Youth and Sports, and Humanitarian and Disaster Management (Garowe Online 2017). Since then, two women ministers have been replaced by men.

Implementation of the quota at the cabinet, regional, and local levels appears to rely on men's goodwill. For example, one mayor of Mogadishu, Thabit Mohamed, committed to a 50 percent quota for women and appointed five women as district commissioners out of fifteen; the deputy mayor and secretary general for the Benadir region were also women. When the mayor was fired, the deputy mayor and the general secretary also lost their positions. Soon after, two of the district commissioners were replaced with men.

Conclusion

Increasingly, women are running for local and regional offices. The 2023 local elections were the first time that direct elections took place in Puntland since 1969, and women won 17 percent of the seats. In the 2021 federal parliament elections, women's representation in the lower house dropped by 4 percent to 20 percent. Paradoxically, women's representation in the Senate rose by 2 percent to 26 percent.

Some women activists believe that the only way for women to be accepted is to compete with men, considering that this would eliminate the opposition by men to women entering politics. Others believe that if women were to compete with men, this would lead to the election of qualified women (interview, July 2018, Mogadishu). Others believe that Somalia's eventual transition to one-person-one-vote will lead to more women in office. Unfortunately, the example of Somaliland shows that even in a political system where the people vote, the

clan is the primary criterion for deciding for whom to vote. Recognizing this barrier to women's political participation, Somaliland recently tabled a 20 percent
quota for women in the parliament. In Somalia, it was hoped that one-person-
one-vote would be implemented in time for the 2020 election, but that did not
happen. Out of the thirty-five political parties that have temporarily registered,
only one is headed by a woman.

A study by SIDRA found that many participants believed that "the involvement of men is key to the success of the gender-equality movement in Somalia
but changing long-held social structures and convincing men of the importance of equal opportunities for women will not happen overnight" (Koshin
2016). The men who need to be convinced are the clan elders, the religious actors, and male politicians, and most do not see any value in women's participation in politics. Somaliland's 2021 local and parliamentary elections serve as a
warning of what will happen to women's political participation without a gender quota. In that election, twenty-eight women ran for local and parliamentary seats, and only three were elected to the local council (Hassan and Abdi
2022). In 2023, Amina Fareed was appointed to the lower house of the parliament. Somali women continue to push for their political inclusion through the
gender quota, knowing that there is no other way to ensure that they have a
seat at the decision-making table, but they will continue to be hindered by their
division along clan lines, lack of agreement on the important of the quota system, and the absence of a national women's movement.

Notes

1. The survey part of the research was funded by the Heritage Institute for Policy
Studies based in Mogadishu, Somalia. The qualitative interviews were conducted by
Zainab Hassan and Ladan Affi.

2. The idea of the sixth clan came from Zakiya Abdisalan Alin, who was a woman
activist.

3. The parliament was to have 245 members, with 44 seats allocated to each of the
four major clans, 25 to women and 24 to the alliance of minority clans, and 20 seats to
be used to address any shortcomings in the parliament.

4. These were Omar Abdirashid, Mohamed Abdullahi Farmaajo, and Abdiweli
Gas, all members of the diaspora.

5. When women asked why they were excluded, they were told that they had been
invited but did not come and were told to organize their own meetings. The Toronto
meeting included Abdi Hosh, the late Constitution minister, and Mohamed Abdullahi

Farmaajo, former prime minister (2010) and former president of the federal government (2017–22).

6. In 2012, out of 2,088 candidates, women made up 135; in 2019, the number of female candidates was only 27 (Gaheir and Jama 2018, 5).

References

Abdullahi, Abdurahman M. 2016. "Somalia: Historical Phases of the Islamic Movements." *Somali Studies* 1 (1): 19–49.

Abdullahi, Abdurahman. 2017. *Making Sense of Somali History*. Vol. 1. London: Adonis and Abbey.

Abdullahi, Abdurahman. 2018. *Making Sense of Somali History*. Vol. 2. London: Adonis and Abbey.

Abdullahi, Abdurahman. n.d. "Islamism in Somalia." Accessed January 25, 2024. https://www.academia.edu/79482340/Islamism_in_Somalia.

Affi, Ladan. 2020. "The Old Men Who Hold Us Back: Clan Elders, Elite Bargaining and Exclusionary Politics." *Journal of Somali Studies: Research on Somalia and the Greater Horn of African Countries* 7 (2) (December): 125–45.

Affi, Ladan. 2021. "No Going Back: Somali Women's Fight for Political Inclusion." In *Women and Peacebuilding in Africa*, edited by Ladan Affi, Liv Tonnessen, and Aili Mari Tripp. Suffolk: James Currey.

Ahmed, Ali Jimale. 1995. *The Invention of Somalia*. Lawrenceville, NJ: Red Sea Press.

Ahmed, Hassan. 2015. "Global Somali Women Launch Movement to Play an Important Role in Politics." *Sahan Journal*, June. http://sahanjournal.com.

Alexander, Amy C. 2012. "Change in Women's Descriptive Representation and the Belief in Women's Ability to Govern: A Virtuous Cycle." *Politics and Gender* 8 (4): 437–64.

Berry, Marie E. 2017. "Barriers to Women's Progress after Atrocity: Evidence from Rwanda and Bosnia-Herzegovina." *Gender & Society* 31 (6): 830–53.

Bush, Sarah Sunn. 2011. "International Politics and the Spread of Quotas for Women in Legislatures." *International Organization* 65 (Winter): 103–37.

Convention on the Elimination of Discrimination against Women (CEDAW). n.d. United Nations. Accessed January 25, 2024. http://www.un.org/womenwatch/daw/cedaw/.

Dahlerup, Drude. 2008. "Gender Quotas—Controversial but Trendy: On Expanding the Research Agenda." *International Feminist Journal of Politics* 10 (3): 322–28.

Dini, Shukria. 2013. "Women in the Government of Somalia." *Afrikas Horn—Horn of Africa Journal* 2:1–11.

Elmi, Afyare, and Abdullahi Barise. 2006 "The Somali Conflict: Root Causes, Obstacles, and Peace-Building Strategies." *African Security Review* 15 (1): 32–54.

Eno, Mohamed A., and Omar A. Eno. 2009. "Intellectualism amid Ethnocentrism: Mukhtar and the 4.5 Factor." *Bildhaan: An International Journal of Somali Studies* 9:137–45.

Federal Republic of Somalia, Provisional Constitution. 2012. Accessed January 25, 2024. http://hrlibrary.umn.edu/research/Somalia-Constitution2012.pdf.

Gaheir, Maria Abdilahi, and Guleid Ahmed Jama. 2018. "Somaliland: A Male Democracy." *Horn Diplomat*, November 13. https://www.horndiplomat.com/2018/11/13/somaliland-a-male-democracy/.

Garowe Online. 2017. "Somalia's PM Names His New Cabinet, Reinstates Former Ministers." March 21. https://www.garoweonline.com/en/news/somalia/somalias-pm-names-his-new-cabinet-reinstates-former-ministers.

Gelle, Asha. n.d. Puntland Development Research Center video. Garowe, Somalia. Copy in author's possession.

Goobjoog. 2015. "Prime Minister Omar Announces 66 Cabinet Members." February 6. http://goobjoog.com/english/prime-minister-of-somalia-announces-new-cabinet-with-26-ministers/.

Hassan, Sahra Abdi, and Ayan Abdilahi Abdi. 2022. "The Role of Women in Somaliland's 2021 Elections." Institute for Peace and Conflict Studies, University of Hargeisa, July.

Heritage Institute. 2017. "Somalia's Parliament Should Produce a Constitution by and for the People." Heritage Institute for Policy Studies, February 28. https://heritageinstitute.org/somalias-parliament-should-produce-a-constitution-by-and-for-the-people/.

Hughes, Melanie M. 2009. "Armed Conflict, International Linkages and Women's Parliamentary Representation in Developing Nations." *Social Problems* 56 (1): 174–204.

Interview recorded by Lul Kulmiye. 2016. YouTube, October 22. https://www.youtube.com/watch?v=tVTdg1Wtorw&feature=youtu.be.

Jama, Faiza. 2010. "Somali Women and Peacebuilding." *Accord* 21:62–65.

Koshin, Sahro Ahmed. 2016. *2016 Elections in Somalia: The Rise of Somali Women's New Political Movements*. Garowe: SIDRA Institute.

Mareeg Online. 2014. "List of the New Somali Cabinet Revealed by Prime Minister Abdiweli Sheikh Ahmed." https://mareeg.com/en_gb/list-of-the-new-somali-cabinet-revealed-by-prime-minister-abdiweli-sheikh-ahmed/.

Menkhaus, Ken. 2002. "Political Islam in Somalia." *Middle East Policy* 9 (1): 109–23.

Mohamud, Maimuna. 2017. "Women, Piety and Political Representation: Islamic Discourses in Contemporary Somalia." *Journal of Women of the Middle East and the Islamic World* 14 (September): 166–86.

Osman, Abdulahi A. 2015. "The End of Transition in Somalia and the Role of the Technical Selection Experience." *Journal of Somali Studies: Research on Somalia and the Greater Horn of African Countries* 2 (1–2): 99–126.

Second Somali National Consultative Constitutional Conference. 2012. Garowe, Somalia, February 15–17.

Somali Roadmap Signatories. 2012. "Protocol Establishing the Somali New Federal Parliament (Adopted June 22, 2012)." https://peacemaker.un.org/somalia-transitionalcharter2004.

Somali Women and Human Rights Development. 2020. *Somali Women Forging Alliances to Safeguard Equal Rights for All*. Mogadishu: Somali Women and Human Rights Development.

Tripp, Aili Mari. 2015. *Women and Power in Post-Conflict Africa*. Cambridge Studies in Gender and Politics. New York: Cambridge University Press.

Voice of America. 2016. "A Heated Debate—Gender Quota." October 13. https://www.youtube.com/watch?v=xQ6Ni1nl8OE&t=265s.

Young, Crawford. 2000. "Africa: Democratization, Cultural Pluralism, and the Challenge of Political Order." *Macalester International* 9 (1): 3–30.

Young, Crawford. 2006. "The Heart of the African Conflict Zone: Democratization, Ethnicity, Civil Conflict and the Great Lakes Crisis" *Annual Reviews Political Science* 9:301–28.

Young, Crawford. 2012. *The Postcolonial State in Africa: Fifty Years of Independence, 1960–2010.* Madison: University of Wisconsin Press.

11

Territorial Nationalism, Cultural Pluralism, and Women's Peace Mobilization in Cameroon

Melinda J. Adams

As a first-year graduate student, I had the good fortune to take Crawford Young's Survey of African Politics seminar. Later, I took his graduate seminar in cultural pluralism. As I reread his work, I am transported back to these classes. I can picture the rooms and almost hear his voice as he shared his vast knowledge of African politics. Rereading his work has made me realize how much his teaching and scholarship have shaped my understanding of African politics and my orientation to the discipline. While his scholarship was wide-ranging, he particularly focused on the state and cultural pluralism. For Young (1976, 66), these two topics are inextricably linked as the state is the "cast-iron grid superimposed upon the culturally diverse populace." His approach helps us understand much of contemporary politics in Cameroon—the focus of this chapter.

One gap, however, is the relatively little attention that he devoted to gender. In identifying categories of cultural differentiation in *The Politics of Cultural Plu-*

ralism (1976), Young highlights ethnicity, race, religion, caste, and regionalism. Notably absent from this list is gender. His later work begins to address this omission. In *The Postcolonial State in Africa* (2012, 326), for example, he acknowledges that "there is some evidence that men and women experience and enact ethnicity differently. Given the near universality of patriarchal norms embedded in societal structure, one may ask whether the resulting asymmetries influence ethnic consciousness." While he briefly considers the ways that gender interfaces with other forms of identity, his treatment of gender is less developed than that of other forms of cultural pluralism.

In this chapter, I highlight how Young's work helps us understand contemporary politics in Cameroon. His scholarship helps us comprehend the stickiness of the geographical parameters of the Cameroonian state, the efforts by Cameroonian presidents Ahmadu Ahidjo and Paul Biya to promote a national identity, the framing of contemporary Anglophone movements, and the multifaceted, situational, and evolving nature of identity in Cameroon. I then extend his work to look more deeply at how gender intersects with other forms of identity in Cameroon. In Cameroon and elsewhere, gender influences how individuals experience and embody national identity and ethnicity (Mougoué 2019). Identity is particularly salient in Cameroon given the current Anglophone crisis, which began with protests in fall 2016 by lawyers, educators, and students against government policies that marginalized Anglophone populations and has led to the deaths of an estimated six thousand people, the destruction of more than 250 villages, and the displacement of more than 600,000 people (OCHA 2022; International Crisis Group 2022a). I argue that Young's work provides a useful framework for understanding contemporary Cameroonian politics, particularly the territorial and identity components of the Anglophone crisis, but a full picture requires highlighting the ways that gender intersects with other forms of identity and how women have contributed to Anglophone national identities and peace movements.

Cameroonian Context

In *The African Colonial State in Comparative Perspective* (1994, 283), Young wrote: "Although we commonly described the independent polities as 'new states,' in reality they were successors to the colonial regime, inheriting its structures, its quotidian routines and practices, and its more hidden normative theories of governance." In the Cameroonian context, the legacies of French and British colonial rule permeate local government structures, language policies,

educational policies, legal systems, and more. Some of the challenges associated with creating a national identity are linked to the stickiness of these formal
and informal colonial institutions.

Cameroon's "Anglophone problem" is linked to the country's mixed colonial heritage. Germany established control over Cameroon in 1884. Following
Germany's defeat in World War I, France and Britain divided the German colonial territory between them. First, as a League of Nations mandate and later
as a United Nations trust territory, Britain controlled the smaller Western section, while France oversaw the rest of the territory. During this period, Camer-
oonians experienced different local governance structures, educational systems,
administrative languages, and legal systems. These differences contributed to
the development of distinctive identities. Despite an ongoing conflict with the
Union des populations du Cameroun (UPC) party, French-controlled Cameroon gained independence on January 1, 1960. On February 11, 1961, the United
Nations organized a plebiscite in the British-controlled territories of Northern
Cameroons and Southern Cameroons. Voters were given just two choices: joining Nigeria or joining Cameroon. The preferred outcome of many in British
Cameroons—becoming an independent state—was not an option (Konings
and Nyamnjoh 2019). Within this framework, Northern Cameroons voted to
join Nigeria, while Southern Cameroons voted to join Cameroon. This led to
the creation of the Federal Republic of Cameroon on October 1, 1961. The
newly independent state included two federal units: East Cameroon, the former French-controlled territory, and West Cameroon, the former British-
controlled territory. The "Anglophone problem," as it is often referred to, stems
from the two territories' different colonial experiences, the limited options provided in the plebiscite, and the marginalization of Anglophone regions in the
postcolonial period.

From the mid-1960s until the 1990s, there was little space for activism
around Anglophone identity. By 1966, the first president of Cameroon, Ahmadou Ahidjo, had eliminated all opposition parties and established a single
legal party, the Cameroon National Union (CNU). On the heels of the single
party came a new, stricter law on association. The 1967 law required most civil
societal groups either to dissolve or to join state-led organizations. While the
federation was weak from its inception, with few powers or financial resources
distributed to subnational entities, Ahidjo continued to centralize power. In
1972, he established a unitary state. While the transition to Paul Biya as president in 1982 initially sparked some optimism regarding the position of Anglophones within Cameroon, Biya continued to concentrate power within the
unitary state. In 1984, Biya renamed the state the Republic of Cameroon

(rather than the United Republic of Cameroon), which referenced the former French-controlled territory before the two entities merged in 1961. Under both Ahidjo and Biya, Anglophones have felt politically and economically marginalized. As evidence of this marginalization, they point to the small number of Anglophones in positions of power within the government and the lack of investment in the country's two English-speaking regions.

Opportunities for opposition parties and civil society grew in the 1990s with the return of multipartyism and greater associational freedom. On May 26, 1990, opponents of the single-party state launched the Social Democratic Front (SDF) in Ntarinkon Park in Bamenda. The government responded with violence and repression, killing at least six people as the crowd was dispersing. Facing external and internal pressure, the state shifted its stance by December 1990, passing a law reintroducing multiparty politics. It also passed a new law on association in 1990 that facilitated the growth of civil societal organizations. Greater political and associational space and the recognition that the SDF only lukewarmly embraced Anglophone concerns contributed to the emergence of a more public and active Anglophone movement in the form of organizations such as the Free West Cameroon Movement, the Ambazonia Movement, the Cameroon Anglophone Movement, and the All Anglophone Conference (Konings and Nyamnjoh 1997, 2019). The return to multiparty politics is also associated with the increased salience of ethnic and regional identities as Biya utilized divide-and-rule tactics to foment tensions among Anglophone communities (Fonchingong 2004).

The Cameroonian government responded to peaceful protests organized by lawyers, teachers, and students with violence, arrests, and an Internet shutdown. The protests transformed into armed conflict in 2017, leading to the deaths of an estimated six thousand people and the internal displacement of more than six hundred thousand (OCHA 2022). The crisis has also produced tens of thousands of refugees, mostly in Nigeria. Schools in Anglophone regions have been largely closed since 2017 (International Crisis Group 2022a). Even as schools are slowly reopening, university lecturers, teachers, and students continue to face attacks, and fewer than half of schools in the two regions were functioning in the 2022–23 academic year (OCHA 2022).

The international response to the conflict has been limited. Cameroon topped the Norwegian Refugee Council's list of the ten most neglected displacement crises in 2018 and 2019. It was ranked second in 2020 and third in 2021. During his July 2018 visit to Cameroon, Moussa Faki Mahamat, the chairperson of the African Union Commission, encouraged inclusive dialogue but also indicated the AU's "commitment to the unity and territorial integrity of Cameroon" (African Union 2018). Switzerland offered to lead negotiations in 2019, but the Cameroonian government ended the Swiss-led mediation process in September 2022. In January 2023, Canada announced that some separatist groups had agreed to enter a process to resolve the conflict, but the Cameroonian government quickly denied that it had authorized Canadian mediation.

Territorial Nationalism

Young's work helps us understand the contemporary Anglophone crisis, particularly the links between colonial boundaries and postcolonial states. He highlights the centrality of territorial nationalism, noting that the code of decolonization was territoriality (Young 2012). The concept of self-determination gained traction after World War II, but international support was generally limited to instances where calls for new states aligned with existing colonial boundaries. In Young's words, "the elixir of sovereignty hardened the map lines of the colonial partition into a permanent array of containers" (2012, 89). Young notes that the traditional building blocks of national identity—a deep historical narrative, shared culture and language, and a common religious identity—are missing in most African states. In this context, "territorial identity itself became the primary component [of national identity], erected with few exceptions on a shallow historical narrative, recent shared memories, and a limited repertoire of common icons" (Young 2012, 309). Nationalism in Africa has been associated with territory. During the process of decolonization in Cameroon, "A curious form of ghostly territoriality excavated from German times appeared . . . asserting a natural claim to the restoration of the pre-1914 geographic frame" (Young 2012, 91). A return to these earlier colonial boundaries was not inevitable. It was linked to the UN's refusal to offer independence as an option and intra-Anglophone struggles for political influence (Konings and Nyamnjoh 2019).

Once African states gained independence, they faced the challenge of creating a national identity that overlapped with the state boundaries. Cameroon was no exception. Highlighting the ascendency of the nation-state, Young (2012, 309) notes: "The now universalized international state system had come to rest on a premise that its individual components were 'nations.' In everyday language 'state' and 'nation' were interchangeable terms. If states fell short of corresponding to a recognizable version of nationhood, then they were summoned to improve themselves. African states thus required nation building not only for internal legitimation but also for international respectability." The first generation of African leaders, including Cameroon's Ahmadou Ahidjo, promoted national unity by establishing a single party that integrated major social groups such as women and youth into the party apparatus. Political opposition was framed as diversionary, and Ahidjo employed the concept of national unity as a way of silencing dissent and eliminating competing organizations. In Cameroon under Ahidjo, as elsewhere in newly independent African states, "nation-building, or national unity, provided ideological support for concentrating political and economic power in his office and person" (Konings and Nyamnjoh 2003, 4).

In the Anglophone regions, political liberalization in the 1990s led to the creation of new groups advocating for the return of federalism and secessionism. Leaders of these movements invoked the League of Nations mandate and United Nations trust territory to justify their claims for an independent state. Organizations with names that initially highlighted Anglophone identity changed them to emphasize their association with the territorial entity of Southern Cameroons. Piet Konings and Francis Nyamnjoh (2003, 90–91) describe this strategic shift:

> The AAC [All Anglophone Conference] was renamed Southern Cameroons People's Conference (SCPC), the Anglophone Council was renamed Southern Cameroons National Council (SCNC), and the Anglophone Advisory Committee was renamed the Southern Cameroons Advisory Council (SCAC). According to an SCNC press release, "the change of name makes it clear that the struggle led by the former AAC is neither of an essentially linguistic character nor in defence of an alien colonial culture, as had often been alleged, in bad faith, by some misguided critics of the AAC." It stressed that the adoption of the name Southern Cameroons showed that the aim of the struggle had always been and remained to restore, within a newly restructured Federal Republic of Cameroon, the autonomy of a territory—Southern Cameroons—and of a people—Southern Cameroonians—and to put an end to their annexation by *La République du Cameroun*.

Since international support for secessionist movements has been greater when the movement is tied to a previously existing territorial unit, Anglophone organizations sought to emphasize their connection to Southern Cameroons rather than their linguistic identity.

As Young emphasizes in his work, territorial nationalism has been central to the establishment of African states—both in the immediate postcolonial period and in more recent separatist struggles. Nationalist movements that can point to a historic entity are perceived as more legitimate by the international community. The United Nations invoked the pre-1914 territorial boundaries of the German-controlled colony in designing the options for the 1961 plebiscite.

Contemporary movements seeking a return to federalism or separation from the Republic of Cameroon have also invoked the territorial entity of Southern Cameroons. Across Africa, separatist movements—like the anticolonial nationalist movements that preceded them—have generally been linked to colonial boundaries. As Young (2012, 301) writes: "The small number of separatist movements of significance that have developed have invariably invoked a claim to territorial standing of colonial origin, never ethnic self-determination . . . or to special standing as kingdoms." The Anglophone movement in Cameroon fits the first pattern. Konings and Nyamnjoh (2003, 19) observe: "Secessionist demands have been on the increase since the early 1990s but appear mostly to revolve around the re-establishment of colonial partition-lines that were once erased or transformed into internal administrative boundaries." Young's work helps us understand why certain options become more "thinkable" than others (Schatzberg 2001). He highlights the centrality of territorial nationalism, which helps us understand key cleavages and framing strategies in Cameroon. This focus on territorial nationalism, however, does not highlight how gender intersects with national identities.

Cultural Pluralism

Young is arguably best known for his work on cultural pluralism, and the Cameroonian case, with its ethnic, religious, and linguistic diversity, also connects with his work on cultural pluralism. For Young, cultural pluralism is based on three main dimensions: common attributes, shared consciousness, and the presumption of an "other" (2012, 314). Common attributes can include "language, shared cultural practices and symbolic resources, belief in common ancestry, and historical narratives" (Young 2012, 314). Shared consciousness means that members of a group must recognize the name and self-identify with the group. Finally, identity is relative: there are boundaries and a sense of what differentiates "us" from "them." Young also emphasizes that identity is situational: in different contexts, different roles become salient.

Young's scholarship helps us understand the multifaceted and dynamic nature of identity in Cameroon. While linguistic identities are particularly salient right now, given the Anglophone conflict, it is important to recognize that ethnic, religious, and regional identities cut across linguistic divides in Cameroon. Konings and Nyamnjoh highlight this complexity: "Colonial boundaries have had an ambivalent impact on what has come to be known as the Anglophone problem. On the one hand, the boundary between Anglophone and Francophone Cameroon has laid the foundation for the construction of Anglophone and Francophone identities and the development of cleavages between the two elites. On the other hand, this boundary has failed to erase the existing ethnic relations between both territories altogether, enabling the Anglophone and Francophone elites to cement alliances if they were felt to be opportune" (2003, 9). Konings and Nyamnjoh emphasize that there are cultural similarities that unite ethnic groups across the linguistic divide, particularly between the Grass-fields ethnic groups that span the Northwest and West regions and the Sawa ethnic groups that cross the Southwest and Littoral regions.

In addition to ties with groups across linguistic boundaries, there have also been tensions within the Anglophone community itself. Both Ahidjo and Biya have exploited these differences by creating two different provinces (now regions) and utilizing divide-and-rule tactics that focus on coopting elites, particularly from the Southwest region, to support the government. Describing the division of the Anglophone region into two administrative units, Konings and Nyamnjoh (2003, 16) write: "This decision . . . would exacerbate these divisions that in the future would be the Achilles' heel of most attempts at Anglophone identity and organisation." Biya similarly sought to exacerbate intra-Anglophone tensions (often by coopting Anglophone elites) and tried to counter the Anglo-Bami (referring to Bamileke) alliance between the Northwest (predominantly Anglophone) and West (predominantly Francophone) regions with a Grand Sawa Movement that linked the Southwest (predominantly Anglophone) and Littoral (predominantly Francophone) regions. In the Southwest region, those from the Northwest have been pejoratively characterized as settlers, *graffis*, and *kam-no-go*, and non-indigenes have been excluded from voting and running for election (Fonchingong 2004).

Young's approach to cultural pluralism highlights the multifaceted and dynamic nature of identity. For Young (1976, 11), "the definition and boundaries of cultural groups are fluid rather than static." Young's nuanced approach to cultural pluralism, which eschews parsimony for complexity, captures the reality of identity in Cameroon. Individuals are not defined by a single element of their identity. Instead, different elements of identity become relevant in different contexts. In the current climate, linguistic identities are generally the most salient, but at times intra-Anglophone tensions, which fall along regional and ethnic lines, become important. Women and men also experience identity differently, and gender intersects with other identities; however, Young did not systematically explore the ways that gender shapes norms and expectations associated with ethnic and national identities.

Gender and Identity in Cameroon

While Young's work recognizes some relevant feminist scholarship, particularly the work of his University of Wisconsin–Madison colleagues like Aili Mari Tripp (2000, 2015) and Virginia Sapiro (1993), his own scholarship only briefly considers how gender intersects with national and ethnic identities. Similarly, accounts of Cameroonian nationalism (with the important exceptions of Mougoué 2019 and Terretta 2013) largely exclude women's contributions. They tend to focus instead on the male political leaders (e.g., John Ngu Foncha and Emmanuel Endeley) who led the campaigns leading up to the UN referendum in 1961 and/or on male-led political organizations such as the SDF, AAC, and SCNC. The SDF, the leading opposition party throughout the 1990s and early 2000s, was founded in 1990 by John Fru Ndi, who, along with other early leaders, has been dubbed one of the "Founding Fathers" of the party (Krieger 2011, 46). The AAC was established in April 1993 by four male leaders. Accounts that focus on women's roles and contributions are rare, and most focus on either Anlu, a 1958–61 uprising led by Kom women to protest colonial tax and agricultural policies (Ardener 1975; Konde 1990), or Takumbeng, a prodemocracy movement in the 1990s that protected Fru Ndi and enforced the "ghost town" campaigns (the closure of markets, other businesses, and transportation to turn towns and cities into "ghost towns") (Fonchingong and Tanga 2007; Kah 2011). While Milton Krieger (2011) mentions the role that women played in secretly circulating information and documents in the Northwest region as the SDF was being established, most accounts of Anglophone activism provide little information on the ways that women have contributed, though Jacqueline-Bethel Tchouta Mougoué's (2019) monograph is an important exception.

Mougoué (2019) shows how elite Anglophone women in the terminal colonial and federal periods constructed a distinctive gendered Anglophone identity. Prominent women, including women serving in newly created political institutions, the wives of male politicians, and the leaders of women's organizations, promoted the construction of a West Cameroon/Anglophone culture through the promotion of local dances, a national dress, local dishes, and beauty pageants. Through these activities, they constructed a unified Anglophone identity that elided ethnic differences, promoted pride in a distinct Anglophone identity, and emphasized "Anglophone separatism and cultural autonomy" (Mougoué 2019, 98). National identity was gendered: the characteristics associated with Anglophone women (e.g., a good mother and homemaker who eschewed gossip) were different from the expectations placed on men. The ideal Anglophone woman was also juxtaposed with stereotypes of

Francophone women. Mougoué (2019, 51) notes that there was a "widespread belief that Anglophone women were more authentically African, traditional, and sexually conservative," while Francophone women, in contrast, "were considered sexually loose, with poor public comportment and conduct." The activities of these elite Anglophone women—organizing in civic groups, holding contests to establish a national West Cameroon dress, participating in beauty pageants that celebrated West Cameroon, and creating cookbooks that highlighted indigenous foods—contributed to the construction of a distinct Anglophone national identity that continues to be used by Anglophone nationalists today. As Mougoué (2019, 56) observes: "In many ways, today's male leaders of Anglophone self-determination organizations use the past efforts of these women as a foundation to invoke tangible signifiers of Anglophone nationalism." While not focused specifically on Anglophone nationalism, Meredith Terretta's (2013, 5) study of the Union démocratique des femmes camerounaises similarly shows how women shaped "the collective consciousness" and brought women's concerns, such as inadequate medical and educational institutions, restrictions on women's commerce and agricultural practices, and the rights of women and children, to the anticolonial nationalist struggle.

Young (2012, 327) recognizes that women experience ethnicity differently and are more likely to come together across identity divides, writing that Aili Tripp "offers compelling evidence that women are more successful than their male counterparts in sustaining cooperation across ethnic lines in their organizations." In Cameroon—as in Uganda, Liberia, and elsewhere—women have mobilized across ethnic, regional, and linguistic divides to advocate for peace. Women in Cameroon have advocated for the peaceful resolution of conflict in formal and informal ways, organizing peace conventions, utilizing social media, engaging in public demonstrations, and drawing upon traditional organizations. The Anglophone crisis has affected men and women in different ways (Adams and Fonjong 2023). Women have taken on additional economic and care responsibilities and are more likely to face sexual violence. The closure of schools has been associated with an increase in teenage pregnancies. Women have drawn on these roles and experiences to build coalitions for peace. This is to say not that tensions do not exist within these organizations but rather that women are actively working to overcome these differences.

A diverse group of women—including urban women active in nongovernmental organizations and rural women with close ties to grassroots communities—are involved in the peace movement. Women involved in peace activism are motivated by their firsthand experiences of the negative effects of the conflict and by the marginalization of women in formal peace processes and political leadership. In addition to women's peace organizations, there are mixed-gender groups organizing for peace, including religious organizations and human rights groups. The Center for Human Rights and Democracy in Africa (CHRDA) and the Network of Human Rights Defenders in Central Africa have documented human rights abuses related to the conflict. Documenting these violations strengthens peace movements by highlighting the costs of the violence. In December 2022, CHRDA engaged twenty-five youth (women and men) from the Southwest region in a peacebuilding workshop. The Catholic Church, particularly under the late Cardinal Christian Tumi, the former Archbishop of Douala, established the Anglophone General Conference (AGC) with support from Protestant and Muslim leaders as a forum to prepare for a national dialogue. The Cameroonian government, however, has prevented the AGC from taking place. At least initially, the government seemed more willing to allow women to organize public demonstrations than male-led movements/mixed-gender groups (International Crisis Group 2022a).

Women have taken the lead in creating networks and coalitions promoting peace (Crawford et al. 2022). Organizations such as the Southwest Northwest Women's Task Force (SNWOT) and the Cameroon Women's Peace Movement (CAWOPEM) are registered with the state, invite government officials to participate in some of their events, and maintain social media accounts and websites. A coalition of more than 150 representatives of women's organizations and individual activists, SNWOT was founded in May 2018 and is the "first women-led local peace building network created purposefully to address the ongoing armed conflict in the country who called for a ceasefire from parties to the conflict" (Mbondgulo-Wondieh 2020, 137). It has scheduled meetings with parties in conflict and convened press conferences (Mbondgulo-Wondieh 2020). In August 2022, it jointly released a press statement with the Cameroon Women Peace Movement on the right to education of all children in Cameroon.

The Cameroon Women Peace Movement (CAWOPEM), another women's peace network, was established in 2019 by seventeen Cameroonian women who participated in a weeklong residential training program on conflict resolution, mediation, and negotiation run by Africans Rising and Action Aid Kenya. Its mission is to "offer diverse and innovative ways to create lasting peace," and it calls attention to the conflicts in both the Extreme North (Boko Haram) and in the Northwest and Southwest regions (CAWOPEM 2022). It brings together women-led civil society organizations from all ten regions of the country.

Both SNWOT and CAWOPEM are coalitions of women's groups. Tripp and Alice Kang (2018) argue that coalitions are particularly adept at naming problems, proposing specific policy solutions, and signaling broad domestic support for an issue. While Tripp and Kang focus on the relationship between domestic women's coalitions and the adoption of gender quotas, their findings suggest that coalitions as an organizing strategy may also help women's peace movements achieve their goals. One challenge associated with coalitions, however, is that there can be tensions within the networks regarding which individuals and organizations are most visible and benefit most directly from the opportunities provided to those associated with the network. Opportunities to travel abroad, participate in conferences, and be appointed to commissions are limited, and only a few women associated with these coalitions directly benefit from these opportunities.

With support from the Friedrich Ebert Stiftung (FES), a committee representing thirty-eight civil society organizations from all ten regions of Cameroon (and all fifty-eight divisions and 360 subdivisions) organized a Women's National Convention for Peace in July 2021. The convention brought together more than a thousand women peacebuilders in the capital city, Yaoundé, for a three-day event to draw attention to the consequences of the war and to advocate for peace. It included a welcome from the Cameroon Women's Peace Movement, testimonies from women in the Far North, Northwest, and Southwest who had been directly affected by the conflict, and presentations by Cameroonian academics and leaders of civil societal organizations (National Women's Convention for Peace in Cameroon Programme 2021). The convention concluded with the presentation of a "Solemn Proclamation of the Women's Call for Peace in Government" in English, French, Fulfulde, and Pidgin. It was designed to be inclusive: it brought together participants from all ten regions, focused on the conflicts in both the Far North and the Anglophone regions, and published all conference documents in English and French. Despite these efforts, the convention was exclusionary in several ways. The location, Yaoundé, was not accessible to many women, and the decision to limit attendance to invited participants meant that some women who were interested in participating in the proceedings were not able to do so.

As a follow-up to the July 2021 Women's National Convention for Peace, the FES supported the National Women's Negotiations for Peace in Cameroon in September 2022, a simulated peace negotiation. Women came together in Yaoundé for three days, September 19–21, 2022, and the event was livestreamed over Zoom. The National Women's Negotiations for Peace culminated in the launch of a peace treaty on Wednesday, September 21, the International Day of Peace. The event highlighted the need to include women and other marginalized voices (including youth and the disabled) in peace negotiations. Like the previous convention, it focused on the conflicts in both the Far North and the Anglophone regions. It emphasized the need for an inclusive dialogue, something that has not happened in the past. The event embraced bilingualism: the peace treaty was published in both English and French with the statement that "the two texts will always appear side by side on the same page, not in separate documents." Like the peace convention, in-person participation was by invitation only, and the location in Yaoundé was not convenient for many women. While the event was also accessible to watch (but not participate in) via livestream, many in Cameroon do not have adequate Internet bandwidth or data to stream hours of live coverage. In addition, technical issues including poor sound quality made it difficult to follow the events from afar. Accessibility also has costs. Some women were fearful that their public association with the simulated negotiations could put themselves or their family members at risk of violence.

As in other contexts (e.g., Argentina and Liberia), women have drawn on their identities as mothers and their association with peacebuilding to carve out space for public protest not accessible to other groups. The Cameroon Anglophone Civil Society Consortium (CACSC), a male-led organization of teachers, lawyers, and other interest groups, led the strikes protesting the appointment of Francophone magistrates and teachers to courts and schools in Anglophone regions and the lack of English translations of laws in fall 2016. In January 2017, the government banned CACSC and arrested four of its leaders. Nancy Annan et al. (2021, 712) highlight how SNWOT has been able to act in ways not accessible to other civil societal groups such as CACSC: "SNWOT is probably the foremost example of resistance to the unprecedented violence in the Anglophone regions, yet its actions and public protests have been largely tolerated by government, without mass arrests or disruption. It may be that SNWOT learnt from the fate of CACSC at the beginning of the crisis. CACSC was established as an alliance of CSOs in December 2016 to be a voice for the Anglophone population and to lead the peaceful protests. However, CACSC's advocacy of a return to the two-state federation, as created at independence in 1961, could not be countenanced by the government." In a report on women in Cameroon's Anglophone conflict, the International Crisis Group (2022a, 14) indicates: "Paradoxically, as authorities silence the larger, male-led civil organisations in the Anglophone regions, making it increasingly dangerous for men to criticise the government or advocate for peace, the advocacy space for women's groups gradually expanded, allowing them to thrive, at least for a period of time." Describing the lamentation campaigns organized by women in Northwest Cameroon, including SNWOT, Kefen Ivoline Budji (2021, 452) notes that "usually these armed forces are more lenient in their crackdown on women than on men." While the male-led CACSC was banned, women—at least for a time—retained the ability to mobilize publicly. It is important to note, however, that this space has constricted and that women do face potential backlash for their activism. Zoneziwoh Mbondgulo-Wondieh (2020, 142) notes: "When different women's groups and networks like SNWOT have spoken out against the conflict, they have encountered abuse, harassment, threats of physical attacks and are the targets of hate speech."

Like the Takumbeng, who mobilized in the 1990s to protest the government's use of violence to suppress leaders and supporters of the political opposition, women have come together to highlight the negative effects of the Anglophone crisis and advocate for peace. This form of mobilization draws on long-standing women's secret societies like the Takumbeng, but it also transforms these organizations in important ways by integrating younger women, building global connections, and using the Internet to reach broader audiences (Mougoué 2018; Mbondgulo-Wondieh 2020). The Takumbeng is a secret society that mobilized in the 1990s in Northwest Cameroon to protest the violent repression of the political opposition and to support the transitions to multiparty politics (Fonchingong and Tanga 2007). Angry after the government killed six people at the launch of the SDF in Bamenda in May 1990, Takumbeng members drew on their roles as mothers to enforce opposition-sanctioned "ghost town" campaigns and to protect John Fru Ndi, the leader of the SDF, from security forces. Members of the Takumbeng—generally postmenopausal women—employed a strategy of disrobing and shaming; those who did not respect their procreative capacity invited bad luck (Fonchingong and Tanga 2007, 128).

Cameroonian women are utilizing similar protest strategies to call attention to the contemporary Anglophone crisis. Budji (2021, 454) notes that "when the northwestern Grassfields women marched in Bamenda on May 9, 2019, they emulated the Takumbeng." They carried *nkeng* (dracaena), a plant that serves as a symbol of peace, and linked their activism to their roles as mothers. While members of the Takumbeng in the 1990s noted that "as mothers, they could not be unsympathetic to their children dying in the streets for want of a genuine democracy" (Fonchingong and Tanga 2007, 124), contemporary activists emphasized their maternal connections, carrying placards with slogans such as "We cry for our children, we cry for our future" (Budji 2021, 447).

Lamentation campaigns "are passionate expressions of grief or sorrow over the ills of lived violence by women who sit, carry messages of peace and peace plants, roll on the ground and mourn as an appeal to the key actors of violence to cease fighting and engage in peaceful negotiation" (Crawford et al.

2022, 81). Women publicly engage in mourning rituals—crying, weeping, wailing—to draw attention to the effects of the violence and their grief. On May 9, 2019, women in Bamenda organized a lamentation campaign to coincide with the prime minister's visit. As a participant explained to the media:

> These are the women of the North West region who have been in pain for the past three years, and because we heard that the prime minister is coming here today we decided that we should come out and cry aloud because the flow of blood has been too much. There is pain! We don't sleep! There are incessant killings every day. We think that as women we have to do our own part of the job by coming out to cry, to tell the powers that be that they should try to put an end to this. (Budji 2021, 443)

The women marched to the hotel where the prime minister was visiting. When he arrived, they shared their experiences and called for peace. The protest was effective in that it led to an audience with the prime minister, and there was no violence.

In contrast to the Takumbeng of the 1990s, the new manifestation of women's mobilization includes younger women. As described by Mbondgulo-Wondieh (2020, 144), "unlike historical political crises where frontline leaders were usually older people, the advent of social media has expanded the engagement of younger women who are claiming their civic rights and democratic freedoms of speech and organising." The use of the Internet as a medium for peace activism amplifies the voices of younger women who are more adept at utilizing YouTube and social media. While the Takumbeng of the 1990s took to the streets of Bamenda, the new forms of mobilization includes using social media and operating globally in places like Canada, the United States, and Europe (Mougoué 2019). The use of new strategies has, at times, contributed to intergenerational power struggles between an older generation that wants to continue to lead and a younger generation that feels that it should be given the opportunity to speak for the future of Cameroon.

Despite their mobilization, women remain largely excluded from official peace processes. Activists indicated that the Cameroonian government consulted them before the Major National Dialogue but then failed to include them in the dialogue (International Crisis Group 2022b). As Mbondgulo-Wondieh (2020, 139–40) notes: "In the ongoing Anglophone crisis, the proactive involvement and engagement of women in calling for a ceasefire and pushing for dialogue should have led to their inclusion as a key pillar in the political process. However, in the strategic stages of the 'attempted' peace processes, women, especially young women, remain marginal." Cameroonian women want to have their voices heard by the government and separatist groups, and they seek to be included in dialogues and peace processes. To date, however, they have largely been marginalized.

Conclusion

Crawford Young's approach to African politics is inductive and integrative. He starts with a deep understanding of the empirics and then engages in a "search for what is general from the wealth of particular detail" (Young 1976, 505). Young read widely and sought to learn from everyone—from his colleagues, his students, and visiting speakers. One of his most important contributions to the field of African politics is his ability to synthesize vast amounts of information to make innovative contributions. His approach helps us understand how concepts like territorial nationalism and identity apply to Cameroon because he emphasizes the historical origins of contemporary states and the multifaceted nature of identity, and he resists simplifying complexity. While his work displays these many strengths, he devotes relatively little attention to gender.

I argue that we can supplement Young's approach to studying cultural pluralism by more systematically examining how gender intersects with ethnic and national identities. Women have complex identities, and these various identities, including language, region, ethnicity, and gender, intersect and shape women's experiences and responses to the Anglophone crisis. Studies by Mougoué (2019) and Terretta (2013) show how Cameroonian women contributed to the construction of a national identity that continues to be used by political actors today. Contemporary women's peace movements draw on women's distinctive experiences in the conflict, gender-specific indigenous institutions and practices, and the greater space sometimes afforded to women for public activism. Gender shapes women's experiences and the tools available to them for action. Young's work highlights the situational and dynamic nature of identity. We can build upon his contributions and increase our understanding of contemporary African politics by incorporating gender in our analyses.

References

Adams, Melinda, and Lotsmart Fonjong. 2023. "Anglophone Conflict, New Institutions, and Women's Access to Political Power in Cameroon." *Africa Today* 69 (4): 79–100.

African Union. 2018. "Readout of the Visit of the Chairperson of the African Commission to Cameroon." July 18. https://www.peaceau.org/en/article/readout-of-the-visit-of-the-chairperson-of-the-african-commission-to-cameroon.

Annan, Nancy, Maurice Beseng, Gordon Crawford, and James Kiven Kewir. 2021. "Civil Society, Peacebuilding from Below and Shrinking Civic Space: The Case of Cameroon's 'Anglophone' Conflict." *Conflict, Security & Development* 21 (6): 697–725.

Ardener, Shirley. 1975. "Sexual Insult and Female Militancy." In *Perceiving Women*, edited by Shirley Ardener, 29–54. London: Malaby Press.

Budji, Kefen Ivoline. 2021. "Utilizing Sounds of Mourning as Protest and Activism: The 2019 Northwestern Women's Lamentation March within the Anglophone Crisis in Cameroon." *Resonance: The Journal of Sound and Culture* 1 (4): 443–61.

Cameroon Women's Peace Movement (CAWOPEM). n.d. "Peace Building! Cameroon Women's Peace Movement." Accessed June 28, 2023. https://cawopem.org/.

Crawford, Gordon, James Kiven Kewir, Nancy Annan, Ambo Abuo Gaby, Henry Kame Kah, Terence Nsai Kiwoh, Albert Mbiatem, Zoneziwoh Mbondgulo-Wondieh, Atim Evenye Niger-Thomas, et al. 2022. "Voices from 'Ground Zero': Interrogating History, Culture and Identity in the Resolution of Cameroon's Anglophone Conflict." Centre for Trust, Peace and Social Relations, Coventry University.

Fonchingong, Charles C. 2004. "The Travails of Democratization in Cameroon in the Context of Political Liberalisation since the 1990s." *African and Asian Studies* 3 (1): 33–58.

Fonchingong, Charles C., and Pius T. Tanga. 2007. "Crossing Rural-Urban Spaces. The Takumbeng and Activism in Cameroon's Democratic Crusade." *Cahiers d'études africaines* 47 (185): 117–43.

International Crisis Group. 2022a. "Rebels, Victims, Peacebuilders: Women in Cameroon's Anglophone Conflict." *Africa Report*, no. 307, February 23. https://www.crisis group.org/africa/central-africa/cameroon/rebels-victims-peacebuilders-women -cameroons-anglophone-conflict.

International Crisis Group. 2022b. "Women and the Search for Peace in Cameroon." March 3. https://www.crisisgroup.org/africa/central-africa/cameroon/women -and-search-peace-cameroon-online-event-3rd-march-2022.

Kah, Henry Kam. 2011. "Women's Resistance in Cameroon's Western Grassfields: The Power of Symbols, Organization, and Leadership, 1957–1961." *African Studies Quarterly* 12 (3): 67–91.

Konde, Emmanuel. 1990. "The Use of Women for the Empowerment of Men in African Nationalist Politics: the 1958 'Anlu' in the Cameroon Grassfields." Working Papers in African Studies, no. 147. Boston: African Studies Center, Boston University.

Konings, Piet, and Francis B. Nyamnjoh. 1997. "The Anglophone Problem in Cameroon." *Journal of Modern African Studies* 35 (2): 207–29.

Konings, Piet, and Francis B. Nyamnjoh. 2003. *Negotiating an Anglophone Identity: A Study of the Politics of Recognition and Representation in Cameroon*. Leiden: Brill.

Konings, Piet, and Francis B. Nyamnjoh. 2019. "Anglophone Secessionist Movements in Cameroon." In *Secessionism in African Politics: Aspiration, Grievance, Performance, Disenchantment*, edited by Lotje de Vries, Pierre Englebert, and Mareike Schomerus, 59–89. New York: Springer International.

Krieger, Milton. 2011. *Cameroon's Social Democratic Front: Its History and Prospects as an Opposition Political Party (1990–2011)*. Bamenda, Cameroon: Langaa RPCIG.

Mbondgulo-Wondieh, Zoneziwoh. 2020. "Women and the Anglophone Struggle in Cameroon." In *Gender, Protests and Political Change in Africa*, edited by Awino Okech, 131–47. London: Palgrave Macmillan.

Mougoué, Jacqueline-Bethel Tchouta. 2018. "Gender and (Militarized) Secessionist Movements in Africa: An African Feminist's Reflections. *Meridians: Feminism, Race, Transnationalism* 17 (2): 338–58.

Mougoué, Jacqueline-Bethel Tchouta. 2019. *Gender, Separatist Politics, and Embodied Nationalism in Cameroon*. Ann Arbor: University of Michigan Press.

National Women's Convention for Peace in Cameroon Programme. 2021. July 29–31. https://camerounpeaceconvention.org/.

Office for the Coordination of Humanitarian Affairs (OCHA). 2022. "Cameroon: North-West and South-West Situation Report No. 47." October. https://reliefweb .int/report/cameroon/cameroon-north-west-and-south-west-situation-report-no -47-october-2022.

Sapiro, Virginia. 1993. "Engendering Cultural Differences." In *The Rising Tide of Cultural Pluralism: The Nation-State at Bay?*, edited by Crawford Young, 36–54. Madison: University of Wisconsin Press.

Schatzberg, Michael G. 2001. *Political Legitimacy in Middle Africa: Father, Family, Food*. Bloomington: Indiana University Press.

Terretta, Meredith. 2013. *Petitioning for Our Rights, Fighting for Our Nation: The History of the Democratic Union of Cameroonian Women, 1949–1960*. Mankon: Bamenda: Langaa Research & Publishing CIG.

Tripp, Aili Mari. 2000. *Women and Politics in Uganda*. Madison: University of Wisconsin Press.

Tripp, Aili Mari. 2015. *Women and Power in Postconflict Africa*. New York: Cambridge University Press.

Tripp, Aili Mari, and Alice J. Kang. 2018. "Coalitions Matter: Citizenship, Women, and Quota Adoption in Africa." *Perspectives on Politics* 16 (1): 73–91.

Young, Crawford. 1976. *The Politics of Cultural Pluralism*. Madison: University of Wisconsin Press.

Young, Crawford. 1994. *The African Colonial State in Comparative Perspective*. New Haven, CT: Yale University Press.

Young, Crawford. 2012. *The Postcolonial State in Africa: Fifty Years of Independence, 1960–2010*. Madison: University of Wisconsin Press.

12

"Who Will Open the Door?"

Women in Parliament and Cabinet in Ghana

Gretchen Bauer and Akosua K. Darkwah

It is time to be [in] power. . . . Let the failure of politics and policy be your inspiration; channel the anger from the misrepresentation of your favorite politician and get deeply involved. So, when the man who created the office of the special prosecutor in a minute by putting pen to paper is asking you WHO WILL OPEN THE DOOR, you are not sitting helplessly aghast wondering why a man who can change the system, legislations and policies or advance parity is asking you rhetorical questions.

Nuong Faalong, "Navigating Parity—Who Will Open the Door?"

At the 2019 Women Deliver Conference, in Vancouver, Canada, Ghanaian president Nana Akufo-Addo stated that the reason there are so few women in political office in Ghana is that "we are not seeing enough dynamism and activism on the part of those who are seeking [office]. I am talking about dynamism where it matters . . . electing people to parliament, controlling political parties because they are the instruments by which our societies make decisions." When the United Nations High Commissioner on Health, Employment and Economic Growth, Dr. Alaa Murabit, responded to his comments, President Akufo-Addo interrupted her, asking her how doors to women were going to open (Ahorney 2019). Akufo-Addo's rhetorical and disingenuous question and comments were roundly decried and derided by women activists and women politicians across Ghana and on social media more broadly (though some from his own party defended him). The Network for Women's Rights (NETRIGHT 2019) issued a statement in which it reminded the president and others that for "change to occur in the lives of Ghanaian women and girls, the state and its agencies must fulfill constitutional, regional and international commitments to gender equality, and regularly report on progress to citizens." Blaming women for their low level of political representation is a time-honored tradition but long-discredited argument, along the lines of opposing electoral gender quotas and other affirmative action measures because they will elect "unqualified" women who "lack merit."[1]

While women in Ghana have a long history of political participation and leadership and may be found in leadership positions across the economy and society today,[2] they have remained underrepresented in all branches of government, no matter which political party is in power. Since the political transition in 1992, when Ghana held competitive multiparty elections, governments have alternated every eight years between the National Democratic Congress (NDC) and the New Patriotic Party (NPP), and today, Ghana is considered among the most promising emerging democracies in Africa (Botchway 2018; Nsiah 2021). And yet, since the transition to democracy, Ghana has moved from center to bottom in global rankings with respect to women's representation in parliament, though women's presence in cabinets has been slightly higher.[3] What, then, accounts for Ghana's surprising lack of women in elected and appointed office since the political transition of the early 1990s?

This chapter focuses on the Fourth Republic and some factors working against women's election to parliament, as well as factors working against more women's appointment to cabinet. The chapter argues, as has been stated in the recent NETRIGHT (2019) communiqué, that until the government, political parties, and some political officeholders fulfill long-standing stated commitments around gender equality in politics and decision making, the obstacles facing potential women politicians are unlikely to be overcome. In the remainder of the Introduction we discuss our theoretical approach and Crawford Young's enduring contributions to our work as scholars before turning briefly to women's political leadership in precolonial and colonial Ghana and the limitations on women's political participation during decades of military rule. Next, we outline the challenges facing women seeking elected office (parliament) in Ghana during the Fourth Republic. Thereafter, we reveal how women under consideration for appointed office (cabinet) have fared during the Fourth Republic, based on an assessment of the cabinet appointment process. Finally, we conclude that unless and until there are changes to the election and selection processes for parliament and for cabinet, respectively, Ghana will continue to lag regionally and internationally in women's representation in politics.

Beginning with the section on women in parliament, this chapter relies upon a feminist institutionalist theoretical framework, with feminist institutionalism understood as the ways in which institutions reproduce patterns of disadvantage and discrimination even as ideals of equality may be espoused. Feminist institutionalism focuses on the ways in which rules, norms, and practices produce gendered outcomes (Krook and MacKay 2011). This chapter pays particular attention to institutions relating to parliament, such as electoral systems, electoral laws, the formal and informal rules that govern primary and general elections, political party practices around candidate recruitment and selection—and the ways in which they may work to disadvantage or discriminate against women aspirants and candidates for parliament. With regard to the cabinet, the chapter focuses on the formal and informal rules of the cabinet appointment process, how they interact with the primary "selector"—the president—and those who are eligible for appointment to the cabinet—"the ministrables"—and to what extent they gender the outcome of the appointment process (Annesley, Beckwith, and Franceschet 2019).

One of the legacies of Crawford Young was his mentoring of women scholars, a good many of whom worked on gender and politics. Crawford Young was dissertation adviser to one of us and a knowledgeable scholar of Africa to the other. Like most male scholars of his generation, Young paid scant attention to gender or women in African politics in his research and writing. In his magisterial book on the colonial state in Africa, he devoted a mere two pages to a discussion of the ways in which "colonial state doctrine and policy had an unequal impact on males and females, enlarging whatever gender inequality pre-existed" (Young 1994, 231). Indeed, it would be subsequent generations of feminist scholars who would restore African women to accounts of African politics and history.[4] And yet, especially in his later years, Young carefully mentored women graduate students and colleagues who would focus their own scholarship on questions of gender and women in African politics.

Just as important, Crawford Young infused in all of us a spirit of respect and collaboration between scholars across the ocean and a belief in the importance of interdisciplinarity, as evident in our collaboration: we are an American political scientist and a Ghanaian sociologist who have been working together for years on women and politics scholarship on Ghana. Indeed, Young coauthored and coedited many journal articles and books with other scholars, but especially with his former students and colleagues, providing an example to us all. Finally, in his own practice, Young modeled the importance of extensive reading broadly, especially writings by African scholars, and of intensive periods of hands-on empirical research in those places we choose to study. In an interview for an oral history project, he related the importance of training his students in "field research," which he described as "indispensable" (Teicher 2003). As such, Young's legacies live on in the work of many of us, even if more so the form (the training and mentoring) than the content (the research and scholarship) for some of us (including the authors of this chapter).

Before the Fourth Republic

Although the current number of women in parliament and even cabinet in Ghana is low by African and global standards, Ghanaian women have historically held important political and leadership roles. The most celebrated of these historical figures is Nana Yaa Asantewaa, the Queen Mother of Ejisu, who is famous for having taken on the British during the last Anglo-Asante War, in 1900.[5] She played no mean role in the war, which is evident in the fact that it is known to Ghanaians as the Yaa Asantewaa War (Boahen 2000), and the British found it necessary to punish her by exiling her to the Seychelles Islands (Aidoo 1985; Brempong 2000). While Yaa Asantewaa stands tall as the Ghanaian heroine of all time, she is not unique in her superb leadership qualities. Ghanaian precolonial and colonial history is replete with women who took up various leadership roles, including officiating at religious festivals, presiding over their own courts, guiding councilors in government, leading their citizens out of exile, and meeting with foreign dignitaries to sign treaties or to discuss the potential for missionary work in their communities (Aidoo 1985; Manuh 1988). In the Independence movement as well, market women were an important force in contributing finances and time to the effort (Adomako Ampofo 2008).

The critical roles played by women and their organizations in the precolonial, colonial, and early independence years were disrupted by successive military regimes, beginning as early as 1966 (and lasting until the political transition in 1992, with the occasional civilian governments in between). Many scholars have noted the ways in which military rule impacted negatively on women's participation in politics (Allah-Mensah 2007; Musah and Gariba 2013; Bauer 2017). Beyond the fact that there were very few women in the military and certainly even fewer in any leadership positions during military regimes, women's posttransition political participation may have been affected in at least two ways by years of military rule.[6] First, there was the scapegoating, intimidation, and violence against women under military rule (Manuh and Anyidoho 2015), and, second, the femocracy and First Lady Syndrome that were prevalent in Ghana and neighboring Nigeria during periods of military rule (Mama 1998; Ibrahim 2004)—and the potential enduring legacies of both. Indeed, to understand the current situation of women's low level of representation in political office in Ghana, it is important to bear in mind the history of women's political leadership in the precolonial and colonial periods, followed by the active repression of women and their organizations under military rule in the first decades of independence.

Women in Parliament

Like most former British colonies in Africa, Ghana uses the (woman- and quota-unfriendly) single-member district (SMD) electoral system for parliament and has no electoral gender quotas (Bauer 2019). Unlike more than a dozen other African countries with 30 percent women or more in parliament, Ghana falls at the bottom of the world ranking in terms of women in parliament, with 14.5 percent women representatives since the 2020 election, the highest ever in Ghana's history (www.ipu.org). In elections since the political transition in 1992, it is evident that women aspirants and candidates who stand in party primaries and general elections for parliament win in proportion to their candidacies (in fact, they usually do a little bit better), suggesting that Ghanaian voters do not discriminate against women candidates in the general elections (see table 12.1).[7] There are just very few women candidates. Bauer and Darkwah (2019, 2020, 2021) have focused on party primaries as the mechanism for recruiting and selecting candidates and identified "the cost of politics" and a "politics of insult" as conspiring to deter Ghanaian women from standing for parliament, as well as the overall weakness of the legislature vis-à-vis the executive. In attempting to understand why there are so few women in parliament in Ghana, it is imperative to focus on the "secret garden of politics"—the recruitment and selection of candidates first and foremost during party primaries (Wang, Muriaas, and Bauer 2023).

The Cost of Politics

Gretchen Bauer and Akosua Darkwah (2019, 2020) have identified the (financial) "cost of politics" as one of the major disincentives for female aspirants and candidates for parliament in Ghana (see also Westminster Foundation for De-

Table 12.1. Women Elected to Parliament, Ghana, 1992–2020

Election year	Number of women MPs	Total number of MPs	Percentage of women MPs	Percentage of women candidates
1992	16	200	8.0	5.2
1996	18	200	9.0	7.3
2000	19	200	9.5	8.7
2004	25	230	10.9	10.9
2008	20	230	8.7	9.5
2012	30	275	10.9	10.0
2016	36	275	13.1	11.7
2020	40	275	14.5	13.8

Source: Bauer and Darkwah (2019, 135); Nyabor (2021b); BusinessGhana (2020).

mocracy 2018), with the costs accruing as soon as an individual indicates an interest in standing in a party primary. The "social welfare provisioning" expected of aspirants may include the payment of school fees and medical bills as well as donations toward weddings and funerals and often extends beyond the campaign (whether one wins or not). Staffan Lindberg (2010, 124) confirms the long-lasting obligations incurred by many members of parliament (MPs) in Ghana: "The personal assistance/benefits type of accountability relationship is the most common in MPs' relationships with their constituents, and the one that puts the most pressure on MPs."

These "social welfare" costs (both before and after elections) are in addition to the costs associated with running primary or general election campaigns, including publicity costs (posters, T-shirts), meeting costs (rental space, refreshments), and transportation and communication costs, with the prices of these services rising during an election year as vendors capitalize on the increased demand. On average, it cost interviewees who stood in the party primaries for the 2016 election cycle the equivalent of between $38,000 and $100,000 to vie for their party's nomination (Bauer and Darkwah 2019). Moreover, with each election cycle, the cost of politics may rise. The Westminster Foundation for Democracy (2018, 5) notes a 59 percent increase in the cost of standing between the 2012 and 2016 elections, with most candidates relying heavily on their personal incomes.

The cost of politics is gendered in Ghana and elsewhere. Clientelist or patronage politics make costly campaigns even more expensive. Around the world, women have fewer resources—less wealth, fewer assets, and less access to resources than men. As Abena Oduro, William Baah-Boateng, and Louis Boakye-Yiadom (2011, 34) note, based on a 2010 household survey in Ghana, "women own [only] 30.2 percent of total gross physical wealth" in the country. On the one hand, this lack of resources places women at a disadvantage relative to men in financing political campaigns. On the other hand, women are also at a disadvantage in seeking access to resources. Fundraising for a campaign is not a simple alternative to depleting one's own resources, especially for female aspirants and candidates, who often face demands for sexual favors in return for resources. In the interviews for our study, female informants revealed that they perceive the monetized nature of Ghana's elections as unfair and off-putting in principle (Bauer and Darkwah 2019). In discussing the injustice of the system, female respondents focused not only on their relative lack of funds and their relative inability to raise funds but also on the principle undergirding an election system that relies so heavily on money.

The political parties themselves have recognized the "cost of politics" in Ghana as a problem, and at least one of them attempted to ameliorate the situation ahead of the 2016 election (Ichino and Nathan 2021; Dodsworth et al. 2022). In the primary elections leading up to the 2016 election, the NDC expanded its electoral college on the assumption that this would encourage aspirants to sell their message to voters instead of buying the support of delegates—because it would be impossible to buy all the votes of an expanded electoral college. The majority of our NDC interviewees, however, felt that this strategy had not worked and may rather have exacerbated the situation—leading to even more costly primary campaigns. While the NDC emerged from the primaries with more women candidates than the NPP, in the end, more NPP women won their contests; following the 2016 election, twenty-four women MPs were from the NPP and twelve from the NDC.[8] In the 2020 election, in which the two main parties nearly tied in the number of members of parliament, they did in fact, elect the same number of women MPs, twenty each.

The Politics of Insult

In addition to the problems posed by the cost of politics, women face other challenges referred to by one of our respondents, a female Convention People's Party (CPP) candidate in 2012 and selectorate in 2016, as the "politics of insult"

(Bauer and Darkwah 2019, 2020). Baba Iddrisu Musah and Ibrahim Gariba (2013, 466) have argued that aspersions are likely to be cast on women who run for political office in Ghana, for example, that they may be "suspected as flirts and prostitutes." The insults and lies directed at women aspirants and candidates do not come only from opponents. They may come even from one's own party members, noted more than one of our informants. The "politics of insult," with regard to women aspirants and candidates, is by no means confined to Ghana. They have been documented among women candidates for political office in Botswana, Nigeria, and Uganda, to name just a few other African countries (Tamale 1999; Ibrahim 2004; Bauer 2010).

On top of facing insults being hurled at them, women who choose to run find that their bodies are scrutinized, and they are penalized for not conforming to conventional norms about women's appearance and behavior. One NDC aspirant recounted the kind of policing that women faced: "no dyeing of hair, no painting of nails different colors, no wearing trousers for women aspirants and candidates!" In addition, in a country where marriage and motherhood are prized, being single and/or not having children may be cause for further insults (Bauer and Darkwah 2020). While we did not encounter reports of physical violence against women who stand for parliament in Ghana, in contrast to the manifold reports of such from around the world (Krook 2018), cyberbullying directed toward women candidates and hate speech have also been rife in recent Ghanaian elections, according to the International Republican Institute and National Democratic Institute (IRI and NDI 2020, 10). Moreover, the politics of insult can carry over to the halls of parliament as well. One female NPP MP reported to us that she has been referred to as "my wife," "my sister," or "my mother" by male colleagues in parliament.

Weak Legislatures and MPs

Another strong disincentive to women considering standing for parliament in Ghana is a concern about what they will—or, more likely, will not—be able to do once they get there. For example, the "cost of politics" described earlier can carry over to parliament, distracting MPs from their real work and seemingly leading to a misunderstanding about the role of an MP. Our interviewees noted that the need to raise funds to repay debts incurred during the campaign or to secure funding for the next election cycle diverted the attention of MPs from the real work of legislation, one of their central functions. There is also the problem of patronage politics—legislators' fifth function as identified by Lindberg (2010) and mentioned earlier.

Moreover, having fewer women in parliament means that it is even more difficult to represent women's interests—something that women MPs in African countries with large numbers of women MPs have been able to do (Bauer 2021). Not surprisingly, with the low representation of women in Ghana's parliament, moving women-friendly laws through parliament is much more challenging, with some of the greatest successes for women, such as the 2007 Domestic Violence Bill, coming from mobilization outside rather than within the parliament (Adomako Ampofo 2008).

Another part of the problem, according to one NPP female MP, is that parliament does not have the respect and power it should have in relation to the other two branches in Ghana. In her words: "until parliament recognizes or comes into its own and actually performs its constitutional duties the way it should, we will always be treated as the poor cousin of the executive and the judiciary. And it will devalue our democracy" (Bauer and Darkwah 2020). As H. Kwasi Prempeh (2008) has observed, national legislatures in Africa remain the weakest branch of government, especially vis-à-vis the executive. Some years into Ghana's political transition, Lindberg and Yongmei Zhou (2009, 148) found that parliament was not "flourishing" due to limited resources for the legislature, weak capacity of the parliamentary service, a high turnover among MPs, and demands for constituency services. There is also the requirement in Ghana's constitution that at least half of cabinet ministers come from parliament. Many see this requirement as problematic, contributing to a "hybrid" government in which the executive is dominant over the legislature (Boafo-Arthur 2005; Prempeh 2008). This can also dampen women's interest in standing as they consider the likelihood (or not) of accomplishing legislative and other goals.

In sum, having to use a candidate-centered electoral system with no electoral gender quotas, women in Ghana have been deterred from contesting for parliament not just by the nature of electoral politics (marked by the high cost of politics and an insidious politics of insult), which greatly diminishes the appeal of standing for office, but also by the nature of elected political office. Many Ghanaian women have little incentive to stand for an office (MP) that is poorly understood and generally misused because the parliament is weak and has limited powers vis-à-vis the other branches of government; because of these constraints, a limited number of members are likely to be able to accomplish very few legislative or other goals.[9] In addition, a strong contemporary women's movement mobilization in Ghana specifically aimed at increasing women's representation in the parliament is lacking.[10]

Women in Cabinets

We know relatively little about women cabinet ministers in Ghana since independence. As noted in earlier sections, many studies have considered some women's notable roles in politics in the precolonial and colonial periods as well as in the early years of independence. Overviews from independence on, of which there are many, have tended to privilege women activists and their organizations or women in parliaments, with almost no research and scholarship on women in cabinets.[11] Melinda Adams, John Scherpereel, and Suraj Jacob (2016) have published the only study before our own (Bauer and Darkwah 2022) to focus on women in the cabinet in Ghana. Indeed, they observe that Ghana has been one of those countries in Africa that has a higher percentage of women in the cabinet than in parliament, and they suggest three factors that may have promoted women's incorporation into the cabinet—a conducive institutional environment, an international context stressing gender-balanced decision making, and an autonomous domestic women's movement (Adams, Scherpereel, and Jacob 2016, 146–47). We found slightly different factors at play.

We used a model developed by Claire Annesley, Karen Beckwith, and Susan Franceschet (2019) to understand the cabinet appointment process and whether it is gendered. We investigated the cabinet appointment process in Ghana to try to find out why so few women have been appointed to the cabinet in Ghana (Bauer and Darkwah 2022). We examined initial cabinets appointed by presidents for five new administrations from 2001 to 2017 (two terms for President Kufuor and one each for Presidents Mills, Mahama, and Akufo-Addo). Like Annesley, Beckwith, and Franceschet (2019), we relied on interviews with selected informants, news reports during discreet periods for each new administration, insider accounts, and other primary and secondary sources. To date, the cabinet with the most women ministers (32 percent) has been that of President Mahama, appointed upon taking office in 2013 (see table 12.2). Indeed, according to one member of Mahama's "kitchen cabinet," he was urged to appoint a gender parity cabinet but ultimately was constrained from doing so by the formal and informal rules of appointment we discuss in our article (Bauer and Darkwah 2022) and in the paragraphs that follow here (see also Awuni 2019).[12]

According to one former cabinet minister, the cabinet in Ghana is "a creature of the constitution," and, indeed, the constitution sets out several rules and guidelines for the composition of Ghana's cabinet. First, according to Article 76(1) of the constitution, the cabinet consists of the president, the vice president, and not fewer than ten and not more than nineteen ministers. Article

Table 12.2. (Initial) Appointments of Women to Cabinet, Ghana,
1993–2021

Election year	Party/president	Women/total ministers	Percentage of women ministers
1993	NDC/Rawlings	2/19	10.5
1997	NDC/Rawlings	3/19	16.0
2001	NPP/Kufuor	2/19	10.5
2005	NPP/Kufuor	2/19	10.5
2009	NDC/Mills	4/19	21
2013	NDC/Mahama	6/19	32
2017	NPP/Akufo-Addo	4/19	21
2021	NPP/Akufo-Addo	3/19	16

Source: Bauer and Darkwah (2022, 554); Nyabor (2021a).

78(2) further stipulates that the president may appoint the number of ministers
that he deems necessary "for the efficient running of the state." Further, Article
78(1) of the constitution notes that ministers are appointed by the president,
with the prior approval of parliament (so they must be vetted), from among
members of parliament or persons qualified to be elected as members of parliament, except that the majority of ministers shall be appointed from among
MPs (Republic of Ghana 1992). Finally, the Directive Principles of State Policy,
Article 35(6b) of the constitution, state that the government "shall take appropriate measures to achieve reasonable regional and gender balance in recruitment and appointment to public offices" (Republic of Ghana 1992). In short,
the cabinet ministers are appointed by the president, though vetted by parliament; at least half must come from parliament; and there should be some regional and gender balance among the cabinet ministers (and the president may
appoint as many additional ministers outside the cabinet as he sees fit).

In using the framework developed by Annesley, Beckwith, and Franceschet
(2019) we found that, in practice, Ghana, indeed, has an "empowered executive"
easily able to exercise his "presidential prerogative," as it was often referred to in
the media, to appoint cabinet ministers of his choosing. Seldom, except for the
early years after the political transition, are any nominees not approved by parliament. Additionally, the president determines which ministers and ministries
are in the cabinet. For example, during both of the African Union Gender

Champion President Akufo-Addo's terms, the Ministry of Gender, Children, and Social Protection has not been in cabinet for the first time since the ministry was created, in 2000. The president is constrained, however, by the requirement that at least half of all ministers be from parliament. Indeed, in all of the Fourth Republic cabinets, there has always been a 9/10 split between those ministers drawn from outside parliament and those who are "minister MPs," with the balance tipping either way. As for the principle of regional and gender balance among appointees, we found region to be by far the more important concern, with some news reports and informants suggesting that the minimum of ten ministers in the cabinet was meant to indicate that there would be at least one minister from each of Ghana's ten regions (the number of regions had increased to sixteen by the time of the 2020 election, which is not included in our earlier study). Indeed, regional balance (sometimes described in ethnic terms) appears to be a strong imperative in cabinet appointments. Gender balance, by contrast, hardly appears in the composition of cabinets (despite being called for in media reports and by women's organizations), either because it is of little concern to the empowered executive or because it is of less importance than (and precluded by) other norms and practices. We also found that dozens of ministers are appointed outside the cabinet in Ghana as regional ministers, deputy ministers, ministers of state, and other such posts. These are often referred to by the media as including "friends and family appointments." We find this to be potentially problematic to the extent that, on one hand, dozens of ministerial appointments outside the cabinet can serve as alternate sites of power, diluting the power of actual cabinet ministers. On the other hand, the many additional ministerial appointments, of whom some are women, allow senior government leaders to claim the appointment of significant numbers of women ministers, who may not, however, have the power and authority that cabinet ministers have.

Annesley, Beckwith, and Franceschet (2019, 59) suggest that "cabinet construction is akin to putting together a puzzle: the individual cabinet ministers are not as important on their own as they are in how they fit with each other." In Ghana, we found the same. While presidential candidates typically have in mind during the campaign an initial set of cabinet appointments—the most important ones—the final appointments can be determined only after the election and in accordance with the election results—how the party fared in the election, which constituencies the party won and lost, which MPs were elected, which people and places need to be rewarded or otherwise paid attention to, and so on. Moreover, it is also with the final appointments that the required representational balance is met and that the balance between minister MPs and others is met. As one member of a presidential kitchen cabinet illustrated the balancing act to us: "We needed the female MP from Ada" because she was a woman, she was an MP, and she was from a certain region (Greater Accra). Still, since it is the president alone who appoints cabinet ministers (though they are vetted by parliament), he alone should be able to "open the door" to more women in the executive, at least, just as presidents and prime ministers have done in Ethiopia, Seychelles, Rwanda, South Africa, and Mozambique, among other African countries, bringing in gender parity cabinets.

Conclusion

In the contemporary period, the number of women in political office in Ghana belies the long history of women in leadership positions. Yet, there is no question that in Ghana, there are more than enough talented and capable women available to be appointed (or elected) to political office. Adams, Scherpereel, and Jacob (2016, 158) report: "In December 2012, immediately after the elections, Women in Law and Development in Africa (WiLDAF) presented a petition to [President] Mahama that included the names of 65 women who could be considered for government posts and called on the parliamentary appointment committee to reject any list of appointments that did not include 40 percent women." Similarly, Darkwa (2015, 246), in her study of women in parliament in Ghana, refers to a "directory of qualified and available women, ready to participate in the political decision-making process" as a resource for her study. As she further notes: "since one of the often-cited reasons for the low numbers of appointment of women into key decision-making processes had been the unavailability of women to participate in politics, the objective of the directory was to obtain and collate information on women who were willing and available to be appointed by government should there be a need."

For a time, leading civil society organizations flush with donor funding sought to convince the main political parties and to train potential women candidates to bring more women into parliament, according to the director of one such organization. But, given the challenges of standing for parliament and the likelihood that they would be able to have little impact once there, some highly accomplished and talented women show a complete lack of interest even though friends, family, and others may have encouraged them. We heard more than once that some women who stood in primaries and the general election lost their interest after they obtained a fuller understanding of the mechanics of the electoral system and the limitations of elected office.

Ghana's situation in terms of women's political leadership in elected and appointed national-level positions is not unlike that of several other countries in

Africa that use the quota- and woman-unfriendly SMD electoral system. In Ghana, there is less apparent women's movement mobilization specifically around an electoral gender quota (Amoah-Boampong 2018), despite a long history of affirmative action for women and girls in other arenas (Tsikata 2009a) and despite calls for quotas from some politicians and associates (Awuah 2017; Oquaye 2017). At the same time, it appears that some Ghanaian women may eschew the opportunity to stand for a parliament in which many members and even more constituents appear to have a limited understanding of the role of the MP or the parliament and which is, in any event, a weaker branch of government. Over the years, political parties have shown little commitment and no enduring successful interventions to bring more women into parliament.[13] Women may, however, easily be appointed to other political offices such as cabinet minister. And yet, for cabinet, too, we have shown the obstacles to the appointment of more women ministers, most notably the formal rules and informal practices used by Ghanaian presidents. Until gender balance gains the same respect as regional balance in the cabinet appointment process, the requirement that half of cabinet ministers must be "minister MPs" is removed, and presidents begin to exert their authority as empowered executives to appoint gender-balanced cabinets, women will remain underrepresented in cabinet in Ghana. As Afrobarometer surveys reveal, ordinary Ghanaians (too) expect their government to act on the gender inequalities that persist across the country.[14] Unless, and until, some of the many protocols and conventions that Ghana has signed are respected and implemented, Ghana will continue to lag behind other African countries and the world in women's presence in the executive and in the legislature.

Notes

This chapter's epigraph is from Nuong Faalong, "Ghana Rising with Nuong Faalong: Navigating Parity—Who Will Open the Door?," GhanaWeb, June 13, 2019, https://www.ghanaweb.com/GhanaHomePage/features/Ghana-rising-with-Nuong-Faalong-Navigating-parity-Who-will-open-the-door-754721#.

1. See Murray (2014); Nugent and Krook (2016).

2. In March 2020, Mastercard reported that Ghana was ranked first in the world on its Index of Women Entrepreneurs, with 46.4 percent of businesses owned by women. "The Mastercard Index of Women Entrepreneurs: 2020 Report," https://www.mastercard.com/news/media/1ulpy5at/ma_miwe-report-2020.pdf.

3. That said, it is also understood that there is no necessary correspondence between democracy and more women in politics (Dahlerup 2017). Ghana's move from the center to the bottom of the rankings can be accounted for by many other countries surpassing Ghana over the years while Ghana remained relatively stable.

4. For example, Jean Allman, Ife Amadiume, Susan Geiger, Takyiwaa Manuh, Oyeronke Oyewumi, and Dzodzi Tsikata.

5. Female leaders who co-rule with chiefs, although the extent of their co-ruling powers varies across the various ethnic groups in Ghana. See Stoeltje (2003) and Steegstra (2009) for more on some Queen Mothers in contemporary Ghana.

6. For an elaboration of this argument, see Bauer (2017).

7. Relying on primary data from Belinda Glover, we have confirmed this finding for the party primaries held in advance of the 2020 general election, though not for previous elections.

8. Dodsworth et al. (2022) examine the NDC's opening up of the primary process in 2016 and the NDC's return to the more exclusive system in 2020, even though members of both parties stated their preference—in the abstract—for the more inclusive primary process.

9. See Owusu-Mensah's (2019) recent study of Ghanaians' perceptions of their members of parliament.

10. Efforts to pass an affirmative action law in parliament—with aspirational goals for increasing women's presence in politics and decision making—have been delayed for more than a decade (Madsen 2021).

11. See Prah (2004, 2007), Allah-Mensah (2005, 2007), Tsikata (1997, 2009b), Nketiah (2010), Sossou (2011), Bawa and Sanyare (2013), Musa and Gariba (2013), Darkwa (2015), Bauer (2019), among others.

12. Similarly, Adams, Scherpereel, and Jacob (2016, 155) report that in 2009 President Mills was unable to follow through on an NDC promise to have women constitute 40 percent of government (cabinet) as only five women from his party were elected to parliament and he was required to draw the majority of ministers from parliament, as is further discussed here.

13. In a comparison of Cabo Verde and Ghana, Wang, Muriaas and Bauer (2023) examine how the institutional context impacts political party responses, or lack thereof, to fewer women aspirants and candidates.

14. According to Twum and Zupork (2022, 1), based on Round 9 Afrobarometer findings in Ghana: "Survey findings show that in Ghana, women still lag behind men in educational attainment, ownership of key assets, and financial autonomy. Strong majorities of citizens express support for women's right to equality in hiring, in land ownership, and in political leadership." Further, "A majority of Ghanaians say the government needs to do more to promote equal rights and opportunities for women."

References

Adams, Melinda, John Scherpereel, and Suraj Jacob. 2016. "The Representation of Women in African Legislatures and Cabinets: An Examination with Reference to Ghana." *Journal of Women, Politics & Policy* 37 (2): 145–67.

Adomako Ampofo, Akosua. 2008. "Collective Activism: The Domestic Violence Bill Becoming Law in Ghana." *African and Asian Studies* 7 (4): 395–421.

Ahorney, Makafui. 2019. "Gender Champion? Women's Rights Allies and the Case of Ghana's President Akufo-Addo." AfricanFeminism, June 10. https://africanfemi nism.com/gender-champion-womens-rights-allies-and-the-case-of-ghanas-presi dent-akufo-addo/.

Aidoo, Agnes Akosua. 1985. "Women in the History and Culture of Ghana." *Research Review* 1 (1): 14–51.

Allah-Mensah, Beatrix. 2005. *Women in Politics and Public Life in Ghana.* Accra: Friedrich Ebert Foundation.

Allah-Mensah, Beatrix. 2007. "Women and Politics in Ghana 1993–2003." In *Ghana: One Decade of the Liberal State,* edited by Kwame Boafo-Arthur, 251–79. London: Zed Books.

Amoah-Boampong, Cyrelene. 2018. "Historicising the Women's Manifesto for Ghana: A Culmination of Women's Activism in Ghana." *Legon Journal of the Humanities* 29 (2): 26–53.

Annesley, Claire, Karen Beckwith, and Susan Franceschet. 2019. *Cabinets, Ministers, and Gender.* New York: Oxford University Press.

Awuah, Sandra. 2017. "Addressing Gender Imbalance in Ghana's Parliament." Background Paper, no. 2. Parliament of Ghana Research Department, January. https:// www.parliament.gh/publications?research&gp=4.

Awuni, Manasseh Azure. 2019. *The Fourth John: Reign, Rejection & Rebound.* Self-published.

Bauer, Gretchen. 2010. "'Cows Will Lead the Herd into a Precipice': Where Are the Women MPs in Botswana?" *Botswana Notes and Records* 42:56–70.

Bauer, Gretchen. 2017. "'Did You See What Happened to the Market Women?' Legacies of Military Rule for Women's Political Leadership in Ghana?" *Contemporary Journal of African Studies* 5 (1): 31–59.

Bauer, Gretchen. 2019. "Ghana: Stalled Patterns of Women's Parliamentary Representation." In *The Palgrave Handbook of Women's Political Rights,* edited by Susan Franceschet, Mona L. Krook, and Netina Tan, 607–25. New York: Springer.

Bauer, Gretchen. 2021. "Women in African Parliaments: Progress and Prospects." In *The Palgrave Handbook of African Women's Studies,* edited by Olajumoke Yacob-Haliso and Toyin Falola, 335–52. London: Palgrave Macmillan.

Bauer, Gretchen, and Akosua K. Darkwah. 2019. "'Some Money Has to Be Going': Discounted Filing Fees to Bring More Women into Parliament in Ghana." In *Gendered Electoral Financing: Money, Power, and Representation in Comparative Perspective,* edited by Ragnhild Muriaas, Vibeke Wang, and Rainbow Murray, 133–53. London: Routledge.

Bauer, Gretchen, and Akosua K. Darkwah. 2020. "We Would Rather Be Leaders than Parliamentarians: Women and Political Office in Ghana." *European Journal of Politics and Gender* 3 (1): 101–19.

Bauer, Gretchen, and Akosua K. Darkwah. 2021. "Party Primaries and Women's Representation in Ghana: How Can More Women Aspirants Win?" In *Women and Power in Africa: Aspiring, Campaigning, and Governing,* edited by Leonardo Arriola, Martha Johnson, and Melanie Phillips, 61–84. Oxford: Oxford University Press.

Bauer, Gretchen, and Akosua K. Darkwah. 2022. "'The President's Prerogative?' The Cabinet Appointment Process in Ghana and the Implications for Gender Parity." *Politics & Gender* 18 (2): 546–73.

Bawa, Sylvia, and Francis Sanyare. 2013. "Women's Participation and Representation in Politics: Perspectives from Ghana." *International Journal of Public Administration* 36 (4): 282–91.

Boafo-Arthur, Kwame. 2005. "Longitudinal View on Ghana's Parliamentary Practices." In *African Parliaments: Between Governance and Government*, edited by Mohammed Salih, 120–41. New York: Springer.

Boahen, Albert Adu. 2000. "Yaa Asantewaa in the Yaa Asantewaa War of 1900: Military Leader or Symbolic Head?" *Ghana Studies* 3 (1): 111–35.

Botchway, Thomas Prehi. 2018. "Ghana: A Consolidated Democracy." *Asian Research Journal of Arts & Social Sciences* 5 (4): 1–13.

Brempong, Arhin. 2000. "The Role of Nana Yaa Asantewaa in the 1900 Asante War of Resistance." *Ghana Studies* 3 (1): 97–110.

BusinessGhana. 2020. "Election 2020: Provisional Results Show Slight Rise in Women Elected to Parliament." December 9. https://www.businessghana.com/site/news /politics/228553/Election-2020-Provisional-results-show-slight-rise-in-women -elected-to-parliament.

Dahlerup, Drude. 2017. *Has Democracy Failed Women?* Hoboken, NJ: John Wiley & Sons.

Darkwa, Linda 2015. "'In Our Father's Name in Our Motherland': The Politics of Women's Political Participation in Ghana." In *Constitutionalism, Democratic Governance, and the African State*, edited by Boniface Y. Gebe, 239–74. Accra: Black Mask Limited.

Dodsworth, Susan, Seidu M. Alidu, Gretchen Bauer, and Gbensuglo A. Bukari. 2022. "Parliamentary Primaries after Democratic Transitions: Explaining Reforms to Candidate Selection in Ghana." *African Affairs* 121 (483): 275–97.

Ibrahim, Jibrin. 2004. "The First Lady Syndrome and the Marginalisation of Women from Power: Opportunities or Compromises for Gender Equality?" *Feminist Africa* 3 (September): 48–69.

Ichino, Nahomi, and Noah L. Nathan. 2021. "Democratizing the Party: The Effects of Primary Election Reforms in Ghana." *British Journal of Political Science* 52 (3): 1168–85.

IRI and NDI. 2020. *Ghana Election Watch, December 2020 General Elections*. Washington, DC: International Republican Institute and National Democratic Institute.

Krook, Mona L. 2018. "Violence against Women in Politics: A Rising Global Trend." *Politics & Gender* 14 (4): 673–75.

Krook, Mona L., and Fiona Mackay. 2011. *Gender, Politics and Institutions: Towards a Feminist Institutionalism*. Basingstoke: Palgrave Macmillan.

Lindberg, Staffan I. 2010. "What Accountability Pressures Do MPs in Africa Face and How Do They Respond? Evidence from Ghana." *Journal of Modern African Studies* 48 (1): 117–42.

Lindberg, Staffan I., and Yongmei Zhou. 2009. "Co-optation Despite Democratization in Ghana." In *Legislative Power in Emerging African Democracies*, edited by Joel D. Barkan, 147–66. Boulder, CO: Lynne Rienner.

Madsen, Diana Hoglund. 2021. "Affirmative Action in Ghana? Patriarchal Arguments and Institutional Inertia." In *Gendered Institutions and Women's Political Representation in Africa*, edited by Diana Hoglund Madsen, 217–40. Uppsala: Nordic Africa Institute.

Mama, Amina. 1998. "Khaki in the Family: Gender Discourses and Militarism in Nigeria." *African Studies Review* 41 (2): 1–18.

Manuh, Takyiwaa. 1988. "The Asantehemaa's Court and Its Jurisdiction over Women: A Study in Legal Pluralism." *Institute of African Studies Research Review* 4 (2): 50–66.

Manuh, Takyiwaa, and Nana Akua Anyidoho. 2015. "'To Beijing and Back': Reflections on the Influence of the Beijing Conference on Popular Notions of Women's Empowerment in Ghana." *IDS Bulletin* 46 (4): 19–27.

Murray, Rainbow. 2014. "Quotas for Men: Reframing Gender Quotas as a Means of Improving Representation for All." *American Political Science Review* 108 (3): 520–32.

Musah, Baba Iddrisu, and Ibrahim Gariba. 2013. "Women and Political Decision Making: Perspectives from Ghana's Parliament." *Journal of Alternative Perspectives in the Social Sciences* 5 (3): 443–76.

NETRIGHT. 2019. Press Statement by Network for Women's Rights in Ghana (NETRIGHT). Accra, June 10. http://twnafrica.org/wp/2017/wp-content/uploads/2019/06/NETRIGHT-PRESS-STATEMENT10.06.2019.pdf.

Nketiah, Eric Sakyi. 2010. *A History of Women in Politics in Ghana 1957–1992*. Milton Keynes: AuthorHouse.

Nsiah, Isaac Owusu. 2021. "Emergent Programmatic Politics and Gradual Demise of Neopatrimonial Tendencies in Ghana's Electoral Democracy." *Open Journal of Political Science* 11 (4): 721–38.

Nugent, Mary K., and Mona Lena Krook. 2016. "All-Women Shortlists: Myths and Realities." *Parliamentary Affairs* 69 (1): 115–35.

Nyabor, Jonas. 2021a. "Akufo-Addo Announces 19-Member Cabinet for Second Term." *CitiNewsroom*, June 10. https://citinewsroom.com/2021/06/akufo-addo-announces-19-member-cabinet-for-second-term/.

Nyabor, Jonas. 2021b. "Women Representation in Ghana's Parliaments." *CitiNewsroom*, January 12. https://citinewsroom.com/2021/01/women-representation-in-ghanas-parliaments-infographic/.

Oduro, Abena D., William Baah-Boateng, and Louis Boakye-Yiadom. 2011. *Measuring the Gender Asset Gap in Ghana*. Accra: Woeli Publishing Services.

Oquaye, Aaron Mike. 2017. Inaugural Address as 7th Speaker of Parliament. January 7. parliament-full-text/http://citifmonline.com/2017/01/07/mike-oquayes-inaugural-address-as-speaker-of-7th-parliament-full-text/.

Owusu-Mensah, Isaac. 2019. "Assessment of 275 Members of Parliament—Perspectives from the Constituents." University of Ghana Legon, Accra.

Prah, Mansah. 2004. *Chasing Illusions and Realising Visions: Reflections on Ghana's Feminist Experience*. Dakar: CODESRIA.

Prah, Mansah. 2007. *Ghana's Feminist Movement: Aspirations, Challenges, Achievements*. Accra: Woeli Publishing Services.

Prempeh, H. Kwasi. 2008. "Progress and Retreat in Africa: Presidents Untamed." *Journal of Democracy* 19 (2): 109–23.

Republic of Ghana. 1992. Constitution of the Republic of Ghana. Accra: Republic of Ghana.

Sossou, Marie-Antoinette. 2011. "We Do Not Enjoy Equal Political Rights: Ghanaian Women's Perceptions on Political Participation in Ghana." *Sage Open* 1 (1).

Steegstra, Marijke. 2009. "Krobo Queen Mothers: Gender, Power, and Contemporary Female Traditional Authority in Ghana." *Africa Today* 55 (3): 105–23.

Stoeltje, J. Beverly. 2003. "Asante Queen Mothers: Precolonial Authority in a Postcolonial Society." *Institute of African Studies Research Review* 19 (2): 1–19.

Tamale, Sylvia. 1999. *When Hens Begin to Crow: Gender and Parliamentary Politics in Uganda.* London: Routledge.

Teicher, Barry. 2003. Interview #642. M. Crawford Young. Oral History Project. University of Wisconsin Madison Archives.

Tsikata, Dzodzi. 1997. "Gender Equality and the State in Ghana: Some Issues of Policy and Practice." In *Engendering African Social Sciences*, edited by Ayisha Imam, Amina Mama, and Fatou Sow, 381–412. Dakar: CODESRIA.

Tsikata, Dzodzi. 2009a. *Affirmative Action and the Prospects for Gender Equity in Ghanaian Politics.* Accra: Friedrich Ebert Stiftung.

Tsikata, Dzodzi. 2009b. "Women's Organizing in Ghana since the 1990s: From Individual Organizations to Three Coalitions." *Development* 52:185–192.

Twum, Maame Akua Amoah, and Mavis Zupork. 2022. "Amid Persistent Gender Inequalities, Ghanaians Call for Government Action to Bridge the Gaps." Afrobarometer Dispatch, no. 573. Accra: Afrobarometer.

Wang, Vibeke, Ragnhild L. Muriaas, and Gretchen Bauer. 2023. "Funding Demands and Gender in Political Recruitment: What Parties Do in Cabo Verde and Ghana." *International Political Science Review* 44 (1): 77–90.

Westminster Foundation for Democracy. 2018. "The Cost of Politics in Ghana." https://www.wfd.org/sites/default/files/2022-02/Cost_Of_Politics_Ghana.pdf.

Young, Crawford M. 1994. *The African Colonial State in Comparative Perspective.* New Haven, CT: Yale University Press.

Afterword

Edmond J. Keller

I am honored to write the afterword for this collection of essays dedicated to celebrating the contributions to the study of African and comparative politics of Professor M. Crawford Young, of the University of Wisconsin–Madison (1963–2020). I joined the UW Department of Political Science as a graduate student in 1969, after completing three years of military service. It was the height of the civil rights movement. These were tumultuous years of change both in the United States and Africa, and this was the context that inspired me to pursue an Africa-focused PhD in political science. My goal was to contribute to rectifying the glaring absence of highly qualified Black academics at the leading institutions of higher learning, especially in the South. I was acutely aware that there was a need for African Americans in the professorate at all institutions of higher learning in the country. I was interested in the new nations of Africa, but I was then more keenly interested in urban politics in the United States. Thus, during my first year of graduate studies, I focused on American and comparative politics as well as basic methods courses.

I joined the department and discovered the rapidly emerging University of Wisconsin–Madison African Studies Program. The University was in the process of becoming one of the leading US universities with multidisciplinary African Studies programs. Crawford Young had been a faculty member in the department for only six years. Although primarily known for his work on the former Belgian Congo, Young, at the time I arrived, was engaged in research on Uganda's political economy of agricultural development. Importantly, by then, Young had acquired a bevy of graduate students, including John Harbeson, Tom Turner, Catharine Newbury, Joel Samoff, Georges Nzongola-Ntalaja, and others engaged in research in Africa, gathering data for their dissertations. I spent five years in the program, and throughout much of that time, Crawford was a campus administrator. Yet he taught his signature undergraduate course in African politics when not in Africa. My first encounter with him in a class was in this course, which met two times a week at 7 a.m.! In terms of working with him in graduate seminars, at the beginning of my second year, he arranged for a small group of us to participate in an independent study seminar, which rotated every two weeks among each of our apartments and his own home. He found time to keep in touch with our progress in the program and the classes we were enrolled in.

Right away, Crawford became a mentor to me. He soon became my rock! When it was time for the dissertation, I initially wanted to follow up on some of his research in Uganda on producer cooperatives and development. I had already secured funding from the Ford Foundation for dissertation research when the Ugandan dictator Idi Amin Dada went *berserk*, so I switched to a study of the political economy of education and development in Kenya. During the year I spent in Kenya, Crawford was a dean at the University of Lubumbashi in Zaire.

My first academic job was at Indiana University (1974–83). My dissertation had been published, and I was hoping to do a second major project in Ghana, but when funding for that project did not materialize, I was given an opportunity for a one-year research/administrative position at the UN Economic Commission for Africa (ECA) in Addis Ababa. It was also a time when I was trying to find a second project following the publication of my first book. The Ethiopian Revolution was in the process of unfolding, and although I was not able to do any academic work during my time at the ECA, I had the good fortune to live through the beginning of the revolution and to interact closely with colleagues from Ethiopia and other parts of Africa undergoing dramatic socio-political changes wrought by the ending of European colonization.

On my return to Indiana University, Crawford, along with my colleagues in political science at IU, pushed me to use my experience of living through the onset of this revolution to carve out a new research agenda relating to identity politics, revolution, and social change in Africa. This fit well with Crawford's new project on ideology and development in Africa. Exchanges with him helped me sharpen the historical and theoretical underpinnings of my 1988 book, *Revolutionary Ethiopia: From Empire to People's Republic*. It is important to note that Crawford Young played a major role in encouraging me to undertake further research on how historical bureaucratic empires were created and how they collapsed under the weight of demands for revolutionary change. This helped me crystallize my understanding of the emergence and the continued importance of multiethnic states in Africa, particularly identity politics in Ethiopia today. Our ongoing exchanges on identity politics in contemporary Africa enriched my research and my long-term mentoring relationship with Crawford.

The present book, *The State, Ethnicity, and Gender in Africa: Intellectual Legacies of Crawford Young*, is composed primarily of essays written by some of Crawford's graduate students and centered on the major themes that characterize the corpus of his academic contributions: the colonial and postcolonial state and identity politics in Africa. For the remainder of his academic life, Crawford's research journey focused on issues relating to the quests of independent African states to create and implement democratic institutions and practices on the continent. In the process, he was drawn to understanding the emerging political cultures in different parts of newly independent Africa, democratization, and the structure of identity politics in independent African states. The essays included in the book are representative of Young's major theoretical, historical, and methodological contributions to our understanding of the pre-and postcolonial state and identity politics in Africa today.

In 2012, M. Crawford Young published his must-read, *The Postcolonial State in Africa*. The current volume reflects his impact on the study of postcolonial Africa and the importance of his theories related to identity politics in Africa, as well as his career-long quest to understand the roots of cultural pluralism and identity politics in Africa today. The contributors to this veritable *festschrift* reflect the impact Young has had as an internationally distinguished scholar of postcolonial African politics as well as a mentor and a friend.

Contributors

Dauda Abubakar received his PhD from the University of Wisconsin–Madison. He taught at the University of Maiduguri, Nigeria, where he was the chair of the Department of Political Science. From 2003 to 2009 he taught at Ohio University, Athens. Dr. Abubakar is a professor of political science and Africana studies at the University of Michigan–Flint. His research agenda is at the intersection of sectarian identity politics and its implications for democratization in postcolonial Africa. Professor Abubakar is a coeditor of the book *Violent Non-State Actors in Africa: Terrorists, Rebels and Warlords* (2017). He has also contributed several book chapters to edited volumes on peace, conflict, and security in Africa, including *The Routledge Handbook on Counter-terrorism and Counter-insurgency in Africa*, ed. U. A. Tar (2021).

Melinda Adams is a professor of political science at James Madison University in Harrisonburg, Virginia. Her research focuses on women's movements, gender and politics, and women's political representation, particularly in West Africa. Her work has been published in *Politics & Gender, Governance, International Feminist Journal of Politics, Journal of Women, Politics & Policy, Women's Studies International Forum*, and elsewhere.

Ladan Affi received her PhD in political science from the University of Wisconsin–Madison and is an associate professor of political science in the Department of International Affairs at Zayed University in the United Arab Emirates. She has also taught and done research at Vassar College, the Université de Djibouti, and Qatar University. Born in Somalia, she has carried out extensive research in Somalia and published in the area of gender and politics in Somalia, piracy off the Horn of Africa, the role of diaspora in Somalia's development, and conflict and governance within fragile states. She has conducted numerous studies for USAID. She is currently working on comparative research on Somali women's political participation in the Horn of Africa (Somalia; Somaliland; Djibouti; Ethiopia; and Kenya). She is a coeditor (with Liv Tonnessen and Aili Mari Tripp) of *African Women in Peacebuilding* (2021).

Gretchen Bauer is a professor of political science and international relations at the University of Delaware, where she teaches African and comparative politics and gender and politics. She researches women's political leadership in Africa with a current focus on women in parliament and cabinet in Ghana and West Africa. She has been a visiting researcher at the Institute for Public Policy Research in Windhoek, Namibia (2002), and the University of Botswana in Gaborone (2009). She was a Fulbright scholar at the University of Ghana in 2016 and a senior fellow at the Merian Institute for Advanced Studies in Africa (MIASA) at the University of Ghana in 2023. From 2014 to 2018 she directed the Young African Leaders Initiative Mandela Washington Fellowship at the University of Delaware.

Akosua K. Darkwah is an associate professor of sociology at the University of Ghana. Her primary area of research interest is in the ways in which global (economic) policies and practices reconfigure the nature and character of Ghanaian women's work. In recent years, she has been particularly interested in the ways in which policies such as gendered electoral financing reconfigure the landscape for Ghanaian women in politics. Together with Gretchen Bauer, she co-convened an Interdisciplinary Fellows Group at the Merian Institute of Advanced Studies in Africa based at the University of Ghana that explored West African women's participation in politics. She has held visiting positions at Duke University and the University of Bergen, Norway. From 2012 to 2016, she directed the Centre for Gender Studies and Advocacy at the University of Ghana.

Joshua B. Forrest is a professor and the chair of the Department of History & Political Science at La Roche University in Pittsburgh, Pennsylvania. He previously taught at the Graduate School for Public & International Affairs at the University of Pittsburgh and in the Department of Political Science at the University of Vermont. In his most recent book, *Local Autonomy as a Human Right* (2021), he analyzes the worldwide effort by local communities to achieve greater policy autonomy and explains why this ought to justify the establishment of a human right to local control. His earlier publications focused on interethnic nationalist movements in sub-Saharan Africa (*Subnationalism in Africa*, 2004);

rural civil society in Guinea-Bissau (*Lineages of State Fragility*, 2003); and decentralization in Namibia (*Namibia's Post-Apartheid Regional Institutions*, 1998).

John W. Harbeson is professor of political science emeritus at the City University of New York (Graduate Center and City College). He is the author/editor of fourteen books. He has been an elected member of the American Political Science Association Governing Council, founding chair of the African Politics Conference Group, and cofounder of APSA's Democracy and Autocracy section. He has been a Jennings Randolph Senior Fellow at the US Institute of Peace. He has served as the US Agency for International Development's Regional Democracy and Governance Advisor for East and Southern Africa.

Cédric Jourde is a professor in the School of Political Studies at the University of Ottawa. He specializes in the politics of religion and ethnicity in West Africa as well as in democratization and authoritarian restoration in sub-Saharan Africa. He is the coauthor, with Jean Schmitz and Abdel Wedoud Ould Cheikh, of *Le Sahel musulman entre soufisme et salafisme: Subalternité, luttes de classement et transnationalisme* (2022), and with Muriel Gomez-Perez and Marie Brossier, of *The Politics of the Hajj in a Comparative Perspective: States, Entrepreneurs, and Pilgrims* (2024).

Edmond J. Keller is a Distinguished Professor Emeritus and former chair of Political Science, director of the UCLA Globalization Research Center-Africa, and former director of the James S. Coleman African Studies Center at the University of California–Los Angeles. He specializes in comparative politics with an emphasis on Africa. Keller received his PhD from the University of Wisconsin–Madison. Keller is the author of three monographs, including *Education, Manpower, and Development: The Impact of Educational Policy in Kenya* (1980) and *Revolutionary Ethiopia: From Empire to People's Republic* (1988). Most recently his research has been detailed in his monograph *Identity, Citizenship, and Political Conflict in Africa* (2014). Keller has also written more than fifty articles on African and African American politics and has coedited four books: *Afro-Marxist Regimes: Ideology and Public Policy* (with Donald Rothchild, 1987); *South Africa in Southern Africa: Domestic Change and International Conflict* (with Louis Picard, 1989); *Africa in the New International Order: Rethinking State Sovereignty and Regional Security* (with Donald Rothchild, 1996); and *Africa-US Relations: Strategic Encounters* (with Donald Rothchild, 2006).

Timothy Longman is a professor of political science and international relations at Boston University, where he serves as Associate Dean for Academic Affairs in the Pardee School of Global Studies. He is also the director of CURA: the Institute on Culture Religion and World Affairs and previously served as director of the African Studies Center for nine years. His research focuses on state and society in Africa, particularly human rights, transitional justice, the politics of race, ethnicity, and gender, and religion and politics. He has published two books on Rwanda, *Christianity and Genocide in Rwanda* (2010) and *Memory and Justice in Post-Genocide Rwanda* (2017), coauthored a textbook on South Africa, *Confronting Apartheid* (2018), and is currently writing a book on church-state relations across Africa. He has previously held teaching or research appointments at Vassar College, the University of California, Berkeley, Columbia University, the National University of Rwanda, and the University of the Witwatersrand, and he has served as a consultant for USAID, the International Center for Transitional Justice, the Justice Department, and Human Rights Watch in Rwanda, Burundi, Uganda, and the Democratic Republic of Congo.

Kaden Paulson-Smith is an assistant teaching professor in the Department of Crime & Justice Studies at the University of Massachusetts–Dartmouth. Their research and teaching crosscut critical carceral studies, law and society, African politics, and feminist and postcolonial studies. They received a PhD in political science from the University of Wisconsin–Madison.

William Reno is a professor and chair of the Department of Political Science at Northwestern University who specializes in research on the politics of violence and state collapse in sub-Saharan Africa and the Middle East. He is the author of three books: *Corruption and State Politics in Sierra Leone* (1995), *Warlord Politics and African States* (1999), and *Warfare in Independent Africa* (2011). These and other works inform Reno's current research on the politics of foreign assistance to security forces in very weak states, how patronage-based regimes that are reluctant to rely on their own armed forces wage counterinsurgency campaigns, and a project on the impacts of surveillance technologies on the exercise of authority in states that have very weak institutional capacities.

Rachel Beatty Riedl is the John S. Knight Professor of International Studies and the director of the Einaudi Center for International Studies at Cornell University. She is a faculty member in the Department of Government and the Brooks School of Public Policy. Riedl is an expert on democracy and authoritarianism, institutional development, local governance and decentralization policy, and religion and politics, with a regional focus in Africa. Riedl is the author of the award-winning *Authoritarian Origins of Democratic Party Systems in Africa* (2014) and a coauthor of *From Pews to Politics: Religious Sermons and Political Participation in Africa* (2019). She is the president of the Scientific Council at the Institute for Advanced Studies (Nantes), an editorial committee member at World Politics, and a coeditor of the Elements series Politics of Development at Cambridge University Press. She has held fellowships with Fulbright (Zambia and France), Yale University, Notre Dame, Princeton University, and has conducted policy analysis with USAID, the World Bank, State Department, Carter Center, US Institute of Peace, and other organizations on issues pertaining to governance reforms, elections, democratic representation, and identity politics. She is a full member of the Council on Foreign Relations, Scholars Strategy Network, and served as Chair of the Democracy and Autocracy section of the American Political Science Association. She is a co-host of the podcast Ufahamu Africa, about politics on the African continent. She holds a PhD from Princeton University.

Joel Samoff is an educator, researcher, and evaluator who combines the scholar's critical approach and extensive experience in international development. He studies the links among research, public policy, and foreign aid. At Stanford University since 1980 and a research associate at the University of Johannesburg, he holds honorary doctorates from the University of Pretoria and the University of the Free State. Recent publications include *Capturing Complexity and Context: Evaluating Aid to Education*, with Jane Leer and Michelle Reddy (2016); *Higher Education for Self-Reliance: Tanzania and Africa* (2019); and "Institutionalizing International Influence" (2023).

Scott Straus is a professor of political science at the University of California, Berkeley. He studies political violence, genocide, human rights, and post-conflict politics with an empirical focus on sub-Saharan Africa. He is the author or editor of nine books, including *Making and Unmaking Nations: War, Leadership, and Genocide in Modern Africa* (2015), *The Order of Genocide: Race, Power, and War* (2006), and *Introduction to International Studies: Global Forces, Interactions, and Tensions*, coauthored with Barry Driscoll (2022, 2nd ed.). Straus has published articles in *American Journal of Political Science*, *World Politics*, *Politics and Society*, *Foreign Affairs*, *Perspectives on Politics*, *African Affairs*, *Journal of Peace Research*, *Terrorism and Political Violence*, *Genocide Studies and Prevention*, *Journal of Genocide Research*, and other journals. Prior to his academic career, Straus was a freelance journalist based in Nairobi; he was nominated for a Pulitzer Prize for his 1996 coverage of the war in the Democratic Republic of Congo.

Linda Thomas-Greenfield holds a bachelor's degree from Louisiana State University and a master's degree from the University of Wisconsin, where she also did work toward a doctorate with Professor Crawford Young. She received an honorary Doctor of Law degree from the University of Wisconsin in May 2018 and an honorary Doctor of Philosophy from the University of Liberia in May 2012. Thomas-Greenfield was the 2017 recipient of the University of

Minnesota Hubert Humphrey Public Leadership Award, the 2015 recipient of the Bishop John T. Walker Distinguished Humanitarian Service Award, and the 2000 recipient of the Warren Christopher Award for Outstanding Achievement in Global Affairs.

Linda Thomas-Greenfield serves as the Representative of the United States of America to the United Nations as well as the Representative of the United States in the UN Security Council since 2021. Prior to this, she has had a distinguished career in foreign service for thirty-five years, holding positions that include Assistant Secretary of State for African Affairs (2013–2017), Director General of the Foreign Service and Director of Human Resources (2012–13), ambassador to Liberia (2008–12), and postings in Switzerland (at the United States Mission to the United Nations, Geneva), Pakistan, Kenya, The Gambia, Nigeria, and Jamaica. In Washington, she served as Principal Deputy Assistant Secretary of the Bureau of African Affairs (2006–8) and as Deputy Assistant Secretary of the Bureau of Population, Refugees, and Migration (2004–6).

Aili Mari Tripp is Vilas Research Professor of Political Science at the University of Wisconsin–Madison. Her research has focused on gender/women and politics, women's movements in Africa, transnational feminism, African politics, and the informal economy in Africa. She is the author of several award-winning books, including *Seeking Legitimacy: Why Arab Autocracies Adopt Women's Rights* (2019); *Women and Power in Postconflict Africa* (2015); *African Women's Movements: Transforming Political Landscapes*, with Isabel Casimiro, Joy Kwesiga, and Alice Mungwa (2009); and *Women and Politics in Uganda* (2000). She has served as the president of the African Studies Association and vice president of the American Political Science Association. She currently is an editor of the *American Political Science Review*.

Index

Africa and the Diaspora: History, Politics, Culture

Edited by Neil Kodesh and James H. Sweet

Postcolonial Paris: Fictions of Intimacy in the City of Light
Laila Amine

Spirit, Structure, and Flesh: Gendered Experiences in African Instituted Churches among the Yoruba of Nigeria
Deidre Helen Crumbley

Farming and Famine: Landscape Vulnerability in Northeast Ethiopia, 1889–1991
Donald Crummey; edited by James C. McCann

A Hill among a Thousand: Transformations and Ruptures in Rural Rwanda
Danielle de Lame; translated by Helen Arnold

Spirit Children: Illness, Poverty, and Infanticide in Northern Ghana
Aaron R. Denham

Defeat Is the Only Bad News: Rwanda under Musinga, 1896–1931
Alison Liebhafsky Des Forges; edited by David Newbury

Entrepreneurial Goals: Development and Africapitalism in Ghanaian Soccer Academies
Itamar Dubinsky

Education as Politics: Colonial Schooling and Political Debate in Senegal, 1850s–1914
Kelly M. Duke Bryant

Power in Colonial Africa: Conflict and Discourse in Lesotho, 1870–1960
Elizabeth A. Eldredge